THE
GARDENER'S
ASSISTANT

Editor

WILLIAM WATSON

F.R.Hort.S.

Curator, Royal Botanic Gardens, Kew

With Preface by

PROFESSOR SIR FREDERICK W. KEEBLE

C.B.E., F.R.S., Sc.D.(Cantab.)

VOLUME II

APLES

(From left to right): Rival, Crimson Bramley's Seedling (behind), Baxter Pearmain, Charles Ross, Cox's Orange Pippin

CONTENTS

VOLUME II

v

LIST OF PLATES

THE GARDENER'S ASSISTANT

VOLUME II

ORCHARDS

Orchard planting has received great attention in the British Isles at different periods of our history, and for different objects. The establishment of orchards on an extensive scale dates from the seventeenth century, when the production of cider as a substitute for foreign wines was the principal aim of the planters. Many of the ancient orchards in the West of England had their origin about that time, and as the cider industry advanced in importance the area devoted to fruit-trees was largely extended. During the following century beer gradually took the place of cider as a general beverage amongst the working-classes, while the consumption of imported wines increased greatly amongst other classes, to the loss of the cider-makers and fruit-growers. Then a long period of neglect succeeded; the varieties of Apples that had been chiefly planted were not adapted for any other purpose, and in consequence a large extent of orcharding became practically valueless. In the course of the nineteenth century, however, the demand for Apples and other fruits increased as the population advanced, with the result that orchards of a different character were planted, for the production of Apples that could be utilized either for sale or home consumption in a fresh or cooked state. With this object the attention paid to orchards is increasing every year, and the subject has now assumed an importance it has never previously possessed.

It will be convenient, in dealing with this matter, to divide it into three sections: 1st, the formation of new orchards; 2nd, the management of established orchards; and 3rd, the improvement of neglected orchards. Under each division of the subject some consideration will be devoted to the three general types, namely, the commercial orchard, or fruit plantation, the sole object of which is profit; the farm orchard, for home supply and the sale of surplus crops; and the garden or home orchard, which is usually on a smaller scale, and is intended mainly to furnish supplementary supplies to those afforded by garden trees, or it constitutes a portion of the garden itself.

THE FORMATION OF NEW ORCHARDS

The establishment of a new orchard is not a matter that can be lightly undertaken if success is to be ensured. So many conditions exercise a bearing upon the results that the most careful consideration is requisite to provide for probable contingencies. Even on a small scale the expense of forming permanent plantations is heavy, and a long period often elapses before it is perceived whether the outlay has been judiciously directed or otherwise. In the event of failure occurring from the operation of causes that might have been foreseen, not only is the loss serious, but the disappointment is such as to prevent any further attempt.

Much harm has in this way been done to fruit culture generally, and to orchard planting in particular, by ill-advised schemes, or by defective attention to essentials at starting. These essentials we now purpose to briefly review.

In selecting a site for a permanent plantation of fruit-trees the points that demand attention are the elevation, aspect, and shelter of the land. Each of the characteristics named exercises a marked effect upon subsequent progress and returns. With elevation is included not merely the actual height above sea-level, but also the relative altitude as compared with neighbouring land, for that is often of even more importance. It is well established that on low-lying land, and in enclosed valleys, frosts are frequently severe and destructive in the flowering season of fruit-trees, and the difference in this respect is often strongly marked when there is higher land in the immediate neighbourhood occupied with similar crops. Unfortunately it is a matter that has been many times overlooked when choosing sites for fruit plantations, with the result that repeated disasters have been experienced.

It is impossible to formulate a rule that

unfavourable effects are produced when the more elevated land is on the south or south-west side, and when the lower sites are more or less enclosed, preventing the escape of the cold heavy air.

The necessity for what is termed atmospheric drainage has received some consideration in the United States, and, as Professor L. H. Bailey says, the " escape of cold air is the secret of much of the success of fruit-growing on rolling and sloping land." This is unquestionably the fact, and many examples could be found in this country where,

Fig. 1.—Apple Orchard at Aldenham.

will apply to all districts, as local conditions often exercise a complicated influence, but in general, as regards the central portion of England, most distant from the coast in every direction, a lower elevation than from 150 to 200 feet above sea-level is exposed to considerable risks from spring frosts. As the coast is approached the minimum altitude of comparative safety falls until near the sea, where the lowest point is reached. As already indicated, this is affected to some extent by the neighbourhood of higher land, as the low temperatures are mainly due to the descent of cold air from greater elevations, and to air-stagnation. Especially

though the actual elevation of the orchard is lower than might be considered safe, yet owing to the proximity of still lower land the ill effects are avoided to a large extent.

The aspect of an orchard site has a bearing upon success in several ways, especially if the land slopes in a particular direction. A northerly slope is obviously unfavourable to wood and fruit ripening, but such inclines can occasionally be utilized on a small scale for the prolongation of supplies. An easterly direction is a source of danger in time of frost, because the rapid thawing of slightly frozen flowers, caused by exposure to the rays of the early morning sun, will often bring a destruction that might have been avoided under other circumstances. A direct south-west exposure necessitates adequate shelter, or when the trees are laden with fruit the gales commonly reaching us from that quarter will do much damage.

The question of shelter generally requires careful consideration, for it is certainly extremely disadvantageous to plant fruit-trees in very exposed positions unless some protection can be afforded. It is not only that the trees themselves are often damaged, but the fruits, particularly Apples, even if not blown off, are so bruised as to be rendered almost worthless.

Belts of trees will afford this shelter, and these can be formed at moderate expense if there be land available for the purpose. Where quickly developed protection is required nothing surpasses the Poplars for rapid growth, but they are objectionable in some respects, chiefly as the haunt of many insect pests. Mixed plantations of deciduous trees with Conifers also constitute efficient shelters, while for hedges near the orchard as wind-breaks, the Cherry Plum or Myrobalan (*Prunus cerasifera*) is admirably adapted, being of strong growth in all suitable soils, and forming a thick fence in a few years.

SOIL AND ITS TREATMENT

Soil.—An ideal soil for almost all the hardy fruits employed in the formation of orchards and plantations is a substantial loam resting on a well-drained subsoil. For Apples it may be fairly heavy, cool, and moist, but even for them it should be of a nature that admits of free cultivation. A near approach to clay is as objectionable as a sterile sand.

The physical condition of a soil is often of more importance than its actual constituents, as by mechanical means and the employment of suitable manures great improvement can be effected if the soil be neither excessively tenacious nor too sandy. Still, if it is possible to make a choice, preference should be given to a moderately heavy soil rather than a light one, if Apples are to constitute the whole or major part of the plantation.

It has been shown by chemical analysis that all our hardy fruits abstract from the soil a large proportion of phosphoric acid and potash, therefore land that is to be utilized successfully for fruit culture must contain plentiful stores of these essentials. An analysis of a soil is a useful guide in this respect as indicating what is present in it, but even the best analysis cannot tell precisely what proportion of the substances present are immediately available to the roots of fruit-trees or plants generally. In consequence it sometimes happens that on land showing widely different results in analysis equally marked success in fruit culture may be obtained. But the analysis of a soil is valuable in another way, namely, it shows whether an important constituent is seriously deficient, and it also points out the presence of a substance that may be positively injurious. Therefore it is advisable, before undertaking the expense of

preparing a large area of land for fruit plantations, to secure a reliable analysis of the soil.

As examples of the variation in the chemical constitution of soils equally well adapted for orchard cultivation we give the four following analyses from land in Kent, Sussex, and Herefordshire, where fruit has been largely and successfully grown during many years. The first two are by Sir A. D. Hall, F.R.S., and Dr. E. J. Russell, the second two are by Dr. A. J. Voelcker :

ORCHARD SOILS.

	In Kent. Per cent.	In Sussex. Per cent.
Moisture	3.47	1.82
Loss on Ignition	4.65	5.98
Nitrogen	0.141	0.182
Alumina	2.69	4.26
Oxide of Iron	3.78	3.57
Oxide of Manganese	0.06	0.03
Magnesia	0.41	0.24
Lime	1.02	0.34
Carbonates	0.26	0.09
Potash	0.74	0.49
[1]Available	0.048	0.074
Phosphoric Acid	0.143	0.256
[1]Available	0.066	0.082
Sulphuric Acid	0.06	0.006

ORCHARD SOILS.

	In Kent. Per cent.	In Hereford-shire. Per cent.
[2]Organic matter and loss on heating	5.07	4.39
Oxide of Iron	3.63	4.81
Alumina	3.51	6.75
Carbonate of Lime	1.48	.79
Magnesia	.42	1.29
Sulphate of Lime	.34	.02 [3]
Potash	.30	.72
Soda	.01	.15
Phosphoric Acid	.01	.06
Insoluble silicates and sand	85.74	81.02
	100.00	100.00

1 Soluble in 1 per cent citric acid.
2 Nitrogen=.19=to Ammonia=.23.   3 Sulphuric Acid.

To prove what enormous quantities of the most important constituents are present in good soils Dr. Voelcker calculated that in 6 inches depth of the Hertfordshire soil he analysed, the following were the total weights of the respective substances per acre :

	lbs. per acre.			
Phosphoric Acid	4,569	= over	2	tons.
Potash	10,483	= ,,	5	,,
Lime	74,188	= ,,	33	,,
Magnesia	9,676	= ,,	4	,,
Sulphuric Acid .	4,569	= ,,	2	,,
Nitric Acid	22			
Nitrogen	2,397	= ,,	1	ton.

Soil Preparation and Improvement.—The land selected for a new orchard may have been subjected to ordinary garden cultivation, it may be a portion of the arable land of a farm, or it may be a pasture. In the first case probably no special preparation will be needed, but in the other two it will. If on the arable land shallow ploughing only has been adopted during a long period, one of two courses will be necessary, *i.e.* deep or subsoil ploughing, or trenching by hand. If a " pan " has been formed, as is frequently the case in some soils, it must be broken up to permit the roots of the trees free extension, and to ensure due circulation of moisture in the soil. If standard Apples, Pears, or Plums are to be planted at distances of 20 to 30 feet apart, and the intervening spaces occupied only with vegetable crops, then double ploughing, supplemented by trenching for each station to be filled by the trees, will be sufficient. If, however, it is proposed to form a commercial plantation comprising both standard and dwarf trees with bush fruits between, the preparation of the whole of the ground by means of trenching, costly though the process be, is at the same time more economical in the end. In any case, should the land be foul with weeds, particularly those with creeping roots like Twitch, not only will a thorough forking be essential, but a season's close cropping, with the attendant cultivation, is most desirable prior to the orchard planting.

Grass land to be devoted to orchards offers several important problems for solution. It has been demonstrated by experiments both in the United States and in Great Britain, that grass growing over, or in close proximity to the roots of newly-planted young fruit-trees is injurious to them, stunting the growth, starving the tree, and either crippling it for many years, or rendering it entirely useless. Many attempts at the formation of new orchards, or the restoring of old ones, have failed through this cause.

If it is desired to plant fruit-trees in a thriving pasture, this can be done if a portion of the ground surrounding each tree is kept clear of grass. For standard Apples on crab stocks a space 6 feet in diameter will suffice at least for the first four or five years, after which the trees should be able to take care of themselves.

Bastard trenching is preferred for orchards, *i.e.* two full " spits " of soil are moved and broken down, but each is kept in the same relative position, *i.e.* the lower spit is kept below, and the upper one on the top. In addition, the soil beneath the second spit is also stirred or broken with the spade or fork if it be heavy or hard. If the preparation is for immediate planting, without an intermediate course of cropping, the trenching cannot be too well done, as in all heavy soils it will be the means of unlocking abundance of pent-up plant food. After planting, digging can be of only a partial and imperfect character.

It is assumed that farm land to be appropriated to the orchard has been previously properly drained, and that there is a porous subsoil, or the natural surface drainage is sufficient, otherwise it will be necessary to have the land efficiently drained.

Manures.—In the application of manures before planting several points require consideration. While it is not desirable that fruit-trees should be stunted in their early stages, it would be unwise to induce excessively vigorous growth, the effect of which would be to unduly postpone the period of fruit-bearing. As a general rule, a moderately heavy well-worked soil can supply all that a young fruit-tree requires for its early development. On the other hand, if the soil is somewhat poor and light, and there is reason to believe that owing to defective cultivation in the past it is not in a condition to ensure continued growth, a liberal admixture of old stable or farmyard manure (12 to 20 tons per acre) may be very beneficial. It is a case for the exercise of the cultivator's judgment. In one instance the application of manure may be not only wasteful, but injurious ; in the other it may be found a profitable investment.

But there is another respect in which natural and bulky manures prove beneficial, and that is in their physical or mechanical action of opening the soil, ensuring better aeration, and consequently a more rapid breaking down of the various compounds to fit them for the use of the trees. This applies specially to heavy soils, and we have seen remarkable effects produced on the growth of Apple-trees by the incorporation of such an unpromising substance as fibrous peat in a very heavy soil prior to planting.

For the same reason the growth of green crops to be ploughed or dug in previous to planting is also beneficial on such soils.

ARRANGEMENT OF ORCHARD

The arrangement of the orchard and the general plans for fruit plantations require some discussion. As regards the orchard proper there are four systems upon either of which the trees can be conveniently arranged. These are :

1. The Square system (see fig. 2). In this the trees are arranged at equal distances each way, so that each tree stands at the

lines, and thus they stand in triangular form, the trees in the adjoining rows being slightly farther apart than those in the rows. This also is best adapted for a permanent plantation, as it does not admit of convenient or equal thinning.

4. The Hexagonal arrangement (see fig. 5) permits a more equalized occupation of the ground than any other, as all the neighbour-

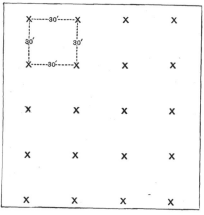

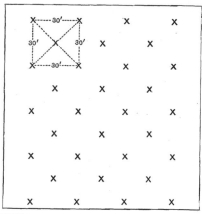

SCALE: 50 FEET TO 1 INCH

Fig. 2.—The Square System.
X = Standard Fruit-trees : 30 feet × 30 feet.

Fig. 3.—The Quincunx System.
X = Standard or Dwarf Fruit-trees. The lines can, however, be formed with Standards and Dwarfs alternately.

corner of a square. This is convenient for planting and working, and is best adapted for permanent plantations, although it admits of fewer trees per acre than the others at the same distances.

2. The Quincunx (see fig. 3) is a modification of the square system, in which an additional tree is planted in the centre of each square. This obviously allows of a much larger number of trees to the acre, and is to be preferred where the intention is to reduce the number of trees by thinning.

3. The Triangular or alternate system (see fig. 4) is still another modification of the last, the trees being arranged so that they are equi-distant in the lines, and the rows are the same distance apart ; but each alternate line is commenced opposite the centre of the space between two trees in the adjoining

ing trees are the same distance apart, each three trees forming the corners of an equilateral triangle. This does not lend itself to ready or equal thinning without the removal of a large number of trees. It must be remembered that the distance between the rows is less than between the trees in the row.

The question as to whether there is any advantage in the rows of trees running in any particular direction is a difficult one, as the results mainly depend upon local circumstances, which are rarely repeated under precisely the same form. As a general rule, it may, however, be taken that the less the trees are shaded by their neighbours the better, and there is also the prevailing direction of the winds to be considered. For this reason in many places there seems to be a material advantage in allowing the rows of trees to run due north and south, thus permitting a free exposure to the sun's rays at the most important part of the day, and at the same time preventing the southwest winds from sweeping up the rows of the trees, though this is effected at the expense of the part of the plantation which is exposed to that quarter. Due shelter, as already advised, should always be provided on that side.

The foregoing remarks refer mainly to the arrangement of standard trees planted from 20 to 30 feet apart, though of course it is obvious they are equally applicable to bush or pyramid trees at smaller distances.

are formed, the 30-feet distance is most convenient, allowing ample space between the lines for intercropping, an important matter where quick returns and constant occupation of the land with crops of some kind are needed. We shall, therefore, take this as the best adapted to illustrate the arrangement of plantations, and it can be modified according to circumstances and requirements.

One of the simplest methods is that shown in fig. 6, and it has been adopted in several market orchards with satisfactory results. In this, standard trees are arranged at 30 feet apart each way (on the square system), with bush or pyramid Apples or half-

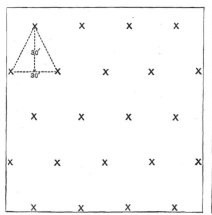

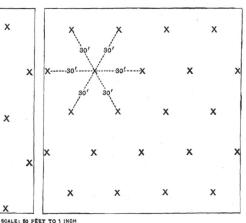

SCALE: 50 FEET TO 1 INCH

Fig. 4.—The Triangular System.
X=Standard Fruit-trees.   Distance between the rows and
between the trees in the rows=30 feet.

Fig. 5.—The Hexagonal System.
X=Standard Fruit-trees.   All the trees 30 feet
apart in each direction.

Under each of the systems described it is also possible to form commercial plantations in which the interspaces can be filled in various ways with bush and small fruits. We will illustrate some of the most approved methods for such arrangements ; but as these depend chiefly upon the distances at which the permanent standard trees are to be planted, this matter must be referred to first.

Standard Apples and Pears can be planted at any distance from 20 to 30 feet apart, but they can be classed according to their habit of growth in three groups, i.e. small growers at 20 feet, medium growers at 24 feet, and strong growers at 30 feet. The first-named distance is also a suitable one for most Plums, and the last one for Cherries. But in many respects, where mixed plantations

standard Plums between these in the rows at 15 feet apart, and Currants and Gooseberries again between these at 5 feet apart. The spaces between the rows are then subjected to alternate cropping in this way. One space is planted with vegetables, the second with Gooseberries, the third with Currants, and the fourth with vegetables, repeating this order throughout the plantation. When the bush fruits give signs of exhaustion, or cease to be profitable, they are removed, and the vegetable quarters are devoted to fresh plantations ; the spaces previously occupied with the bushes are then devoted to vegetables. In this way there is always a succession of young bushes in free bearing, and the land is kept in well-worked fertile condition. Strawberries or Raspberries can be substituted either for

Gooseberries or Currants, or both, or they can be employed in addition ; and a system of alternate cropping such as this is most suitable where Strawberries are grown.

If the land is to be devoted entirely to fruit, some modification of the scheme shown in fig. 7 can be adopted. There we again take the standards at 30 feet apart in the square system, with two rows of bush Apples, Pears, or Plums between at 10 feet apart, the intermediate spaces being again filled with small fruits at 5 feet. In planta-

tions of this kind the process of thinning simply consists of the removal of the small fruits first, and the bush Apples, &c., later as they become too crowded, ultimately leaving the standards the whole of the ground. Protective and useful boundaries to any of these plantations can be formed with Damsons and Nuts, either as hedges or as part of the general arrangement. As a rule, however, the former method is preferable, as there is then no interference with the general design.

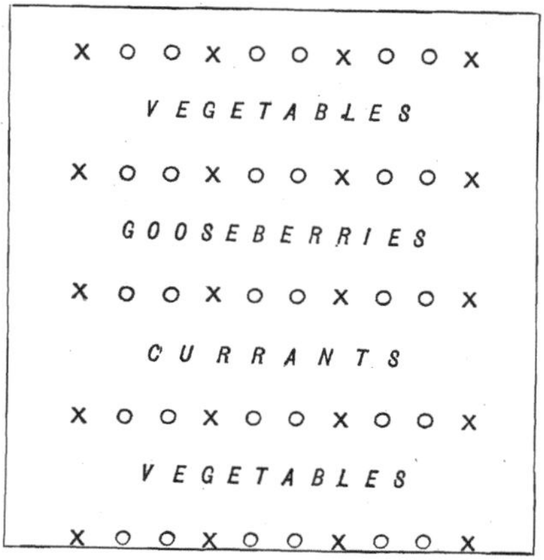

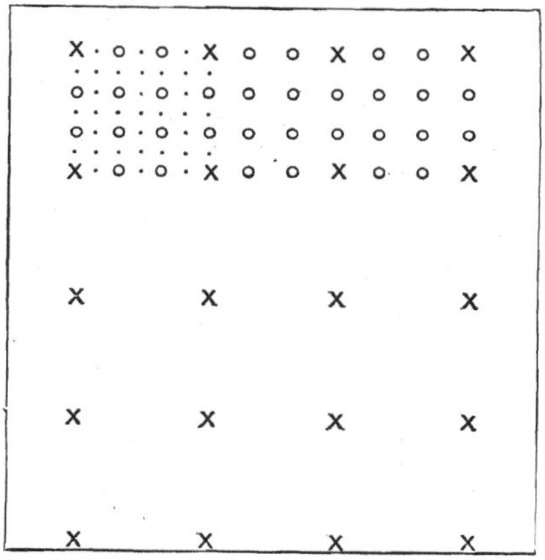

SCALE, 50 FEET TO 1 INCH

Fig. 6.—Mixed Plantation.
X=Standard Fruit-trees—30 feet × 30 feet. O=Dwarf Apples, Pears, or Plums 10 feet apart in the rows. Intermediate spaces cropped with vegetables and bush fruits alternately.

Fig. 7.—Mixed Plantation.
X=Standard Fruit-trees—30 feet × 30 feet. O=Dwarf Apples, &c., at 10 feet. • =Gooseberries and Currants at 5 feet.

MANAGEMENT

General Management of Orchards. — One of the first considerations in regard to an established orchard is how the ground is to be treated in the plantation. If the trees have been planted in grass, a space of six feet diameter (as previously advised) being cleaned around them, they require protection if cattle, sheep, &c., are turned in to graze. Even if fowls or pigs only are in the orchard, some means must be adopted to prevent their disturbing the soil over the roots of the trees. We have seen young trees repeatedly ruined by their roots being bared, and it is one of the difficulties of the farm orchard, but a few stakes and a ring of wire-netting will usually suffice to prevent this. If the grass is cut for hay and not grazed, the land must be treated generously in the application of manurial dressings, especially in the neighbourhood of the trees.

When the trees have made free growth, and the roots have reached the limit of the prepared soil, it becomes a question whether the area cleared of grass round the trees should be farther extended or not, and the matter has a wider bearing than appears at first sight. When a tree is well rooted and developing freely, a moderate check would have a tendency to promote earlier fruit-bearing than if it continued to make unrestricted growth. It is upon this the opinion rests, which prevails in some fruit-growing districts, that it is advantageous to have some trees (especially Plums and Cherries) entirely in grass when they have passed their earliest stages. It is found, also, that the fruit of Plums particularly is usually obtained under such circumstances in better saleable form, brighter, cleaner, and of higher flavour than in open cultivated soil. As regards Apples and Pears, the presence of grass also has a decided tendency to increase the colour of the fruits, but when these trees are on the Paradise or Quince stocks respectively the effect in reducing the size of the fruits is just as marked. A strong established standard tree on the free stock is not, of course, affected to the same extent, and the influence on the colour and appearance of the fruit is then an advantage.

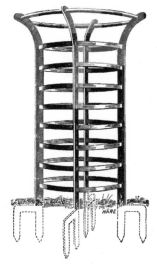

Fig. 8.—Wrought-iron Tree Guard.

The firmer soil round the prepared area into which the roots penetrate further aids in the restriction of growth and the promotion of fertility. It is therefore largely a matter for close observation to determine whether the cultivated area round a tree in grass should be extended or not. When the trees have made ample vigorous growth and do not appear to be getting into a fruit-bearing state, we should allow the restricting influences to exercise their effect. If, on the contrary, the trees are not developing freely, we should endeavour to encourage increased root action.

Where the whole of the ground in an orchard is cultivated or cropped, the hoe should be freely used. The destruction of weeds is an important service, but the constant moving of the surface soil is of greater benefit in preventing cracking and the excessive loss of moisture in dry weather. If the plantation is wholly occupied with fruit-trees and bushes planted closely, very little more can be done to the land in the way of cultivation. When, however, alternate spaces are devoted to vegetables, deep cultivation is requisite. In many market orchards continuous cropping with both flowers and vegetables is carried on to within a foot or two of the tree stems. In plantations near large towns, whence constant and large supplies of stable manure have been obtained and applied to the land over a long period, it is probable that the rough system of root pruning, which is performed in the digging and planting, may tend to prevent the undue luxuriance of growth that would otherwise result in such soils. In general practice such close cropping is not desirable, and we have found that in the early years of a plantation it is not advisable to crop to within a less distance than five feet from the stems.

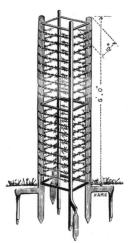

Fig. 9.—" Porcupine " Tree Guard.

At several of the experimental stations in America attention has been given to catch-cropping, with the object of preventing the nitrates formed in the soil during the summer from being washed out during the autumn and winter, but the matter has not received much attention here, and it is a question how far such cropping will pay. In the ordinary way crops are grown which can be sold from the ground in winter or spring, either flowers or vegetables.

Cultivating orchard-land with leguminous crops has also been tried rather extensively with the object of enriching the soil and testing the effect on the trees. But it appears from observation in this country that while the tree is young, and at the season of full growth, any kind of crop will inflict some injury on the trees simply by the withdrawal of water from the soil.

When manurial aid becomes needful to an established orchard either from defective growth or sterility (provided the latter is not due to extreme vigour), moderate dressings of old manure from the stables or farmyard applied to the surface at the rate of 10 or 12 tons per acre every year until an im-

of potash can be used, the former at the rate of 2 to 3 cwts. and the latter at 1½ to 2 cwts. per acre, the smaller dressings being preferable in each case. These can be mixed together and applied in the autumn after the leaves have fallen. There are many other artificial manures, which with crushed bones and bone meal are excellent fertilisers, but where the soil is deficient in lime, Basic Slag at 4 cwt. per acre is very helpful.

The routine work in an orchard comprises many matters in which the most watchful care must be exercised. Pruning and the development of the trees require to be

Fig. 10.—Apple—Blenheim Orange, unpruned.

provement is effected will generally accomplish its purpose. Failing this, recourse may be had to artificial or mineral manures. If growth is weak, nitrate of soda at the rate of 1½ cwt. to 2 cwts. per acre will in many soils produce a marked effect in a short time, provided other needful soil constituents be present ; or sulphate of ammonia may be employed instead at about 1¼ cwt. to 1¾ cwt. for the same space. The first should be applied just as the leaves are expanding and when the soil is moist ; the second should be given at least two months before growth starts. In cases of defective fertility superphosphate of lime and sulphate

studied closely, the bark injuries resulting from friction with stakes must be guarded against, and the first signs of disease or insects should bring the cultivator to the rescue. When young trees are in full bearing, judicious thinning of the crops will demand attention, and if the trees fail to bear from excessive vigour, root-pruning and lifting are laborious but usually effective remedies. The spraying of fruit-trees is so important a matter that it is treated in a separate chapter.

One other point only in connection with established orchards and fruit plantations need be referred to here, and that is the removal of trees or bushes where close planting has been adopted with a view to subsequent thinning. If this is deferred too long not only are the surplus trees injured, but the permanent ones also suffer to such an extent that no after-care will restore them. It is a matter that is too often overlooked, to the serious loss of the cultivator.

IMPROVING OLD ORCHARDS

There are many old orchards which would admit of only one kind of profitable improvement, and that would be their total destruction. Decayed, cankered, insect-infested specimens may be very picturesque when laden with moss and lichen, but they are painful objects for a gardener to contemplate, and if he should be expected to restore them to health and usefulness he is deserving of sympathy. There are, however, thousands of acres of orchards that would admit of improvement, and difficult though the task might be, the labour would under some conditions be well repaid. If trees are badly diseased they should be removed and burnt, root and branch. If the varieties are worthless, they may be cut down and grafted with approved sorts, Trees may present a thicket of entangled intercrossing branches, depriving each other of light and air. To reduce these branches to something like order often necessitates the removal of the greater portion. The branches should be sawn off cleanly, the surfaces smoothed where possible with a knife, and the wounds tarred. The next point is to wash or spray the trees thoroughly for the destruction of insect pests and the cleansing of the bark. Both operations can be readily performed even with large trees if the necessary appliances are at command.

Finally, the restoration of the food supplies in the soil must be considered, as where a tree has occupied the ground for half a century, during a large portion of which time it has been neglected, the principal available constituents of the soil have probably been exhausted. If the trees are in grass, take an area corresponding to the spread of the branches, clear off the grass, and give this a liberal dressing of stable manure. Where there are tanks in a stable-yard for the collection of drainings, dilute this with water and apply it when the soil is moist in summer. Where the trees are not in grass the manure can be lightly dug into the surface, and the liquid may be supplied as in the other case. Should the trees fail to respond to this treatment, add a dressing of superphosphate of lime and sulphate of potash or other similar mineral manures. In many instances within our experience most gratifying results have followed persevering attention of the character advised, though it is naturally a more pleasing task to plant a new orchard than attempt to restore an old one.

The gathering of fruit, the storing, packing, or marketing, do not come within the scope of this chapter, but are dealt with fully in other portions of this work.

SPRAYING FRUIT-TREES

The devastation amongst fruit-trees caused by insect and fungus pests has been serious during the past quarter of a century. The causes of this are various. The trees may be weakened and predisposed to attacks by the excessive use of stimulating manures, by overcropping, or by poor cultivation. Careful selection of sites, planting only healthy young trees, and good cultivation are the best preventives. Still, even where these are provided, atmospheric and other conditions may prevail which favour the development and increase of both insects and fungi, and organized methods of prevention or cure become necessary. The adoption of such means is now compulsory in some British Colonies and foreign countries, while the Board of Agriculture now has the power to enforce regulations for dealing with certain pests, especially the American Gooseberry Mildew.

Important assistance has been rendered to cultivators by the invention of improved apparatus for the distribution of liquid substances over trees and plants. The ordinary syringe which has long been used in gardens is both wasteful and inefficient for the purpose, and the majority of garden-engines or hand-pumps are almost as unsatisfactory. When, however, the various forms of spray-nozzles were introduced, and the knapsack-machines came into use, both economy and efficiency were secured. With knapsacks of the "Eclair," "Notus," "Enots," "Alpha," "Holder," "Four Oaks," and "Antipest" types any liquid can be distributed over small trees, on the upper and under surfaces of the foliage, and a man with a machine strapped on his back can effectually spray hundreds of trees in a day.

In the ordinary form of knapsack the reservoir, which is of thin copper, will carry three gallons of liquid, and the whole machine, when full, weighs about 35 lbs. It is furnished with a pump and agitator which are both worked by the same action, and the object of the latter is to ensure the thorough mixing of the solution while in use.

This is forced into a small chamber, and thence through a perforated cap or nozzle in a finely-divided spray. The regulation of the fineness is provided for in most of the knapsacks used in this country by nozzles having different-sized apertures which can

Fig. 11.—Knapsack Spraying Machine ("Four Oaks").

be removed or affixed as desired, but in one form in use in America and Canada this can be regulated by a small T-shaped tap on the nozzle itself. Forms of nozzles for affixing to hose-pipes are shown in figs. 12, 13, and 14. Fig. 12 represents a "Vermorel" nozzle with two discharges, each fitted with a "degorger" to clear the chamber and aperture of any temporary obstruction. This furnishes a conical and fine spray for small trees. Fig. 13 shows another "Vermorel" with four discharges similar in construction to the last. Fig. 14 depicts the Mistifier (Junr.) Patent Spray Nozzle, which is designed to perform the work of several nozzles. By screwing the cap up or down, all varieties of spray can be obtained.

With brass and india-rubber pipe connections of sufficient length it is possible, with good knapsacks, to spray fruit-trees thoroughly up to the height of 10 feet; they are therefore specially adapted for bush or pyramid trees. For standards and larger trees more powerful machines are required. They can be had now as barrels on wheels, to be worked by one or two men, or in still larger sizes to be drawn by horses, the capacity of the reservoirs being from 50 to 100 gallons (or more), and the pumps having a power equal to the distribution of the liquids over the largest orchard trees.

Useful portable forms of spraying apparatus for plantations of small trees are illus-

whole machine being only 22 inches wide. The same kind of machine is made with tanks to hold 30, 40, 50, or 60 gallons, the last two being 26 and 32 inches wide. The tanks are of steel, copper, or wood, as required. Lead-lined iron tanks can also be had.

There are also pumps that can be fixed to any ordinary strong barrel holding 20 or 30 gallons. Most of the larger machines are constructed to discharge from at least four sets of hose at the same time, thus greatly facilitating the work. The more powerful and best-made garden-engines can be utilized for the same purpose, as, with a suitable pipe attached, any form of nozzle can be fitted to them. For large trees and some infestations greater force is essential than can be obtained in the ordinary knapsack, and then these hand-engines are useful.

For spraying large orchard trees many powerful machines are manufactured and

Fig. 12.
" Vermorel " Two-discharge Nozzle.

Fig. 13.
" Vermorel " Four-discharge Nozzle.

Fig. 14.
" Mistifier " Spray Nozzle.

trated in figs. 15 and 16. Fig. 15 represents the Weeks' No. 1 Hand-Spraying Machine, which is employed in mixed fruit plantations where comparatively close planting is adopted, as it requires but little space, and can be readily wheeled between the rows of trees or bushes. The apparatus shown is the smaller size, with a tank of 12 gallons capacity, fitted with one hose, branch, and nozzle. A larger size is constructed with a tank holding 20 gallons of liquid. The pumps are powerful, and the valves are formed to deal with all kinds of materials. Other machines of a similar character are made with tanks holding 30, 35, 50, 100, and 200 gallons, which are used for both fruit and hops. The illustration fig. 16 represents one of Messrs. Drake & Fletcher's excellent Mistifier Machines, which are made in several forms and of various capacity. That shown is the M.M. type, with a tank holding 20 gallons, fitted with two 20-feet hose pipes and nozzles, the

in general use, which perform the requisite work much more efficiently than the earlier forms. That represented in fig. 17 is Drake & Fletcher's Power Spraying Machine, which secured the second prize at the Royal Agricultural Society's Trials at Gloucester. The power is supplied by a petrol engine of the Daimler pattern. It has two suction and delivery pipes, and can supply several hundred yards of piping with 8 to 12 nozzles.

For the distribution of insecticides or fungicides in the form of dry powder (which is important in some cases) there are machines constructed on the bellows principle, i.e. the alternate indrawing and expulsion of air. One of the best of these is the " Coronette." This is like the knapsack machine for liquids, and is carried on the back of the operator in the same manner, the handle working the bellows, the powder being expelled through a metal tube with the mouth formed as a distributor.

The "Torpille" and "Holder" are useful sulphur pumps, but for dwarf bushes the Dustifier is excellent and expeditious. *Winter Spraying* is recommended as a

Fig. 15.—Weeks' No. 1 Hand-Spraying Machine.

preventive measure against fungus and insect attacks on fruit-trees. When the trees are in a dormant state powerful remedies can be applied with safety which at other seasons would be injurious. The cleansing effect alone is valuable, for when the bark is covered with a dense growth of lichens and other minute forms of plant life, not only is the health of the tree directly affected, but they afford protection to innumerable insects, their larvae, or their eggs.

A simple and inexpensive wash for winter dressings is caustic soda (sodium hydrate) dissolved in water at the rate of about 3 oz. to 1 gallon of water for small quantities, or 3 lbs. to 10 gallons for large, this being nearly equivalent to what is termed a 2 per cent solution. It should be sprayed on the trees during the winter as weather permits, avoiding times when frosts or strong winds prevail. If more than one dressing be applied, the last should be given shortly before the buds expand. We have found it an advantage to add 2 to 4 oz. of soft soap to each gallon of water, as it causes the solution to adhere to the bark of the trees better, and thus increases its efficacy while adding little to the cost. Whenever soft soap is used for admixture with other solutions it should be dissolved in a little hot water first, and then added to the principal liquid.

A winter dressing that is used at the Wye Agricultural College, Kent, consists of 1 lb. of ground commercial caustic soda, ¾ lb. pearlash (crude carbonate of potash), and 10 oz. of soft soap to each 10 gallons

of water. This solution, with the addition of pearlash, is more destructive to the eggs of many insects than when the soda is used alone.

In the application of all caustic and poisonous washes to trees two points should be remembered : one is, that the efficiency of the wash chiefly depends upon the substance being evenly distributed over the whole of the infected surface, whether bark or foliage ; the other is, that due precaution should be taken to protect the clothes and body of the operator. Work as much as possible to the windward of the trees if there is a breeze, protecting the hands with leather or india-rubber gloves if the spraying is to be done with the stronger mixtures. A suit of oilskin, such as is worn by sailors, is an efficient protection.

The application of insecticides and fungicides to trees in growth requires care and forethought if they are to be effective and at the same time harmless to the trees. As a rule, the spraying should be done when the bark and foliage are moist, or, if the weather be bright, in late afternoon. The surface should be thoroughly moistened without there being sufficient to run.

As many of the substances used cannot be

Fig. 16.—Mistifier Spraying Machine, M.M. Type
(Drake & Fletcher.)

reduced to a state of complete solution to ensure a thorough mixture, it should be well stirred each time the knapsack or engine is filled. The strainers with which all spraying machines should be furnished must have extremely fine meshes, and all liquids must be passed through them before use, otherwise the nozzles will be continually blocked and cause endless trouble.

Insecticides must either kill the insects immediately by contact, or poison them through their food. For the former it is difficult to find a compound that will destroy the pests without injury to the plant. The insects which infest plants can be classed in two groups, namely " sucking " and " biting " insects, indicating roughly both the habits of the pests and the best methods for their destruction. The sucking insects comprise those that absorb the juices of the foliage, as the numerous kinds of aphis, red spider, &c.; while the biting insects include those which consume the leaf itself, as the hosts of caterpillars and other larvae.

For sucking insects paraffin, particularly in the form of an emulsion with soft soap, is

ture can be obtained ready for use on a small scale, but for extensive work it is cheaper to make it. The Quassia chips should be first steeped in enough cold water to cover them for two hours, and then boiled for ten hours, adding 10 lbs. of chips to each 10 gallons of water, which can afterwards be diluted to 100 gallons; to this, ½ lb. of soft soap for every 10 gallons is added, previously mixed as already directed.

The indirect method, *i.e.* poisoning the food of the pests, is applied for the multitude of " biting " insects which, if unchecked, soon render the trees leafless or injure the fruits. For this a mixture of Paris Green and lime in water is most effective. It is a powerful

Fig. 17.—Power Spraying Machine (Drake & Fletcher).

extensively used. Where injury to foliage has resulted from its use this has been traceable to neglect of ordinary precautions. One of the simplest preparations we have tried is the following : Dissolve two quarts of soft soap in a gallon of hot water, and while it is still warm add a quart of paraffin, stirring the whole together, preferably with a hand-syringe. To this add 20 gallons of soft water. This mixture is destructive to aphides of all kinds, while with the addition of about 2 oz. of liver of sulphur the efficacy of the wash against red spider is increased.

Quassia extract with soft soap is also largely used against sucking insects, but it varies in its effects, and is not so reliable as the petroleum mixture. The Quassia mix-

poison, and therefore great care is required in handling it. It is sold both as a powder and as a paste, the latter form being preferable in all respects, and this can be employed at the rate of ½ lb. with 1 lb. of fresh lime to each 100 gallons of water. The Evesham Committee of fruit-growers a few years since recommended the use of 1 oz. of Paris Green to 8 gallons of water for growing foliage, or 1 oz. to 6 gallons of water when the foliage is matured. The weaker mixtures, however, are usually effective, and are less likely to injure the trees. It should be impressed upon operators that Paris Green does not dissolve in water, and therefore requires frequent agitation to keep it thoroughly mixed. Owing to its poisonous nature it must not be sprayed over fruit blossom, or the bees will be killed ; nor over fruit within a few weeks of the time for gathering it. The best time for the first application is immediately after the flowers have set and when the young leaves are expanding, and subsequently as occasion demands until the fruit is approaching maturity.

London Purple, a somewhat similar poison to Paris Green, varies more in its composition, is more uncertain in its effects on insects, and more frequently injures the foliage. Its advantages are that it is very finely divided and more easily mixed. It can be used at the rate of 6 oz. of London Purple and 12 oz. of lime to 100 gallons of water.

Arsenate of lead has been tried in England with satisfactory results as a destroyer of caterpillars. It is prepared by mixing 27 oz. acetate of lead with 10 oz. of arsenate of soda to 100 gallons of water. Mixtures can be made with this and paraffin emulsion, or with Bordeaux mixture, thus securing a wash containing the properties of several.

Fungicides.—The chief fungicide in general use on a large scale for fruit-trees and orchard spraying is the Bordeaux mixture, and this is most efficacious. The mixture used consists of 12 lbs. of copper sulphate and 8 lbs. of quicklime to 100 gallons of water. The copper sulphate is placed in a coarse canvas bag and suspended in the water to dissolve gradually, the fresh lime is mixed with water to form a paste, and is then added. Another form is that in which copper sulphate, lime, and treacle are mixed at the rate of 10 lbs. of each to 100 gallons of water ; the treacle causes the liquid to

adhere to the foliage. Soft soap is occasionally substituted for treacle, or, instead of either, ½ lb. of Paris Green per 100 gallons can be added to the copper sulphate and lime, and will constitute a valuable combined fungicide and insecticide, the lime in the Bordeaux mixture rendering the Paris Green quite innocuous to the leaves.

Bordeaux mixture should be applied in advance of fungus attacks or at the first signs of disease, as it is essentially a preventive. Where fungus diseases have been prevalent in the previous season, winter dressings should be applied two or three times, especially just before the flowers expand and again when they have fallen.

A fungicide which is coming into general use, especially against the American Gooseberry Mildew, is the lime-sulphur mixture, to which salt is sometimes added. This has been well tested at Wye, also by some of the large fruit-growers in Kent and elsewhere. It has been used in preference to Bordeaux mixture for dormant trees, and as an insecticide in some instances (Pear leaf Blister Mite). The chief modes of preparation are as follows : Quicklime, 7 lbs. ; sulphur, 3 lbs. ; salt, 3 lbs. ; water, 10 gallons. The two first boiled for an hour and the rest added. It has been found better in some cases to have twice as much sulphur as lime. Great care is needed in all first trials.

Potassium sulphide or liver of sulphur is a useful fungicide, used at the rate of 1 oz. to from 5 to 10 gallons of water, with the addition of soft soap. The reader should also consult the chapters on " Insect Pests " and " Fungus Diseases."

THE APPLE

The Apple takes first rank amongst the more important hardy fruits cultivated in the United Kingdom, and owes its high position to many valuable qualities. In hardiness it is unsurpassed, for, as regards the larger number of varieties in British gardens, it is rare that the lowest temperature experienced ever affects the trees themselves to any serious extent. In very low situations, and in seasons when the minimum temperatures have fallen to near the zero of the Fahrenheit scale, we have known occasional instances of bark injury resulting, but this has been confined to a few varieties and generally to trees on unsuitable stocks. Even in the spring, frosts seldom damage the young foliage, though unfortunately we have not yet secured a race of Apples with flowers that can resist frost.

The Apple can be grown with a fair measure of success over a greater area of our country, and in a greater variety of soils and situations, than any other fruit, but its best qualities and fullest capabilities are only developed under special circumstances of soil and climate.

Then, too, the season during which the fruits can be had for use extends throughout the whole year, no other fruit being so easily kept in a fresh state for six to nine months, and at the same time retaining all its characteristic properties.

Though the Apple in its different forms does not present such a variety of rich aromatic flavours as the Pear, yet there is a wide range of variation in degrees of sweetness and acidity, as well as in flavour and other characters. In appearance the Apple is unequalled in form and colour variations, which alone would render the fruit an interesting and delightful study.

From a utilitarian or commercial point of view also the Apple is highly important. The rapidly-extending and well-founded appreciation of the fruit as an essential part of the food of the people, has led to an enormous increase in its cultivation in temperate climates, and there appears to be every probability that for many years to come this extension will be continued. The safety with which the fruit can be packed and transported long distances by road, rail, or sea, has aided the advance in this respect, and increased facilities in the future will still further help in the same direction.

In seasons of great abundance drying Apples for home use or export has become a great part of the fruit-preserving industry in America. It has also been tried here when prices were very low and the markets glutted, but as a rule the demand for fresh Apples is sufficient to render this method unnecessary. The usual form in which the dried fruits are stored or sold is that of Apple rings, which retain the flavour well and are readily prepared for use.

Several machines are in use for the purpose of paring, coring, slicing, and drying or evaporating Apples, and service-

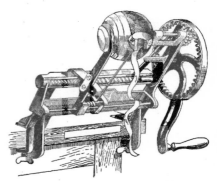

Fig. 18.—Mayfarth's Apple Parer, Corer, and Slicer.

able forms which have been tried in Great Britain, as well as on the Continent and in the United States, are shown in the illustrations figs. 18 and 19. Mayfarth's Apple

parer, corer, and slicer is a simply constructed appliance which can be readily
affixed to the edge of a table or bench, the
operations of removing the peel and core
being effected in succession after the fruit
is placed in position, by turning a handle
at the side, the slicing being then performed
by another simple action. The fruit is then
sulphured or dipped in salt and water, and
is ready at once for the drying-machine.
Mayfarth's American Evaporator (fig. 19)
has been subjected to several trials in Eng-

demonstrations at Leicester a few years
ago, and the same machine has been used at
the Woburn Experimental Fruit Farm. In
this the principle is similar to that in the
Mayfarth Evaporator, but the trays are
arranged immediately above a hot-air
chamber.

The utilization of Apples for the production of jelly on a commercial basis is extending, and several flourishing enterprises have
been started for this purpose in recent
years. There is also a partial revival of

Fig. 19.—" American " Evaporator.

land, notably at the Royal Horticultural
Society's Gardens, Chiswick, and has given
satisfactory results both in efficiency and
economy of fuel 'when carefully managed.
It consists of a stove and a series of trays
upon which the Apple rings are arranged,
and through which hot air is passed until
desiccation is sufficiently effected to ensure
the keeping of the fruit when properly
stored.

Another form of evaporator, the " Geisen-
heim Fruit and Vegetable Drier," was employed in the Royal Agricultural Society's

cider manufacture in some districts. Greater
attention is being paid to the matter, improved systems are in operation, the cider is
presented to the consumer in a more pleasing
form, and the better brands are decidedly
superior to many of the cheap foreign wines.

In short, the Apple merits all the attention
that can be accorded to it, whether it be
grown simply for home consumption or for
general commercial purposes, and we purpose in the course of this chapter to review
the aspects of the subject which most concern
the cultivator generally.

EVOLUTION AND IMPROVEMENT

Evolution of the Apple.—The origin of the innumerable varieties of cultivated Apples is attributed to the Common Crab—*Pyrus Malus* (fig. 20)—still found wild in many districts of Great Britain, and having a wide

Fig. 20.—Crab Apple (*Pyrus Malus*). (⅓.)

distribution throughout the temperate countries of Europe and part of Asia. There is evidence that it has been used as food and cultivated by man for upwards of four thousand years, and specimens of the dried or carbonized fruits have been found in the lake dwellings of central Europe dating from prehistoric times. Where the first varieties and the first cultivation commenced is not known, but the evolution of the Apple as we know it has been a long and gradual process. The wild Crab of our hedgerows does not vary so much in its fruits as it does in its habit and vigour of growth, though in some districts in England a distinction is made by the country people between Crabs and Crab-Apples, the latter being regarded as a larger type. Some differences of this kind are, however, no doubt due to accidental advantages of soil or situation. In raising seedlings for stocks from the Crabs gathered in the hedgerows it is remarkable what surprising diversities of growth are obtained, indicating the capacity for variation which exists in the plant. The average size of the

wild fruits found at the present time in Great Britain is from 1 inch to 1¼ inches in diameter, and this does not differ materially from the size of the Apples found amongst the remains of the Swiss lake dwellings. We have seen a marked improvement in the fruit of the Crab in one generation, from the seed of a wild type, when grown under favourable conditions. There is no doubt that we owe the greater number of the finely developed and varied Apples of the present time to selection, at first slow, but considerably accelerated within the past two hundred years by the increased number of breeders and cultivators.

Until grafting and budding became the general method of propagation for the Apple the usual means was by seed. At the present time there are thousands of old seedling Apples scattered about the country which originated in this way, many of which have been perpetuated locally. Some of these are good and distinct, but the majority are either worthless or not superior to others in general cultivation.

A glance at the list of old varieties will show that nearly all, to within recent times, were practically chance seedlings of unknown origin. It has been claimed that the Api or Lady Apple, now so much grown in America, and frequently seen in London shops in neat little boxes, is the oldest Apple in cultivation, as it is believed to have been known to the Romans. Continental pomologists dispute this, however, and state that it was found as a wilding in the forest of Api in Brittany, and that it was so recorded early in the seventeenth century. The Old English Pearmain was regarded by the late Dr. Hogg as " the oldest English Apple on record," as it was cultivated in Norfolk before the year 1200, though nothing is known of its origin. The Costard was probably contemporaneous, as it was known before 1292. Next amongst the ancient Apples must be placed the London Pippin, which was in cultivation prior to 1580, while in the seventeenth century the best known were Catshead, English Codlin, Golden Pippin, Golden Reinette, Joanneting, Pomewater, Summer Pearmain, and Winter Quoining, concerning the origin of which nothing whatever is known, though they were all doubtless seedlings selected for their marked characters. Some of them are still grown in gardens, and there are many other well-known Apples which have come to us in a similar way, such, for instance, as Ribston Pippin, Blenheim Pippin, Dumelow's Seedling, and Devonshire Quarrenden, which have no recorded parentage, while Claygate Pearmain is said to have been found in a hedge, Keswick Codlin on a rubbish heap, and Cornish Gilliflower in a cottager's garden. In some cases the name of the seed parent is known, as for example, Cox's Orange Pippin is from Ribston Pippin, Worcester Pearmain from Devonshire Quarrenden, and Waltham Abbey Seedling from Golden Noble. Many more could be given, but these will suffice to illustrate that the advance of the Apple has been largely due to chance seedlings and selection.

Systematic Improvement of the Apple.— Raising seedlings, even from varieties of proved merit, is an uncertain task ; the prizes are few and the blanks many. We cannot rely upon perpetuating any good qualities the parent tree may possess, but we can be sure of having a large proportion of seedlings that are utterly worthless. It is slow and unsatisfactory work, and the improvement of so valuable a fruit as the Apple deserves more systematic and scientific treatment. It may be said : Why seek to obtain more varieties when there are too many at the present time ? Varieties of poor quality, or those with insufficiently marked characters, are indeed too numerous, but we have not too many good Apples, and there is still room for material advance in the right directions. Thus early Apples of better quality are required, the productiveness and constitutional strength of many shy and weakly varieties of high merit could be improved, first - class, richly flavoured, late-keeping dessert sorts are not too numerous. The flavours of the fruits could also be diversified. In fact, there is plenty of work for those who have the time, the opportunity, and the desire to do it.

Thomas Andrew Knight, at the end of the eighteenth and the beginning of the nineteenth century, set an admirable example to horticulturists in the systematic improvement of fruits, including Apples, but until comparatively recent years very little has been done on the same lines. Mr. Knight feared that the old varieties of Apples were dying out owing to repeated propagation by grafting and budding, and he sought to obtain a re-invigorated race by calling in the aid of the varieties that approached more nearly to the original stock. In several instances vigorous, hardy-constitutioned, and fertile forms resulted, but they could only rank as high-class Cider Apples. The most

notable of these were the Siberian Bittersweet and the Siberian Harvey, both of which originated in crosses between the Yellow Siberian Crab and Golden Harvey or Brandy Apple, the latter being the pollen parent. Foxley was another of the same

Fig. 21.—Siberian Crab (*Pyrus baccata*). (½.)

type, and resulted from a cross between the Scarlet Siberian Crab *Pyrus baccata* (fig. 21) and Golden Pippin. If these crosses had been continued for another generation or two, some remarkable results might have been obtained. The best of Mr. Knight's other seedling Apples are Downton Pippin from Isle of Wight Orange Pippin fertilized with Golden Pippin (Yellow and Red Ingestrie are from a similar cross), and Bringewood Pippin from Golden Pippin crossed with Golden Harvey.

Not only was the principle of systematic cross-fertilization thus introduced amongst fruits, but the greatest care was adopted to prevent self-fertilization, by removing the stamens from the seed parent before the anthers were mature. It is also essential that the flowers be protected by small muslin or paper bags before and after the pollen is applied. Whatever is employed for protection must be light and translucent, and be removed immediately the fruit is set, or failure will result.

Some good Apples have been recorded from direct crossing since Knight's time, such as Sturmer Pippin, raised at Sturmer in Sussex from crossing Ribston Pippin with Nonpareil. The late Mr. Thomas Laxton also commenced crossing amongst Apples, but his attention was diverted to Strawberries before he had accomplished very much, though several of his seedlings are now in cultivation. In more recent times Mr. Charles Ross, Welford Park Gardens, Newbury, has done some systematic crossing

Fig. 22.—Hybrid Crab Apple—Leopold de Rothschild (John Downie Crab × Cox's Orange Pippin). (¼.)

with the result that several seedlings appear likely to take a high place, such as Mrs. Phillimore from Cox's Pomona and Mr. Gladstone, and Charles Ross (see Plate) from Cox's Orange and Peasgood's Nonesuch, with several others which are described in the list of varieties. Messrs. J. Veitch & Sons have also raised several remarkable seedlings, such as Langley Pippin from Mr. Gladstone crossed with Cox's Orange, and Leopold de Rothschild (fig. 22) from John Downie Crab crossed with Cox's Orange. The latter is a similar experiment to some of those tried by Knight, and the resulting cross has small fruits very freely produced, and it is both ornamental and useful.

Good progress is being made in England in the cross-breeding of fruits on a sys-

tematic and scientific basis, and there is a strong probability that a greater advance will be accomplished in the near future. Of the varieties added to the Apples in the present edition of this work, no less than eleven are the results of direct crossing. Amongst these five have Cox's Orange Pippin for one of the parents, namely, William Crump, Feltham Beauty, Rival, St. Everard, and the Houblon, the objects of the raisers being to secure the high quality of Cox's with improved habit of growth and of cropping. In the crosses referred to, the other parents were Worcester Pearmain, Mr. Gladstone, Peasgood's Nonesuch, and Margil. In the total Peasgood's was one of the parents in three cases, Ribston Pippin in two, Blenheim Orange and Warner's King also in two each.

The application of the Mendelian principles to the cross-breeding of Apples does not seem at present to have carried us far, but Laxton Brothers state that in examining the records of crosses made by their father and themselves amongst Strawberries they have found ample confirmation of Mendel's experiments and theory. The subject is very important, and all interested should study the following works : *Breeding and Mendelian Discovery*, by A. D. Darbyshire ; and *Mendelism*, by R. C. Punnett.

Besides the improvement of the fruit, which is of course the most important object in crossing, attention should be given to securing robust habit, a disease-resisting constitution, and early fertility. It might be possible to obtain varieties whose flowers were more likely to escape frost, either by changing their time of flowering or from the form and texture of the flowers themselves. That considerable differences in these respects already exist amongst the Apples grown at the present time, comes within the knowledge of cultivators who have had large numbers of varieties under their observation. Several varieties with large flowers and petals of thick substance, especially if these are turned in somewhat, or cupped at the points, are good frost-resisters. An example of this is furnished by Stirling Castle, which on many occasions within our own experience has been exposed to considerable frost at flowering time, but has escaped with few losses, while other varieties in the same situation have had the whole of their flowers destroyed.

FLOWERING AND FERTILITY

Flowering Period.—The time of flowering differs greatly amongst the varieties of Apples, and although this is affected by situation and climate, an approximate order is kept. Three groups may be formed according to the time at which the flowers are fully expanded—namely : 1. early, 2. midseason, 3. late ; and as regards a large part of central and southern England, these periods roughly correspond to the dates : May 1st to 8th, 9th to 16th, and 17th to 24th, with local variations as earlier or later extensions of these times. A few examples in each may be given from our own observations over a wide area, but it is impossible to arrange the varieties in exact order :

1. Early.

Keswick Codlin.	Hanwell Souring.
Irish Peach.	Flower of Kent.
Tower of Glammis.	Golden Spire.
Duchess of Oldenburg.	Hubbard's Pearmain.

2. Midseason.

Lord Suffield.	Baumann's Red Reinette.
Warner's King.	
Devonshire Quarrenden.	Dutch Mignonne.
Kerry Pippin.	Sturmer Pippin.
Manx Codlin.	Bramley's Seedling.
Emperor Alexander.	Royal Russet.
Yellow Ingestrie.	Cellini.
Scarlet Nonpareil.	Norfolk Beefing.
Stirling Castle.	Lord Grosvenor.
Adams' Pearmain.	Minchall Crab.

3. Late.

Blenheim Pippin.	Lord Derby.
Worcester Pearmain.	Ecklinville.
Cox's Orange Pippin.	Annie Elizabeth.
Dumelow's Seedling.	Alfriston.
Margil.	Golden Noble.
Cox's Pomona.	King Edward VII.
King of the Pippins.	Royal Jubilee.
Fearn's Pippin.	Court Pendû Plat.

Interpollination and Fertility. — Another matter in reference to the fertility of Apples is receiving more attention now than formerly, especially when forming large plantations, as the occasional defective pollen supplies can be remedied by pollination from other varieties. If the sterility arises from insufficient or unsuitable soil-food the remedy is a cultural one, which will be discussed later in this chapter ; but where

it is peculiar to the variety other means must be adopted.

Observations in various districts prove that some Apples are under ordinary conditions usually self-fertile, while others are as frequently self-sterile, and this is so generally recognized that mixed planting is much more common than formerly. It should not, however, be carried out in a haphazard or indiscriminate fashion, or the purpose will be partly or wholly defeated. When a variety selected for planting is known to be sometimes self-sterile, it is a wise precaution to select others that flower about the same time which can be relied upon as pollen producers. These should be planted either in alternate rows or alternately in each row. Bees are always valuable helpers, but are now, unfortunately, too scarce.

The following lists are founded mainly upon our own observations extending over many years, but those of Mr. Cecil H. Hooper, who has given much attention to the subject, are also included :

Usually Self-fertile.	*Usually Self-sterile.*
Adams' Pearmain.	Allington Pippin.
Annie Elizabeth.	Beauty of Bath.
Baumann's Red Reinette.	Belle de Pontoise.
	Ben's Red.
Braddick's Nonpareil.	Blenheim Orange.
Bramley's Seedling.	Cox's Pomona.
Cellini.	Duchess's Favourite.
Cockle's Pippin.	Egremont Russet.
Court Pendû Plat.	Fearn's Pippin.
Dutch Mignonne.	Golden Noble.
Early Victoria.	Golden Shire.
Ecklinville.	Hambling's Seedling.
Forge.	Hawthornden.
Gascoyne's Scarlet Seedling.	Hoary Morning.
	Lady Henniker.
Irish Peach.	Lady Sudeley.
James Grieve.	Lord Suffield.
Keswick Codlin.	Mère de Ménage.
King Edward VII.	Old Nonpareil.
King of the Pippins.	Red Astrachan.
Lord Grosvenor.	Ribston Pippin.
Margil.	Rival.
Murfitt's Seedling.	Sandringham.
Newton Wonder.	Striped Beefing.
New Northern Greening.	Sturmer Pippin.
	The Queen.
Pott's Seedling.	Waltham Abbey Seedling.
Royal Jubilee.	
Scarlet Nonpareil.	Warner's King.
Stirling Castle.	William's Favourite.
Washington.	
White Transparent.	

CULTURE

General Culture.—The Apple grows and fruits under so many different conditions of soil and climate that the limits to its adaptability appear to be widely placed. Unfortunately, this elasticity of constitution has led in some districts to a course of neglect which now shows serious effects. All earnest cultivators must desire the highest possible results that intelligent care can ensure, and the Apple is worthy of the best efforts. Every detail should have the fullest consideration, for even with the closest study there are always sufficient difficulties to contend with and problems to perplex when dealing with plant life. In British gardens the greatest success has been attained in the cultivation of the Apple, yet examples of failure can usually be found very near them, just as in some of our largest markets the finest fruits may be seen almost side by side with others comparatively worthless. Experience throws a light on many divergencies in results, and teaches that success in fruit culture is largely dependent upon attention to details that at first sight often appear unimportant.

Situation.—Where the site for a garden has been selected with judgment, there should always be ample provision for the satisfactory culture of the Apple as well as of other fruits. But we have here to consider the special requirements of this fruit alone, and the chief preliminary matters demanding attention are the situation where the trees are to be grown, including altitude, aspect, climate, and rainfall, and the nature of the soil. Throughout the British Isles there is scarcely a district where the Apple cannot be grown, except where local conditions of exposure, soil, sterility, or excessive soil-moisture are prohibitory. From Caithness to Cornwall, in Great Britain, from Antrim to Cork, in Ireland, Apples take the leading place amongst hardy fruits.

Altitude.—The range is proportionately as wide in altitude. At the Royal Caledonian Society's Apple and Pear Congress in Edinburgh, examples of twenty-seven varieties of Apples were shown which had been grown at Monaltrie, Ballater, Aberdeenshire, at an elevation of 1350 feet above sea-level. Farther south there are many instances of successful Apple plantations at considerable elevations, one of the best known being that at Mentmore, Lord Rosebery's estate in Buckinghamshire, which has an altitude of 650 feet. Grown on the higher elevations in the North of Britain the fruits are usually small and wanting in colour, while the dessert varieties are seldom satisfactory except with the protection of walls. The only extremes of altitude which are really dangerous to the Apple are in low inland districts where late spring frosts too frequently destroy the flowers, as they are also apt to do in valleys or near sluggish watercourses.

Important differences in temperature may often be caused by local conditions where the elevation is very slight. For instance, at the Woburn Experimental Fruit Farm there are two stations for meteorological observations, and the difference in the elevation is only 15 feet, yet at the lower station the minimum radiation temperature on the ground has occasionally been 5 degrees lower than that at the upper one. This means that with such a small difference in height, and within a distance of about 700 feet, all prospects of a crop of fruit might be destroyed in the one place. The air temperature registered in stands 4 feet from the ground seldom shows such marked differences. Further reference to this matter and to air-drainage will be found in the chapter on Orchards.

Aspect.—The aspect of the site chosen for Apples usually has a much greater influence on results than either latitude or altitude—at least as far as the United Kingdom is concerned. Remarkable illustrations of this fact occur in many counties, especially in the north and along the east coast. A favourable slope of the land and a little shelter make more difference between two neighbouring situations than a hundred miles north and south. For example, at Dunrobin Castle, Golspie, in Sutherlandshire, Apples are grown with success, although it is so far north ; but the situation is open to the sea on the south and well sheltered on the north, north-east, and north-west sides. Also at Skibo Castle, Dornoch, in the same county, Apples are satisfactory, but that also is well sheltered from the north. From both these gardens collections of good Apples, representing respectively twenty and sixteen varieties, were contributed to the Edinburgh Apple and Pear Congress. In each collection Devonshire Quarrenden and Stirling Castle were noted as of special merit. Yet in a large proportion of that and neighbouring counties in unfavourable aspects, Apple culture would not yield such encouraging results. Coming south some hundreds of miles, there are gardens both on the east and west sides of this island where the aspect has not been well chosen in the respects named, and where the skilled efforts of the cultivator fail to produce as good results as have been attained in the North of Scotland under better local conditions.

An essential part of the conditions included in aspect is the slope of the land, as a slight inclination in a suitable direction often ensures Apples being cultivated in unfavourable districts. The preferable directions are south, south-east, and south-west, in the order named, the respective advantages of which are reviewed in the chapter on Orchards, where also the disadvantages of an eastern inclination are noted. A fall of 2 feet in every 100 feet is a good medium incline ; if it is less than that the full benefit of the sun's heat and light is not obtained, and if it is greater other difficulties connected with too rapid surface drainage are introduced. On very steep slopes the terrace method of planting must be adopted, similar to that in the Vine-growing countries of South Europe.

In the southern counties of England the northerly slopes may be utilized under some circumstances, but such are best suited for early cooking Apples, when it is desired to prolong the supply of those varieties. The chief difficulty is in securing the thorough maturation of the wood, so that health and fruit-bearing may be continued. For this reason the upper portions of such aspects, or a side open to the west, help somewhat by providing exposure to the sun's rays for a part of the day, though they necessarily reach the trees very obliquely.

Shelter is also important as already indicated, and further details will be found in the chapter on Orchards. It affects the trees in several ways and at different times. When the flowers are expanded, protection from high winds often means the saving of a crop, if no other adverse influences intervene. After the fruit is formed, and especially when it is approaching the ripening state, shelter is even more important ; while there is the general safety of the trees to be considered.

Rainfall is a point that should have consideration, for the Apple thrives under moist atmospheric conditions, and an ample supply of moisture in the soil without stagnation is essential. The east and west counties of Great Britain differ greatly in the annual rainfall, without taking into consideration the exceptional records from high localities in Devonshire and Westmorland. In the eastern counties of England there are many places where the yearly rainfall ranges between 15 and 20 inches, while near the western coast the average would be almost double these figures. This has a material bearing upon Apple culture, for in districts where the rainfall is from 20 to 25 inches success can be obtained in heavier soils than where the annual average is nearer 40 inches. On the other hand, in the region of heavy rainfall the trees can be grown in lighter soils than in the dry counties. This matter is too frequently overlooked, yet in selecting positions for large plantations it demands close attention. It often affords an explanation of the diverse soil-conditions under which Apples give good results.

SOIL

Soil.—The majority of substantial loams and other fertile soils suited to the Apple contain ample supplies for the growth of the tree in its early stages, provided there be sufficient moisture present to render the various substances available to the roots. By chemical changes, and by the action of soil organisms, various compounds are slowly reduced to a state in which they can be absorbed by the roots ; and as far as growth only is concerned, this is usually sufficient. When fruit - production commences, a much larger additional strain is imposed upon the resources of the soil. From analyses at the Cornell Experiment Station (U.S.A.) it was determined that "five bushels of Apples remove in round numbers 11 lbs. of nitrogen, nearly 1 lb. of phosphoric acid, and 16 lbs. of potash, and that the leaves of a tree large enough to produce the Apples would contain 10 lbs. of nitrogen, nearly 3 lbs. of phosphoric acid, and 10 lbs. of potash." If the bearing of heavy fruit crops continues over a succession of years, there will be a gradual exhaustion unless the soil is very rich in the constituents named, or it receives the best cultivation with judicious manurial treatment. This distinction must be remembered, namely, that a soil which can ensure the development of a vigorous Apple-tree to fruit-bearing age, may yet prove unequal to the task of maintaining it in good condition over a long period of fruit-bearing when so much is being annually removed from the land.

It is evident, therefore, that the elements of fertility must either be present in considerable proportions, or sufficient must be added to compensate for what is being lost.

The physical constitution of the soil and mechanical means of amelioration will exercise a material influence on the results. The water-retaining power of soils and the conditions favouring the even distribution of moisture are mainly dependent upon the coarseness or fineness of the particles, and upon the proportion of clay, sand, or humus that may be present. By the various operations of digging, trenching, and hoeing, some of these conditions can be modified to such an extent that the nature and productiveness of a soil can be greatly altered without direct manurial additions. The extremes most difficult to deal with are where coarse stony gravel, clay, or chalk forms a deep subsoil immediately below a thin surface soil. As regards the Apple, the first-named is the worst, and should be avoided whenever possible. Gravel forms an effective barrier to the circulation of moisture, as while rain passes away with great rapidity, there is little rising of water from below. In the case of clay and hard chalk, water circulation is very slow and ineffective in times of drought. With a good surface soil 2 to 3 feet deep the subsoil is of less importance, provided it be not of a nature to induce the accumulation of water, and that of course can be prevented by drainage.

The consolidation of the soil has a bearing upon cultural problems. A hard condition checks root development and hinders free growth, but it has a tendency to induce greater subdivision of the roots, and in a degree may promote earlier fruit-bearing. In the opposite direction a loose condition of the soil encourages rapid growth, and if such a soil be rich as well, it often results in excessive growth with corresponding unfruitfulness.

Preparation of the Soil.—To prepare the ground properly, the directions given in treating of the formation of the kitchen garden should be followed. If circumstances will not admit of their being carried out to their full extent, they should be kept in view, and acted upon as far as possible. If the ground requires draining, that should be seen to in the first place. It must then be well trenched, whether the plantation be of small or large extent, for in either case the trees will amply repay the trouble of the operation. In trenching let the good soil be thrown up where it is deep ; let all inequalities which may then appear in the bottom of the trench be reduced, and when all is trenched over, the surface can either be levelled or made to form a regular slope

or slopes, such as may be found to agree best with its general inclination. In wet or cold subsoils it has been recommended to plant the trees on the surface, or on raised mounds or ridges. This may succeed very well for a time, but ultimately the roots will go down after moisture if this should in some dry summers be deficient near the top. It is therefore a much better plan to drain the subsoil effectually, and thus render high planting unnecessary, so far as regards too much moisture at the root. A tree cannot thrive when the extremities of the roots are in a dry medium, even although the soil close to the stem may be moist in consequence of the tree being placed in a hollow. If, on the contrary, the soil at the root extremities be moist, it is of less consequence if it is dry near the stem.

Where the soil is light, and not naturally rich enough, it should be well manured. We do not wish to encourage over-luxuriance in any case, but a healthy vigorous growth should be promoted. If, consistent with this, a tree make annually twice the quantity of shoots and foliage that another does that is stinted of nourishment, the former will be able to bear double the quantity of fruit, although it may not be disposed to commence bearing at so early a period.

Instead of applying manure from the farmyard in a fresh state, it is better to form it into a compost with a proportion of a soil that would by itself prove beneficial. Turfy loam will in all cases be suitable. The compost should be worked in as the trenching proceeds, and it should be placed chiefly between 1 foot and 2 feet below the surface. Some good compost ought to be reserved for mixing with the soil when planting the tree.

TREES

Selecting Trees.—Healthy young Apple-trees can be obtained in any quantity from the leading British nurseries. It is possible to secure trees of some varieties by thousands, even in size and moderate in price. Still, it is well for all who are purchasing in large numbers to inspect the plantations themselves, and at least select a sample of what they require. The propagation of Apple-trees is seldom resorted to in gardens at the present time, except for the perpetuation of special varieties that are not readily procurable, or on large estates where trees are raised for the tenants. This part of the subject is reviewed later in this chapter as a needful part of the gardener's knowledge, but one which he is only called upon to exercise in special cases. The selection of

Fig. 23.—Feathered Standard Apple.

trees, the different forms of training and their particular merits, the character and advantages of the various stocks, are matters which come within the experience of all, and therefore demand prior attention.

The natural form of the Apple-tree, that which permits the full-est development and the greatest durability, is the standard on the Crab or free stock. For orchard purposes these are obtainable with clean stems 5 to 6 feet high from the root to the head ; but for ordinary planting, or at least where cattle will not have access to the trees, low or half standards, with stems 3 to 4 feet high, are often preferred. Usually these form their heads more quickly, and they are more convenient for cultural attendance. The main objection to standards in gardens, or wherever fruit is in urgent demand, is the

length of time the majority of varieties in this form require before profitable cropping commences. Ten years or more will elapse with some varieties before fruit is produced in quantity, and Blenheim Pippin is a notable example of the extreme in this respect, as the above limits are sometimes exceeded. Some of the more prolific Apples reach a bearing state much earlier, such as Lord Grosvenor, which we have known to produce good crops when five or six years old. As a permanent plantation, and for the improvement of an estate where the future has to be regarded as well as the present, standard Apples are certainly desirable, as if well grown and in suitable soil they will often continue bearing profitable crops for over 100 years. The value of a finely-developed Apple-tree that yields 20 bushels and upwards of good fruit can be easily estimated.

For gardens and plantations where early returns from the land are essential, and as a portion of an orchard of standards where livestock is not admitted, dwarf trees on Paradise stocks (fig. 24) are by far the most useful. In any case of short tenancy it hardly pays to plant standard Apples, as though compensation may be secured at the termination of the occupancy for the then value of the trees, this does not represent the loss to the growers in the land they have occupied unprofitably as regards actual returns in the meantime. Either as bush or pyramid

Fig. 24.—Dwarf or Low Standard Tree on Paradise Stock.

trees on suitable stocks, Apples will produce fine fruits in the second and third year, and with the best cultivation and attention the more robust can be relied upon for twenty to thirty years, and under very favourable circumstances for longer periods. For general purposes the dwarf Apple on the best English stocks is one of the most useful trees that can be grown. The bush form is naturally adapted to the habit of most varieties, and if grown with clean stems 1 to 2 feet high, handsome freely-branched trees can be formed in a few years. The

Apples of some varieties are grown on the Crab or free stock, and prove very satisfactory.

The more formally trained trees are exclusively adapted for gardens, and are especially suited for planting near walks and as divisional lines in kitchen gardens. The larger of these are the espalier in the horizontal or vertical forms, the first—the horizontal espaliers—having the lateral branches trained at right angles to the central stem (fig. 25); the second—the vertical espalier or " gridiron " trees—having the main branches taken to the right and left of the stem, from which vertical branches are trained up at intervals, all branches in both forms being in the same plane, so that they can be secured to trellises or walls. The principal other form adapted for the Apple is the cordon, which is a still more restricted and artificial style of training. This is usually grown in the horizontal form, either with a single stem in one direction, or with two in opposite directions (double horizontal cordon). The trees can also be formed with stems inclined at an angle either as single, double, or triple oblique cordons, but these are not much in use in this country, the horizontal cordons being preferred as edges to walks, &c., where, under skilful treatment, very handsome exhibition fruits can be obtained.

Fig. 25.—Espalier Apple-tree—horizontally trained.

pyramid form can be adopted with many varieties that naturally grow with a stout leading stem, but the Apple does not retain this form so well as the Pear. In addition to the early fruit-bearing, dwarf trees offer many advantages. They are convenient for pruning, for fruit gathering, for spraying and cleaning. A large number of trees can be planted in comparatively small spaces, and the produce of thriving fruitful dwarf Apple-trees has exceeded 500 bushels per acre in a few years from planting where the conditions have been favourable. Bush

The bush form admits of several variations of a more artificial character than the type; of these the most notable is the bowl-shaped, in which all the central stems and branches are removed, a series of even outer branches being trained outwards and then vertically, and treated after the manner of upright cordons. Fine fruits can be had in this form, and well-balanced trees have a distinct appearance in a garden, but they require a good deal of attention in pruning and training to keep them in the right condition.

Whatever form of tree is required, endeavour to select such as are free from any indication of disease or deformity. Let them be trees that appear to have grown freely but naturally from the bud or graft; excessively vigorous or stunted trees are to be avoided, but the latter are the worst. See that the juncture of stock and scion is even and the union complete, as that is occasionally a source of material weakness. The characteristic habit of the variety must be remembered, and it is not always the most symmetrical tree that is the most fruitful, though symmetry is a point that must be considered.

Stocks and their Effects.—The great majority of Apple-trees raised in nurseries are worked upon stocks of some kind. The principal important difference between stocks is in regard to their origin, namely whether they have been raised from seed or from layers. Plants differing widely in strength will be obtained in both methods, but generally the layers are more even, because only the best and most suitable branches are selected for the purpose. The chief point is that there is a material difference in the root systems of the two classes of stocks, which may occasionally be only asserted temporarily, while in other cases it will be found to be permanent. The vigorous vertical tap-root of a seedling Crab, Apple, or Pear gives rise in the early stage to the correspondingly strong upward growth of the stems and branches, hence the name " Free Stock " that is commonly applied to them. With layers of all the Paradise stocks, or those raised in a similar way, the root system differs in the fact that there is no direct downward extension of the main axis into the tap-root, but the first roots produced are fibrous, similar to those of a rooted cutting around that part of the branch covered with soil, and from the callus formed on the cut portion. In the case of the seedling Crab or Apple we have a natural unrestrained root system, and in the layered Paradise or dwarfing stock the root system is restricted. In consequence there is a broad distinction in their initial stages between trees budded or grafted upon the " free " and the " dwarfing " stocks, for stem and branch growth correspond in degree to the root vigour and character. Experience with many varieties of fruits in differing soils and situations proves, however, that it is impossible to lay down a definite rule even with regard to the behaviour of any one variety under all circumstances on the respective stocks. Observation, too, will show that this is not surprising, for it is possible to have a seedling stock with abundant fibrous roots, and it is equally possible to have a layered stock with few fibres. We have seen many that possessed all the characters considered to be peculiar to the others. Then again the root growth of the " free " stocks can be to some extent

modified by shortening the tap-root, or bending it into a horizontal direction, while in some soils a strong rooting habit is induced in the Paradise and other layered stocks. In the true types of each the differ-

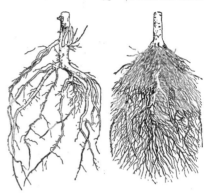

Fig. 26.—Wild Crab Apple Stock.   Fig. 27.—Paradise Stock.

ence is clear, but they are rarely selected in that way, and the result is all the divergent experiences recorded by horticulturists regarding the adaptability of certain varieties to different stocks. Apart from this, some varieties of fruits possess an overpowering vitality, the effects of which in a few years are visible on both stocks and roots, completely extinguishing all special peculiarities of the former.

We may therefore take it in a general way that seedling stocks encourage free growth and postpone fruiting, but prolong tree life, while the layered stocks restrict growth, promote early fruit production, and possibly shorten the average life of the tree.

Many nurserymen now employ Paradise stocks of their own selection, and use layers from these almost exclusively. There are several types of the broad-leaved Paradise thus employed, as well as the Nonesuch, all of which have originated from selected seedlings. The whole of these show greater strength than the French Paradise, the Doucin, and others of Continental origin, and are better adapted for the Apple as cultivated in Great Britain, ensuring fully developed and lasting trees. The French Paradise stocks are used for producing miniature trees, which flower very early.

The Crab stocks raised from seed of trees growing wild in the country usually present a marked difference from " free " stocks, which often are raised from the seeds of refuse Apples. The latter are most variable, and produce corresponding differences in the behaviour of the Apples worked upon them ; the true Crab after the first few years makes moderate growth, and rarely produces fruit in less than eight to ten years.

The Age of Trees.—The age of trees at the time of planting has a bearing upon growth as well as upon fruit production. It is frequently asked : At what age is an Apple in the best state for planting in its permanent quarters ? and various answers are given in accordance with equally varied experience. As regards growth only, it has been proved in some instances that a tree one year old from the bud or graft becomes better established and forms a proportionately more vigorous specimen in three or four years' time from the planting, than an older tree will do that has been subjected to several removals. The effect on fruit production is not so easily determined ; but even in this respect there are many cases where the ultimate advantage has proved to be in favour of the younger trees. If one-year-old trees are planted they require extra care in the early pruning and training, there is also a longer time to wait before crops can be obtained ; but against this we have to take the lower cost of the trees and their quick establishment. Well-developed two-year-old trees are very serviceable, and for garden purposes generally three-year-old properly-prepared trees are usually preferred, as fruit is secured early. These remarks apply specially to dwarf Apples on Paradise stocks ; in the case of standards it is seldom advisable to purchase trees under three or four years old.

In all instances the due preparation in a nursery means that they should have been lifted and replanted to keep the roots within moderate limits. If a young tree has been left undisturbed for a long time, and it has become strongly rooted in the soil, the transference to fresh quarters necessitates considerable root injury, and a corresponding check to the growth, which is not recovered from very readily.

Time to Plant.—The Apple can be planted at any time from the falling of the leaf until the buds start in spring. The success of the trees depends mainly upon their condition and the state of the soil at the time of planting. There are, however, several good reasons for the early autumn being preferred for this operation. In the first place the weather and soil conditions are usually more favourable for preparing the land and lifting and transferring the trees. Then,

too, if trees are selected in a nursery, the earlier the choice is made the better chance there is of securing what are required. Above all, if trees are planted before the soil has lost the heat accumulated during summer and autumn, and before winter rains have saturated it, the injured roots have a better opportunity to heal. The tree also has time to recover from the check before growth commences in the spring.

But it is by no means essential that Apples should be planted in October or November. It might, for instance, be advisable to postpone the work on account of excessive wet, especially on heavy land. On light soil the rain might not interfere with the work, and in many cases it would prove beneficial.

Very early planting, *i.e.* before all the leaves have fallen, is not recommended ; in moist districts and seasons it can be done without much risk, but there is always danger of the young growth shrivelling.

Trees planted late in the season are often injured by drought, and if the buds start before the roots are able to meet the demands upon them failure will probably result. This may be partly avoided by close attention to watering and syringing. We have planted young Apple-trees in April, when the buds are expanding, without the loss of a single specimen, but the cost of the needful attention renders such planting an expensive proceeding. The particular season must always be taken into consideration, as there may be quite a month's difference in the starting of growth in the different years, and what may be safe in one season would be dangerously late in another. It is therefore impossible to fix definite dates for such work without the risk of their proving misleading to the inexperienced. The simplest rule is :

Plant Apples as soon after the leaf falls as the soil is in a suitable condition, avoiding frost at all times, and a wet state on heavy or adhesive soils.

Distances for Trees.—If a large plantation or orchard of Apples is to be formed, it will be needful to determine the arrangement and distances before the trees are secured. The principal methods of placing the trees are described in the chapter on Orchards, and it is only necessary here to give the most suitable distances for Apples.

Standards of the moderate-growing varieties may be planted 18 or 20 feet apart, but in orchards or mixed plantations where other fruit-trees are introduced between the trees as temporary crops, it is always advantageous to allow more space. There is a tendency to plant such trees too closely. A distance of 30 feet should be allowed whenever possible, and all strong-growing varieties must have this space at least, while even 35 or 40 feet may be allowed where growth is vigorous. The greater distances are advantageous for plantations in rich soil and moist districts, where, unless provision is made for a free circulation of air amongst the trees, they soon become loaded with lichens. Crowding is bad under any circumstances, but in such localities as those referred to, of which abundant examples will be found in some of the western counties, close planting produces in a few years its worst effects.

We have seen standard Apples planted 10 feet, 12 feet, and 15 feet apart with the intention of "thinning" the plantation as soon as necessary, but in too many instances the thinning is deferred until all the trees have suffered from crowding, and the removal of the extra trees is then attended with danger to those which remain, both as regards root disturbance and wind effects on the weakened permanent trees. This is a defect that is perhaps more frequently demonstrated in commercial or market plantations than in private gardens, as when the possibility of danger from "thinning" is recognized the trees are often left from year to year until a dense and useless thicket is formed. It is safer and preferable in every way to allow minimum distances of 20 feet or 30 feet, for medium and strong sorts respectively as standards, and fill the intermediate spaces either with dwarf trees or other kinds of fruit of bushy habit. Thinning will not then be such a serious matter, as the heads of the standards can develop freely.

Dwarf Apples on Paradise stocks, either as bushes or pyramids, can be planted at 6 feet to 12 feet apart, but there are few varieties which will stand many years at the first distance, unless they are pigmy trees on some very dwarfing stock. In the list of select varieties at the end of this chapter we indicate separately some of the best small-growing varieties; these can be planted as stated.

Examples of useful small-growing sorts are Seaton House, Stirling Castle (fig. 24), and Margil, which under ordinary circumstances can be grown for ten years at 6 feet apart, and sometimes even permanently.

For the majority of dwarf Apples 10 feet is the most suitable distance, and this allows space for the free development of the trees, and permits intermediate cropping or culti-

vation. Bush Apples on the free stocks (either seedling Apple or Crab) should be at least 12 feet apart, and in the best soils 15 feet is not too much for the strongest varieties.

Espaliers on trellises or walls require 20 feet distance to permit full development, and fan-trained trees (though they are seldom grown now) need similar distances. Single horizontal cordons should be 10 feet apart, and double horizontal cordons 20 feet, thus allowing an extension of 10 feet in each direction. If single oblique or vertical cordons are grown they can be planted at 2 feet apart, and are then useful for filling up the intermediate spaces on a trellis or wall while espaliers are attaining their full size.

Marking the Stations.—When the plan and distances have been decided upon, the next point is setting out the places for the trees, and though this is a matter that does not present any great difficulties several details require attention. A well-designed and carefully-laid-out orchard or plantation has a very pleasing appearance, and it is worth a little extra trouble at the beginning to ensure this. If a good base-line is secured to start with, it is not a difficult task to set off a plantation of fruit-trees with rod or tape, line, and pegs, in any shape and at any required distances. The chief points to be observed are to have the first line straight, to be accurate in measuring off the distances, and to set the pegs each time in the same position on the tape or rod marks. Mistakes are often made by the inexperienced in this work, by sometimes setting the pegs inside and at others outside the mark, and in a large plantation this soon leads to considerable irregularity that will take a good deal of time to correct when the trees are set out. If pegs of equal diameter are used, and approximately equal to the diameter of the stems, the measurement may be conveniently made from the inside of one stake to the inside of the next in the same line. But in this case allowance must be made for the diameter of the pegs in the total length of the row. For example, if fifty trees are to be set out in one line at 10 feet apart, the total length required, if the stakes or pegs are 2 inches in diameter, will be 508 feet 4 inches, not 500 feet. If the stations are set off exactly at 10 feet, the measurement must either be made from centre to centre of the pegs, or from the inside edge of one to the outside edge of the next, or *vice versa*. There is more risk of mistakes in taking the centres of the stakes than in measuring to the edge, provided they are all equal in size. These appear simple matters to dwell upon in detail, but we have seen troublesome errors arise from ignoring them, which are necessarily more marked in the largest plantations.

If the pegs are only used for the purpose of marking off the plantation, and are to be removed as planting proceeds, it is a material help if a tree is first planted at the end of the line, and one in the centre, as they can then be sighted from either end of the row, and afford a guide for keeping the others in line.

Stakes.—If staking is an essential procedure to ensure the safety of the trees, as it is in many situations, there are several advantages in using the stakes for marking out the ground and at once putting them in position for the trees. Under the best circumstances staking can only be regarded as a necessary evil, and whenever such support can be dispensed with it is desirable to do so. But it is only in very sheltered situations, or where one- or two-year-old trees are selected, that stakes are not needed. They are especially requisite for standards; but even dwarf trees, if well developed, require securing in some way. The operation should be simplified as much as possible if the object is only to protect the trees from damage by wind until they are well rooted. Where trees are planted in grass-land used for grazing, more elaborate precautions will be required. These are referred to under the head of protection. I light, loose soils staking is particularly important, and it is necessary to have the stakes of sufficient length to allow them to be driven deeper into the soil than in heavier land. For standard Apples they should be from 5 to 7 feet long, proportionate to the length of the stems, allowing from $1\frac{1}{2}$ to 2 feet of the stake in the soil; for dwarf trees a length of $2\frac{1}{2}$ to 3 feet is usually sufficient, and a foot length in the ground is generally enough to keep the trees steady.

Stakes with rough surfaces or edges are objectionable, as there is more danger of stem abrasion, and those with the bark attached, especially if somewhat loose, provide retreats for insect pests. The stakes should preferably be round, as the edges of square ones are sometimes a source of trouble; and they must be of sufficient diameter to give the requisite rigidity, not less than $2\frac{1}{2}$ inches. The base should be evenly pointed, as they can then be driven into the ground with more regularity; if cut wedge-shaped they are easily thrown out

of their places by stones or hard clogs of earth when being forced into the soil. When sufficient time can be allowed for the stakes to dry before they are wanted for use, they should be well tarred; and sound stakes so prepared will last for years, probably, indeed, until the trees are independent of their aid.

The preceding remarks refer to cases where a single stake is employed for each

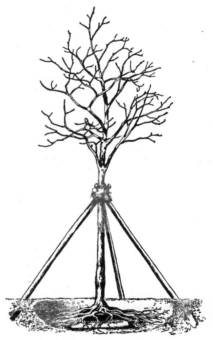

Fig. 28.—Method of Planting and Staking.

tree, which is planted up to the support, and therefore is exposed to some risk of bark injury unless due precautions are adopted to avoid this by suitable tying, or by pads between the tree and the stake. It is sometimes found more advantageous to have two or three stakes to each tree (fig. 28), which cannot then be placed close to the stem, and they cannot be readily utilized for marking out the exact stations, but the method is convenient where extra protection is needed.

Size of Holes.—If the whole of the ground has to be cultivated as directed earlier in this chapter, it will not be advisable to make the holes for the trees until planting can be proceeded with. In grass-land the stations must all be prepared in advance, removing the turf from a space 4 to 6 feet in diameter (preferably the latter), and either cutting up the turf for incorporation with the soil in digging or, if that is not desirable, taking it away altogether. In the lighter or poor soils the addition of the broken-up turf is beneficial, but in those of a heavier and more fertile character it is not necessary.

Treatment of Trees on Arrival.—The majority of nurserymen now give special attention to the careful packing of fruit-trees for sending by road or rail, in fact, the packing of plants constitutes a most important department in a nursery. The result is that Apple-trees can be sent some hundreds of miles absolutely secure from external injury. As, however, railway journeys are occasionally unduly prolonged, risk is incurred in the drying of the roots and stems. More failures arise from this cause than from any other in connection with the removal of Apples, yet it is frequently overlooked, and disasters are attributed to everything but the right cause. The most serious results in this direction are seen in very early autumn or late spring planting, but it has been found that evaporation from the bark of Apple-trees is considerable, even in the winter when the air is dry. As regards the smaller twigs, the moisture evaporated has been found to exceed 10 per cent of their total weight in a few hours. It is not desirable to expose either roots or trees to severe frosts, but with ordinary care the roots of Apple-trees are uninjured by frost, whereas we have seen many either seriously checked or killed by undue drying in transit.

If the trees arrive at a time when the weather or soil is unfavourable for planting immediately, they should be unpacked and carefully laid in by the roots in trenches in a sheltered position. When the soil is frozen too hard for this proceeding, if cool sheds are available the trees should be placed in them, and the roots covered with damp mats or soil. For late spring planting in dry weather it is advisable to dip the roots of the trees in water as soon as they are received, and if they appear to have been much dried this can be repeated before planting.

Planting.—In the operation of planting Apple-trees one of the most important conditions is the state of the soil at the time, and particularly on heavy land. If the holes are made in adhesive soil when wet, the sides will often dry into a brick-like consistency almost impervious to roots and water. Thus moisture is excluded in dry weather, and in wet times it cannot pass away freely, as the base of the hole will probably be in a similar puddled state. Trees planted in this way often show the ill effects for years.

The soil must in all cases be broken down into a moderately fine state, and the more numerous the roots of the trees to be planted, the more important this is. In rough soil carelessly filled in a large proportion of the roots are for a time inoperative, and some are permanently injured. It is impossible to plant trees satisfactorily where the soil is in coarse clod-like lumps.

The size of the hole must be proportionate to the extent of the roots, but it is well to allow at least 6 inches more than the spread of the roots, as they can be regulated more thoroughly. The depth also will depend upon the roots, as Apples on Crab or free stocks, which produce strong downward roots, must have a greater depth than those of the surface-rooting Paradise stocks. In the former case the advice usually given, to " spread the roots," is often quite impracticable, as with three- or four-year-old trees these are as strong and inflexible as the main branches, and all that can be done is to carefully fill in the soil amongst them. Such trees may need holes 1 to 1½ feet deep, while the more horizontal-rooted dwarfing stocks may require only 9 to 12 inches.

These directions will need modification by the nature of the soil and the moisture present. For instance, it is not only safe to plant deeper in light soils than in heavy ones, but it is sometimes a preferable course if there is no danger of getting into an unsuitable subsoil, as the roots are less likely to suffer from drought than when near the surface. In very dry soils and climates deep rooting should be encouraged for this reason, whereas in heavy soils shallow planting is advantageous. The often repeated direction to plant Apples or other trees at the same depth as they have been in the nursery is usually a safe course to follow.

Planting on the surface and mounding up the roots is advocated and practised in wet situations and in extremely heavy soils, but Apples should only be planted under such conditions in very exceptional circumstances. It would be unwise to attempt to form a commercial plantation in that way. A thorough system of tile-draining would be a preferable proceeding, or, if the situation is too low for this, superficial draining may be attempted by means of shallow trenches running across the ground.

The Apple-trees intended for planting should be carefully examined, and all damaged roots cut clean at the points with a sharp knife, either straight across, or with a slight slope on the upper side, the former being better for all downward roots, and the latter for the horizontal roots. If any branches start too low down the stem they can also be more readily removed before the tree is planted.

If the stakes are in position and the holes prepared as directed, it is only necessary to place the trees by the stakes at the required depth, spread out the roots as evenly as possible in all directions, and fill in the soil. The latter part of the operation should be done gradually and with care ; some workmen throw large spadefuls of soil on, or roll it in from the sides, as if the only object was to conceal the roots as quickly as possible. The work is never done satisfactorily in this way. Small quantities of the finer soil should be placed over the roots first and worked in among them with a stick if necessary ; after this the remainder can be completed with more speed. Where stout roots start from near the base of the stem in a downward direction it often leaves a hollow that should be provided for by making a slight mound for the base of the tree to rest upon, otherwise it is often difficult to fill in properly afterwards. With the exception already referred to, the roots should be arranged as near the surface as seems safe, and with a slight upward rather than a downward bearing at the points. It is advisable to go over the plantation several times in the season after planting for the purpose of treading the soil firmly about the roots. In light soil, if the weather be very dry at the time of planting, a thorough watering will help to settle the soil. On heavy soils treading over the roots requires more care, or, if wet, it will be forced into a solid mass that can never be restored to its former condition without moving the trees. When the soil is fairly dry, light treading only is needed to render the trees sufficiently firm, and it is better to let the process be effected gradually by the sinking of the soil than to tread it hard.

Treatment after Planting.—The first consideration after planting a well-developed Apple-tree, either a standard or dwarf, is whether the branches shall be cut back immediately or left for a season. Opinions and practice differ on this question, and

varied experience as to the merits of each method has no doubt resulted from the different circumstances under which each may have been carried out. Cutting back at once after planting is supported by the view that in reducing the branches the balance between those and the roots which have suffered in the removal is maintained. There is, therefore, less demand upon the latter until they have had time to become established and can perform their proper functions, than if the branches are allowed to remain their full length and produce a larger number of leaves. Another point in favour of this plan is that the lower buds on the branches are later in starting to grow, and this gives the tree a better chance to recover before the leaves expand.

Those who prefer postponing the cutting back for a season do so on the ground that the greater number of leaves produced by the unpruned branches assist the formation of roots, and this helps to restore the tree more quickly. In moist, cloudy springs this is probably true, but in hot, dry weather the benefit derivable from the leaves is reduced by the great evaporation which takes place from them, and the ill effects are visible both in the dying back of the young shoots and in the shrivelling of the wood unless the roots have become well established. In a general way, therefore, we have found it safer to cut back at once, better formed and more compact trees being usually the result.

GENERAL PRUNING AND TRAINING

In the following directions the procedure necessary to secure well-balanced trees is detailed for each form of training, and the treatment is traced in most cases from the maiden stage, though it is more usual and convenient in gardens to purchase trees which have passed through the first degrees of training in the nurseries.

Standards.—It is highly important that these should be reared with clean straight stems ; that the stem should be self-supporting ; that the head should be commenced at the proper height ; and that it should be formed with regularity. The mode formerly adopted to obtain clean stems rendered continuous staking essential ; and a tree for which staking is absolutely necessary in its youth will always be liable to lean and twist after it has attained a considerable size. When the maiden tree had been well transplanted, and was in a vigorous state, it was not an unusual practice to keep the stems well trimmed, that is to say, every shoot that appeared upon them was cut closely in till the desired height was attained. A few shoots at the top were only to be seen, and a slender stem unable to keep itself upright was the consequence. This is an artificial stem, for the Apple does not grow in a natural state to the height of 6 or 7 feet without side branches, which bear leaves to thicken and strengthen the lower part of the stem. When the tree with the artificially-formed stem is transplanted, it has, however, this advantage, that though

To rear a straight substantial stem incurs little additional trouble in the first instance—much after expense is saved—and at the same time a satisfactory result is ensured. It has been explained in the chapter on Pruning that roots and wood are produced in proportion to the amount of foliage. In rearing a properly-constituted stem we must bear in mind that important fact. We cannot by any means get so much work done by a few leaves at the top of a stem as we can by ten times the number produced partly at the top and partly along the sides.

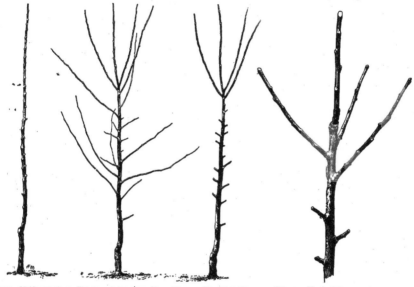

Fig. 29.—Maiden tree (one year from bud). Can be cut down to form a dwarf or espalier, or remain the full length for a standard.

Fig. 30.—A two-year-old standard, unpruned.

Fig. 31.—The same tree with lateral growths shortened and head prepared for the first pruning.

Fig. 32.—Head of the same tree enlarged to show pruning for the leading shoot and the three main branches.

liable to bend from feebleness, it can be easily lashed straight to a stake, and so far some good comes out of evil ; but on the other hand the stem will require support for years. Rather than have crooked trees, it is better to make sure of straight ones by supplying a fresh set of stakes, and by the time these become decayed, the trees, on their removal, will exhibit straight and apparently self-supporting stems ; but left to their own strength to support their tops, now large enough to be acted upon with considerable effect by the wind, the stems bend, and cannot then be straightened.

We want thickness of stem, for if we have that, the desired height will be attained in one or two seasons ; but if the stem is tall and disproportionately slender, it is very difficult to render it inflexible. A slender stem, 6 or 7 feet high, and which has no leaves to thicken it except those above that height, will increase equally along its whole length. To be self-supporting it should be thickest at the base, as would have been the case had it not been for the injudicious use of the knife.

A well-grown stem should have the following dimensions : Height, 6 feet ;

diameter at base, 3 inches ; in the middle, 2½ inches ; and at 6 feet high, where the top begins to branch, 2 inches ; this will be self-supporting. A stem that has once assumed a tapering form will retain that form as long as it exists. The whole tree may be torn up by a hurricane, but the stem will not become crooked, and this is precisely the kind of stem that is wanted. We shall therefore endeavour to show how it may be obtained.

Commencing with the maiden shoot from the graft or bud, we find it during summer furnished with leaves from near its base to its extremity. If at the end of the growing season we girth the shoot at the top and successively below each leaf downwards, we shall find that every girth is greater and greater as we descend. The difference between each measurement will be greater or less according to the health, nature, and size of the leaves. Where a portion of a shoot is deprived of leaves such gradation does not take place, but if there are leaves below the naked portion, there will be a sensible difference in the increase of girth below the first of them, and so on to the base. From what has been stated it is evident that all the leaves on the first shoot from the graft or bud should be encouraged. When the leaves fall in autumn, buds more or less prominent will be seen along the stem, and perhaps some may have grown into laterals ; the latter should be shortened to two buds.

In the second season the terminal bud will start into vigorous growth if no accident has happened to it, as will also several others along the shoot, and some will remain dormant, especially those near the base. The shoots that do start should be allowed to grow, taking care, however, to check any that are likely to compete with the leader. Foliage should be encouraged on the latter, and likewise on the young shoots of the previous year. With regard to the laterals on the former year's shoots, they may be allowed to grow till the end of July, and their extremities should then be pinched or cut off. The reason for allowing them to grow is in order that they may bear foliage to give additional strength to the stem below them. The foliage of these laterals also encourages root growth.

In autumn, when the growth of the second season is completed, the tree will exhibit a stem consisting of the first summer's shoot, now two years old, and, in continuation, the young shoot or leader which has just ceased growing. The laterals stopped

in July should now be shortened to one or two buds, with the exception of two or three of the lowest, which should be cut close to the stem. The same mode of proceeding with regard to the side shoots on the stem should be adopted every year. As the head of the tree is in course of formation, and is producing abundance of foliage, the side shoots can be gradually dispensed with. The quantity of foliage on a young tree should considerably exceed every year that of the previous one ; therefore in gradually removing side shoots, care should be taken that the consequent diminution of foliage should bear only a small proportion to the increase made by the new branches and shoots at the top. The rate of increase of these must regulate the more or less gradual removal and final clearance of the side shoots.

If the tree has been planted in rich soil, and has consequently grown vigorously, the upright leader will have attained the height of more than 6 feet. But whatever may be the intended height of the clear stem, the leading shoot ought to be cut three buds above that height, which would be a few inches above 6 feet from the ground for a stem 6 feet high. Supposing, however, that the extremity of the shoot reached very little above the intended height of stem, the buds immediately below the cut, and which are to commence the main limbs of the tree, would be situated on the softest part of the shoot. Instead of this it would be desirable that these limbs should originate from buds on the more substantial part of the shoot ; therefore, if it happen that the shoot is not firm at the required height, it will be advisable to let it grow for another season, and then cut it back.

In the following spring three shoots should be encouraged from the three buds just below the place where the leader was cut. Three main branches are better than two, as regards the formation of a well-balanced head ; four are too many from the same point, or so nearly from the same point that when they become large they appear to have so originated.

As the shoots grow they should receive particular attention throughout the summer, for much depends on the limbs being fairly and equally started. If left to themselves, they will rarely proceed at an equal rate of growth. The uppermost will incline to take the lead, and will endeavour to grow upright to form a stem. This tendency must, however, be checked in good time. The shoot having this inclination should be made to diverge at a lower angle than either of the others ; and, on the other hand, the weakest shoot ought to be elevated the most. In short, equality of growth between these primary shoots must be maintained.

Before the growing season is over, 1 foot at least of the lower part of each shoot ought to be made straight, and all three should be trained equidistant, and to diverge from the stem at an angle of about 45°. At the autumn or winter pruning each of the shoots should be cut back to within 9 inches or 1 foot of its base, observing to cut above

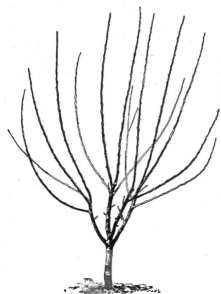

Fig. 33.—Three-year-old dwarf Apple, before pruning.

two buds as nearly opposite to each other as possible, and pointing in the direction which it is desirable the shoots springing from them should take.

In the following season two shoots, and no more, should be encouraged from each of the three original ones. The head will then consist of six shoots, originating six principal branches. By a little attention in summer, these can easily be kept at equal distances from each other, and also from the centre. The tree, it is presumed, being vigorous, many shoots will grow from the branches formed as above directed. If these were allowed to remain till autumn,

and then cut back, many more would again start in the following spring ; or if they were cut off closely, the branches would be too naked. It will therefore be advisable to pinch them in summer, when they have grown 6 inches, commencing with the strongest. By this process shoots that would otherwise cause confusion can be made to assume the character of fruit-spurs, from which some of the largest and fairest fruit will be obtained. This is also the way to turn to account any strong shoot, or rather any one that would evidently become such, and which, if allowed to proceed, would occupy a position where it was not wanted.

It is better to attend to this in summer than to allow the shoot to grow till autumn and then cut it back ; and this again is better than permitting it to remain for some years and form a thick branch which must then be cut out. In short, the head being fairly started with its six equidistant branches,

Fig. 34.—The same tree, after pruning either for a pyramid or a bush.

it may be left to itself, with the exception of pinching, as above recommended, any badly-placed shoot, and checking leaders that are likely to become too strong.

Dwarf Pyramids and Bushes.—In order to have a well-formed pyramid tree, it is best to begin with a maiden and merely top it. Allow it to establish itself for a year, then cut it down to about 1 foot from the ground. Train upright a shoot from the uppermost bud, and outwards the shoots that may push below. After the leaves have fallen, shorten the upright leading shoots to 15 inches above where it was cut in the preceding year. Proceed thus every year till the tree attains the desired height. This may be from 6 feet to 12 feet, according to the distance from other plants or trees that would be injured by shade.

In the formation of a well-shaped bush Apple, the points to be borne in mind are practically the same as in the preceding, but a more open character is aimed at, and the main central stem is not so essential as it is to the pyramidal form. The branches should be disposed as evenly as possible, and induced to grow outwards by pruning to a bud pointing to the circumference of the tree's branches. Some varieties on the

The last thinning of the shoots, and final stopping, should take place about the end of August. The fruit-buds will form, and both the young wood and fruit will have a chance to ripen satisfactorily. If the pruning is well managed, any other training is seldom necessary.

Dwarf Bowl-shaped Trees.—If the tree has made one season's growth from the graft or bud, it may be planted in autumn ; the extremities of the shoots must be shortened a little, and it should be allowed to grow at full freedom till next autumn, when it must be cut down to within 9 inches of the ground.

Fig. 35.—A well-developed six-year-old pyramid Apple, after pruning.

The tree, having been a year established, will now be able to produce vigorous shoots, three of which should be selected, as in forming the head of a standard. During the summer, care should be taken that the three shoots make equal growths. They must be cut back at the winter pruning to between 6 and 9 inches in length, and thus, as in the case of standards, six branches will be originated. These should be allowed to grow freely during the summer, so as to be tolerably straight, and if kept equidistant so much the better.

It would be advisable to regulate these six shoots in winter by training them to a hoop, which ought to be 6 feet in circumference, and the branches, secured at equal distances, would then be just 1 foot apart. In many cases materials for hoops might not be at hand, and the purchase of them might be found too expensive. If so, three straight or nearly straight sticks, about 2 feet long, may be substituted. Three such lengths can be much more easily procured than a hoop 6 feet round. At $\frac{1}{2}$ inch from each end of the 2-feet sticks cut a notch, so that a piece of bass, tied round, may not slip. Place the stick across the centre of the tree, and secure the two opposite shoots by the ties, near the end of the stick. Stretch the sticks in a similar manner between the other two pairs of opposite branches. When this is done, each branch ought to be exactly 1 foot from those next to it ; if any are wider apart than that distance, let them be brought

dwarfing stocks require very little pruning after the first year or two, as they make but moderate growth, indeed it is occasionally difficult to keep such trees sufficiently furnished with fresh shoots.

Some varieties may be both pruned and trained in summer by removing the young shoots where they are crowding each other, for if sun and air are not freely admitted to the centre of the trees, fruit-buds will be formed sparingly or not at all. The shoots allowed to remain should be shortened, 6 inches of the young wood to remain afterwards. When the trees have grown to the required size, and are in full bearing, the young wood should be closely cut in.

to it. Whether a hoop or this contrivance be employed, the shoots, after being secured, should be shortened to a few inches above the hoop or place where they are 1 foot apart, in order that each of the six branches may be there subdivided into two, making twelve in all. In shortening, where the leading branch is not intended to be subdivided, observe to cut above a bud pointing away from the centre, or in the direction that the shoot forming a prolongation of the branch is desired to take. From the inclination of the branches, and favoured by the open space which they form, strong shoots from the upper sides of the inclined branches will be apt to start in the middle of the tree, where their presence would prove injurious. The means already pointed out for converting what would otherwise prove worse than useless shoots into fruit-spurs, should therefore be employed.

Cordons. — This system of training is adapted both for large and small gardens. The usual forms are the simple lateral (fig. 38) and the bilateral (fig. 39). The lateral consists of a single shoot bent in a horizontal position, and trained along a single wire fixed about a foot from the surface of the ground. This wire is fixed at one end to a stout iron support, which is best kept in position by being soldered into a solid block of stone. This is rather expensive at first, but when its durability is taken into consideration, it is as cheap and far more satisfactory than posts made of oak or other wood, which in some soils soon decay. One of these permanent iron supports may be placed at each end of a very long border, and to keep the wire steady, iron supports should be placed at every 10 or 12 feet; these should have a hole drilled near the top, and the wire be run through these holes before it is permanently fixed.

For tightening the wires the useful little appliance termed the raidisseur, which has been in use for many years in French gardens, and is now manufactured in England at a cheap rate, is the best, as however tightly the wire may be strained at first, in the course of a year or two it will hang loosely, then by simply turning the key of the raidisseur it can be made firm at once. It may be fixed on any part of the wire between the two end-posts.

For training as cordons, plants one year from the graft may be selected, or if required to come into immediate bearing, trained trees can be obtained. Beginning, then, with maiden plants, we plant one in a sloping position, at every 6 feet along the wire, and all that is required is to bend down the

Fig. 36.—A well-developed six-year-old bush Apple, after pruning.

shoot and fasten it to the wire; being placed in such a position, buds will start growing regularly along its whole length, and the wire thus be furnished in two or three years. Sometimes each tree is in-arched on the one next it, as represented in fig. 36, so that the whole of the branches form a continuous line. This is frequently practised on the Continent. Persistent summer pinching will soon throw the trees into bearing if the same stocks are used as are recommended for bushes. Double or bilateral cordons are formed by heading down the young trees to within ten inches of the ground, and two shoots of equal strength are trained in opposite directions along the wire. The general management is the same as recommended for lateral cordons.

In cold and unfavourable districts the finer sorts of Apples may be grown as

Fig. 37.—Three-year-old Apple with branches tied to ring to form a bowl-shaped or open bush.

upright cordons and trained to walls. The leading shoot requires to be stopped twice during the growing season, in order that the spurs may form regularly. Trees of this description are sometimes planted between the usual fan-trained wall-trees,

Fig. 38.—Lateral Cordon.

marking the division between them, and from such trees very fine fruit may be obtained.

The best position for horizontal cordons

Fig. 39.—Bilateral Cordon.

is by the side of walks in the kitchen garden. No doubt many other positions would suggest themselves to the intelligent culti-

vator, such as the front of a warm border for choice varieties. By this method of culture fruit of the highest quality is obtained, and at the same time an interesting feature is added to the garden.

Espaliers (fig. 42).—This mode of training is well adapted for the Apple either in large or small gardens. The trees are easily managed ; and the fruit can be well exposed to both sun and air, whilst it is more secure from being blown down by wind than when it is grown either on standards or dwarfs.

Fig. 40.—Young Tree of Apple Cellini.

These advantages ought to more than counterbalance the only drawback, namely, the expense of the espalier rail. Many espalier trees may be seen that produce scarcely anything but wood ; and, of course, annual disappointment is the result. It may be well, therefore, to point out the cause of this. We will suppose that the horizontal branches have been trained at proper distances, and that the intended number of them has been obtained. A number of shoots will grow in an upright direction from the upper sides of each horizontal, but more especially from the topmost ones. Each of the shoots on these will, from their position, command more sap than the shoots which constitute the leaders of the horizontals. Let us take one of them : if we allow it to grow during the season, and then cut it off, it is so much of the vigour of the tree wasted ; if it is cut to within a few inches of its base at the autumn or winter pruning, two or more equally strong shoots will start in the ensuing season ; and if each of these is treated at the next pruning like the original, a mass of shoots will result, so that that which was in the beginning but a single bud, will soon

not afford a satisfactory result if that be neglected.

First Season.—This may date from the planting of the tree in autumn ; it should then be cut down to 1 foot above the ground. Train the shoot from the uppermost bud upright in summer ; also a shoot to the right and another to the left, at an angle of 45° in the first instance, and if one grow stronger than the other, depress the strong and elevate the weak.

Second Season.—Cut back the upright shoot to about 1 foot from where it was formerly shortened, or to one bud above

Fig. 41.—Espalier Apple-tree at Madresfield Court.

become a sort of burr, yielding crops of shoots like a Willow stool. The sap flows in greatest abundance into the upper branches to be again fruitlessly expended instead of being equally distributed throughout the whole of the tree, and unproductiveness is the consequence. The cause having been traced to the buds on the upper branches, and more especially the buds on the higher sides of these branches being allowed to develop strong shoots, it is evident that the remedy consists in checking that tendency, and this is in fact the principal object to be kept in view in managing espaliers ; for, however well they may be attended to in other respects, they will

two buds eligible for forming a second pair of horizontals. These two buds should be a little below the horizontal line along which the shoots from them are ultimately to be trained. Let the lowest two be brought to the horizontal position if strong, but only nearly to that position if weak. These lowest branches cannot be too strong ; therefore, the shoots they produce should be allowed to grow unchecked, except so much as may be found necessary to prevent their competing too much with the leaders.

Third Season. — Cut back the upright shoot as before, and shorten the laterals on the horizontals to about 2 inches. Shoots will start from the parts left, and they

should be pinched when about 6 inches in
length.

Proceed in this manner till the requisite
number of horizontals is obtained. When
the upright shoot is cut in order to obtain
the two uppermost horizontals, only two
buds should be allowed to grow, a third one,
for an upright, being no longer required.

The direction of the branches being that
of horizontal lines at equal distances, the
leaders have only to be trained in that
direction, and the intended form of the tree
will be ensured. This part of the manage-

vigorous than those that are older, such
ought not to have been the case, and equality
must if possible be restored. The shoots
on the strong branches must be kept well
pinched in, commencing early ; as soon as
they have extended to five or six leaves,
they should be pinched immediately below
the fifth one. The shoots on the weak
branches, on the contrary, ought not to be
pinched till they have attained a considerable
length, and then they should be left long
enough to bear a greater amount of foliage
than those which are over-vigorous. By

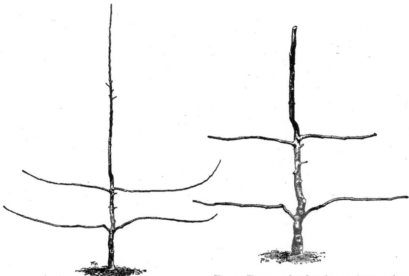

Fig. 42.—Two-year-old espalier Apple, before pruning.

Fig. 43.—The same enlarged to show pruning to produce a
third pair of horizontal branches and a continuation of the
growth in the others.

ment is so simple that it requires no comment. It is, however, necessary to direct
particular attention to the way in which the
flow of sap should be equalized, and consequently an equal degree of vigour maintained
amongst the respective branches, and according as that equality is maintained, the more
healthy and productive they will be ; moreover, the fruit will be of better flavour than
when some of the branches are starved
whilst others are over-luxuriant.

When the shoots begin to grow in the
early part of the season, inspect the tree, and
take especial notice of the strongest branches,
and also of the weakest. If any of the
younger branches are thicker and more

these means the weak branches will gain
upon the strong. When that equality is
regained, which indeed ought never to have
been lost, it will still be necessary to commence summer-pruning the upper branches
first. Presuming that in the spring all the
branches possessed an equal degree of
vigour, and if, when the shoots started,
they were all stopped or pruned equally and
at the same time, the upper ones would
gain an advantage over the lower, from the
natural disposition of the sap to flow into
the former in preference to the latter. Hence
the necessity of always checking the young
shoots in the upper parts of the tree before
those in the lower.

Wall-trees.—Although Apples are grown in perfection in the southern parts of the kingdom as standards, dwarfs, and espaliers, yet certain sorts are very generally provided with a wall in northern situations. Apple-trees do not require the minute care that some other kinds of wall-trees do ; yet, as walls are expensive, every kind of tree planted against them ought to be well managed and productive.

The first consideration is the mode of training which should be adopted. If the wall is low, the horizontal espalier is decidedly the best, and it is also suitable for those of the usual height. In some particular cases, as against the high gable end of a house, the tree may be trained in the fan manner, in order that the wall may be the sooner covered. If the horizontal mode is the one adopted, the next consideration is the distance between the horizontal branches. For the weaker-growing varieties of dessert Apples, the distance may be four courses of bricks, or 9 inches ; but for vigorous, large-leaved sorts, 12 inches, or four courses of bricks, will be preferable. In cold situations this width is not too much ; for if part of the surface is not covered with foliage, the sun's rays, acting directly against the naked bricks, will heat the wall to a much higher degree than if the surface were entirely covered with foliage. Whether the distance between the branches be 9 or 12 inches, the lowest should be 1 foot from the ground. But the upright leading shoot ought to be cut back, so that the two buds intended to originate the lowest pair of horizontals may be about 9 inches above the surface, thus allowing them 3 inches of an ascent to the line by which they are afterwards to be trained. The next pair of horizontals may be allowed nearly as much ; the third course of horizontals somewhat less than the preceding ; and so on to near the top, where the branches may proceed at right angles from the stem. In some cases two courses of horizontals may be taken in the same season, cutting back the upright shoot to one bud above the place from which the side shoots are required to push. This should not be done later than June.

The directions for maintaining equality of vigour among the branches of espalier-trained trees apply also to those trained on walls. The summer pruning, and the pruning of the spurs in winter, are conducted in the same manner as for the Pear, in the chapter on which further particulars will be found.

Root-pruning.—This means of checking the excessive vigour of the Apple is described at some length in the chapter on the Pear, it is only needful to point out here that it is often practised to check excessive growth and to promote fruitfulness in both cases. In fact, in the case of large established trees it is the only method available, as though lifting the trees can be adopted when they are young, it is a very expensive process when they are more fully developed, and could not be followed out on a large scale.

Sterility may result from other causes than excessive growth, and apart from the introduction of varieties to assist in pollination, a remedy may sometimes be found in increasing or changing the manurial supplies. The subject of manures is so fully dealt with in the chapter on that subject that it is unnecessary to enter upon it here except to call attention to one or two facts. A healthy young Apple-tree in a substantial and suitable soil is practically independent of manurial aid in its early stages. When the fruiting stage is reached the exhaustion is greater, and the cultivator must then watch closely the behaviour of the tree, and if there are indications that the strain is too great, prompt resort to suitable manures will often restore them to their right condition. In the same way, if the trees be weakly in their early stages, the application of manure will bring them into a better state, provided they are not diseased and there is no serious defect in the soil.

THE CROP

Gathering and Storing the Crop.—The period for gathering any particular sort of Apple cannot be precisely stated, for it varies in different localities according to the soil and climate, and even in the same locality in different seasons. In light dry soils the fruit will not hang so long as in those that are of a stronger nature. The falling of unsound fruit is no criterion ; but when that which is sound begins to fall, the crop may be gathered. Or, the fruit may be tried without pulling, and if the stalk then parts easily from its connection with the spur, it is fit to gather ; but if it hold firmly at that place, so that in order to separate the fruit it must be twisted and broken, the fruit has not attained full maturity. When ripe, the seeds are of a brownish or nearly black colour. Some early sorts of Apples ripen in succession, and should be gathered accordingly; such, indeed, require párticular attention in respect to gathering; for if taken a few days too soon they are watery, if a few days too late they are mealy.

Fig. 44.—Storing trays for Apples, &c.

Dry weather is to be preferred; but if the season is wet, the fruit must sometimes be gathered when damp, in which case they should be spread thinly in an airy place to dry.

In gathering, great care should be taken not to injure the fruit. The gathering-baskets or trays ought to be lined with some

soft substance, and too many fruits should not be placed above each other. Indeed, choice sorts, and such as are intended to be kept through the winter and spring, should be laid singly on a light hand-barrow, the bottom of which is of large area and lined with a mat or cloth; over this first layer another mat or cloth should be spread, and then a second layer may be placed in the barrow. The fruit should be taken out by hand and not tumbled out of the baskets.

The late-keeping sorts should be stored in a place where the exhalations from ripe and nearly ripe fruit cannot reach them. The latter could be kept in baskets lined with some well-dried straw, and placed above each other. If the quantity of Apples fit for use be too large for the space that can be allowed for them in the fruit-room, they may be laid on the floor of a loft or other place where there is a free circulation of air, which, though necessary, cannot how-ever be admitted at all times without occa-sioning vicissitudes of temperature. If the air is cold for several days and nights, the fruit will also become cold; and if the air should get suddenly warm, the fruit will get wet from condensation. In order to protect them from being affected to any considerable extent by sudden changes of temperature, it is advisable to cover them about 1 inch thick with straw made very dry by exposure to the sun, or by placing it on a kiln. The straw will absorb any moisture that may arise from the fruit, which will ripen of a fair colour and be more plump than if fully exposed to the air.

The most essential points in keeping Apples are coolness and a steady temperature, with no greater circulation of air than is absolutely necessary to prevent exhalations from accumulating, and they should be kept in the dark. When hermetically enclosed, fruit becomes insipid, although it may seem quite perfect as regards external appearance. For information on the best methods of storing consult chapter on STOR-ING FRUITS.

PROPAGATION AND GRAFTING

Propagation.—The Apple may be in-creased in several ways, but different methods are adopted for perpetuating the varieties, and to obtain stocks upon which to place them. For the first-named purpose by far the most important are budding and grafting, which are now very extensively employed, indeed it may be said almost

exclusively. Inarching is occasionally re-sorted to, and cuttings still more rarely. To obtain new varieties and free stocks for budding, &c., seed-raising is the method, while for dwarfing or Paradise stocks layering is the plan followed. As all these are described in detail in other chapters it will not be necessary to refer to them further here except with regard to seed-raising and grafting, which demand a few words.

Seeds selected from fruits that have been obtained by special cross-fertilization, or which have been chosen from the fruits of good varieties with the object of raising new sorts, are best sown in deep pots of light soil in a frame or cool house. The seeds should be sown soon after they are thoroughly ripe, and must be protected from mice, which are very partial to them. Sow thinly and do not let the young plants remain long enough in the pots to become stunted. Crab seeds for stocks are best sown out-of-doors, and the method adopted in raising free stocks from the seeds of Apples employed in the manufacture of cider can be followed. In Normandy, where Apples are extensively cultivated, the pomace is taken and rubbed between the hands in a vessel of water, in order to separate the pulp from the pips. After allowing some time for settling, a part of the contents of the vessel is poured off so as to get clear of the pomace and bad seeds, the pips at the bottom being the only ones that should be made use of. These are dried, and kept in a dry place till they are sown. The sowing is then performed as soon as the sharp frosts are over, as the seeds do not long preserve their germinative powers.

The soil in the seed-bed is prepared by being finely pulverized, and enriched with manure. Drills are made 1 inch deep, and from 7 to 9 inches apart, and in these the seeds are deposited, then covered with fine soil, and afterwards rolled, or pressed close with the back of the spade. It is sometimes advisable to mulch the surface, to prevent its becoming too dry. When the plants are 1 or 2 inches high, they are thinned in rainy weather; otherwise the seed-beds should be watered, to settle the earth about the roots of the plants left. In thinning, care should be taken to leave the strongest plants. The bed must be kept clear of weeds.

When a year old the plants are ready for transplanting. Stout plants are preferred to tall ones. In light soils transplanting takes place in November, but in strong ones in February or March. The plants are put in at from 20 to 24 inches apart, in rows distant from each other 40 inches. In light soils the rows are made to run east and west, but in cold soils north and south, in order that the rays of the noon-day sun may penetrate between them and warm the ground. The stem is not shortened in the same year in which transplantation takes place, unless it is very tall and slender, and

then the third, or one-half at the utmost, is cut off, but at the same time a sufficient number of buds is left to produce leaves, which encourage the formation of roots.

If it is intended to graft the trees standard-high (though this is rarely practised now), the upward growth of plants that are inclined to grow straight should be encouraged, by pinching the young shoots on the sides, in order to divert the sap into the terminal shoot; and such plants as are crooked ought to be cut down to obtain a vigorous upright shoot.

The shoots on the young stem should be preserved until it has attained a sufficient size to be grafted, but they must not be allowed to grow too large. They ought to be shortened to 8 inches or 1 foot in the beginning of June, earlier or later according to the season. The stubs or shortened shoots left on the stem should not be cut off at once, but partial removals should be annually made in autumn or spring. They should be removed by an upright cut, at about one-tenth of an inch from the stem, and parallel to the circular wrinkles or rings at the base of the shoot, for if cut off in the direction of these the wound soon heals.

The above are the essentials of what is considered, in Normandy, the best mode of raising Apple-trees from seed, and of rearing them with a tall stem, fit for standards. In this country they are raised for stocks nearly in the same manner, but they are transplanted, first from the seed-bed, again when they are strong enough for bedding out, and finally when they are to be placed in nursery rows.

Grafting.—Any of the methods detailed in the chapter on grafting may be employed, but of all others whip-grafting is to be preferred. It may be well, however, to remark, that the stocks should be grown in well-manured soil, so as to be healthy and vigorous, and at least as thick as the finger. They ought to be pruned back to where the graft is to be placed, in January if the weather is not too severe, but in any case before vegetation becomes active. It is not advisable to cut them down in hard frost, as in that case small splits often take place at the wounded part. If the weather permit, the heading-back should not be deferred to a later period than the end of January or beginning of February.

The scions ought to be cut from the healthiest trees that can be found. Where canker is observed in any part of a tree, the apparently healthy shoots from that tree should not be taken if others can be obtained from a healthy one. They ought to be cut in January, but not when they are in a frozen state ; and to preserve them till the time for grafting arrives, a spade-deep trench should be dug out from east to west, throwing the soil on the south side, so as to form a ridge, on the north side of which the cuttings should be laid in, but not in bundles, the inner portion of which would be hardly, if at all, in contact with the moist soil, and would consequently be apt to become dried up. Each cutting should have its side laid against the slope of the trench, and its end in contact with the soil at the bottom. The lower portion of the cutting must then be covered with soil, which may be drawn up to nearly its entire length, and pressed close. Scions may also be preserved until the time of grafting, by sticking their ends in moist sand ; and they may be kept alive for a year by shortening them a little, and inserting to the depth of 5 inches in moist, shaded ground. Treated in this way, we have seen cuttings taken in January, and grafted successfully in the March of the following year, fourteen months after their removal from the tree.

Grafting is performed close to the surface of the ground for dwarf trees, and also for standards when the sort worked is calculated to form a good straight stem, as is the case with many of the strong-growing kitchen Apples.

Budding is generally preferred to grafting because it is more expeditious, and with young stocks an excellent union is obtained.

DISEASES

Canker, it is well known, attacks some varieties more than others growing in the same soil. Hence, it must be inferred that some varieties are constitutionally more disposed to this disease than others ; again, in some soils almost every variety is more or less subject to canker, whilst in others the whole of them are comparatively free from it. Amongst predisposing causes to attacks of canker are sudden checks to the vegetation of the tree, especially in spring and the early part of summer, from vicissitudes of heat and cold, as well as of moisture and dryness, unskilful and severe pruning, and deleterious substances in the soil or subsoil.

When a tree grows rapidly in consequence of high temperature, and is then suddenly checked by cold, small lateral shoots that have pushed to the length of 1 or 2 inches are apt to die, and in that case canker appears round their bases. As soon as this is observed, the dead shoot should be cut in very closely to the branch from which it springs, the cankered wood and bark cut away, and the wound dressed with tar. If this is done when the tree is in full growth, the wounds will heal rapidly. If canker appears where the soil has not been drained, draining should be immediately proceeded with, and beneficial results will certainly follow. Severe and untimely pruning unquestionably favours the attacks of canker. If it appears in varieties that are not usually subject to it, and if the trees have not suffered from any of the above-mentioned causes, the evil may reasonably be attributed to some defect in the soil. If the canker is evidently increasing, and if the trees are not too old for removal, they had better be taken up, and the soil ameliorated by trenching and other means. In some cases a considerable portion of a bad substratum may be turned up to the top, where it will be comparatively harmless, and besides, by exposure to the weather, and by cultivation, it must there undergo a change for the better ; and when the soil turned down from the top to the bottom is reached by the roots of trees, the latter generally thrive well.

Mildew frequently attacks the foliage of the Apple, and sometimes the extremities of the shoots. The soil should be examined, and care taken that it is not at any time too dry at the extremities of the roots. Taking up the tree, trenching the ground, and replanting, have often proved beneficial.

Moss and lichens should be scraped off, but it is better if the trees can be made to thrive so well as to throw off the old bark, moss and all, as we have seen ill-thriving, moss-grown Apple-trees do, in consequence of draining the soil. After scraping the bark, brushing the branches with a solution of soft soap and caustic soda, well working it in, has been found an effectual remedy.

Bark Enemies.—American Blight, Apple Mussel Scale, Woeberian Tortrix. *Bud and Flower Enemies.*—Apple Blossom Weevil. *Fruit and Seed Enemies.*—Apple Sawfly, Birds. *Leaf Enemies.*—Apple Aphis, Brown Tail Moth, Figure-of-8 Moth, Garden Chafer, Lackey Moth, Lunar-spotted Pinion Moth, Mottled Umber Moth, Pale Brindled Beauty Moth, Pear-leaf Blister Moth, Red-

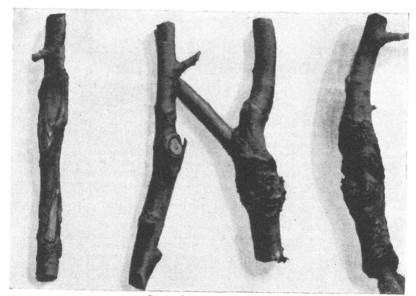

Fig. 45.—Canker in Apple branches.

1. Injury caused by branches rubbing : a common wound, favouring the invasion of canker. 2. An early stage in canker, probably due to improper pruning, leaving a rough exposed surface. Excision and dressing a possible remedy in this case. 3. A more advanced stage of canker injury; excision still possible, but the results doubtful. 4. Branch practically destroyed, entire removal the only course.

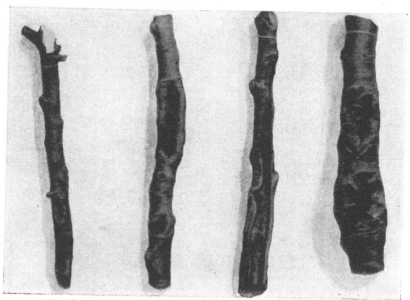

Fig. 46.—Canker in Apple branches : various stages of healing after excision and dressing.

1. A slight injury, nearly healed. 2. A larger wound, healing proceeding favourably. 3. A very long wound, branch healing slowly. 4. A large stem and deep wound, healing but leaving an unsightly scar.

footed Beetle, Small Ermine Moth, Winter Moth, Yellow-Tail Moth. *Root Enemies.*— Cockchafer. *Stem Borers.*—Apple Clear- wing Moth, Goat Moth, Stem-boring Weevils, Wood Leopard Moth. See INSECT AND OTHER PLANT ENEMIES, Vol. III.

APPLES FOR MARKET

The disposal of surplus garden supplies of Apples, as well as of other fruits, is now so general that it is necessary gardeners should have some knowledge of the commercial side of fruit culture. In the early stages of their career it is difficult to gain the requisite information, unless they serve in establishments where marketing is carried out on a business basis ; but no opportunity should be lost in that direction. Apart from the sale of surplus produce, the number of plantations founded solely for commercial purposes is increasing, and there is a demand for practical men who are familiar with the duties of such positions. It is desirable, therefore, that all young men engaged in horticulture should be well informed on the whole subject, alike as to the prospects, the difficulties, the methods, the expenses, and the results. It is the purpose of the following hints to convey an idea of the commercial aspect of Apple culture, which may be modified according to varying circumstances, and adapted to either small or large undertakings. Though specially directed to the requirements of Apple growers, most of the particulars will be found to have a bearing upon the market culture of fruits generally, as they embody the results of many years' experience in several counties and under widely different circumstances.

It has been urged that the land cultivator, to ensure prosperity, should plant acres of Apple-trees. On the strength of this some have invested a considerable amount of capital, and then construed their instructor's advice so literally that they have thought and acted as if nothing more were needed than to wait for the result. Experience moderates enthusiasm. We are thoroughly convinced of the benefits which, under the right conditions, can be derived from Apple culture. Still, we have been so impressed with the evils arising from extravagant statements that induce persons to enter a business for which they are unqualified, and under circumstances which do not afford a reasonable chance of satisfactory results, that we are compelled to urge caution on the part of beginners.

The cultivation of hardy fruits is a pleasurable and healthful occupation to those who have vigour of body and mind, who are able and willing to work, who are naturally persevering, not easily daunted by difficulties, who are energetic, resourceful, and quick to adapt themselves to circumstances. For such men, adding the essential knowledge and experience of the business, there is ample room. Keen as the competition may be, they can make a living, and may even do more than this. They may be able in the course of years to contemplate a comfortable balance at the bank as the result of well-directed labour.

If it were possible to obtain the exact figures we should probably find that the total amount of fresh or preserved fruit consumed in this country is quite double what it was a quarter of a century ago. The increased attention paid to dietetic matters can only result in still further advance in this respect, though we do not anticipate that the Briton will ever entirely subsist on a fruit and vegetable diet. There can, however, be no question respecting the advantages of plentiful supplies of good fruit and vegetables in improving the health of the people ; and this is becoming so generally recognized, and is so frequently enforced by the highest sanitary authorities, that it would be safe to predict an even greater proportionate demand than now exists. The British fruit-grower has therefore nothing to fear on the ground of demand, but what he has to face is the competition of cultivators in other countries who are less heavily burdened.

When our own growers prepare fruit for market, they have to remember that not only have they to compete with their neighbours or fellow-countrymen in other counties, but they have to contend with enormous supplies from abroad. Supplies, too, that, in the case of Apples, usually arrive in an excellent condition, well packed, tastefully displayed, and of uniform quality. Briefly, therefore, British growers must not only possess a thorough knowledge of their work, with all the qualities requisite to success in a difficult business—they have not only to contend with climatic peculiarities of an exceptional character, heavy expenses and high carriage rates, and to compete with home growers, but they have to equip themselves for a still fiercer conflict. On the other hand, there is no danger of a falling off in the demand for fruit, and the producer who is close to his own markets ought to stand the best chance in the struggle as compared with those who are many hundreds, or even thousands of miles away.

Preliminaries — Business Methods — Economy. — As cultivators generally British growers have nothing to fear. Their skill is unquestioned, and their keenest rivals freely admit their superiority, but they are occasionally lacking in some other respects which have a material bearing upon financial results. A business man in these days who expects to command a share of success must be methodical in his work and economical in his expenses ; he must provide a good article at a moderate price ; and he must present this for sale in a form that will attract buyers. Method can be displayed both in the commencement and the routine of Apple culture, and it all means economy of the right kind, namely avoidance of waste. It is on this basis that we advocate economy in land, economy in labour, and economy in materials. It does not mean a reduction in the amount of labour, or the payments, but it does mean that waste of any kind must not be permitted. Economy is effected by a well-considered system of planting. We should endeavour to secure the utmost the soil will produce.

The true economy of labour may be summed up as " efficiency." That is the employment of skilled and well-directed labour sufficient to accomplish the required work at the best time, and under the most favourable circumstances. It applies to all the operations of Apple growing, planting, pruning, gathering, sorting, and packing. Much is lost for want of knowledge or carelessness in execution, and this is generally the result of cheap labour. An employer who has a long labour bill to meet every week may well be excused for wishing to reduce it, but he often errs by the substitution of lower rates. It is better to find out the most intelligent men or lads, and, if possible, teach them, and encourage them to work with their brains as well as their muscles. Attentive, thoughtful men, who take a true interest in their work, are wanted to assist in the competition of the day, and they should see that they have a common interest with their employers.

Essentials.—Beyond the requirements of good soil, favourable aspect, and other conditions, which have been fully described in the chapter on Orchards and under the general culture of Apples, there are several matters to which the market-grower must give his attention in selecting a position. If the undertaking is on a moderate scale, and it is intended to chiefly depend upon local markets and home sale, the district must have most careful consideration. There are many country districts which are at the present time inadequately supplied with home-grown Apples, and there are others where the local produce is ample to meet the demand. This, in consequence, should be ascertained carefully, as if a mistake is made the system of marketing will have to be altered or failure must result. When a good local market is found, the proximity to a railway-station is of little importance provided there are good roads. With well-constructed carts, and due care in packing, it is possible to convey such fruit as Apples 12 to 15 miles direct to the market, shop-keeper, or consumers with greater economy, greater despatch, and greater safety than when sending by rail. This obviously affords the grower a better chance of selecting suitable land at a moderate rent than if it be very near a station or a town. For larger plantations, where other markets will have to be utilized, the distance from a station must be taken into consideration, as much time is wasted and great expense is incurred in carting large quantities of fruit to the rail. But there is one point here worth attention, namely, it is often preferable in every way to cart produce a few miles by road and put the consignment direct on a main line, than to send them on a branch line where either delay or transference of goods to other trains is necessary on the way.

As regards the large establishments, another matter is of great importance, namely, the availability of labour in the district. This does not affect the routine work so much as the periods of pressure, either for land-cleaning or fruit-gathering, but at such times it is serious if sufficient labour of the right kind is not obtainable. Where market-gardening and fruit-growing is an established industry, more skilled or practically-trained workmen are usually to be had, at a higher scale of wages, of course, than in country districts at a distance from a town. In the latter case, if villages of from 400 to 600 inhabitants are within a mile or two, women can often be had for the lighter work of gathering and packing, and with a little tuition prove both useful and reliable. The more intelligent lads should also be engaged as they leave school, and if they can be sufficiently interested in the work, and afforded due encouragement, they become useful assistants in a short time. Any one who starts in a rural district must be prepared to face these difficulties, and if they are overlooked at the commencement it will only cause increased trouble later on. In extreme cases arrangements are occasionally made at fruit-gathering time, when sufficient labour is not obtainable in the district, to convey helpers by road or rail from the nearest neighbouring town, but this is seldom necessary where Apples alone are grown, though it is often requisite where large mixed plantations are formed in which Strawberries or other small fruits preponderate.

Land Tenure.—Though surrounded by many difficulties still, it is possible now to ensure some security for outlay to a man who plants Apple-trees or other fruits on land of which he is not the owner. Recent Acts of Parliament have provided that fruit plantations formed upon land let for market-garden purposes are subject to valuation at the end of the term for which the land is held, with compensation to the outgoing tenant. But in other cases it is rarely, difficult to obtain an agreement with the landlord, or his consent to the planting (which is practically equivalent). For a man who is about to invest a considerable amount of capital in planting, there can be no question that it is preferable to secure the freehold of the land if possible, especially as the purchasing price at the present time is generally low, except near towns. Frequently, however, it is extremely difficult to obtain freehold land in suitable districts, and of the desired extent. Large farms or estates are often offered for sale, the major portion of which would be unfitted for fruit, and moderate-sized plots of from 20 to 50 acres are rarely obtainable with a house. It is much easier to rent land on lease, as occasionally, when large farms fall into the hands of the owner, they may be divided, or a few fields separated for the purpose. For the benefit of the tenant who intends planting Apple-trees to form a lasting plantation, the longer the lease the better, and anything less than twenty-one years is not of much value, unless there is an equitable arrangement for renewal at the termination of shorter terms.

Methods.—The principal systems of arranging trees in plantations are described and illustrated in the chapter on Orchards; it is only needful therefore to briefly recapitulate the methods which are practicable and profitable.

A. Apples without other fruits.
Under this head the chief systems are :
1. Apple-trees with intercropping of vegetables, or flowers.
2. Apple-trees in open cultivated soil, without intercropping.
3. Apple-trees in grass.
The last is the least desirable method, as it is not suitable for dwarf trees. Where standards are employed, some years should elapse before the grass is allowed to extend to the tree stems, and poultry-keeping may then well be combined with such a system.
B. Apples in conjunction with other fruits.
Necessarily this offers the widest scope to the fruit-grower for market, but it also requires a larger outlay at starting and in subsequent maintenance ; but in a well-devised system there are earlier and heavier returns, a matter of the greatest importance where capital is limited. To some extent the constitution of such mixed plantations should be regulated by the distance from the markets to be principally depended upon. For the home trade and local markets Strawberries and Raspberries are profitable, while for the more distant markets Gooseberries for gathering green are more serviceable.

Expenses.—Whatever may be the amount of capital at the command of the cultivator who is about to launch out into Apple-growing for market, it is essential that the expenses to be incurred should be carefully reviewed. Numbers have failed, who were in all other respects well qualified to succeed, simply because they have not first enquired into the question of expenses, or because they have underrated some of the leading items.

In taking land for the special purpose we have in view it is needful to ascertain whether it is efficiently drained and fenced, or otherwise after-expenses may be incurred that will make a substantial addition to the outlay. Again, there is the actual condition as regards cleanliness to be considered, for foul land may mean trouble and expenditure in labour for years. With reference to fences, it will be necessary to decide between the merits of a " live fence " and a " dead fence," *i.e.* hedges and rail fences respectively. The disadvantage of a hedge is its liability to become a refuge for insect pests, and as regards old hedges this is often an evil of a very serious character. A young hedge, with due care in spraying, can be kept clean and form a useful boundary.
The expense of soil preparation or cleaning

APPLES

(From left to right): Cox's Pomona, Lane's Prince Albert (behind), S. T. Wright, Rev. W. Wilks

may be one of the most serious items, depending chiefly upon the condition of the land and whether horse or hand labour is to be employed. If a season's course of cultivation and cropping be adopted for cleaning the land, the preparatory expense may be greatly reduced, or even wholly extinguished, by the sale of the crops. The digging and trenching of the spaces only that are to be occupied with the trees would, in the case of dwarf Apples, at 12 feet apart, with prepared spaces 2 yards square for each tree, reduce the outlay to a little more than one-fourth of that where the whole ground is cultivated. When the trees are to be planted in rows, with bush fruits between them, and intermediate spaces of 30 feet for other crops, preparing the land in the rows 2 yards wide by hand labour will effect a saving of about one-half, if horse-power can be employed for the other parts.

Trenching in the best land for Apples is a costly process, and though it may be undertaken in gardens or plantations for special purposes, it is rarely essential in a plantation exclusively for profit.

The provision of roads in the plantation must be considered ; but in some districts, where suitable materials have to be carted a long distance, the expense is practically prohibitive to a market-grower, and in consequence the work cannot be done as thoroughly as might be desired. Near large towns the coarser refuse, cinders, &c., can often be readily obtained, and the basis of serviceable roads may be thus formed cheaply. In districts where clay abounds, if small coal can be had at a moderate price, hard burnt ballast is useful, but in wet or soft land it does not make a lasting road if there is much heavy traffic.

The next important item in the expenses is obtaining the trees, either by purchasing healthy young trees from a nurseryman or by raising them at home. Many market-growers, now not only raise their own trees, but also sell their surplus. It is well to have a few stock trees true to name to furnish buds of the required varieties, as sometimes they are difficult to obtain when needed, except at extravagant prices. The same remark applies to scions for grafting, but to obtain the numbers for a large plantation, trees of good size are needed.

Planting and staking constitute a portion of the expenses of establishing an Apple plantation, but if one- or two-year-old dwarf trees are selected the staking can

usually be dispensed with. Planting can be done by piece-work at an agreed price per 100 trees, but this is not an advisable procedure. It is preferable in all ways to entrust this work to careful men, under the personal supervision of the grower. A horse or pony and cart will be required wherever general cropping and home marketing are carried out. Much labour can also be saved on a plantation by the use of a horse or strong pony if some of the best forms of light cultivators are employed.

The provision of storing-, sorting-, and packing-rooms also needs attention ; but if sheds or similar outbuildings already exist on the place they can usually be readily, and with small expense, adapted for the desired purposes. If, however, they have to be erected it is a rather serious matter on small undertakings.

An excellent fruit-room, shown in figs. 47, 48, and 49, is in the gardens at Aldenham House. It is handsome in appearance, simple in construction, comparatively inexpensive, and in every way satisfactory. It is 35 feet long, $15\frac{1}{2}$ feet wide, and 16 feet high. The walls are formed with matchboards and reeds, the latter being about 7 inches in thickness, and kept in place by strips of wood fixed horizontally at equal distances apart, as shown in the illustration. The base of the walls is formed with concrete, and the floor is formed of the same material. Access is obtained to the structure by double doors, one opening outwards and the other inwards, the duplication of the door being for the purpose of preventing the fruit being influenced by the temperature of the external air. A ventilator is fixed over the door, and at the other end of the fruit-room is a window with a ventilator over it, and from this window sufficient light is obtained. Internally the fittings comprise a central set of shelves arranged in four tiers and 4 feet wide, and a range of shelves round the side 2 feet 6 inches wide, and also in four tiers. At the end of the central shelves next the door a fixed table 4 feet by 3 feet has been provided for packing and for the fruit selected for dessert. The shelves are made with deal laths 3 inches wide, and with slightly rounded edges to prevent injury to the fruit. Eighteen inches is allowed between each shelf, and this is found sufficient to allow of the fruit being readily examined.

Beyond this, the water-supply may occasion some expense, as, wherever spraying is systematically and thoroughly carried out, sufficient water must be at command whenever it is needed. Near towns the usual services are available, and, though

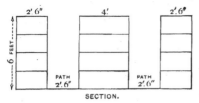

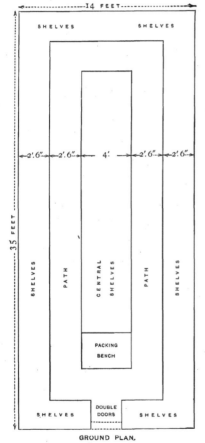

SECTION.

GROUND PLAN.

Fig. 47.—Section and Ground Plan of Fruit Room.

costly, are convenient ; in rural districts, wells and water-sources have to be depended upon. Well - sinking is expensive work, especially in some soils ; while if the water has to be raised to higher levels from rivers or brooks, rams in some form will be necessary, or the light iron or steel windmills, now frequently used, are serviceable and essential in all extensive plantations. If capacious tanks are placed on the most elevated part of the land, or sufficiently raised for the purpose, the water can be distributed by gravitation, the expense of the requisite pipes being a profitable set-off against the hand labour otherwise needed.

Working Expenses.—The cost per acre of conducting and maintaining an Apple plantation for market supplies must necessarily be influenced by many circumstances. The extent, the methods of planting and cropping, the nature of the soil, the freedom from weeds or the reverse, the system of sale adopted, and how far horse labour can be substituted for, or utilized as additional to, hand labour. The proportionate expenses are greater per acre in the smaller undertakings, but will be materially modified by the part taken by the grower himself ; if he exercises an active superintendence and takes a lead in all work the reduction may be considerable. As regards the number of hands required permanently, or at least for the greater portion of the year, it may range from one man per acre up to one man per 4 acres, with a lad for every two or three men. This will suffice for the routine work, but extra help would be needed at fruit-gathering on most plantations from 5 acres upwards. Gathering apples can be done by piece-work where the permanent labour is not equal to the task. Where ladders have to be used and the work is necessarily slow, the cost will, of course, be greater. Sorting, packing, and storing Apples are preferably performed by the regular workmen, and may therefore be included in the routine expenses.

If the fruit is sent direct to a wholesale market, most salesmen provide baskets, so that in such cases the grower is relieved of a heavy expense ; but for home and retail trade he requires either boxes or baskets of his own. Baskets are expensive, but when well made are very durable, especially the " rounds," such as half-sieves and bushels. Boxes are slowly coming into more general use in the British trade, and they can be purchased of several large firms at moderate prices. Some of the railway companies also now provide boxes, but the sizes for holding half a bushel or a bushel of Apples are too slight to stand much travelling and they are too expensive to be given with the fruit. Where boxes are used the best plan is to employ the permanent hands in making them during wet or bad weather in the winter. In this way, if the wood is bought in quantity, ready sawn, it is possible to produce useful half-bushel boxes which, with ordinary care, will last for several years. In the case of choice dessert Apples, packed in boxes to hold from 1 dozen to 2 dozen, the box can be given with the fruit.

There are several other expenses of a minor character, such as the cost of materials

these, size, colour, and quality affect the prices ; which are again still further influenced by home crops, by the American crops, and later in the season by the colonial supplies. With all these complicated conditions it is not surprising that prices vary enormously, and sometimes with a rapidity that seems mysterious to the inexperienced.

Dessert Apples that are distinguished by earliness, good appearance, or quality, almost invariably command fair prices and frequently yield very profitable returns. Some growers rely almost exclusively upon

Fig. 48.—Fruit-room at Aldennam.

for spraying, &c., that need not be particularized. The use of manures will depend upon the system of intercropping adopted. On substantial soils for Apples this need not be a serious item for some years, or when heavy crops of fruit begin to try the strength of the trees.

Prices and Profits.—To gain something like an approach to an accurate knowledge of the market value of Apples the whole matter requires to be studied very carefully in all its bearings. The use to which the fruit is applied, *i.e.* for cooking or dessert ; the season when it is available : early, midseason, or late ; and then under each of

such varieties as Devonshire Quarrenden, Yellow Ingestrie, Worcester Pearmain, and Cox's Orange Pippin. There are, however, many Apples of prepossessing appearance, though not of high quality, such as Duchess of Gloucester (or Duchess's Favourite), which command a ready sale for eating, especially in some seasons. The demand for early cooking Apples is also considerable, but market prices rule lower for these, except for unusually early or very fine samples in a season of scarcity. The selling advantage of cooking Apples is the long general demand that exists for them, and the heavy crops that are usually obtained from healthy trees of the best varieties. As regards season, if Apples can be disposed of before the American supplies lower the prices, or after they are exhausted and before the Tasmanian Apples reach our markets, it is to the advantage of our own growers. But there is an increasing difficulty in this now, for the Tasmanian supplies have been increased and prolonged, and the first of the American Apples arrive earlier than formerly.

The importance of grading all Apples for market is being forced on the attention of

is the more important quality. We have repeatedly had cases under notice where samples of such varieties as Cox's Orange Pippin, of equal size and quality, for eating, have differed in price from 10 to 15 per cent, the difference being in favour of the more highly-coloured fruits. It sometimes happens, in fact, that finely-coloured samples of an Apple that is of indifferent quality will realize a better price than the duller fruits of a superior variety. There is a limited demand for the highest quality Apples, unless they are recommended by

Fig. 49.—Interior of Fruit-room at Aldenham.

British growers by their over-sea competitors, and the money value of such sorting can be easily proved by any grower who will take the trouble to make the comparison. There is no question that all the care which can be devoted to gathering Apples without injury, grading, and packing is well repaid in the higher prices realized, and this can be carried still further in the case of the choicest dessert varieties by displaying them to the best advantage in small quantities.

Size in Apples has a distinct market value, especially as regards cooking varieties, but to a less extent it also applies to dessert varieties, though as regards the latter colour

other more evident properties, or unless they are popular varieties. For instance, Ribston Pippin and Blenheim Pippin are so widely known as " names " that in the shops it is common to see many other Apples displayed under those titles. ·Cox's Orange Pippin is also advancing rapidly in popularity, and a few others of merit are becoming known, but there are many excellent dessert Apples grown in gardens that would have but a poor chance in a market, as the probable purchasers who knew their value would be very few.

The varieties of Apples for market must combine many good qualities. They must be hardy, healthy, prolific, and regular croppers ; the fruit should be large, or at least of medium size, preferably even and handsome in form, or brightly coloured. They should also be either early, late and good keepers, or of exceptional quality.

In the list given in another part of this chapter, some of the best-proved varieties possessing these qualities are included, and their respective characters are indicated in the descriptive list.

From the review of the expenses attendant upon Apple culture for market, it is evident that all the qualities set out in our preliminary remarks are essential to those who would command a chance of success. Notwithstanding the outlay in starting and maintaining a plantation of Apples for profitable purposes, there is an ample chance of making the investment a profitable one, as many

have proved in the face of numerous difficulties. But all the conditions should be as favourable as experience and judgment can ensure, and there must be but one object in view—commercial success.

It is difficult to gauge the actual average returns from a plantation, because the results depend upon a variety of causes, but where Apples are the sole fruit crop it is possible to form an estimate that may be modified in different cases. If dwarf trees are principally relied upon, and about four hundred are planted to the acre, crops ranging from one hundred to five hundred bushels of fruits may be secured when the trees are fully developed and in their best condition. These would include both cooking and dessert varieties, and at an average price of 10s. per bushel would yield from £50 to £200 per acre.

SELECT APPLES

There are probably 2000 varieties of Apples in cultivation in the British Isles at the present time, a large proportion of which have distinctive names. Many of these are, however, either worthless or so much like others in general cultivation that they are seldom grown outside the locality where they originated. To all engaged in the commercial departments of horticulture, either as nurserymen or as market-growers, it would be a great advantage if the number of cultivated varieties could be materially reduced. There are few private gardens where large collections are required so long as a supply can be maintained throughout the year. But wherever much interest is taken in hardy fruits, it is a source of considerable satisfaction to have a collection that will show somewhat of the wonderful range of variation in form, colour, and flavour, which Apples present. Experience differs also as well as taste, and when certain varieties have been found to succeed better than others they are naturally in demand ; this, in fact, is one of the principal reasons why so large a number of varieties continue to be grown, and nurserymen find it exceedingly difficult to reduce their stocks as they might desire.

Apart from the pleasure derivable from a large collection of good Apples there is a substantial advantage also, because it is found which varieties give the best and most constant results, and these can be increased accordingly.

The following list includes only those Apples which have proved satisfactory either

generally or under some special conditions. The well-proved recent varieties are also included, and some of the older varieties which have been superseded by later introductions have been omitted. Old varieties of first-class quality that still maintain their position are, however, included, even though the fruits may be small as compared with some modern productions. For dessert purposes many persons naturally object to large fruits, and although many varieties are indicated that can be employed either for dessert or cooking, in the majority of such cases the latter is the principal use, and the variety need only be taken to table when the supply of dessert varieties runs short.

The list is intended for reference as to the more important characters of the varieties, while the selections which follow will enable those who require a moderate number only to choose what are likely to suit them. In every case the stocks referred to as " Dwarfing " or " Paradise " are the best types employed by British nurserymen, and not the pigmy stocks so often used on the Continent. The term " Free " stock includes both Crab and seedling Apples, unless the former is specially named.

ADAMS' PEARMAIN.—Dessert. November–February. Useful as a late variety, keeping well. Tree of moderate growth, forming a good bush on the Dwarfing stocks, and very prolific. Fruit medium, distinctly conical yellowish with russet spots and red streaks. Rich flavour.

ALFRISTON.—Culinary. November–March. A late variety of free-cropping habit. Tree of moderate growth as a bush on the Paradise, and is best on the Free stock, either as a large open bush or a standard. Fruit very large, rounded and angular, yellow with some russet ; juicy and of fine flavour when well ripened.

ALLEN'S EVERLASTING.—Dessert. March–May. A very late keeper of considerable merit ; it shrivels quickly and is worthless if gathered too early. Tree dwarf and compact as a bush, slender in growth. Thrives on both stocks, but is best on the Paradise in most soils. Fruit small to medium, yellow with red streaks, juicy and aromatic, can also be used for culinary purposes early in the season.

ALLINGTON PIPPIN.—Dessert. November–February. A late variety of the Cox's Orange Pippin type. Grows vigorously and does well as a bush on the Paradise, or as a small standard on the Crab. Healthy and prolific. Fruit medium, round or conical, yellow streaked with red. Of good flavour on warm soils, and early in the season.

AMERICAN MOTHER.—Dessert. October–November. Of American origin ; has proved very satisfactory in Great Britain. Tree much branched, of moderate growth, free, adapted for the bush form on either stock. Fruit medium, round to conical, yellow streaked with red, sweet and aromatic.

ANNIE ELIZABETH. — Culinary. December–April. A late keeper of excellent quality, much valued in the midland counties. Tree of moderate growth, erect and freely branched, healthy and prolific on the Paradise, also strong on the Crab, especially useful as a standard. Fruit large, round and ribbed, yellow with a red tinge. Late in the season it is suitable for dessert.

ARD CAIRN RUSSET. — Dessert. February–March. One of the best late Russets. Tree of vigorous habit, upright, and prolific. The fruit is conical, rich golden russet and crimson, flesh yellow, aromatic and of delicious flavour. Lately introduced from Ireland.

ATALANTA.—Dessert and culinary. November–January. A useful apple of English origin. The tree a regular bearer. Fruit medium to large, yellow, handsome, good flavour. It has been found to stand exposed situations.

BARNACK BEAUTY.—Dessert and culinary. November–February. Tree of upright growth, a regular and prolific bearer, likely to be valuable for market to follow Worcester Pearmain. Fruit medium, conical, golden yellow with crimson flush, and some stripes. Flesh crisp, sub-acid distinct flavour. Keeps well, and the tree succeeds in chalk districts.

BARON WOLSELEY.—Culinary. December. This is said to have been raised in New Zealand, where the tree is reputed to be proof against American Blight. Tree of rather loose habit, but strong and a good bearer. Fruit very large and of angular form, an excellent cooker, and valued for exhibition. Somewhat like Warner's King.

BAUMANN'S RED WINTER REINETTE.—Dessert and culinary. December–March. Tree erect in habit with strong branches, not very compact as a bush but ,prolific on the Paradise, also forms a good standard. Fruit medium, round or flattened, rich deep-red, firm, pleasant flavour when ripe, keeping its weight well and not shrivelling.

BEAUTY OF BATH. — Dessert. July–August. Valuable as an early variety both in gardens and for market, distinct and prolific. Tree spreading, bushy, freely branched, but compact. Growth medium. Forms a fertile bush on the Paradise, and a large tree on the Crab or Free stocks.

Fruit medium, round, yellow and red, flavour refreshing and good when newly gathered.

BEAUTY OF KENT.—Culinary. November–January. Tree well branched, compact, and forming a good bush on the Dwarfing stock, or moderate-sized standards on the Crab, the latter preferable. Fruit large to very large, round, yellow, green and red, moderately acid, and well-flavoured, sometimes used for dessert late in the season.

BEAUTY OF STOKE. — Culinary. November–March. An excellent long-keeping Apple. The tree is of good habit and productive as a pyramid or a standard, well suited for orchards. Fruit large, conical in form, covered with brown russet ; cooks well. The quality is good, and when ripe the fruit is used for dessert.

BELLE DE BOSKOOP.—Dessert. November–Feb-

Fig. 50.—Apple. Blenheim Orange. (⅓.)

ruary. A useful late variety of good habit, free, very prolific as a bush or pyramid on the Paradise. Fruit large, globular, yellow with red streaks, of a brisk rich flavour, somewhat acid.

BELLE DE PONTOISE.—Dessert and culinary. December–March. A fine late variety, keeping its weight and quality well. Tree erect with long shoots, free and vigorous on both stocks, but especially so on the Crab. Forms a good standard. Fruit large, round, yellow and red, moderately acid, with agreeable flavour as it matures.

BEN'S RED.—Dessert. September. A handsome Apple from Cornwall, where it has long been a favourite. The tree is of compact habit, but vigorous and a regular cropper. Fruit rich bronze-red in colour, with a fine aromatic flavour, of medium size and flat.

BISMARCK. — Culinary. October – February. Valuable for its free-cropping qualities and handsome appearance. Tree rather lax on the Paradise, but exceedingly prolific and produces fine fruits. As a standard or half-standard on the Crab it forms a vigorous handsome orchard tree, producing fruit early and heavily. Fruit medium to large, round or slightly conical, rich dark-crimson, moderately acid, pleasantly flavoured when fully ripe.

BLENHEIM ORANGE (PIPPIN) (fig. 50). — Dessert and culinary. November–February. Highly valued when productive, which it usually is on well-established trees. Excellent quality. Tree open and of vigorous growth, forming a shapely bush or large standard on the Free stock, but slow in coming into bearing. Smaller trees on the Paradise are quicker, but they often do not grow

BRABANT BELLEFLEUR.—Culinary. November–March. A fine kitchen Apple, keeping well. Tree of moderate growth, but free and healthy, forming good bushes or pyramids on the Paradise, and very prolific where it succeeds. Fruit large, conical, ribbed, yellow or streaked, very handsome, brisk flavour.

BRADDICK'S NONPAREIL. — Dessert. October–December Of high quality and a regular cropper. Tree upright, free, compact; forms excellent bushes on the Dwarfing stocks, and also succeeds on the Free. Fruit medium, round, green and russet with a slight red tint, richly flavoured and aromatic.

BRAMLEY'S SEEDLING (fig. 51). — Culinary. December–May. An excellent variety, cropping well on established trees, and keeping sound till late. Profitable for market. Tree vigorous on both stocks, branching widely; forms strong standards on the Crab, with stout stems and large

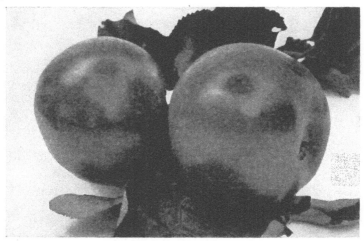

Fig. 51.—Apple. Bramley's Seedling. (½.)

freely. Fruit large, round, green and yellow, slightly acid, but richly flavoured at its best.

BLUE PEARMAIN. — Dessert and culinary. November–January. A handsome Apple of good quality, cropping well. Tree free in growth, forming on the Paradise useful bushes or pyramids. Fruit large, round or conical, purplish red, with a slight bloom, sweet and sometimes very rich.

BOSTON RUSSET. — Dessert. February–April. One of the latest keepers and of good quality. Tree of moderate growth on the Paradise stock as a bush. Fruit medium, round or conical, green with russet and slight red tint, excellent flavour.

BOWHILL PIPPIN.—Dessert and culinary. October–February. A fine exhibition variety, the fruits of great size when well grown. Tree of moderate growth but free and healthy, succeeds on the Paradise as a bush, and also forms an excellent medium-sized standard. Fruit large to very large, globular, slightly coloured, rich flavour when fully ripe.

heads. Fruit large to very large, round or slightly flattened, green, sometimes tinged with red, sharply acid at first, becomes softened with keeping.

BROWNLEES' RUSSET. — Dessert. November–March. Appreciated in gardens for the quality of the fruit and free-bearing. Tree irregular in habit, fairly strong, erect, suited on the Dwarfing stocks as a bush, thriving on Free stocks in some soils. Fruit medium, round, green and brown or reddish-russet, flavour rich when matured; can also be used for cooking early in the season.

BUXTED FAVOURITE. — Dessert. December–January. A Sussex Apple, supposed to be the result of a cross between Blenheim Orange and Winter Queening. Tree hardy, fertile, and forms a neat pyramid. Fruit of medium size, deep green and red, quality good.

CALVILLE BLANCHE D'HIVER. — Dessert and culinary. January – March. Handsome, rather tender in Great Britain, requires a warm situation or protection. Tree an excellent grower and forms strong bushes on the Paradise, for which it is best adapted, and under the best conditions is very prolific. Fruit large, round, with prominent ribs, pale greenish-yellow, flavour brisk and aromatic.

CALVILLE MALINGRE. — Culinary. January–March. Not so tender as the other Calville's. Tree extremely strong in habit, and requires a vigorous Paradise stock, or preferably a Free stock, growing it in bush form. Fruit very large, rather oblong, and ribbed, yellow with a reddish tint, handsome.

CARDINAL.—Dessert and culinary. August–September. A handsome prolific early variety. Tree erect and strong in habit, forming a well-proportioned bush on both stocks, very fertile

Fig. 52.—Apple. Catshead.

on the Paradise. Fruit medium, round or slightly conical, of even and beautiful shape, yellow and bright-red, soft but pleasant flavour when freshly gathered.

CASTLE MAJOR.—Culinary. October–November. Frequently grown in Kent and other home counties for market. Tree of moderate growth, forms a good bush on the best Paradise stocks. Fruit large, round or oblong and ribbed, acid, and aromatic.

CATSHEAD (fig. 52).—Culinary. Fruit large, about 3 in. wide and high, oblong, with prominent ribs, and several knobs round the eye, which is open and set in a deep basin; stalk short and slender, cavity shallow; skin green, with minute russet dots. Tree a strong grower, and best in the orchard. An old and favourite cooking apple, in use from October to January.

CELLINI. — Dessert and culinary. August–

November. A free-bearing and useful variety where it succeeds, but subject to canker in some soils. Tree of moderate growth, rather lax and irregular on the Paradise, but usually healthy longer on that stock, though stronger trees are obtained in the early stages on the Free stocks. It can be grown as a short standard. Fruit medium, round or conical, even, striped with red, soft and pleasant flavour when fresh, but soon loses its quality.

CHARLES EYRE.—Culinary. December. This is one of the numerous seedlings raised by Mr. Charles Ross, and the tree is of sturdy habit, but varies in fertility in different soils and situations. It should be tried on both Crab and Paradise stocks. The fruit is large, conical, and pale green.

CHARLES ROSS.—Dessert. September–December. A recent variety of much promise, handsome and good quality. Tree of free growth and can be worked on both Paradise and Crab stocks. Fruit medium to large, round, even, yellow, flushed and streaked with bright crimson, flavour rich and aromatic. Obtained from a cross between Cox's Orange Pippin and Peasgood's Nonesuch.

CHELMSFORD WONDER (fig. 53).—Culinary. January–April. A useful late variety of good quality. Tree often irregular in growth as a bush on the Paradise, but strong and well developed on the Free stock. Fruit medium, round or slightly flattened, green and yellowish, sharply acid, and good for cooking.

CHRISTMAS PEARMAIN. — Dessert. November–December. A free cropper of good constitution. Tree bushy and upright, very strong and freely branched on Free stocks, also good on the Paradise. Fruit medium, round or conical, green, with bright-red and russet, of brisk pleasant flavour.

CLAYGATE PEARMAIN. — Dessert. January–February. An excellent late Apple of first-class quality. Tree spreading, much branched, but bushy and strong, succeeds equally well on both classes of stocks, but is more fertile on the Paradise. Fruit medium, conical, green with reddish-russet, flavour remarkably rich and sweet.

COBHAM.—Dessert and culinary. November–February. Handsome, of the Blenheim Pippin type, but earlier. Tree vigorous, adapted for the best Paradise or Free stocks as a large bush for early bearing, or as a standard for orchards. Fruit large, even, round or oval, yellowish-green with few crimson streaks, flavour sweet and rich when ripe.

COCKLE'S PIPPIN. — Dessert. January–March. An old variety of high quality, and keeps well. Tree erect, strong, and much branched, forming compact bushes on the Dwarfing stocks, but useful medium-sized standards; also good on the Crab. Fruit medium, somewhat conical, green and yellow, very rich and sweet at its best.

CORNISH AROMATIC. — Dessert. October–January. A high-class Apple of fine quality. Tree of free growth but not strong, it does well on the Paradise as a bush, and is fairly prolific. Fruit medium to large, round, yellow-russet and red, richly flavoured.

CORNISH GILLIFLOWER. — Dessert. January–May. One of the best, but a shy bearer. Tree of moderate growth, and can be had either on the Paradise or the Crab. Requires careful pruning as it bears near the points of the previous season's wood. Fruit medium, rather angular and irregular, dull-green and reddish. flavour rich aromatic, and sweet.

CORONATION.—Dessert. November–December. A handsome table Apple, valued for exhibition. Tree hardy, compact, and fertile. Fruit of medium size, yellow flushed red, flesh tender, juicy, crisp, and often highly flavoured, but varies

Fig. 53.—Apple. Chelmsford Wonder. (⅓.)

in different soils. Colour and appearance excellent.

COURT - PENDÛ - PLAT. — Dessert. February–April. A useful late variety, keeping very soundly. Forms a dwarf bush of slender growth on both kinds of stocks ; difficult to obtain in a vigorous condition. Fruit medium, round but much flattened, very distinct, green, yellow, and deep-red, firm, and pleasant flavour late in the season.

COX'S ORANGE PIPPIN (fig. 54).—Dessert. November–February. One of the best. Tree free and vigorous with slender wood and much "spray," very fertile on good Paradise stocks ; especially adapted for the open-bush style of growth ; also strong on Free stocks as a bush or standard, bears freely at an early age. Fruit medium, round, inclined to conical, yellow and bright-red, juicy, richly flavoured, and retains its qualities, if carefully kept, until it shrivels.

Fig. 54.—Apple. Cox's Orange Pippin. (⅓.)

COX'S POMONA. — Dessert and culinary. October–November. A handsome and free-cropping variety. Tree forms a dense full bush freely branched and strong, requires to be well

pruned in the centre. Good as a standard. Fruit large, round or conical and angular, yellow and brilliant-red, very beautiful, flavour brisk and pleasant when fresh.

CRAWLEY BEAUTY (fig. 55).—Culinary. March–April. Fruit large, handsome, of even outline ; skin green, covered with bold stripes of red ; flesh white, crisp, juicy of acid, cooking well ; profuse bearer. An Apple of much promise, which was raised in a cottage garden at Tilgate, near Crawley, Sussex, and introduced to notice by Messrs. Cheal. It is late in flowering and vigorous in growth.

CRAWLEY REINETTE.—Dessert and culinary. November–April. A sturdy growing tree, very hardy and prolific, well fitted for heavy soils, on which it thrives better than many varieties. Fruit of medium size, deep green with a bronze-red flush on the sunny side. When well ripened this is of good quality for dessert.

CRIMSON BRAMLEY. — Culinary. November–January. A remarkable sport from Bramley's

Fig. 55.—Apple. Crawley Beauty.

seedling, possessing all the good qualities of that well-known and valuable cooking Apple. In addition the fruit is remarkable for the very rich crimson colour that covers the whole surface, but which is more intensely bright on the sunny side.

DEVONSHIRE QUARRENDEN.—Dessert. August. A favourite and useful early Apple, in considerable demand. Tree inclined to be lax in habit, moderately branched, especially free on the Crab ; also fertile on the Paradise. Not satisfactory in a cold soil. Fruit small to medium, round but flattened, uniform dark-red, juicy, refreshing, and one of the most aromatic of early Apples.

DUCHESS'S FAVOURITE.—Dessert. September–December. A useful market Apple owing to its brilliant colour, very prolific on good stocks. Tree erect, of medium growth on the Paradise, stronger on the Free stocks, forms a good head quickly when grown as a standard. Fruit small, round, brilliant-scarlet, sweet and pleasantly flavoured.

DUCHESS OF OLDENBURG.—Culinary. August–September. Handsome and free, of fine constitution. Tree strong and erect with long shoots. Forms a prolific bush on the Paradise, is also suited for Free stocks when large trees are desired. Fruit medium to large, round and somewhat ribbed, green, yellow, and rich crimson, moderately acid, and pleasantly flavoured when fresh, but soon loses its quality. When at its best it may be used for dessert.

DUKE OF DEVONSHIRE.—Dessert. March–May. Chiefly valued for its late-keeping character. Tree very strong, free, open, much branched, excellent on Free stocks and good as a standard. On the Paradise stock it is rather small but very prolific. Fruit medium, round, aromatic and sweet.

DUMELOW'S SEEDLING.—Culinary. November– March. A favourite acid Apple for cooking. Tree of vigorous growth on the Crab either as a bush or standard. More compact on the Paradise, but more liable to disease. Requires a well-drained soil to ensure the best results. Fruit medium to large, round and slightly flattened. yellowish with a bright soft-red tint, sharply acid but pleasantly flavoured.

DUTCH MIGNONNE. — Dessert and culinary. December–March. An old favourite, an excellent keeper ; prolific and hardy. Tree strong, branching freely but compact and bushy. Does well both on the Paradise and the Crab. Fruit medium, round, yellowish with red and russet markings ; flavour rich and sweet.

EARLY HARVEST.—Dessert and culinary. Aug. Of American origin, but long grown in Great Britain. Tree of moderate growth, and best suited for the Paradise as a bush or pyramid, when it is very prolific. Fruit medium, round, greenish-yellow to yellow, juicy and brisk flavour.

EARLY JULYAN.—Culinary. August–September. Of considerable merit for gardens, being useful and early. Tree dwarf, compact, does well and makes moderate growth on the Paradise. Fruit medium, round, somewhat ribbed, flavour pleasantly acid, slightly aromatic.

EARLY VICTORIA.—Culinary. August–September. A cross between Lord Grosvenor and Keswick Codlin. It has been grown with success at Wisbech. Tree of free growth, prolific on the Paradise as a bush, and can be grown as a standard on the Crab. Fruit of medium size, round or slightly conical, yellow, of brisk flavour.

EASTER ORANGE.—Dessert. March–April. A recent addition to table apples of much promise, and if it maintains its high character it will be a valuable late successor to Cox's Orange Pippin, with nearly as rich a flavour. The fruit is of medium size, green with a flush of crimson.

ECKLINVILLE.—Culinary. September–November. Of large Codlin type, useful and prolific where it thrives, but it fails in some places. Tree vigorous but irregular as a bush, rather better as a pyramid. It forms a large spreading standard on the Free stock. Fruit large to very large, round, flattened, green and yellow with slight red tint, soft and moderately acid.

EDWARD VII.—Dessert and Culinary. February–April. The result of a cross between Blenheim Orange and Golden Noble, raised at Worcester. It resembles the former in flavour and the latter in shape and colour. Tree of upright growth, very fertile, flowering late in the spring, in some districts not until the third week in May. A valuable addition to the lists.

EGREMONT RUSSET.—Dessert. October–November. An excellent autumn Apple of high quality. Tree erect, compact, of moderate growth, but freely branched ; slow in development on the

Paradise, but fruitful. Fruit medium, round, yellow with bright russet, flavour rich and aromatic.

ELLISON'S ORANGE. — Dessert. October. A promising Apple raised by the Rev. C. Ellison and sent out from Lincoln. In general character it resembles Cox's Orange Pippin, but it ripens earlier, is more vigorous and fertile, and appears to be more reliable in constitution. The flavour is excellent.

EMPEROR ALEXANDER.—Culinary. September– December. An exhibition variety, of fine appearance. Tree very strong on the Free stock, but it comes into bearing earlier and is more prolific on a strong Paradise stock. Fruit large to very large, oval and even, yellow streaked, red and orange, juicy and sweet when fully ripe.

ENCORE.—Culinary. February–April. This is said to have resulted from a cross between Warner's King and Northern Greening. Tree robust and fertile. Fruit large, greenish-yellow, keeps well and cooks well.

FEARN'S PIPPIN. — Dessert. January–March.

Fig. 56.—Apple. Gascoyne's Scarlet. (⅓.)

A useful late variety of good quality. Tree forming an open vigorous bush, freely branched ; very prolific on Dwarfing stocks ; may be planted rather closely. Fruit small to medium, yellow and red with some russet, flavour brisk and refreshing, becoming sweet with keeping.

FELTHAM BEAUTY. — Dessert. August. A beautiful early Apple, valuable for garden and market culture. It was raised from a cross between Cox's Orange Pippin and Mr. Gladstone, and possesses intermediate characters. The fruit is of medium size, oval ; the flesh crisp, tender, and sweet.

GASCOYNE'S SCARLET (fig. 56). — Dessert and culinary. November–February. Handsome and useful both for garden and market. Tree of vigorous open habit with long Willow-like growths ; forms a fine bush on the Paradise and an excellent standard on the Crab. Very prolific and a regular cropper. Fruit large, round or somewhat conical and slightly angular or ribbed, resembling Cox's Pomona, yellowish-green and brilliant-red, moderately acid with a distinct pleasant flavour.

GLORIA MUNDI.—Culinary. December–January. Tree erect and tall, almost fastigiate, with clean vigorous growth. Does best on the Paradise, but is not a prolific variety. Fruit very large, one of the largest, round and angular, yellowish with a little red occasionally, juicy and moderately acid.

GOLD MEDAL.—Culinary. September–October. A hardy and prolific variety of good constitution which thrives in the north of England and in cold districts generally. Tree dwarf, compact, good as a bush on the Paradise ; also does well on the Free stock. Fruit large, round or somewhat conical and angular, moderately acid.

GOLDEN HARVEY.—Dessert. December–May. An excellent table Apple. Tree of moderate growth but healthy and forms an excellent small tree on the Paradise stock, bearing freely. Fruit small, round, flattened, yellow and russety, flavour exceptionally rich.

GOLDEN NOBLE (fig. 57).—Culinary. October–December. A handsome and useful variety especially for gardens. Tree of strong free growth, forming a good bush on the Dwarfing stock. but develops into a handsome standard

Fig. 57.—Apple. Golden Noble. (⅓.)

with large, well-balanced heads, and stout stems on the Free stock. Fruit large, round and even, yellow, firm and moderately acid with a pleasant flavour.

GOLDEN PIPPIN.—Dessert. November–April. An old but still valued Apple when true to character. Tree of moderate growth, well suited for the Dwarfing stocks, on which it bears freely, and in good soils and situations continues healthy and productive. Fruit small, round, slightly flattened or elongated, yellow with few russet spots, flavour rich and sweet.

GOLDEN REINETTE.—Dessert. November–February. An old variety of excellent quality. Tree strong, and succeeds either on the Paradise or Free stocks, but is generally more satisfactory on the former if a good type is used. Fruit medium, round and even, bright-yellow with red streaks, flavour rich and brisk.

GOLDEN SPIRE.—Dessert and culinary. October–December. A prolific and regular cropper, good for orchards or gardens. Tree compact and erect, with long growths of moderate strength. It forms a well-shaped bush on either Dwarfing or Free stocks, and also makes a good standard, the stem being very strong. Fruit medium to

large, conical, much elongated and distinct, deep-yellow, firm and moderately acid with a pleasant flavour.

GOSPATRIC. — Culinary. October–December. Of good quality, and can be used for dessert. Tree of moderate growth on the Paradise, but free and compact on the Crab, forming a useful medium-sized standard. Fruit medium, conical, slightly angular, yellowish, with a pleasantly-flavoured acidity.

GRANGE'S PEARMAIN.—Dessert and culinary. January–March. A prolific, hardy variety, especially useful for cooking purposes. Tree forms an open, much-branched bush on both classes of stocks. Fruit large, conical, yellow and green with red and russet, flavour rich and refreshing as it matures.

GRAVENSTEIN.—Dessert and culinary. October–December. A variety of high quality, but rather uncertain in cropping ; a favourite in Germany. Tree of strong growth and spreading habit, forming a large open bush. Good on either stock, but most fertile on the Paradise. Fruit medium to large, round and angular, yellow with red spots, juice abundant, of a peculiarly distinct and aromatic flavour.

GREENUP'S PIPPIN. — Dessert and culinary. October–December. A favourite in the north of England. Tree of moderate growth, free and hardy, grows and bears well on the Paradise. Fruit medium to large, round, pale-yellow with red tint, very juicy and sweet when ripe.

GRENADIER.—Culinary. September–October. Prolific and useful for garden or market ; is sometimes confused with other varieties. Tree of moderate growth, erect, and compact as a bush on the Paradise ; forms a healthy standard on the Crab. Fruit large, round, angular and ribbed, deep-yellow, acid and well-flavoured.

HAMBLEDON DEUX ANS.—Culinary. An old variety much grown in some parts of Hampshire. Tree strong and free, does well on the Crab as a standard, but good early-bearing bushes are obtained on the Paradise. Fruit large, round, yellowish with red tint, very juicy and brisk ; when well ripened sweet and suitable for table use.

HAMBLING'S SEEDLING (fig. 58). — Culinary.

Fig. 58.—Apple. Hambling's Seedling. (⅓.)

December–March. Hardy and free, a good late keeper. Tree of moderate, compact growth on the Paradise, stronger on the Crab ; forms a good standard. Fruit large, round, green, juicy and slightly acid.

HANWELL SOURING. — Culinary. December–March. A late-keeping variety, retaining a powerful acidity. Tree of free growth, adapted to both classes of stocks. Fruit medium to large, yellowish with a red tint, brisk acid juice.

HAWTHORNDEN. — Culinary. October–December. A favourite and useful Apple of first-class quality. Tree of moderate growth, rather irregular, except when on the Free stock. Fruit medium to large, round, green or yellow with red tint, slightly acid, of fine flavour : excellent for cooking.

HECTOR MACDONALD (fig. 59). — Culinary. October–March. A useful variety in the style of Lane's Prince Albert, but keeps much better. The Tree is of free growth, and very prolific. The fruit

Fig. 59.—Apple. Hector Macdonald.

is large, pale yellow with bright red shading. Flavour very good.

HEREFORDSHIRE BEEFING.—Culinary. November–January. A valuable cooking Apple, very heavy, and acid. Tree of free growth, adapted for both Dwarfing and Free stocks. Fruit small to medium, round and flattened, dark-red, very juicy.

HEREFORDSHIRE PEARMAIN.—Dessert and culinary. November–December. An old variety, still valued for kitchen purposes especially, hardy and prolific. Tree rather irregular if not carefully pruned ; grows freely on both stocks. Fruit large, conical, greenish-yellow with a little red, flavour aromatic, slightly acid juice.

HOLLANDBURY.—Culinary. October–December. A handsome and good constitutional variety, but apt to be rather " shy," bearing where it grows strongly. Tree forms a large spreading bush on a Free stock, smaller but serviceable on a Dwarfing stock ; it also makes a fine standard for orchards. Fruit large to very large, round, angular, yellowish-green with brilliant-red, moderately acid and slightly aromatic.

HORMEAD PEARMAIN.—Dessert and culinary. December–April. Hardy and fairly prolific, keeps extremely well. Tree erect, compact, free,

vigorous and clean in growth. Good on both stocks, forms a good bush and a well-developed standard. Fruit medium to large, round, yellow and russety, acid and well-flavoured.

HUBBARD'S PEARMAIN.—Dessert. November–April. An excellent variety of good constitution and high quality. Tree of moderate growth, does well on the Paradise stock. Fruit small, oval or rounded, yellowish covered with russet, richly flavoured.

IRISH PEACH (fig. 60).—Dessert. August. An old favourite, but now closely rivalled by Early Peach and Lady Sudeley. Tree open, moderately

Fig. 60.—Apple. Irish Peach. (½.)

branched ; is best on the Paradise, but can be grown into fine bushes on a Free stock. Careful pruning is needed, as it fruits chiefly at the points of the branches. Fruit small to medium, round, yellow and red, richly flavoured.

KEDDLESTON PIPPIN. — Dessert. December–March. Of high quality, small but useful. Tree of moderate growth, best on the Paradise stock as a pyramid. Fruit small, round, golden-yellow with russet, flavour rich and sweet.

KESWICK CODLIN.—Culinary. August–September. Prolific and excellent for cooking, but rather small as compared with other Apples of the season. An " improved " variety is grown in some nurseries. Tree erect, of medium growth, very prolific on a Dwarfing stock, stronger in growth on the Crab. Fruit medium, conical, ribbed, deep-yellow, moderately acid but well-flavoured.

KING'S ACRE PIPPIN. — Dessert. January–March. An excellent variety derived from a cross between Ribston Pippin and Sturmer Pippin, sent out from Hereford. The Tree is of free healthy growth, and most prolific. The fruit is of medium size, roundish, greenish-yellow with slight red on one side. The flesh is firm, with moderate acidity, and very richly aromatic.

KING OF THE PIPPINS. — Dessert. October–January. A handsome and prolific variety, a favourite for exhibitions, it is most satisfactory in warm soils and districts. Tree somewhat spreading, freely branching, of medium strength ; succeeds on the Paradise as a bush and on the Crab as a small standard ; comes into bearing early, and is usually very prolific. Fruit medium, conical, even, golden-yellow and bright-red, very beautiful, briskly and pleasantly flavoured when fresh, but becomes dry and insipid when kept long.

KING OF TOMPKINS' COUNTY.—Dessert or culinary. December–February. An American Apple which has become a favourite in this country both for use and exhibition. Tree of free growth, does well on the Paradise or Free stocks. Fruit large, round, slightly flattened, deep-yellow streaked with red, flavour sweet and rich when well-ripened.

LADY HENNIKER. — Culinary. December–January. A hardy and usually prolific variety, which often succeeds where other varieties have failed. Tree of lax and irregular growth on the Paradise, but stronger and forms good standards on the Crab. Fruit large to very large, round and slightly conical or angular, yellow streaked with bright rich-red, slightly aromatic and brisk in flavour, essentially a cooking variety.

LADY SUDELEY.—Dessert. August–September. Handsome, very hardy, and prolific. Tree erect

cropping regularly. Tree rather lax and spreading, fertile and healthy on either stock. In the bush form on the Paradise it bears early and continually. For a large bush the Free stock is best; grown as a standard the stems require staking, but in sheltered places it succeeds well in that form. Fruit large, round, even, green or pale-yellow with slight red tint, briskly acid and refreshing, pleasant flavour.

LANGLEY PIPPIN (fig. 62).—Dessert. September. An early new variety of much promise, obtained from a cross between Cox's Orange Pippin and Mr. Gladstone. Tree of moderate growth, but free, healthy, and prolific. Fruit of medium size, conical, yellow streaked and flushed with bright-red, flavour slightly aromatic, refreshing, and juicy.

LODDINGTON.— Culinary. August–December.

Fig. 61.—Apple. Lane's Prince Albert.

and compact, of medium growth; does on both classes of stocks either as a bush or standard. Where large bush trees are required they should be grown on Free stocks. Fruit medium to large, round, even, yellow striped with crimson, soft, richly flavoured, aromatic, and sweet. It should be gathered direct from the tree for use, as it loses its best qualities rapidly when kept for a few days.

LAMB ABBEY PEARMAIN.—Dessert. January–April. A long-keeping, useful Apple, of high quality when at its best. It is said to have been raised from seed of Newtown Pippin. Tree of moderate but healthy growth, well suited for the bush form on the Paradise stocks. Fruit small, round, yellowish-green with red streaks, juicy and richly flavoured.

LANE'S PRINCE ALBERT (fig. 61).—Dessert and culinary. November – March. Valuable for garden or market, coming into bearing early, and

Prolific and hardy, much grown for market in the home counties. Tree strong, spreading, tall, but compact; free and good on the Crab as a standard; also useful on the Paradise, bearing early and freely. Fruit large to very large, round, green, or yellow with red tint, moderately acid, abundant juice.

LORD BURGHLEY.—Dessert. February–March. A table Apple of high quality when well ripened. The tree is a moderate grower, but very prolific and well adapted for bush culture in small gardens. The fruit is yellow with a brownish - crimson flush, soft, and extremely aromatic.

LORD DERBY.—Culinary. November–December. Valuable both for garden and market. Tree erect, much branched but compact, healthy and free on both stocks; grown as a standard on the Free stock it is a regular cropper. Fruit large to very large, round, ribbed, bright-green, acid and pleasantly flavoured.

LORD GROSVENOR. — Culinary. August–September. Of strong constitution, useful, a free cropper, and early. Tree vigorous and erect, forming a shapely bush on a Dwarfing stock ; very prolific as a standard on the Crab. Fruit medium to large, conical, deep-yellow, soft, juicy, and moderately acid. Not so readily damaged as some other early varieties of this type.

LORD HINDLIP (fig. 63).—Dessert. January–

Fig. 62.—Apple. Langley Pippin. (⅔.)

May. A handsome late-keeping Apple of recent introduction, and very promising. Tree of moderate growth, somewhat pendulous in habit, succeeds well as a bush on the Dwarfing stocks. Fruit medium to large, conical, slightly ribbed, yellow with scarlet and crimson, richly flavoured when thoroughly ripened.

LORD STRADBROOKE. — Culinary. January–March. An excellent late cooking variety, which is

Fig. 63.—Apple. Lord Hindlip. (⅔.

finding favour with market growers. Tree of good habit, vigorous, and usually very prolific. Fruit of immense size, solid, slightly ribbed, greenish-yellow with a bright crimson side. This has been known as Fenn's Wonder and was introduced in 1908.

LORD SUFFIELD.—Culinary. August–September. Prolific and handsome, but subject to attacks of canker in cold soils ; the fruit also is easily

bruised. Growth irregular, of moderate strength on the Paradise, stronger but less prolific as a small tree on the Crab. Fruit large, somewhat conical, even and handsome, deep-yellow, soft, briskly acid, and well-flavoured.

MABBOTT'S PEARMAIN. — Dessert. October–December. A prolific variety of high quality ; excellent for the garden. Tree erect and free, the growth slender, best on the Paradise as a bush, but it can also be grown satisfactorily on a Free stock. Fruit medium, round, yellow slightly tinted with red, richly flavoured and aromatic.

MALTSTER. — Culinary. October–December. Prolific and hardy, a favourite in Nottinghamshire. Tree lax and of moderate growth, forming an open bush ; can be grown on either stock, but preferably on the Paradise. It also forms a good standard. Fruit medium to large, round and slightly flattened, yellowish-green streaked with bright-red, briskly acid when fresh, and well-adapted for cooking. It is sometimes used for dessert when matured.

MANKS CODLIN.—Culinary. September–October. Hardy, prolific, and excellent for kitchen purposes. Tree dwarf and of moderate, slender growth on either stock, but is extremely prolific on the Paradise. Fruit medium, conical, and slightly ribbed, yellow, faintly acid, juicy and pleasantly flavoured.

MANNINGTON'S PEARMAIN.—Dessert. November–December. Hardy and prolific, a variety of high quality, valuable in gardens. Tree dwarf, of lax and slender growth ; fairly good on either stock ; is not satisfactory in wet, cold situations. Fruit medium, conical, deep-yellow with russet-red, excellent flavour, brisk and aromatic.

MARGARET.—Dessert. August. Early and of good flavour, fairly prolific. Tree erect, of medium strength, not much branched, suitable for bush or pyramid, rather slow but very fertile on the Paradise. Large bushes and standards are best on the Crab. Requires careful pruning to secure a well-balanced tree. Fruit small to medium, round, yellow with abundant bright-red, flavour brisk and rich for an early Apple.

MARGIL.—Dessert. October–January. Hardy and of the first quality, but the flowers are tender and easily injured by slight frost. Tree dwarf, of compact, slender growth ; on the Paradise it fruits early and freely. Vigorous trees can be grown on a Free stock. Fruit small, conical, deep-yellow and bright-red, juicy and richly aromatic.

MAY QUEEN.—Dessert. January–May. Tree compact in habit, and very fertile. The fruit is of medium size, dark red, the flesh crisp, juicy, and of rich flavour.

MÈRE DE MÉNAGE.—Culinary. December–January. Useful and handsome for general cultivation, a favourite for exhibition. Tree very strong, free, and open, with stout branches ; does well as a large bush or standard on the Crab, which is more adapted to its habit than the Paradise. Fruit large to very large, round, somewhat flattened, or slightly conical and ribbed, remarkable for its dark-red colour, briskly acid and well-flavoured.

MINCHULL CRAB. — Culinary. November–March. A variety much grown in Lancashire and Cheshire. Tree of free growth, but forms a compact bush on the Paradise. Fruit large, round, green and yellow, with russet and red streaks, flavour acid and distinct.

MR. GLADSTONE.—Dessert. July–August. Useful, early, and of fair quality. Tree of rather lax free habit, not much branched, with medium to strong wood. It succeeds on both kinds of stock, but in most soils a Free stock is best ; it also does well as a short standard. Fruit of medium size, round, yellow with red streaks, flavour brisk and refreshing when gathered for immediate use.

MRS. PHILLIMORE. — Dessert. November– December. A recent variety of fine appearance, raised from a cross between Cox's Pomona and Mr. Gladstone ; likely to be a favourite. Tree prolific, of steady growth, and suitable both for bush and standard form. Fruit large, round or slightly conical, ribbed, green or yellow with red, soft and excellent aromatic flavour.

NEW HAWTHORNDEN.—Culinary. November– December. Hardy and prolific, useful both for garden and market culture. Tree compact, freely branched as a bush on the Paradise, stronger on the Crab ; comes into bearing rather slowly. Fruit large, round, flattened, pale-green or yellow, juice abundant and briskly acid.

NEW NORTHERN GREENING.—Culinary. Nov-- ember–April. An excellent late Apple of hardy constitution, good for gardens or market. Tree very strong, erect, much branched ; forms a good bush on a Dwarfing stock, but is best on the Crab as a standard. Fruit large to very large, round, even and handsome, green with rich red colour, pleasantly acid, and very heavy.

NEWTON WONDER (fig. 64).—Culinary. Novem- ber–May. A useful late variety, of excellent

Fig. 64.—Apple. Newton Wonder. (⅓.)

constitution. Tree of vigorous growth as a large bush or standard on the Crab ; satisfactory as a bush on a Dwarfing stock. Fruit large to very large, round, even, yellow and crimson when ripe, firm with a brisk acidity and good flavour.

NEWTOWN PIPPIN.—Dessert. December–April. A celebrated old American Apple, but is rarely obtained at its best in this country even with protection. Tree of slender moderate growth, forming a small bush on the Paradise. Fruit medium, even, round, green, very juicy with a brisk rich flavour.

NONPAREIL.—Dessert. January–May. An old and valuable Apple of first-rate quality. Tree of moderate growth, but free and hardy, forming a compact bush on the Paradise, bearing freely in the best situations. Fruit small, round, yellowish with russet and red, flavour aromatic.

NORFOLK BEAUTY. — Culinary. October–De- cember. A cross between Warner's King and

Waltham Abbey Seedling raised by Mr. Allan of Gunter's Park. Tree strong, and prolific when established. Fruit very large, like Warner's King, but deeper yellow in colour. It cooks well, and has gained favour with many growers.

NORFOLK BEEFING.—Culinary. January–May. A late keeper, very healthy and hardy in the best situations, subject to canker in wet soils. Tree of moderate growth, forming a useful open bush on a Dwarfing stock. Fruit medium to large, round and flattened, green, yellow and dark-red, acid and firm, well flavoured.

NORTHERN DUMPLING.—Culinary. September– October. An especially hardy variety, which succeeds in some of the coldest northern districts.

Fig. 65.—Apple. Peasgood's Nonesuch. (⅓.)

Tree freely branched, compact, and of good habit ; fairly prolific and hardy as a bush on a Dwarfing stock ; also makes an excellent standard. Fruit large, round or somewhat conical, greenish- yellow and red, briskly acid.

PAROQUET.—Dessert. December–January. A particularly handsome Apple that is useful both for private gardens and market, the colour being most attractive. The tree is of good habit and very fertile. The fruit is conical in form, with a bright-red, almost scarlet skin. Flesh white, of fine flavour.

PEASGOOD'S NONESUCH (fig. 65). — Culinary. November–December. A fine exhibition variety, chiefly valued for its great size, but the quality is also good. Tree spreading, dwarf and open as a bush on the Paradise ; strong standards can also be had on the Crab. Fruit large to very large, round or somewhat flattened, even, yellow with abundant red streaks, very handsome, acid and juicy.

POTTS' SEEDLING.—Culinary. August–October. A free cropper of considerable merit for gardens or market. Tree forms an excellent bush or pyramid of medium growth on the Paradise, and is healthy and free and extremely prolific ; also forms a good standard with well-developed heads and a stout stem. Fruit medium to large, round or slightly conical, green, becoming yellow when ripe. Excellent for cooking.

RED VICTORIA.—Culinary. August–October. A valuable early Apple raised near Wisbech and introduced by Mr. Miller. The tree is a free healthy grower, and a prolific cropper. The fruit is large, rather flattened in form, and almost covered with brilliant crimson ; the flesh is white and juicy. It is an excellent cooking variety and has proved most satisfactory.

REINETTE DE CANADA.—Dessert and culinary. November–March. Hardy, prolific, and useful for gardens or market. Tree of strong free open growth ; succeeds on both classes of stocks, but is more prolific on the Paradise. Fruit large, rather conical, yellow with a little russet, finely flavoured and juicy.

REV. W. WILKS.—Culinary. October–November. A handsome cooking variety raised from a cross between Peasgood Nonesuch and Ribston Pippin, sent out in 1908. The tree is dwarf, strong, and fertile. The fruit is very large, flat, even in form, but slightly ribbed, pale-yellow, of good flavour and cooks well.

RIBSTON PIPPIN.—Dessert. December. An excellent old variety of the highest quality, but much subject to canker and often worthless in wet cold soils. Growth lax and spreading on the Paradise, but much more prolific and healthy as a bush on this stock than on the Crab, though larger and better developed trees can be usually obtained on the latter. Fruit medium, round, rather angular, yellowish-green and dark-red, especially rich and sweet, a distinct flavour.

RIVAL.—Dessert and culinary. October–December. The result of a cross between Peasgood's Nonesuch and Cox's Orange Pippin. Tree upright, free, and fertile. Fruit medium, round, gold and scarlet. Flavour brisk and pleasant.

ROSEMARY RUSSET.—Dessert and culinary. December–February. A high-class variety of great merit. Tree erect, growth vigorous, forming a healthy bush, pyramid or standard, as it is suited to both kinds of stock. Fruit medium, ovoid or round, yellow-green and russet-red, excellent flavour, very aromatic.

ROSS NONPAREIL.—Dessert. November–January. Valued for its high quality. Tree compact, bushy, freely branched, growth slender; excellent on the Crab as a large bush or small standard; also satisfactory as a bush or pyramid on the Paradise. Fruit small to medium, round, reddish-russet, firm, rich, and sweet.

ROUNDWAY MAGNUM BONUM.—Dessert. November–February. Of great excellence where it succeeds. Tree of spreading strong growth, small but compact on a Dwarfing stock. In strong soils it often makes too much growth to be fertile, requiring to be lifted or root-pruned. Fruit large, ovoid, somewhat ribbed, yellow and red streaks, flavour remarkably rich and distinct ; it has been considered by some as the best dessert Apple of its season.

ROYAL JUBILEE (Graham's).—Culinary. October–February. A regular cropper, good for gardens and market. Tree of moderate growth, forming an open dwarf bush on the Paradise; also thrives on a Free stock as a standard of moderate size. Fruit large, conical, even, handsome, deep-yellow, briskly acid with a good flavour ; sometimes used late in the season for table, but it is rather large for this purpose.

ROYAL LATE COOKING (fig. 66).—Culinary. December–April. A hardy, healthy, prolific variety. Tree vigorous, and forms a fine bush or pyramid on a Dwarfing stock. Fruit medium, round, even, yellow, slightly acid, well flavoured.

ROYAL RUSSET.—Culinary. November–May. Of the best quality as a kitchen Apple, keeping sound very late. Tree strong, and does well on a Free stock, but is more useful in gardens on the Paradise. Fruit large, round, yellowish with abundant russet, juicy and very sweet when ripe late in season.

ST. EVERARD (fig. 67).—Dessert. September. Raised from a cross between Cox's Orange Pippin

Fig. 66.—Apple. Royal Late Cooking. (¼.)

and Margil. The tree is of good habit and fertile. The fruit resembles Cox's but ripens much earlier.

ST. EDMUND'S RUSSET.—Dessert. September–October. A seedling Apple from Bury St. Edmunds of real value amongst early table varieties. Tree compact and prolific. The fruit is small to medium in size, round, flattish, golden russet in colour, flesh tender, of excellent flavour, and very aromatic.

Fig. 67.—Apple. St. Everard.

SANSPAREIL.—Dessert and culinary. February–April. An excellent and useful late Apple of uncertain origin. Tree compact and prolific. Fruit medium, round, yellowish-red ; flesh crisp and of good flavour ; keeps without shrivelling.

SCARLET NONPAREIL. — Dessert. January – March. This variety is nearly 100 years old, but is still a favourite in gardens and for market. The tree is hardy, healthy, and fertile, of slender but compact growth. Fruit medium, round and even, yellow with much bright-red and russet. Flesh yellowish-white, firm, juicy, sweet, and rich.

SCHOOLMASTER. — Culinary. October–December. Hardy and prolific, does well in the Midland counties. Tree dwarf, compact, and of moderate growth on the Paradise ; freer as a bush or small standard on the Crab. Fruit large, round, slightly angular, green or yellow, tinted red, juicy and moderately acid, well flavoured.

SIR JOHN THORNYCROFT.—Dessert. October–December. A notable table Apple raised in the Isle of Wight, and certified by the Royal Horticultural Society in 1911. Tree of good habit and fertile. Fruit above medium size, yellow with little red ; flesh crisp, juicy, and richly flavoured.

STIRLING CASTLE.—Culinary. October–December. Useful for gardens or market, being hardy and a good cropper. Tree of moderate and rather slender growth as a bush or pyramid either on the Paradise or Crab ; frequently does not make sufficient growth to keep a good form. Requires liberal treatment ; is rather subject to scab in cold wet districts. Fruit large, round and even, slightly flattened, yellow sometimes with a red tint, juicy and briskly acid early in season.

STURMER PIPPIN.—Dessert. February–June. Excellent, late, and of high quality. Tree of moderate growth ; as a bush on the Paradise it is dwarf, and somewhat lax, but very prolific in favourable situations ; it also forms a compact and fertile standard on the Crab. Fruit small to medium, round, yellowish with red and russet, flavour remarkably rich and distinct when at its best.

THE HOUBLON.—Dessert. December–January. A seedling raised from Cox's Orange Pippin by Mr. C. Ross, and worth a place wherever the parent is valued as it prolongs the season greatly. The tree is of moderate growth but prolific and reliable. Fruit of medium size, crimson and russet, richly flavoured.

THE QUEEN.—Dessert and culinary. October–January. Handsome for exhibition, prolific, and of good quality. Tree of free growth on the Crab and forms a handsome standard ; it can also be grown on a Dwarfing stock, and takes a pyramidal shape naturally. Fruit large, round, even, flattened, yellow streaked red, acid, and of good flavour.

THE SANDRINGHAM.—Dessert and culinary. November–January. A fine exhibition variety, hardy and prolific. Tree of excellent habit, erect, freely branched, compact as a bush on a Dwarfing stock ; also succeeds on the Crab. Fruit large, conical, green or yellowish, tinted red, moderately acid, and of good flavour.

THOMAS RIVERS. — Culinary. September–December. A handsome and useful cooking Apple. Tree of free healthy growth either as a bush or a pyramid, very fertile. Fruit large, very bright colour, flesh firm and of an exceptionally rich flavour. One of the best of recent culinary Apples.

TOM PUTT.—Culinary or cider. A favourite Apple in the west of England, where it crops freely. Tree vigorous and erect, much branched and compact as a bush on a Dwarfing stock ; very strong as a bush or standard on the Crab. Fruit medium to large, round, or somewhat flattened, even, yellowish, regularly streaked with dark-red, juicy, sweet, and of fair flavour.

TOWER OF GLAMMIS.—Culinary. November–February. Hardy and prolific, a favourite in Scotland. Tree rather lax in habit, tall, with strong straggling growths if not well pruned. Fruit large, conical and angular, yellow, acid and well-flavoured.

TYLER'S KERNEL.—Culinary. October–December. A fine exhibition variety, also of good quality for garden use. Tree free, vigorous, and erect, good on either stock. Fruit very large, conical and angular, deep-red, slightly acid.

UPTON PYNE. — Dessert. December–March. Raised by Mr. Pyne of Topsham. The tree is a good grower, free, healthy, and prolific. The fruit is large and conical, golden yellow with a pink flush on one side. Flesh firm, white, juicy, and of excellent flavour.

WADHURST PIPPIN. — Culinary. October–January. A fine Apple for general use where it succeeds. Tree of moderate growth, rather lax and irregular as a bush unless carefully pruned ; healthy and fertile on the Paradise, stronger on the Crab. Fruit large to very large, conical, green with red streaks, flavour rich and aromatic.

WARNER'S KING (fig. 68).—Culinary. November–December. Hardy, prolific, and healthy ;

Fig. 68.—Apple. Warner's King.

valuable for garden or market. Tree erect, vigorous ; does well on the Free stock either as a large bush or standard. Fruit large to very large, round, slightly angular, green or yellow, acid and well-flavoured.

WASHINGTON.—Dessert. October–December. Of American origin, a favourite exhibition variety and for orchard-house culture. Tree of free growth, but forms a fine bush or pyramid on the Paradise. Requires a warm or sheltered position. Fruit very large, round or more frequently conical, even, yellow streaked with bright-red, flavour rich and aromatic.

WEALTHY.—Dessert and culinary. November–December. A handsome American Apple which succeeds well in England. Tree erect, rather lax and straggling if not carefully pruned ; does best on a Free stock either as a large bush or standard ; on the Paradise it sometimes becomes rather weakly. Fruit medium, round, even, handsomely streaked with bright-red, rich and distinct flavour.

WHITE ASTRACHAN (fig. 70).—Dessert. Fruit roundish, about 2½ in. diameter, base flattened, sides with obtuse angles extending to the edge of the narrow, plaited basin : skin pale yellow streaked with red and covered with a white bloom; stalk short and thick ; flesh white, juicy, flavour pleasant. Ripe August and September, a bad keeper. Tree a vigorous grower and great bearer.

WHITE TRANSPARENT.—Culinary. July–August. Hardy, prolific and early, good for immediate use. Tree remarkably erect and vigorous with

Fig. 69.—Apple. Worcester Pearmain. (⅓.)

long strong growths : does best on a Dwarfing stock, as it is apt to be too vigorous on a Free stock. Fruit medium, round or ovoid, pale-yellow or nearly white. briskly acid when fresh gathered.

WILLIAM CRUMP.—Dessert. December–January. The result of a cross between Cox's Orange Pippin and Worcester Pearmain. Raised at Madresfield Court. Tree of fine habit and very fertile, inferior in this respect to Cox's. Fruit

medium, conical, bright red and russet. Flavour rich. An excellent Apple.

WINTER GREENING.—Culinary. November–May. An excellent prolific variety for the kitchen, and remarkable for the great length of time it will keep sound—in exceptional cases for eighteen months or two years. Tree of free growth, and adapted as a bush for the Paradise, or as a standard on the Crab. Fruit of medium size, round, deep-green, very firm and acid.

WINTER QUARRENDEN.—Dessert. November–December. Prolific, hardy, and valuable for garden or market. Tree of free growth, but forming good bushes on the Paradise. Fruit medium, resembling Devonshire Quarrenden, deeply coloured. sweet, and of good aromatic flavour.

WORCESTER PEARMAIN (fig. 69).—Dessert. September–October. Prolific, hardy, and profitable ; valuable for gardens or market. Tree much branched, and of medium strength on a Dwarfing stock; in some soils subject to canker. Succeeds on a Free stock, forming a good standard of compact growth, bearing early, and continuing regularly productive. Fruit medium, rather conical, yellowish with abundant bright-red tint, sweet and good flavour early in the season and when fresh gathered.

YELLOW INGESTRIE. — Dessert. September. Hardy and prolific ; a useful market variety, though small. Tree of medium growth ; forms small bushes on the Paradise, vigorous bushes and fine standards on the Crab. Fruit small, conical or oblong, even, deep-yellow, brisk somewhat acid flavour.

YORKSHIRE GREENING.—Culinary. October–January. An excellent variety, hardy, and free. Tree vigorous, suitable for the Free stock as a standard ; can also be grown as a strong open bush. Fruit large, flattened, slightly angular, green with red, sharply acid, but first-rate for cooking.

SELECTIONS FOR SPECIAL PURPOSES

In making these lists the object has been to include only the varieties which have given satisfaction for the particular purposes under different conditions. Many others might be included, but the longer the lists the more perplexing they are to the inexperienced. Sufficient have been named for collections of any extent, and the smaller lists will be found useful to those who only require a few varieties.

Thirty-six Dessert Apples.

Adams' Pearmain.	Nov.–Feb.	Egremont Russet.	Oct.–Nov.
Allen's Everlasting.	Mar.–May.	Fearn's Pippin.	Jan.–Mar.
Allington Pippin.	Nov.–Feb.	Golden Pippin.	Nov.–April.
Ard Cairn Russet.	Feb.–Mar.	Golden Reinette.	Nov.–Feb.
Beauty of Bath.	July–Aug.	Hubbard's Pearmain.	
Ben's Red.	Sept.		Nov.–April.
Braddick's Nonpareil.		Keddleston Pippin.	Dec.–Mar.
	Oct.–Dec.	King's Acre Pippin.	Jan.–Mar.
Brownlees' Russet.	Nov.–Mar.	King of the Pippins.	Oct.–Jan.
Claygate Pearmain.	Jan.–Feb.	Lady Sudeley.	Aug.–Sept.
Cockle's Pippin.	Jan.–Mar.	Langley Pippin.	Sept.
Cornish Aromatic.	Oct.–Jan.	Mabbott's Pearmain.	
Cox's Orange Pippin.			Oct.–Dec.
	Nov.–Feb.	Margaret.	Aug.
Devonshire Quarrenden.	Aug.	Margil.	Oct.–Jan.
Easter Orange.	Mar.–April.	Mr. Gladstone.	July–Aug.

Nonpareil.	Jan.–May.	Scarlet Nonpareil.	Jan.–Mar.
Ribston Pippin.	Dec.	Sturmer Pippin.	Feb.–June.
Ross Nonpareil.	Nov.–Jan.	W. Crump.	Dec.–Jan.
Roundway Magnum Bonum.		Worcester Pearmain.	
	Nov.–Feb.		Sept.–Oct.

Twenty-four Dessert Apples.

Allen's Everlasting.		Keddleston Pippin.	Dec.–Mar.
	Mar.–May.	King of the Pippins.	Oct.–Jan.
Allington Pippin.	Nov.–Feb.	King's Acre Pippin.	Jan.–Mar.
Beauty of Bath.	July–Aug.	Lady Sudeley.	Aug.–Sept.
Brownlees' Russet.	Nov.–Mar.	Mabbott's Pearmain.	
Claygate Pearmain.	Jan.–Feb.		Oct.–Jan.
Cornish Aromatic.	Oct.–Jan.	Margil.	Oct.–Jan.
Cox's Orange Pippin.		Ribston Pippin.	Dec.
	Nov.–Feb.	Roundway Magnum Bonum.	
Devonshire Quarrenden.	Aug.		Nov.–Feb.
Easter Orange.	Mar.–April.	Scarlet Nonpareil.	Jan.–Mar.
Fearn's Pippin.	Jan.–Mar.	Sturmer Pippin.	Feb.–June.
Golden Pippin.	Nov.–April.	W. Crump.	Dec.–Jan.
Hubbard's Pearmain.		Worcester Pearmain.	
	Nov.–April.		Sept.–Oct.

Twelve Dessert Apples.

Beauty of Bath.	July–Aug.	King of the Pippins.	Oct.–Jan.
Claygate Pearmain.	Jan.–Feb.	Mabbott's Pearmain.	
Cox's Orange Pippin.			Oct.–Dec.
	Nov.–Feb.	Roundway Magnum Bonum.	
Devonshire Quarrenden.	Aug.		Nov.–Feb.
Easter Orange.	Mar.–April.	W. Crump.	Dec.–Jan.
Fearn's Pippin.	Jan.–Mar.	Worcester Pearmain.	
King's Acre Pippin.	Jan.–Mar.		Sept.–Oct.

Six Dessert Apples.

Beauty of Bath.	July–Aug.	Fearn's Pippin.	Jan.–Mar.
Cox's Orange Pippin.		King of the Pippins.	Oct.–Jan.
	Nov.–Feb.	Worcester Pearmain.	
Devonshire Quarrenden.	Aug.		Sept.–Oct.

Three Dessert Apples.

Cox's Orange Pippin.	November–February.
Fearn's Pippin.	January–March.
Worcester Pearmain.	September–October

One Dessert Apple.

Cox's Orange Pippin.	November–February.

Thirty-six Culinary Apples.

Alfriston.	Nov.–Mar.	Bismarck.	Oct.–Feb.
Annie Elizabeth.	Dec.–April.	Bramley's Seedling.	
Baron Wolseley.	Dec.		Dec.–May.
Beauty of Kent.	Nov.–Jan.	Castle Major.	Oct.–Nov.
Beauty of Stoke.	Nov.–Mar.	Duchess of Oldenburg.	
			Aug.–Sept.

Lord Grosvenor.	Aug.–Sept.	Potts' Seedling.	Aug.–Oct.
Mère de Ménage.	Dec.–Jan.	Red Victoria.	Aug.–Oct.
New Hawthornden.	Nov.–Dec.	Royal Jubilee.	Oct.–Feb.
New Northern Greening.		Stirling Castle.	Oct.–Dec.
	Nov.–April.	Thomas Rivers.	Sept.–Dec.
Newton Wonder.	Nov.–May.	Warner's King.	Nov.–Dec.

Twelve Culinary Apples.

Bismarck.	Oct.–Feb.	New Northern Greening.	
Bramley's Seedling.			Nov.–April.
	Dec.–May.	New Hawthornden.	Nov.–Dec.
Dumelow's Seedling.		Newton Wonder.	Nov.–May.
	Nov.–Mar.	Potts' Seedling.	Aug.–Oct.
Lane's Prince Albert.		Thomas Rivers.	Sept.–Dec.
	Nov.–Mar.	Stirling Castle.	Oct.–Dec.
Lord Grosvenor.	Aug.–Sept.	Warner's King.	Nov.–Dec.

Six Culinary Apples.

Bramley's Seedling		Lord Grosvenor.	Aug.–Sept.
	Dec.–May.	Newton Wonder.	Nov.–May.
Lane's Prince Albert		Potts' Seedling.	Aug.–Oct.
	Nov.–Mar.	Stirling Castle.	Oct.–Dec.

Fig. 70.—Apple. White Astrachan.

Dumelow's Seedling.		Newton Wonder.	Nov.–May.
	Nov.–Mar.	Norfolk Beauty.	Oct.–Dec.
Ecklinville.	Sept.–Nov.	Northern Dumpling.	
Gloria Mundi.	Dec.–Jan.		Sept.–Oct.
Golden Noble.	Oct.–Dec.	Peasgood's Nonesuch.	
Hanwell Souring.	Dec.–Mar.		Nov.–Dec.
Hawthornden.	Oct.–Dec.	Potts' Seedling.	Aug.–Oct.
Hector Macdonald.	Oct.–Mar.	Rev. W. Wilks.	Oct.–Nov.
Lane's Prince Albert.		Royal Jubilee.	Oct.–Feb.
	Nov.–Mar.	Schoolmaster.	Oct.–Dec.
Loddington.	Aug.–Dec.	Stirling Castle.	Oct.–Dec.
Lord Derby.	Nov.–Dec.	Thomas Rivers.	Sept.–Dec.
Lord Grosvenor.	Aug.–Sept.	Warner's King.	Nov.–Dec.
Mère de Ménage.	Dec.–Jan.	Winter Greening.	Nov.–May.
New Hawthornden.	Nov.–Dec.	Yorkshire Greening.	Oct.–Jan.
New Northern Greening.			
	Nov.–April.		

Three Culinary Apples

Bramley's Seedling.	December–May.
Lane's Prince Albert.	November–March.
Potts' Seedling.	August–October.

One Culinary Apple.

Lane's Prince Albert.	November–March.

Twenty-four Culinary Apples.

Annie Elizabeth.	Dec.–April.	Gloria Mundi.	Dec.–Jan.
Beauty of Kent.	Nov.–Jan.	Golden Noble.	Oct.–Dec.
Bismarck.	Oct.–Feb.	Hawthornden.	Oct.–Dec.
Bramley's Seedling.		Hector Macdonald.	Oct.–Mar.
	Dec.–May.	Lane's Prince Albert.	
Dumelow's Seedling.			Nov.–Mar.
	Nov.–Mar.	Loddington.	Aug.–Dec.
Ecklinville.	Sept.–Nov.	Lord Derby.	Nov.–Dec.

Twenty-four Dessert and Culinary Apples.

Barnack Beauty.	Nov.–Feb.	Herefordshire Pearmain.	
Baumann's Red Winter			Nov.–Dec.
Reinette.	Dec.–Mar.	Hormead Pearmain.	
Blenheim Pippin.	Nov.–Feb.		Dec.–April.
Cardinal.	Aug.–Sept.	King of Tompkins' County.	
Cellini.	Aug.–Nov.		Dec.–Jan.
Cobham.	Nov.–Feb.	Lady Henniker.	Dec.–Jan.
Cox's Pomona.	Oct.–Nov.	Reinette de Canada.	
Dutch Mignonne.	Dec.–Mar.		Nov.–Mar.
Edward VII.	Feb.–April.	Rival.	Oct.–Nov.
Gascoyne's Scarlet Seedling.		Rosemary Russet.	Dec.–Feb.
	Nov.–Feb.	Sanspareil.	Feb.–April
Golden Spire.	Oct.–Dec.	The Queen.	Oct.–Jan.
Grange's Pearmain.	Jan.–Mar.	The Sandringham.	Nov.–Jan.
Greenup's Pippin.	Oct.–Dec.	Wealthy.	Nov.–Dec.

Twelve Dessert and Culinary Apples.

Barnack Beauty.	Nov.–Feb.	Gascoyne's Scarlet Seedling.	
Baumann's Red Winter			Nov.–Feb.
Reinette.	Dec.–Mar.	Hormead Pearmain.	
Blenheim Pippin.	Nov.–Feb.		Dec.–April.
Craw'ey Reinette.	Nov.–Feb.	Lady Henniker.	Dec.–Jan.
Dutch Mignonne.	Dec.–Mar.	Rival.	Oct.–Nov.
Early Harvest.	Aug.	Rosemary Russet.	Dec.–Feb.
		Wealthy.	Nov.–Dec.

Six Dessert and Culinary Apples.

Barnack Beauty.	Nov.–Feb.	Hormead Pearmain.	
Edward VII.	Feb.–April.		Dec.–April.
Gascoyne's Scarlet Seedling.		Rival.	Oct.–Nov.
	Nov.–Feb.	Rosemary Russet.	Dec.–Feb.

Three Dessert and Culinary Apples.

Barnack Beauty.	Nov.–Feb.	Hormead Pearmain.	
Edward VII.	Feb.–April.		Dec.–April.

Twenty-four Richly-flavoured Apples.

Allen's Everlasting.		Fearn's Pippin.	Jan.–Mar.
	Mar.–May.	Golden Harvey.	Dec.–May.
American Mother.	Oct.–Nov.	Keddlestone Pippin.	
Ben's Red.	Sept.		Dec.–Mar.
Boston Russet.	Feb.–April.	King's Acre Pippin.	
Braddick's Nonpareil.			Jan.–Mar.
	Oct.–Dec.	Mabbott's Pearmain.	
Brownlees' Russet.	Nov.–Mar.		Oct.–Dec.
Claygate Pearmain.	Jan.–Feb.	Mannington's Pearmain.	
Cornish Aromatic.	Oct.–Jan.		Nov.–Dec.
Cox's Orange Pippin.		Margil.	Oct.–Jan.
	Nov.–Feb.	Ribston Pippin.	Dec.
Duke of Devonshire.		Rosemary Russet.	Dec.–Feb.
	Mar.–May.	St. Edmund's Russet.	
Easter Orange.	Mar.–April.		Sept.–Oct.
Egremont Russet.	Oct.–Nov.	Sturmer Pippin.	Feb.–June.
Ellison's Orange.	Oct.		

Twelve Richly-flavoured Apples.

American Mother.	Oct.–Nov.	King's Acre Pippin.	
Ben's Red.	Sept.		Jan.–Mar.
Braddick's Nonpareil.		Mannington's Pearmain.	
	Oct.–Dec.		Nov.–Dec.
Cornish Aromatic.	Oct.–Jan.	Ribston Pippin.	Dec.
Cox's Orange Pippin.		Rosemary Russet.	Dec.–Feb.
	Nov.–Feb.	St. Edmund's Russet.	
Egremont Russet.	Oct.–Nov.		Sept.–Oct.
		Sturmer Pippin.	Feb.–June.

Six Richly-flavoured Apples.

American Mother.	Oct.–Nov.	Egremont Russet.	Oct.–Nov.
Braddick's Nonpareil.		Mannington's Pearmain.	
	Oct.–Dec.		Nov.–Dec.
Cox's Orange Pippin.		St. Edmund's Russet.	
	Nov.–Feb.		Sept.–Oct.

Three Richly-flavoured Apples.

Braddick's Nonpareil.		Mannington's Pearmain.	
	Oct.–Dec.		Nov.–Dec.
Cox's Orange Pippin.			
	Nov.–Feb.		

Twelve Handsome Coloured Dessert Apples.

Adams' Pearmain.	Nov.–Feb.	Duchess's Favourite.	
Beauty of Bath.	July–Aug.		Sept.–Dec.
Ben's Red.	Sept.	King of the Pippins.	Oct.–Jan.
Charles Ross.	Sept.–Dec.	Lady Sudeley.	Aug.–Sept.
Coronation.	Nov.–Dec.	Langley Pippin.	Sept.
Cox's Orange Pippin.		Worcester Pearmain.	
	Nov.–Dec.		Sept.–Oct.
Devonshire Quarrenden.	Aug.		

Twelve Handsome Coloured Dessert and Culinary Apples.

Atalanta.	Nov.–Jan.	Greenup's Pippin.	Oct.–Dec.
Barnack Beauty.	Nov.–Feb.	King of Tompkins' County.	
Baumann's Red Winter			Dec.–Feb.
Reinette.	Dec.–Mar.	Rival.	Oct.–Nov.
Cardinal.	Aug.–Sept.	The Queen.	Oct.–Jan.
Cox's Pomona.	Oct.–Nov.	The Sandringham.	Nov.–Jan.
Gascoyne's Scarlet Seedling.		Wealthy.	Nov.–Dec.
	Nov.–Feb.		

Twelve Handsome Coloured Culinary Apples.

Beauty of Kent.	Nov.–Jan.	Maltster.	Oct.–Dec.
Bismarck.	Oct.–Feb.	Mère de Ménage.	Dec.–Jan.
Crimson Bramley.	Nov.–Jan.	Norfolk Beefing.	Jan.–May.
Duchess of Oldenburg.		Peasgood's Nonesuch.	
	Aug.–Sept.		Nov.–Dec.
Emperor Alexander.		Red Victoria.	Aug.–Oct.
	Sept.–Dec.	Tyler's Kernel.	Oct.–Dec.
Herefordshire Beefing.			
	Nov.–Jan.		

Twelve of the Largest Dessert and Culinary Apples.

Barnack Beauty.	Nov.–Feb.	King of Tompkins' County.	
Belle de Pontoise.	Dec.–Mar.		Dec.–Feb.
Blenheim Pippin.	Nov.–Feb.	Lady Henniker.	Dec.–Jan.
Cox's Pomona.	Oct.–Nov.	Reinette de Canada.	
Edward VII.	Feb.–April.		Nov.–Dec.
Gascoyne's Scarlet Seedling.		Rival.	Oct.–Nov.
	Nov.–Feb.	The Queen.	Oct.–Jan.
		The Sandringham.	Nov.–Jan.

Eighteen of the Largest Culinary Apples.

Alfriston.	Nov.–Mar.	Mère de Ménage.	Dec.–Jan.
Baron Wolseley.	Dec.	New Northern Greening.	
Beauty of Kent.	Nov.–Jan.		Nov.–April.
Bramley's Seedling.	Dec.–May.	Newton Wonder.	Nov.–May.
Ecklinville.	Sept.–Nov.	Peasgood's Nonesuch.	
Gloria Mundi.	Dec.–Jan.		Nov.–Dec.
Lane's Prince Albert.		Rev. W. Wilks.	Oct.–Nov.
	Nov.–Mar.	Royal Jubilee.	Oct.–Feb.
Loddington.	Aug.–Dec.	Tower of Glammis.	Nov.–Feb.
Lord Derby.	Nov.–Dec.	Warner's King.	Nov.–Dec.
Lord Stradbrooke.	Jan.–Mar.		

Twelve Early Dessert Apples.

Beauty of Bath.	July–Aug.	Mr. Gladstone.	July–Aug.
Ben's Red.	Sept.	St. Everard.	Sept.
Devonshire Quarrenden.	Aug.	Williams' Favourite.	
Duchess's Favourite.			Aug.–Sept.
	Sept.–Dec.	Worcester Pearmain.	
Feltham Beauty.	Aug.		Sept.–Oct.
Lady Sudeley.	Aug.–Sept.	Yellow Ingestrie.	Sept.
Margaret.	Aug.		

Twelve Early Culinary Apples.

Duchess of Oldenburg.		Lord Grosvenor.	Aug.–Sept.
	Aug.–Sept.	Lord Suffield.	Aug.–Sept.
Early Julyan.	Aug.–Sept.	Manks Codlin.	Sept.–Oct.
Early Rivers.	July–Aug.	Potts' Seedling.	Aug.–Oct.
Gold Medal.	Sept.–Oct.	Red Victoria.	Aug.–Oct.
Keswick Codlin.	Aug.–Sept.	Thomas Rivers.	Sept.–Dec.
Loddington.	Aug.–Dec.		

Twelve Late-keeping Dessert Apples.

Allen's Everlasting.		Easter Orange.	Mar.–April.
	Mar.–May.	Fearn's Pippin.	Jan.–Mar.
Ard Cairn Russet.	Feb.–Mar.	Hubbard's Pearmain.	
Boston Russet.	Feb.–April.		Nov.–April.
Brownlees' Russet.	Nov.–Mar.	King's Acre Pippin.	
Court-Pendû-Plat.	Feb.–April.		Jan.–Mar.
Duke of Devonshire.		Scarlet Nonpareil.	Jan.–Mar.
	Mar.–May.	Sturmer Pippin.	Feb.–June.

Twelve Late-keeping Culinary Apples.

Alfriston.	Nov.–Mar.	Lord Stradbrooke.	Jan.–Mar.
Annie Elizabeth.	Dec.–April.	New Northern Greening.	
Beauty of Stoke.	Nov.–Mar.		Nov.–April.
Bramley's Seedling.		Newton Wonder.	Nov.–May.
	Dec.–May.	Norfolk Beefing.	Jan.–May.
Dumelow's Seedling.		Royal Russet.	Nov.–May.
	Nov.–Mar.	Winter Greening.	Nov.–May.
Hector Macdonald.	Oct.–Mar.		

Twelve Apples for Standards (Dessert Varieties).

Beauty of Bath.	July–Aug.	Duke of Devonshire.	
Christmas Pearmain.			Mar.–May,
	Nov.–Dec.	King of the Pippins.	Oct.–Jan.
Cox's Orange Pippin.		Lady Sudeley.	Aug.–Sept.
	Nov.–Feb.	Margaret.	Aug.
Devonshire Quarrenden.	Aug.	Mr. Gladstone.	July–Aug.
Duchess's Favourite.		Ross Nonpareil.	Nov.–Jan.
	Sept.–Oct.	Yellow Ingestrie.	Sept.

Twelve Apples for Standards (Culinary Varieties).

Annie Elizabeth.	Dec.–April.	Lord Derby.	Nov.–Dec.
Bismarck.	Oct.–Feb.	Lord Grosvenor.	Aug.–Sept.
Bramley's Seedling.		New Northern Greening.	
	Dec.–May.		Nov.–April.
Dumelow's Seedling.		Newton Wonder.	Nov.–May.
	Nov.–Mar.	Potts' Seedling.	Aug.–Oct.
Golden Noble.	Oct.–Dec.	Warner's King.	Nov.–Dec.
Loddington.	Aug.–Dec.		

Twelve Apples for Standards (Dessert and Culinary Varieties).

Baumann's Red Winter		Golden Spire.	Oct.–Dec.
Reinette.	Dec.–Mar.	Hormead Pearmain.	
Belle de Pontoise.	Dec.–Mar.		Dec.–April.
Blenheim Pippin.	Nov.–Feb.	Lady Henniker.	Dec.–Jan.
Cox's Pomona.	Oct.–Nov.	Rival.	Oct.–Nov.
Edward VII.	Feb.–April.	Rosemary Russet.	Dec.–Feb.
Gascoyne's Scarlet Seedling.		Wealthy.	Nov.–Dec.
	Nov.–Feb.		

Twelve Strong Apples for Standards.

Ard Cairn Russet.			Feb.–Mar.
King of the Pippins.			Oct.–Jan.
Mr. Gladstone.	} Dessert.	{	July–Aug.
Yellow Ingestrie.			Sept.
Bismarck.			Oct.–Feb.
Bramley's Seedling.			Dec.–May.
Golden Noble.	} Culinary.	{	Oct.–Dec.
Newton Wonder.			Nov.–May.
Warner's King.			Nov.–Dec.
Blenheim Pippin.	Dessert	{	Nov.–Feb.
Barnack Beauty.	and	{	Nov.–Feb.
Gascoyne's Scarlet Seedling.	Culinary.		Nov.–Feb.

Twelve Prolific Apples as Bushes.

Cox's Orange Pippin.			Nov.–Feb.
Fearn's Pippin.			Jan.–Mar.
King of the Pippins.	} Dessert.	{	Oct.–Jan.
Worcester Pearmain.			Sept.–Oct.
Lord Grosvenor.			Nov.–Mar.
Potts' Seedling.			Aug.–Sept.
Stirling Castle.	} Culinary.	{	Aug.–Oct.
Lane's Prince Albert.			Oct.–Dec.
Baumann's Red Winter Reinette.	Dessert	{	Dec.–Mar.
Cox's Pomona.	and	{	Oct.–Nov.
Gascoyne's Scarlet Seedling.	Culinary.	{	Nov.–Feb.
Wealthy.			Nov.–Dec.

Twelve Hardy Culinary Apples for Northern and Cold Districts.

Alfriston.	Nov.–Mar.	New Northern Greening.	
Bramley's Seedling.			Nov.–April.
	Dec.–May.	Newton Wonder.	Nov.–April.
Crimson Bramley.	Nov.–Jan.	Potts' Seedling.	Aug.–Oct.
Gloria Mundi.	Dec.–Jan.	Winter Greening.	Nov.–May.
Greenup's Pippin.	Oct.–Dec.	Yorkshire Greening.	
Lord Grosvenor.	Aug.–Sept.		Oct.–Jan.
Mère de Ménage.	Dec.–Jan.		

Twelve Hardy Dessert Apples for Northern and Cold Districts.

Adams' Pearmain.	Nov.–Feb.	Fearn's Pippin.	Jan.–Mar.
Braddick's Nonpareil.		Kiddlestone Pippin.	
	Oct.–Dec.		Dec.–Mar.
Claygate Pearmain.		King's Acre Pippin.	
	Jan.–Feb.		Jan.–Mar.
Devonshire Quarrenden.	Aug.	King of the Pippins.	Oct.–Jan.
Early Harvest.	Aug.	Margil.	Oct.–Jan.
Ellison's Orange.	Oct.	Yellow Ingestrie.	Sept.

Twelve Apples for warm Southern Districts or Walls.

American Mother.	Oct.–Nov.	King of Tompkins' County.	
Calville Blanche d'Hiver.			Dec.–Feb.
	Jan.–Mar.	Melon Apple.	Nov.–Dec.
Calville Malingre.	Jan.–Mar.	Newtown Pippin.	Dec.–April.
Cornish Aromatic.	Oct.–Jan.	Reinette de Canada.	
Cornish Gilliflower.	Jan.–Mar.		Nov.–Mar.
Feltham Beauty.	Aug.	Washington.	Oct.–Dec.
Gravenstein.	Oct.–Dec.		

Eighteen Apples for Espaliers or Cordons.

DESSERT.

Beauty of Bath.	July–Aug.	King of the Pippins.	Oct.–Jan.
Cox's Orange Pippin.		Margil.	Oct.–Jan.
	Nov.–Feb.	Worcester Pearmain.	
Fearn's Pippin.	Jan.–Mar.		Sept.–Oct.

DESSERT AND CULINARY.

Atalanta.	Nov.–Jan.	Hormead Pearmain.	
Beauty of Kent.	Nov.–Jan.		Dec.–April.
Bismarck.	Oct.–Feb.	Lady Henniker.	Dec.–April.
Dutch Mignonne.	Dec.–Mar.	Rival.	Oct.–Nov.
Emperor Alexander.		Rhode Island Greening.	
	Sept.–Dec.		Nov.–April.
Golden Noble.	Oct.–Dec.	The Queen.	Oct.–Jan.
		The Sandringham.	Nov.–Jan.

Apples for Scotland.

(Selected by 77 cultivators at the last Scottish Apple and Pear Congress. The numbers in brackets indicate the number of exhibitors who had found the varieties succeed under widely differing conditions.)

DESSERT VARIETIES.

Blenheim Pippin (53).		Irish Peach (43).	Aug.
	Nov.–Feb.	Kerry Pippin (44).	Sept.–Oct.
Court of Wick (24).	Oct.–Mar.	King of the Pippins (63).	
Cox's Orange Pippin (41).			Oct.–Jan.
	Nov.–Feb.	Ribston Pippin (48).	Dec.
Duke of Devonshire (16).			
	Mar.–May.		

CULINARY.

Alfriston (51).	Nov.–Mar.	Northern Greening (21).	
Dumelow's Seedling (51).			Nov.–April.
	Nov.–Feb.	Stirling Castle (62).	Oct.–Dec.
Ecklinville (66).	Sept.–Nov.	Tower of Glammis (25).	
Hawthornden (31).	Oct.–Dec.		Nov.–Feb.
Keswick Codlin (54).		Warner's King (55).	
	Aug.–Sept.		Nov.–Dec.
Lord Suffield (61).	Aug.–Sept.		

SYNONYMS OF APPLES.

Alexander, see Emperor Alexander.
Arundel Pearmain, see Hormead Pearmain.
Arley, see Wyken Pippin.
Belle Dubois, see Gloria Mundi.
Black Blenheim, see Hambledon Deux Ans.
Blenheim Orange, see Blenheim Pippin.
Borovitsky, see Duchess of Oldenburg.
Brandy Apple, see Golden Harvey.
Canadian Reinette, see Reinette de Canada.
Clifton Nonesuch, see Fearn's Pippin.
Counsellor, see Greenup's Pippin.
Crystal Palace, see Gold Medal.
D. T. Fish, see Warner's King.
Duchess of Gloucester, see Duchess's Favourite.
Early Red Margaret, see Margaret.
Emneth's Early, see Early Victoria.
Fair Lady, see Early Julyan.
Fenn's Wonder, see Lord Stradbrooke.
French Crab, see Winter Greening.
Glory of England, see Gascoyne's Scarlet Seedling.
Glory of Flanders, see Brabant Bellefleur.
Golden Drop, see Court of Wick.
Golden Winter Pearmain, see King of the Pippins.
Hick's Fancy, see Early Nonpareil.
Ingestrie, see Yellow Ingestrie.
Irish Pitcher, see Manks Codlin.
Iron Apple, see Brabant Bellefleur.
Jackson's Seedling, see Mr. Gladstone.
Jacob's Strawberry, see Lady Sudeley.
July Pippin, see Early Harvest.
King Apple, see Warner's King.
Lammas, see Margaret.
Leather Coat, see Royal Russet.
London Major, see Lord Derby.
Mother Apple, see American Mother.
Never Fail, see Margil.
Normanton Wonder, see Dumelow's Seedling.
Northwick Pippin, see Blenheim.
Nutmeg Pippin, see Cockle's Pippin.
Old Golden Pippin, see Golden Pippin.
Old Hawthornden, see Hawthornden.
Ox Apple, see Gloria Mundi.
Peter the Great, see Cardinal.
Poor Man's Friend, see Warner's King.
Pope's Apple, see Cobham.
Prince Bismarck, see Bismarck.
Prince's Pippin, see King of the Pippins.
Red Hawthornden, see Greenup's Pippin.
Red Juneating, see Margaret.
Sandringham, see The Sandringham.
Scarlet Incomparable, see Duchess's Favourite.
Shepherd's Pippin, see Alfriston.
South Lincoln Beauty, see Allington Pippin.
Stone's Apple, see Loddington.
Summer Golden Pippin, see Yellow Ingestrie.
Summer Peach, see Duchess of Oldenburg.
Thomason, see Fearn's Pippin.
Tom Matthews, see Golden Spire.
Wellington, see Dumelow's Seedling.
Wise Apple, see Court-Pendû-Plat.
Woodstock Pippin, see Blenheim Orange Pippin.
Woollaton Pippin, see Court-Pendû-Plat.
Yorkshire Beauty, see Greenup's Pippin.

THE PEAR

HISTORY

As one of the most delicious dessert fruits at the command of the British cultivator, the Pear has attained a high degree of popularity amongst those fruits which are generally hardy in this country. On the basis of general utility, and for its dietetic value, it cannot be considered as rivalling the Apple, yet as a garden fruit, and, in favourable situations, for commercial purposes, it must always occupy a prominent place. The fruits are especially appreciated for their remarkably varied, distinct, aromatic flavours, and for the peculiarly melting and butter-like consistence of the flesh of a large number of varieties. Then as regards the period during which the fruit is available for use, the Pear is unsurpassed, as while fresh fruits from the earliest varieties can be had ripe from the trees in July, the latest varieties will retain their good qualities until May or June, thus almost completing the circle of the year.

By far the most important use of the Pear is as a dessert fruit, but this is by no means the only way in which it can be extensively utilized. For stewing or baking some varieties are admirably adapted, and, in fact, this is a purpose for which most of the later sorts are suitable, and they can be so employed especially in seasons or situations where the fruit is not sufficiently matured for table use in a fresh state. In America and elsewhere, where the commercial cultivation of the Pear is conducted on a large scale, " canning " or preserving the fruits in syrup has become an important industry, the popular Williams' Bon Chrêtien, under the name of Bartlett, being the variety chiefly employed.

Drying the fruits for export is another method that has been largely adopted in recent years, and in seasons of great abundance it is a convenient means of utilizing the crop. In some of the British colonies the cultivation of Pears is being considerably extended, and it is probable that similar systems will be tried when the crops are excessive, and the prices realized are too low to pay for export. Here in the United Kingdom, however, there is always an ample demand for the best Pears in a fresh

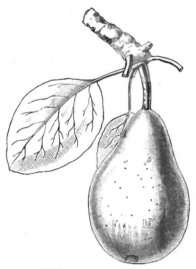

Fig. 71.—Wild Pear (*Pyrus communis*). (Natural size.)

state, and home cultivators in the most favourable districts find them a satisfactory investment.

The manufacture of perry is still of some importance in a few districts of England and France, but it does not receive the same attention as cider production generally, though it is a very palatable liquor at its best.

The numerous varieties of Pears have mainly originated from *Pyrus communis* (fig. 71), which is wild throughout a great part of the temperate and mountainous regions of Europe, and the western portion of Asia. It occurs in many parts of England, but is not so abundant generally as the Crab, and is more frequently found in woods and coppice than in hedgerows. Like the original type of the Apple, the Pear, when really in a wild state, and not merely an escape from gardens as a seedling from cultivated varieties, shows but little difference in the fruits from the earliest known to have been used by man. The fruits which were collected by the lake-dwellers in Switzerland, and either used for food as gathered, or dried and preserved for winter use, were small, hard, and untempting, just as those produced by our wild Pear are at the present time. That variations are induced by special conditions of soil and situation there can be no doubt, but though it has been stated on good authority that there is little difficulty in distinguishing wild Pears from seedlings that have originated from garden varieties, this is open to question. We have raised seedlings from some of the best cultivated varieties, and have found among them forms that could not be distinguished in any character of habit, wood, or foliage, and occasionally even of the fruit, from the wild form.

ensis, a native of China, and cultivated both in China and Japan, possesses a large share of interest in connection with future possible development or adaptation of Pears to different climates, and we shall refer to this more fully in speaking of the improvement of the fruit.

The recorded history of the Pear, as far as

Fig. 72.—*Pyrus nivalis.* (Natural size.)

Another interesting form of Pyrus is that known as the " Snow Pear " or " Sage-leaved Pear," *Pyrus nivalis* or *salvæfolia* (fig. 72), a near ally of *P. communis.* This is the " Poirier Sauger " of the French, and is cultivated in some of the southern countries of Europe. Most of the perry Pears grown in France seem to owe their origin to it, but it is difficult to trace what influence it has had upon the development of garden Pears generally. A third type, *Pyrus sin-*

we are concerned, may be said to commence with the time of the Romans, for Pliny gives the names and brief descriptions of varieties which were distinguished by special flavours, amongst which some were considered to resemble favourite Roman wines ; and even as early as that the musky aroma, which has become a notable character of many fine varieties of modern origin, had been developed. It is impossible at the present time to identify any of the Roman Pears with the oldest varieties still in cultivation, and it is probable that they have long since been lost.

From the earliest historical time much attention has been paid to Pears in France, the climate in a large portion of the country being suited to the best development of the fruit. Some hundreds of distinct varieties

Fig. 73.—Pear. Cuisse Madame. (⅔.)

were grown in French gardens many years before they were counted by dozens here. An example of the progress made in early times is afforded by the catalogue issued by Le Lectier of Orleans in 1628, which is the first exhaustive list published, and which enumerates no less than 260 varieties. These include such names as Cuisse Madame (fig. 73), Jargonelle, Martin Sec, and Bon Chrestien. Subsequently lists became more of the nature of selections, rarely exceeding 100 varieties, until the nursery catalogues of the nineteenth century multiplied the numbers. In Leroy's *Dictionnaire de Pomologie*, the two volumes devoted to Pears (1867–69) included 915 varieties, which were fully described, and the majority illustrated, constituting probably the longest list of varieties of one kind of fruit with systematic descriptions ever printed.

It is probable that the Romans introduced some of their Pears into Britain, but in subsequent years it is certain that a large majority of the varieties grown in this country were brought here from France, and it is difficult to indicate many old

varieties of British origin. Most of the early writers on horticulture notice the Pear. Parkinson, in 1629, refers to 64 varieties ; Wise, seventy years later, names 73, many of which were then considered of little value in this climate. In 1707 Mortimer named 138 varieties, but during that century the number was enormously increased, and, in 1829, G. W. Johnson states in his *History of English Gardening*, that 630 varieties of Pears were then in cultivation in this country. Here, as in France, selection has been in operation, and the late Dr. Hogg described in the different editions of his monumental work, *The Fruit Manual*, the following numbers of Pears as indicating the best grown in the British Isles.

First Edition (1847), 81 varieties.
Second Edition (1862), 279 varieties.
Third Edition (1866), 374 varieties.
Fourth Edition (1875), 581 varieties.
Fifth Edition (1884), 647 varieties.

At a Conference of the Royal Horticultural Society held at Chiswick in 1885, fruits of 616 varieties were represented, but the total number in cultivation in the British Islands would probably far exceed 1000, while on the Continent the number recorded is even greater. There is little doubt that quite three-fourths of these could be discarded

Fig. 74.—Pear. Catherine. (⅓.) (Langley, 1729.)

with advantage, and nurserymen would gladly have their stocks limited to fewer varieties. One method to attain this end would be to adopt the plan of an old trade grower, who classified his Pears under the heads " Good," " Inferior," and " Worthless."

Amongst the known varieties that have been longest in cultivation in Britain the following are still in cultivation, though some of them are difficult to obtain true. Catherine or Katherine (fig. 74) was much valued in Parkinson's time, the Deux Têtes, the Warden (Black Worcester), and the Windsor also belong to the same period, i.e. the sixteenth and seventeenth centuries. The Windsor is, however, believed to be a French Pear of much greater antiquity. Easter Bergamot, Martin Sec, and Jargonelle are also old Continental Pears that have had a place in British gardens for probably 200 years or more, and still retain the characters which distinguished them in earlier days.

EVOLUTION AND IMPROVEMENT

The Evolution of the Pear.—The majority of the older Pears were no doubt simply selections from chance seedlings or wildings, but whether the latter were variations from wild stocks or escapes from gardens there is no means of determining. Amongst the most noted discoveries of wildings are a few Pears that are highly esteemed now. Besi d'Héry, for instance, was found in the forest of Héry in Brittany ; Beurré Bosc was discovered at Apremont ; Beurré Diel was found in a village ; Beurré Giffard near Angers; Chaumontel in a garden ; and St. Germain on the banks of the river La Fare, near St. Germain ; all of those, with the exception of Beurré Giffard, dating from the seventeenth or eighteenth century.

Many Pears, in fact the majority of those now cultivated, including many modern varieties, have originated as chance seedlings. In a few cases we have the names of the seed parent, for instance, Auguste Jurie was raised from seed of Beurré Giffard, Fertility from Beurré Goubault, Huyshe's Prince of Wales from Gansel's Bergamot, and Suffolk Thorn from the same variety. Actually recorded crosses between distinct varieties are by no means numerous. Gansel-Seckle was from Seckle crossed with Gansel's Bergamot ; Huyshe's Prince Consort from Beurré d'Aremberg crossed with Passe Colmar ; and Pitmaston Duchess from a cross between Duchesse d'Angoulême and Glou Morçeau.

Improvement of Pears.—Although we owe the majority of the older varieties of Pears to France, many of the modern varieties were raised in Belgium, chiefly by a few enthusiastic pomologists, who devoted much time and attention to the raising of new varieties. The Abbé Hardenpont of Mons was one of the first to engage in the work, about the middle of the eighteenth century, and to him we are indebted for Délices d'Hardenpont, Glou Morçeau, and Passe Colmar. Early in the nineteenth century Major Esperen at Malines and Dr. Van Mons at Louvain applied themselves systematically to the improvement of Pears, and raised large numbers of seedlings. In British gardens at the present time there are about thirteen of Esperen's Pears in cultivation, and ten of these still merit a position amongst the best, including such well-known varieties as Fondante de Malines, Bergamotte Esperen, Besi Esperen, Joséphine de Malines, and Emile d'Heyst. The work accomplished by Van Mons was, however, of a very extraordinary character, as during his career he is said to have raised 80,000 seedling Pears, and in 1823 he had a collection of 2000 selected seedlings of distinct characters. Many of these were ultimately discarded, and others which are satisfactory in Belgium and France are disappointing here. In most authoritative British lists of Pears about forty of Van Mons varieties are enumerated, but of all these only thirteen can be described as excellent here, though some of them are of exceptional merit, namely : Belle Julie, Bergamotte Heimbourg, Beurré des Béguines, Frédéric de Wurtemberg, Henkel d'Hiver, Maréchal de Cour, Nec Plus Meuris, Sinclair, Surpasse Meuris, and Thompson's.

As illustrating one method of improving Pears, namely, an elaborate system of selection, the plan adopted by Van Mons is interesting, though it has been to some extent superseded by quicker methods. Still, the results prove that a large measure of success attended his efforts.

The plan was based upon the belief that the tendency in cultivated Pears is for their seedlings to revert to a wild form, especially when the seed is from old trees, whereas seed gathered from a young tree of a good variety may produce seedlings of equal or even superior merit. He also considered that similar results followed when taking the seeds from old varieties, which were more likely to give unsatisfactory results than those from a variety of more recent production. Van Mons therefore raised seedlings from young trees of new and meritorious varieties, selecting the most promising of these, as regards habit, to grow on and produce fruit. From these again the best were selected and seed again sown, and this process was continued until the fifth generation (or sowing) was reached, the time required for the fruiting being reduced in each case until the fifth only required three years to produce fruit. When this stage was reached the best varieties were selected for increase by budding or grafting. As part of the system, which was directed to the reduction of the natural vegetative vigour of the seedlings, the fruits were gathered before they were ripe, and then allowed to decay before the seeds were taken from them. Further, the seedlings all had their tap-roots shortened, and were planted close together.

This is probably the most elaborate system of selective improvement that has ever been employed in horticulture, quicker · methods being resorted to now. Still, the principle is suggestive, and is applicable to other fruits and plants, with a less expenditure of time. Downing has pointed out that the theory has had a certain amount of exemplification in the United States of America, because the earlier settlers took seeds there of some of the best old European varieties, the large majority of which proved worthless. But as time went on, and seed was sown from the best of these, there has been a gradual improvement, until numbers of excellent fruits of native origin have been produced in increasing numbers, without any further artificial aid than the continual selection of the most promising.

Another simpler and more expeditious method of improvement by selection is that in which the seedlings, when large enough, are budded or grafted upon a dwarfing or precocious stock, and treated generously to secure the early and full development of the fruit to enable the cultivator to judge whether it is worthy of preservation or not. The chief difficulties in this are : 1st, considerable labour is required ; 2nd, large numbers have to be grafted which are ultimately discarded ; and 3rd, a new Pear, when selected, frequently does not develop its full characters in its early stages, and in the course of a few years may prove to be either better or worse than it was at first thought to be. Practically this method is generally followed by the majority of raisers of new Pears and other fruits both in Britain and elsewhere at the present time.

The third, and most successful method of all, is that of intercrossing the varieties whose characters it is desired to combine or improve. Thomas Andrew Knight was one of the first to commence the work in a systematic manner in England, but though a century has elapsed since he began his experiments in crossing Pears and other fruits, it is only within comparatively recent times that his work has been taken up in the same manner. Unfortunately few of Knight's Pears have withstood the test of time. Amongst these are Althorp Crassane and Monarch (fig. 75), the latter Dr. Hogg considered to be the best of all the Knightian seedlings. It is questionable if the others are in general cultiva-

Fig. 75.—Pear. Monarch.

tion now. Increasing attention is, however, being paid to this work, and the chief difficulty that has to be overcome is the maintenance of a good constitution in the product of the cross, while the quality of the fruit is improved, or the season varied. Many Pears of the highest quality are defective in habit, hardiness, or fertility, and in seeking to correct or reduce these defects there is a danger of inducing the other extreme, i.e. excessive vigour. There is ample room for improvement amongst Pears, although they are so numerous. With early Pears alone many good results might be obtained, while in the production of hardy fertile varieties of general commercial value there is a wide scope for experiments.

As an indication of what can be effected by intercrossing, the results obtained in the United States are especially interesting. The official *Year-book of the Department of Agriculture* recently contained a report upon "Progress in Plant-breeding," in which the following passage occurs :—

"The Pear owes but little of its development to artificially produced hybrids, and yet in no other fruit have hybrids played such an important rôle. The Kieffer, Le Conte, and Garber, all widely-grown commercial Pears, through which this industry

Fig. 76.—Kieffer Pear (after Bailey).

has been greatly extended, are naturally produced hybrids of the European Pear and the Chinese Sand Pear. The European Pear, noted for its excellent quality, succeeds admirably on the Pacific coast, but has never proved wholly satisfactory in the Eastern States, and cannot be successfully grown on a commercial scale south of Virginia. The Chinese Sand Pear comes from a region having climatic conditions very similar to those of the Eastern and Southern States, and thus finds here a congenial home. The fruit is of poor quality, however, and the variety is grown only as an ornamental tree and for stocks on which to bud other sorts. The Kieffer and Le Conte are both seedlings of the Chinese Sand Pear, and from their

characters show that the seeds from which they grew must have been accidentally crossed with the pollen of some good variety of the European Pear. It is probably to the father parent, the European Pear, that the improved quality of the fruit is due, while the vigour and adaptability to growth in warm climates evidently come from the mother parent, the Sand Pear. These hybrid sorts practically revolutionized Pear culture in the eastern United States, extending the limit of profitable commercial Pear-growing several hundred miles southward. From Virginia to Florida the varieties grow luxuriantly, and have practically driven out all other sorts. Even as far north as Philadelphia the Kieffer is by far the most important commercial variety."

The Chinese Sand Pear there mentioned is the *Pyrus sinensis* we have already referred to, and though not in itself very promising as an improver of the many fine Pears now grown in Europe, it is evident from the results referred to that the commercial value of a new race of Pears adapted to hot dry positions and sandy soils would be very great. The variety Le Conte has, for instance, been extensively planted in the neighbourhood of New Orleans, and a consular report states that large shipments of this variety were commenced in 1894. Reports from California state that in quality the fruit there is not equal to the European Pears. At the Hybrid Conference of the Royal Horticultural Society at Chiswick, in 1899, Professor L. H. Bailey of Cornell University, in the course of an interesting paper, had the following remarks : "The European Pear does not thrive in our southern States. But a new race has made Pear-growing profitable there. This race is the product of several hybridizations of *Pyrus communis* and *Pyrus sinensis*. Of this race two varieties, the Kieffer (fig. 76) and Le Conte, are widely planted. The acres upon which they are planted are counted by the tens of thousands. The Kieffer is now the leader. It is a poor Pear in quality, but it is immensely productive, handsome, and a long keeper, and it sells well in the open market. This mongrel race has made Pear-growing possible over an immense region. It must rank as one of the great hybrids of the world." Such a race could well be improved and adapted for many of our British colonies.

FLAVOUR

As regards a large number of the distinct flavours of Pears, it is quite impossible to classify them ; they only differ from each other by delicate gradations. The musk-like flavour so characteristic of many varieties probably originated in the early periods of the Pear's development, a variety known in the time of the Romans being so distinguished. Some of the most marked types of this group in cultivation at the present time are the following : Olivier de Serres, a well-known variety ; Arlequin Musqué, very strongly flavoured ; and the Œuf, which is also remarkably flavoured. With this may be classed the Ambrette d'Hiver, the flavour of which has been compared to the fragrance of the Sweet Sultan, and thence derives its French title ; and Besi d'Héry, with the flavour of Muscat Grapes. Pears of rich aromatic odour form another large group. Prominent amongst them is the Seckle, one of the richest-flavoured varieties in cultivation, and for which we are indebted to the Americans. It is almost unique, but there are a few varieties that present some resemblance to it : such as some of the Rousselets, from which indeed it has been supposed that Seckle may have originated. Beurré des Béguines is another of the same class, and presents some resemblance to Seckle in its aroma. Varieties with almond-like flavour, such as Doyenné Sieulle, Leopold Riche, and Amande Double, form another group ; whilst yet another may be formed of varieties possessing a wine-like flavour represented by Forelle, or the Trout Pear, which, in its best condition, has a peculiar richness. The aroma of Althorp Crassane has been compared to rose-water. Ananas derives its name from the resemblance of its flavour to the Pine-apple. Salviati is the Ratafia Pear, and Franchipanne, which is suggestive of the perfume Frangipanni, derived from the Red Jessamine (Plumeria). The Jargonelle has a distinct flavour, and it forms one of the fruit essences which chemists have succeeded in imitating very closely by artificial products. Sir H. E. Roscoe says : " Amongst the compound amyl ethers the acetate is prepared on a large scale, as it possesses the peculiar odour of Jargonelle Pears, and it is used in flavouring cheap confectionery. This compound is obtained by distilling amyl alcohol with potassium acetate and sulphuric acid ; it can also be prepared by heating the chloride with potassium acetate."

Too much attention has been paid in recent years to the production of varieties with very large or handsome fruits, without due regard to the much more important quality of flavour. Because large finely-coloured fruits, and handsomely-formed Pears are readily sold in the markets, it does not follow that they will satisfy the owners of private gardens or connoisseurs generally.

No hardy fruit varies more in quality and flavour under different conditions of soil, situation, and climate than the pear, and this has been a prolific cause of divergences of opinion concerning the respective merits of well-known varieties. A remarkable, and indeed it may be termed an historical, example of this was afforded by the experience of the late Mr. R. D. Blackmore, who, besides being an eminent novelist, was also a pomologist of a keenly critical character. He formed a large collection of Pears in his garden at Teddington, in Middlesex, and when the late Dr. Hogg was preparing the last edition of his fruit manual he invited Mr. Blackmore to state his opinion concerning the principal varieties in general cultivation. The result was rather startling, as a sweeping condemnation was obtained of varieties which are found satisfactory in many of the best British gardens. Some of the most remarkable instances were afforded by Beurré d'Aremberg, Beurré Berckmanns, Beurré Bronze, Beurré Diel, Beurré de Jonghe, Beurré Langelier, Beurré Six, Catinka, Citron des Carmes, Colmar, Colmar d'Été, Comte de Lamy, Deux Sœurs, Dr. Nelis, Doyenné Boussoch, Durondeau, and Emile d'Heyst. These were variously stigmatized as " worthless," " much overrated," " flavourless," or of " uncertain cropping qualities." These remarks were added by Dr. Hogg to his descriptions, and have provoked much comment, but the object was to indicate how easy it is to misjudge an excellent fruit from a limited experience. If all Pears had failed with Mr. Blackmore the cause would have been traceable to the total unfitness of soil and situation for the culture of this fruit ; but this was not the case, as is proved by the fact that some Pears succeeded there admirably, and received the highest commendation, such, for instance, as Doyenné du Comice. It is obvious, therefore, that there were conditions very unfavourable to some varieties and not to others. They may have been quite local, for Pears are grown admirably in many parts of the Thames valley, though it is not an ideal situation for this fruit. This is only cited as a prominent example, showing that the cultivator is not always to blame for the failure of some Pears. There is always a degree of uncertainty as to the results when Pear-culture is commenced in a fresh district.

ORNAMENTAL USES

A well-grown Pear-tree in full blossom is a beautiful object, as, though the individual flowers are less attractive than those of the Apple, the profusion with which they are produced, and the accompaniment of a few soft green leaves, render the general

Another mode of utilizing Pears for ornamental purposes is that of training them over light metal or wooden arches (fig. 77). The various forms of upright cordons are well adapted for this purpose, and if introduced at suitable positions, especially at the

Fig. 77.—Arched Pergola for Pears.

effect charming. Their period of beauty is brief, but so is that of many popular plants grown exclusively for their flowers, and there is a second period of attraction to anticipate, *i.e.* when the fruit is ripening. Admirers of flowering deciduous trees often include the Pear in ornamental plantations, and some will indeed go further, and form groups in a convenient portion of the flower-garden within sight of the house or favourite walks. Free-growing varieties of distinct habit and profuse flowering are especially useful for this purpose, such, for example, as the erect and stately Old Windsor Pear, or the somewhat pendulous Jargonelle.

intersection of walks, the effect is pleasing. The trees are well exposed to light and air, and often prove exceptionally fruitful as well as ornamental. It is desirable, however, to avoid narrow arches, which have a very meagre appearance and only prove disappointing.

Variegation often appears in Pears, not only in the foliage, but also in the wood and the fruit. Varieties which usually develop this peculiarity are Bergamotte Suisse, Beurré d'Amanlis Panachée, Duchesse d'Angoulême Panachée, and Louise Bonne d'Avranches Panachée.

GENERAL CULTURE

Essentials of Cultivation.— It has been said that wherever the Apple thrives the Pear will grow, and this is perfectly true as far as it goes. But it is not " growth " alone that we require, and unfortunately there are many places where Apples both thrive and fruit though the success of Pears in the same district is mainly confined to growth. The fact is, that there are many places in the United Kingdom where Pears are successful only when great care and skilful cultivation are devoted to them, and there are some where it is useless to plant them. This is a more serious matter in commercial plantations on a large scale than in private gardens, where various means are at command to combat the evils arising from unfavourable conditions. But we have known Pears planted in quantities with a view to profit where various causes have combined to render them a dead loss, yet most of the unsuitable conditions might with due care have been detected before the risk was taken.

Districts for Pears.—There are districts in many of the southern and western counties of England where Pears are particularly successful, but it is occasionally difficult to distinguish between natural advantages and specially skilful cultivation. Kent is obviously a favoured county generally, yet in the neighbourhood of Maidstone, Sittingbourne, and Yalding exceptional results have been obtained, as, for example, at Barham Court, Mote Park, and Kenward as private establishments, and by Mr. A. J. Thomas and Messrs. Bunyard in commercial establishments, the former as a market-grower, the latter as nurserymen. In Sussex the Uckfield, Horsham, and Crawley districts are well suited to Pears, especially the first-named, while Petworth has also contributed in no small degree to the production of fine Pears. In Surrey the fruit succeeds in many districts, but exceptional results are rare. Of the western counties, Hereford, Somerset, Worcester, and Dorset give the best general success ; but there are districts in Devon, Cornwall, and Gloucester where the culture of this fruit might be extended with advantage. The eastern counties are not specially adapted for Pears, except in a few sheltered and warm situations ; but in Essex good results are obtained in many places.

In the midland counties the principal successes with the fruit are scored in private gardens, under the most experienced men ; generally, as regards the colder central districts, on heavy land, the fruit is not seen at its best. In Buckinghamshire, Hertfordshire, and Nottinghamshire, in some favoured localities with fertile soils, Pears are grown with considerable success. The fruit deteriorates in the northern counties of England and the eastern counties of Scotland from bush or standard trees, but with the aid of walls a considerable measure of success is secured even to the extreme north. In part of Wales, especially in the south, Pears are satisfactory, and an admirable example of what can be accomplished with pyramid trees is seen at Cardiff Castle. In Ireland also the climate is generally favourable, at least along the east coast from Antrim to Cork ; and wherever the soil and local conditions are suitable, good fruits are obtained. In fact, Pear culture might be profitably extended in several parts of Ireland, as, though the extreme humidity in the south is not favourable to the fullest development of flavour, yet as regards size much success could be obtained, and fine Pears have a material commercial value.

Situation.—Even in favourable localities the situation in regard to shelter, elevation, and aspect must be carefully considered. The Pear is hardy enough naturally, but the young foliage is produced very early in the season, and in its then delicate condition is perhaps more easily injured by wind than by any other cause. The flowers also expand at an early and critical time, and they are quite as liable to destruction by keen dry winds as by frost. We have seen the prospect of many fine crops ruined by winds that seemed to dry up and shrivel the petals and the essential organs. Shelter, then, is a consideration of the first importance, especially from north and east winds. Protection from south-west winds is equally essential, for the majority of Pears are more easily bruised and rendered practically useless than Apples, and when a heavy crop is ripening, exposure to one gale is sufficient to bring them all to the ground, or at least to materially reduce the value of the fruit. If there is no natural shelter either in the form of timber plantations, rising ground, or buildings, belts or hedges should be planted as indicated in the chapter on Apples. All such protection must be at a sufficient distance, to avoid soil exhaustion by the tree roots in the immediate neighbourhood of the Pears, and over-shading must be avoided.

Elevation is an item of importance amongst the conditions demanding attention. The dangers attending low situations have already been pointed out, and if these are serious in the case of the Apple they are still more so with regard to the Pear. Indeed, it is useless attempting to grow Pears in low positions subject to spring frosts, as, though the trees themselves may thrive and flower, a crop of fruit will seldom be secured. Still, it must be remembered that the requisite elevation is more relative than absolute, and that the more inland the position the higher the altitude must be to give a reasonable prospect of safety. (See section on THE APPLE: Culture, p. 22.)

Aspect is important in reference to Pear culture, the best dessert varieties, especially the early and midseason sorts, requiring the fullest exposure to sunlight to perfect them. The Pear demands a higher temperature than the Apple to develop its finest qualities, and this is one reason why in France and Belgium many sorts have gained favour that are of little use here. We cannot overcome all the difficulties of our climate, but much may be done by choosing an aspect that commands the fullest exposure to the sun, and this is still further aided by a moderate slope towards the south.

These remarks generally apply to plantations of bush, pyramid, or standard trees. In British gardens, however, a large portion of the wall space at command is devoted to Pears, and as we go north this proportion is increased, because they cannot be depended upon without such protection. Another advantage is, that by planting against walls with different aspects the season of some fine Pears can be prolonged, while even the north walls can be turned to account for the varieties employed for stewing, or for some of the latest keeping sorts that require a long period of gradual maturing. It is a rather strange fact, but not inconsistent with what has already been said respecting the variability of the Pear under different conditions, that some varieties develop much higher qualities when trained to walls than they do in the open, while others show the reverse behaviour. They are not constant even in this, as they occasionally give better results on a wall in the north than they do in the south.

Soil.—The most suitable soil for Pears generally is a mellow, fertile loam of moderate depth, and either naturally or artificially drained, as, though a dry soil is antagonistic to the welfare of the tree, yet excessive moisture in a stagnant state is productive of serious evils. As regards the richness and mechanical condition of the soil, the special fitness for Pears will depend to some extent upon the stock on which they are growing. If Pears on a Free stock are planted on a deep, rich soil, an excessive and unfruitful luxuriance will result, necessitating considerable labour to check it, and often leading to disease. On the other hand, the Quince stock will usually thrive in such a soil, and produce healthy, fertile trees. The Quince is a bad stock upon poor, thin soils, the natural vigour of the Pear stock being required under such circumstances.

It is a much less difficult task to ameliorate an unfavourable soil, and adapt it to the needs of the Pear, than it is to alter other conditions that may be adverse to the well-being of the tree. If dwarf bush or pyramid trees on the Quince are to be planted, or trained trees on the same stock, a thorough preparation by digging or trenching should precede the planting, incorporating a good proportion of old stable or farmyard manure where the soil is poor, or if it has been exhausted by previous cropping. It is better to expend a little time in this preliminary work than to rely upon removing defects subsequently, as it can seldom be then performed in a thorough or satisfactory manner. When soil abounds in chalk or lime and is at the same time deficient in humus, this liberal preparation is even more important.

We have known cases where efforts to supply the lacking nourishment by means of top-dressings, or even by generous applications of liquid manures, have absolutely failed to accomplish the desired purpose, the only remedy being lifting and replanting the trees in freshly-prepared borders. With very heavy clay soils (which are naturally the least suited for Pears) no more effective means can be adopted than partially burning a portion and mixing this with the bulk at the time of digging, though abundance of decaying vegetable matter will also assist the work greatly. A rough digging in early autumn and exposure to a winter's frost and weathering will reduce some of the most tenacious soils to workable condition, and they can be then more readily prepared for early planting the next season. In most gardens where the whole of the available space is under a regular system of cropping and liberal cultivation, it is seldom that much special preparation is requisite for Pears. But where a plantation is being formed on fresh ground, or a border near a wall is to be planted, the conditions are very different, and greater attention is demanded.

Pears growing against walls are liable to injury from drought. Rain is prevented from moistening the soil near the wall, a fact which is often overlooked, and it is

early fertility. The Pear stock is often spoken of as if it were derived exclusively from seed of the Wild Pear, whereas it is seldom obtained from this source, and large quantities of Pear seeds or Pear seedlings are exported from France to Great Britain and the United States, practically furnishing the bulk of the Free stocks employed here and in America. These seeds are obtained from various sources, and the resulting seedlings often exhibit marked differences

Fig. 78.—Pear. Pitmaston Duchess on Pear Stock (10 feet high, 6 years old).

Fig. 79.—Pear. Same variety and same age on Quince Stock.

(These figures illustrate nearly equal growth on the two stocks.)

quite possible for wall trees to be suffering through lack of moisture when trees in the open are well supplied.

Stocks for Pears.—The same broad distinctions rule in the stocks used for Pears as in those employed for Apples, namely, the seedling Pear or Free stock is that on which the largest trees are obtained either as standards or pyramids, with a correspondingly tardy arrival at a fruit-bearing stage. The Quince stock usually reduces the luxuriant growth of the trees and promotes

in strength and habit, in the same way as do the Free stocks for Apples (seedlings), and to this may be attributed some of the variations in the behaviour and quality of well-known Pears, where the peculiarities cannot be otherwise accounted for. It is regrettable that a more exact and trustworthy method of securing Pear stocks is not generally adopted, so that the results could be more certain.

Several forms of Quince are used as stocks, such as the Common, the Portugal, the Angers, with others, and very different opinions have been expressed regarding their respective merits. The Portugal and the Angers varieties are, however, the principal favourites ; the first being ~~of free~~ and vigorous growth, but it is not very fertile and is rather difficult to raise in quantity. The Angers variety, on the contrary, is not so strong, but it is compact in habit, very prolific, and comparatively easy to increase, points which have recommended it to nurserymen in Britain, America,

in consequence large numbers of Quince stocks are raised from cuttings for trade purposes. If these are carefully selected and well furnished with roots they are as good as the others ; but this has not always been done, and in consequence a doubt has been cast upon the durability of a very useful stock. It has been said that the sparse-fruiting character of the Portugal Quince affects the behaviour of the variety grafted upon it, but we have never observed an instance of a Pear that is naturally of a

Fig. 80.—Pear. Emile d'Heyst on Pear Stock (9 feet high, 6 years old).

Fig. 81.—Pear. Same variety on Quince Stock (6 feet high, 6 years old).

(These figures illustrate greatly divergent growth on the two stocks.)

and on the Continent. The chief objection against it is that the growth does not always keep pace with that of the scions of the stronger Pears, with the result that the life of the tree is shortened and there is more danger of damage resulting in stormy weather. This partly depends, no doubt, upon the method by which the stocks are propagated and grown previous to budding. Much more strongly-rooted and freely-developed Quinces are usually obtained from layers than from cuttings, but the process does not admit of such rapid increase, and

fertile habit being thus affected. Still, we prefer the Angers type for the reasons already given.

There is no question that the general introduction to gardens of the dwarf-bush or pyramid trees on the Quince stock, which was largely due to Mr. Thomas Rivers, has contributed greatly to the increased popularity of the Pear for general cultivation. In four or five years fruitful trees can be grown, whereas on the Free stock they would not be productive for at least double the time. Then, too, in many cases better coloured and more highly flavoured fruits are secured from trees on the Quince than from those on the Pear, which is apt to induce coarseness until the tree is well established and bearing freely. The objection that trees on the Quince would be of short duration has not proved to be the fact, unless in exceptional cases where the stock has been defective from the start.

Intermediate Stocks — Double-grafting.— Though all Pears will grow on the Free stock, there are some which will not thrive when

Fig. 82.—Pear, double-grafted on Quince Stock, showing the intermediate stock.

placed direct upon the Quince, and this led to the introduction of intermediate stocks or double-grafting, one of the most interesting and important matters connected with the artificial increase of hardy fruits. The principle upon which this depends is that a Pear which grows freely upon the Quince is budded or grafted on that stock and allowed to grow for at least two years; it is then cut back to within a few inches of the Quince stem, and the variety desired to develop into a tree is grafted upon the intermediate stock. It is remarkable what a difference is effected in the behaviour

of the fruiting tree by the introduction of this piece of stem of another variety; handsome, fertile trees are obtained of sorts that had hitherto been unsatisfactory in all respects except on the free stocks. Many varieties have been employed as intermediates which were most suited to special varieties, including the following :—Beurré d'Amanlis, which forms a strong tree on the Quince, suits many Pears as an intermediate stock, especially Jargonelle, Gansel's Bergamot, and several of the Bergamot type. Beurré Hardy is another of free growth on the Quince, and most of the stronger Pears succeed upon it. In France Belle de Berri, known in Britain as Vicar of Winkfield, is largely used. It has also been employed in some English nurseries, Beurré Clairgeau being especially successful upon it. Other varieties that have given good results for a similar purpose are Jaminette, Sucré Vert, Duc de Nemours, and Napoléon Savinien, which naturally form vigorous trees. Bési Goubault is another particularly hardy variety which thrives on the Quince and suits the Jargonelle and Bergamot types. Prince Albert, a Pear of little value in itself, except for its free vigorous habit of growth, has been found well adapted for Marie Louise, Knight's Monarch, with Huyshe's Victoria and Princess of Wales. Marie Louise d'Uccle is extremely vigorous and prolific on the Quince, making a good intermediate stock for Marie Louise, and is also suited for Souvenir du Congrès and Beacon. Beurré Sterckmann is used for Joséphine de Malines, and Bergamotte Esperen for Beurré Rance. That fine old Pear, Brown Beurré, which is satisfactory both on Quince and free stocks, makes a good intermediate for Winter Nelis. For the latter Pitmaston Duchess has also been employed, while this in turn has been worked on Winter Nelis as an intermediate.

Other stocks have been used for Pears, but they possess little value, for instance *Cratægus Oxyacantha, C. Crus-Galli,* and *Cotoneaster affinis* have been tried; while several Continental cultivators have grafted Pears on Apple stocks with some degree of success, though not sufficient to warrant the recommendation of the experiment for general purposes.

Forms of Trees.—The various natural forms of trees suitable for Apples are also adopted for Pears, but the latter lend themselves more readily to artificial training, and many modes are in use, some of which are more fantastic than beautiful or useful. As a standard on the Free stock the Pear makes a very large and long-lived tree, indeed there are specimens still in existence in various parts of Europe that must rank with the oldest of our deciduous trees. When standards are well established and in full bearing they produce enormous crops of fruit during a long period, and though the fruit may be small, they often prove very profitable to their owners. But there is such a long time of waiting for these results that the old saying, " He who plants Pears

Fig. 83.—Pyramidal Pear.

plants for his heirs," fairly expresses the general experience.

For orchards standards or half-standards (which is a preferable form where the trees are not exposed to injuries by cattle) are necessary, and the principal means of avoiding excessive luxuriance and a prolonged period of development is to consider the soil before planting. In rich soil magnificent trees will be obtained, but fruiting will be delayed in proportion to the strength of growth ; in comparatively poor soil or on chalk there is a prospect that crops may be

obtained within a reasonable time. It is desirable that all orchards of Pear-trees on the Free stock should be in grass after they are established, for this exerts an additional check on the vigour. In cultivated land the trees are encouraged to increased growth, unless a close system of intermediate cropping with vegetables is adopted, which necessitates frequent digging, thus performing a kind of rough root-pruning.

By far the most useful form of Pear-trees for general purposes, either in private gardens or commercial plantations, are the bush and pyramid, to the latter of which the natural habit of the tree is most suited (fig. 83). Upon the Free stock large and vigorous pyramidal specimens can be had, and with due care in root-pruning a moderately early fertility can be induced provided the soil and other conditions be favourable. Handsome, well-proportioned, healthy, and prolific trees in this form are both profitable and attractive, and they are worth the trouble they demand, at least as a part of a plantation. Upon the Quince, however, either single or double grafted, we obtain the most serviceable trees for the majority of gardens, and wherever fruit is required as quickly as possible after planting, such trees are indispensable. The most vigorous varieties are moderated in their strength on this stock, and in the early years of the tree's life the difference between those of the same variety on the two classes of stocks is as marked in the flowering and fruiting as it is in the growth. In either of the two principal forms, i.e. bush and pyramid, excellent trees can be had on Quince roots of all the best varieties now that double - grafting has removed the difficulty that at one time rendered it impossible to purchase or raise useful Pears of certain varieties on the dwarfing stock.

A modification of the pyramidal form is the columnar or cylindrical (fig. 84), which is grown of nearly equal width from the base to the apex of the tree. It is convenient for planting where space is limited, but it has not much to recommend it in other respects, and is certainly not so handsome as a well-grown pyramidal or conical tree.

In the artificial and more exact systems of training, the espalier with its various forms is well adapted for the Pear, as it allows more freedom of extension than some of the others.

The horizontal espalier, in which the lateral branches start on each side of the main stem at right angles, *i.e.* horizontally, in successive tiers, until the requisite height is reached,

Fig. 84.—Vertical Cordon in flower.

is that in most general use. The position of the branches tends to check excessive growth, and the tree is especially suited either for training to trellises or walls. The vertical espalier forms a good tree, but is best adapted for the weaker-growing varieties. This is sometimes termed the "grid-iron" form of training, the branches rising vertically from the main stem trained horizontally to the right and left. The individual branches may then be regarded

as similar to and requiring the same kind of treatment as vertical cordons.

The Palmette Verrier (fig. 85) may be considered an extension of the last-named systems of training, and under that method handsome and useful trees can be formed, especially against walls. The lower branches are trained horizontally to the full extent of the lateral space to be allowed to the tree, and then turned up at right angles, thus completing their growth in the same style as the vertical cordon stems. Each successive pair of branches is treated in the same way, at the allowed distance within the others, the whole tree when fully developed thus having a square outline. Mr. E. Luckhurst adopted this method of training Pear-trees in Sussex with great success, and the trees for a number of years have proved highly satisfactory. The wall space is occupied in a very economical manner, and the check caused by the sharp angle at which the branches are turned prevents undue luxuriance of growth and promotes fertility.

Cordon training (figs. 84 to 88), either in the horizontal, vertical, or oblique forms, is adapted for the Pear on trellises or walls, and handsome fruits can be had from such trees under the best treatment. A considerable portion of the finest exhibition fruits which appear at the leading shows are produced by cordon trees in favourable situations. The horizontal cordons, either single or double, are best fitted for marginal borders near paths, but most of the other forms are well adapted for walls or trellises, and permit a number of varieties to be grown in a moderate space, thus obtaining a long succession if that is desired.

Few other forms of training for Pears are adopted in Britain, but in France some very elaborate trees are produced with the expenditure of much time and care. Some of these are formed by the approach grafting of the branches of neighbouring espaliers, so that various geometrical designs are produced. Others are formed by the adjoining branches of the same tree being looped and intergrafted to produce vase or balloon-shaped specimens that are attractive as curious examples of the gardener's art, but which serve no other purpose. Mr. W. Robinson has given some good illustrations of the more remarkable of these in his *Parks and Gardens of Paris*.

Training single cordons or some similar form across each other at an angle, leaving diamond-shaped interspaces, has been advocated as a means of forming Pear-hedges that might be both useful and ornamental, but the same purpose can be more readily accomplished in another way. This is by planting maiden trees, of varieties that grow freely on the Quince, about 2 feet apart, cutting them back and pruning for the first two or three years, when they can be treated in the same way as an ordinary hedge. Some reduction of the growth in the summer is, however, desirable. Free-flowering and fairly compact varieties should be selected, as their appearance is the chief object, though the fruit produced will prove useful in some seasons. One mode of utilizing the Pear need only be mentioned here, as it is referred to at length in another chapter,

gardens. All Pears on the Free stock require a liberal allowance of space, and for orchard standards 30 feet in each direction should at least be allowed. Pyramidal Pears on the same stock should be 15 to 20 feet apart for all the stronger-growing varieties if they are intended to remain where they are planted without thinning. In the columnar style 6 to 10 feet will suffice. Either bushes or pyramids on the Quince seldom require more than 10 or 12 feet, and the weaker-growing varieties will succeed for some years at less than that if necessary. But crowding Pears in any form is very undesirable, if it can be avoided.

As regards trained trees for trellises or

Fig. 85.—Palmette Verrier system of training.

namely growing the trees as pyramids or bushes in pots in orchard-houses. Where early supplies of fine Pears are required, or in districts where soil and climate are unfavourable to obtaining the fruit in perfection out of doors, this is a most valuable addition to the resources of a garden. The trees also possess much ornamental value in flower and fruit.

Arrangement and Distances.—If plantations of Pears are to be formed, the methods of arrangement suitable for Apples and Orchards, of which details are given in their respective chapters, are also applicable. But it is seldom that such are formed wholly of this fruit; they more frequently constitute part of mixed plantations, or are employed as lines or avenues in kitchen-

walls, much will depend upon the height of the support to which the trees are secured. If these do not exceed 8 feet in height, allowance must be made for more lateral extension in the case of all forms of espaliers than where the walls are 10 feet or more high. In the same way the oblique cordons are more fitted for low walls and trellises than the vertical cordons, which demand a greater extent to develop in an upward direction. For espaliers on walls and trellises, from 15 to 24 feet apart may be allowed, according to the habit of the variety, the space at command, or the demands upon the garden resources. Single horizontal cordons may be allowed from 8 to 10 feet, and double cordons of the same type from 12 to 20 feet. Vertical or oblique

Fig. 86.—Oblique Cordon in flower.

Fig. 87.—Oblique Cordon in fruit.

cordons will require a distance of from 1½ to 2 feet for each stem ; thus, double cordons should be at least 3 feet apart, and triple cordons about 5 feet asunder.

Planting.—The directions given respecting the condition of the soil, with the time and method of planting for the Apple, are equally

Fig. 88.—Vertical Cordon (Fondante de Thiriott).

appropriate to the Pear : but this tree starts so early in the spring to produce flowers and foliage that planting cannot be safely deferred so late as with the Apple. Much depends upon the character of the season and the state of the tree ; in moist, warm, and cloudy times late planting can be often safely performed. Mr. T. Rivers has

stated that " Pear-trees on the Quince stock offer a curious anomaly, for if they are removed quite late in the spring—say towards the end of March, when their blossom-buds are just on the point of bursting—they will bear a fine and often an abundant crop of fruit the same season. This is perhaps owing to the blossoms being retarded, and thus escaping the spring frosts ; but it has so often occurred when no frosts have visited us that I notice it, in fact no trees bear late removal so well as Pears on Quince stocks." If this is taken in conjunction with what has been said about weather conditions, it may be relied upon ; but it is not an advisable proceeding to transplant Pears when starting to grow if the characteristic March conditions prevail, *i.e.* drying winds and hot sun.

Deep planting is bad for Pears, especially those on the Free stock. Where the soil conditions are very unfavourable, planting on the surface has been adopted, mounding the roots over with soil. There is a danger in this when very dry seasons follow, as what little rain may fall runs off without penetrating to the roots, and it thus sometimes happens that even in a damp position the trees may suffer through receiving an insufficient supply of water at a critical time. This may be overcome in some measure by ridging the soil on each side of the tree, at the limit of the roots, thus forming a trough-like receptacle.

Pears on the Quince should be planted so that the stock can be covered with soil, unless that is unusually long. Roots are then often formed up to the juncture with the scion, thus strengthening the tree materially. When the stock has not developed in something like the same proportion as the scion, the point of union is always the weak part of the tree, and a source of danger in stormy weather. For this reason careful staking is essential for most bush or pyramid Pears on the Quince, and the stakes cannot be safely dispensed with for some years unless the trees are sheltered or make exceptional progress.

In planting against a wall, it is important to cover it as quickly as possible, consistent with allowing the trees sufficient room. At wide distances trees trained horizontally will reach the top of the wall as soon as others that are planted more closely together, but for many years there will be larger spaces uncovered between those that are widely planted, as will be readily understood on referring to fig. 86. Supposing that the wall is 13 feet high, and that the upright is annually stopped so that one course of horizontals will be made in a year, then in twelve years, the horizontals being 1 foot apart, the leader will reach the top of the wall. Presuming that at the expiration of this period the lower horizontals of the trees 1 and 2 meet, it is then evident that only half of the wall will be covered; for the space covered by the side of the tree No. 1, and that covered by the side of the tree No. 3, are together equal to the unoccupied space *a b c*; whilst the space covered by the tree No. 2 is equal to the

Fig. 89.—Horizontal Training.

other unoccupied space *c d e*. In short, it is easy to observe that the covered spaces form four triangles, and that the uncovered spaces form four similar triangles equal to the former, so that half the wall is covered, and half not.

Supposing the trees had been planted at half the distance apart, as in fig. 90, also that they had grown at the same rate as fig. 89, and accordingly reached the top of the wall in twelve years, it will be observed that at the end of that period all the horizontals, from the base as far as half the height of the wall, will have met. The

Fig. 90.—Horizontal Training.

lower half of the wall is therefore entirely covered, and there is only one-fourth of the surface uncovered. If we calculate the difference in regard to time, we shall find that by planting at half the distance as much surface will be covered in three years as will be the case in four years by the other plan. Now, as walls are expensive, it is desirable that the whole available space should be utilized. Close planting, as above shown, will contribute to that object, and the question is to what extent this may be carried as regards the Pear. In time Pear-trees in good soil will profitably occupy

a wall of ordinary height if planted at 30 feet apart; but at such a wide distance there must be a large space of bare wall for many years. The greatest distance that need be allowed between the trees is 24 feet; but less than this would appropriate the space more rapidly.

When wall-trees were badly managed, when by close planting the branches had to be much shortened to keep them within the prescribed limits, and when in consequence of this shortening a mass of shoots sprung up, one of two things usually happened: these shoots were either allowed to grow during summer and cut off close in winter, entirely wasting so much of the strength of the tree; or they were cut down near to their bases with the view of forming spurs at the portions left, but instead of spurs fresh shoots were usually produced. With such management, close planting was certainly not to be recommended, because it induced growths which, without due care, became an evil. But now it is different; for, by judicious summer pruning, trees can be kept in very small compass; thus, pyramidal-trained Pear-trees can be kept within a space not exceeding 4 or 5 feet in diameter. By employing similar means, a horizontal-trained tree might have its branches limited to an extent of 10 feet. This we know to be possible; but it is not always desirable, and to do it properly would require more strict attention than could, in many cases, be given. We would therefore recommend not less than 15 feet as the minimum distance which should be adopted, and 20 feet as the maximum. If the soil is very rich, 20 feet is a proper distance, and where but moderately so, 18 feet will suffice. It may indeed be said that 24 feet, with "riders" between, would be preferable; but these are not much to be depended upon for fruit, though they answer the purpose of covering the wall; moreover, by the time they are in a good bearing state, they have to be cut away to make room for the permanent trees. The distance to be allowed between these has therefore been considered irrespective of "riders."

Pruning and Training.—The stems of standard Pear-trees should be reared according to the directions already given in treating of the Apple. Three shoots are obtained at the proper height for constituting three main limbs, and each of these should be cut so that two shoots may start at from 9 inches to 1 foot from its base; thus, as in the case of the Apple-tree, six main branches will be produced, a number which will be quite sufficient. For several years all shoots that start from the principal branches should be kept subordinate, until the latter have diverged so far as to afford an abundance of space for an intermediate branch. Where space allows of a greater number of branches being originated, they may be produced at any place by cutting back to suitable buds at that point. It has been explained that three buds will usually start immediately below the section; but in the case of open standards and dwarfs, three branches, with the exception of the three main limbs, should never take their origin from the same point, or at least from three contiguous buds. There ought to be no tridents in the tops of trees so trained, and one of the three growths should either be cut closely off, or shortened and managed so as to form a spur.

When subsidiary branches are encouraged from each of the six main limbs, it is desirable that they should proceed alternately from opposite sides, for when this is the case it will better resist the wind. If each of the six main branches be well balanced by having as many growths on one side as on the other, possessing the same vigour, and further, if equality is maintained between the six principal branches themselves, the tree may be considered to be properly managed.

Whilst encouraging the principal branches, by taking care to check vigorous shoots that otherwise would become competitors, nakedness should at the same time be guarded against. Some varieties are naturally disposed to branch, but others are apt to produce shoots that are bare for nearly their whole length. These, then, require to be shortened, in order that shoots to form branchlets and spurs may be produced. When the top of the tree becomes large, the spurs on the bases of the large limbs will be apt to die, from their foliage not having so full a share of light as those on the outside. This can be prevented to some extent by keeping the branches on the south side thinner than elsewhere, in order to admit the sun's rays more freely into the interior.

After the heads of standard trees have been kept regulated for several years, as above directed, they will generally have to be left to follow their natural mode of growth. Yet all gross irregularities should be prevented: branches must not be allowed to cross each other, and shoots that are taking a wrong direction ought to be cut out. When the tree arrives at a bearing state, branches loaded with fruit will be more or less weighed down; and when a branch is bent during any considerable portion of the growing season, by fruit or any other weight, it retains nearly that form after the weight has been removed. Hence, in full-grown trees, the extremities of the branches are generally turned downwards, a direction unfavourable for the prolongation of shoots, but conducive to the formation of fruit-spurs. In old standard trees, it will be observed that the fruit is chiefly produced at and near the extremities, and there of course it is best situated for light and air. Not unfrequently, however, when the tree is in this condition, vigorous upright shoots push from strong branches in the interior of the head of the tree. These are injurious, for they appropriate the sap that would otherwise contribute to the nourishment of the fruit-spurs at the extremities. The sap will rush into these vigorous shoots as it would into suckers, and the more vigorous they become the weaker are those situated in the older parts. All upright shoots in the centre of the tree should therefore be cut off, or treated so as to form a spur.

Fig. 91 represents a small branch, which has been pruned at *b* above the two spurs *e* and *f*; of the two terminal shoots *c* and *a*, *c* having become too strong is stopped at *d*, *a* is left in order to give vent to the sap which would otherwise have flowed back on the spurs *e* and *f*, and caused them to be abortive. When danger of this is over the branch is cut off at *g*.

Fig. 91.—Pinching and Spur-pruning.

Instead of forming a head from six equally diverging branches, some prefer the pyramidal form, which certain varieties naturally assume. The upright shoot of the young stem should, in that case, be stopped at the proper height; but the shoots which result ought not to be made to diverge equally, but one should be trained as upright as possible; and subsequently, a central perpendicular shoot ought to be encouraged, so that the head of the tree may consist of a central stem with branches proceeding from it. These branches should be kept on an equality, so that the top may be equally balanced.

Pyramid Training.—As regards the form (fig. 92), the main object to be kept in view is a perpendicular stem, with every branch proceeding from it shorter in a horizontal direction than the one below it.

In proceeding to details, it will be best to commence with a maiden tree, which we shall suppose to be planted in November, either in the nursery or where it is to remain. The stem should be topped a little, but not cut so far back as to make the buds start near the ground. Next autumn let the stem be cut back near to the place where it was budded or grafted. If the tree has been well planted, and has made a fair quantity of leaves and roots in the course of the summer, a strong shoot will start from the base, which should be trained as upright as possible. In November cut it back to about 1 foot from the ground, and below this several shoots will start : the uppermost should be trained in a perpendicular direction for a continuation of the central stem, whilst the others will form the lower tier of branches. These may be allowed to grow without restraint till September, and then they ought to be all bent to nearly a horizontal position. But some may be weak and others strong : the latter must be most depressed, whilst the former should be allowed to retain their natural position till they acquire sufficient strength to be bent down in the following summer ; but if likely to interfere with the young shoots above them, they must be trained so as to keep clear of these.

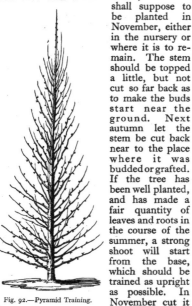

Fig. 92.—Pyramid Training.

In the end of November any laterals that may have been produced on the branches of the lower tier should be cut to within 1 inch of their bases. At the same time the upright leader must be cut 15 inches higher than in the preceding season, if the soil is very rich and the climate moist ; otherwise, only 1 foot higher, more especially if the variety is not a strong-growing one. This will cause shoots to be produced for another tier of branches. By these means the two lower tiers will have been obtained, and in the same manner as many more as may be desirable can be secured.

Instead of obtaining only one stage of horizontals annually, two may very well be produced after the first two, if the trees are growing well. It is advisable to originate the two lower stages from buds on the mature shoot as above directed, for it is important that they should be well established ; but afterwards the upright leading shoot may have its growing point pinched off in summer when it has grown to the height of 12 inches. This will occasion the production of several shoots at or near that height, one of which should be trained to grow upright during the remainder of the season, and afterwards be cut over at 12 inches above where it was pinched, that is, at 2 feet from where it started in spring.

Fig. 93.—Pyramid Training.

Side branches should be pruned and trained to the form of a pyramid or cone, of which, if the tree is intended to be of limited extent, fig. 93 may represent a section. Its total height is about equal to its circumference at the widest part, a proportion which is considered to give the most elegant appearance. If the distance from the base *b* to the apex *a* be 10 feet, the circumference at the widest being as much, the diameter at *d* will be about 38 inches. The branches must therefore be kept within the limits *a c* and *a d*. The upper branches will be strongly disposed to extend, not only beyond the limits represented by the dotted lines, but also much beyond the horizontal extension of the lower branches. This must, however, be prevented by an early stopping of the shoots. In summer, as well as at the winter pruning, the regular outline of the tree must be kept in view and strictly maintained, otherwise the growth of the top will soon be in a condition to draw the greatest share of the sap, which is unfavourable to fruitfulness. If all the branches were of equal length the tree would be like a cylinder, but they would be equal as regards their length and that only, for their vigour would be very different, vegetation being much more active in the upper than in the lower part. When subjected to pyramidal training, the upper branches are shortened so that the quantity of foliage they bear is less than the lower ones do ; and thus the supply of sap will be limited in the part where, otherwise, it would tend to be in excess.

The above remarks will be sufficient to show the necessity of strictly preserving the outline ; but all within will be a mass of shoots unless attention is paid to pinching and summer pruning, for on these the success of trees trained as pyramids chiefly depends.

Summer Pruning and Pinching the Shoots.— It is evident that if the shoots of a pyramid-ally-trained tree were not shortened and thinned, their foliage would suffer from being shaded and crowded. It is also certain that if the laterals were allowed to grow till the winter pruning, they would either have to be cut off, or, if then shortened, a number of shoots would start from their bases, and cause greater crowding in the following season than before. Such being the consequence of cutting back shoots at the winter pruning, in order that little winter pruning may be necessary, recourse must be had to summer pruning, an important operation, respecting which, however, there is much diversity of opinion. We shall consider it in detail, both as regards the parts to be operated on, and the time and manner of performing the operation.

A pyramid-trained tree consists, essentially, of an upright stem, and as many side branches as can be properly trained without overcrowding. There must be space between them for fruit-spurs when these come to be formed. All shoots not required to form the stem or the branches from it must be summer-pruned, either by the knife, or by pinching between the finger and thumb. The operation should be performed on laterals that grow from the young summer shoots that are intended to form a permanent part of the tree, as well as on those of the older wood. The time varies with the earliness or lateness of the season ; and again, as a general rule, the operation should be performed sooner upon the upper and

more vigorous branches than upon the lower and less vigorous.

Allow the lateral shoots to form six leaves, and then pinch them immediately the sixth leaf is formed. There are usually latent or only partially developed buds at the base of the shoot, with occasionally some small imperfect leaves, but in counting the six leaves these should be omitted. The more vigorous shoots will generally be those that will first attain the above extent of growth, and accordingly the first that are stopped or pinched. Many of the shoots will start again after the first stopping, and when these are 3 or 4 inches long they are pinched back to three buds, or to about 1½ inches from their bases.

With regard to the terminal shoots of the branches, those that extend in summer beyond such as are situated below them should be pinched ; but the others ought to be allowed to grow till the beginning of September, when they may be cut to their assigned limits, so that any further shortening at the winter pruning will be unnecessary.

From what has been already stated, any one may rear and maintain handsome and productive pyramid Pear-trees ; nevertheless, the nature of the proceedings having been explained, the chief points may now be briefly recapitulated. The tree having been trained with an upright shoot, is cut back before winter, in order that it may produce side branches near the ground ; and a shoot is again trained upright and cut, so as to produce more laterals and a shoot for the continuation of the stem ; this shoot may be stopped, if vigorous enough, when it has grown about 1 foot. This will tend to throw more sap into the side branches below, whilst the upright leader, from its advantageous position, will soon regain sufficient strength. Laterals from it must be pinched when they have grown 6 or 8 inches ; by shortening them at the winter pruning to within 2 inches of the stem they will produce shoots strong enough for side branches, and, at the same time, the pyramidal form of the tree will be preserved. By stopping the leader in summer, side branches will result, so that at the winter pruning it will only be necessary to cut it 2 feet above where it was cut a year before. Thus, without danger of a deficiency of side branches, an advance of 2 feet in height is gained in one season.

In subsequent years the upright shoot may be treated in a similar manner till the desired height is attained. It is necessary, however, to observe that where the climate is such as not to ripen the wood of the summer shoot properly, it is better to allow the leader to go on without stopping, and originate the side branches by cutting back to 12 inches in autumn. The laterals from the side branches may be made to form fruit-spurs instead of overcrowding the tree ; they must be pinched under the sixth leaf when they have developed that number. The terminal shoots should be allowed to grow till the end of August, when they ought to be shortened to within eight buds or leaves of the stem, not taking into account the buds at the base of the shoot which usually do not push. At the winter pruning, the ends of the branches must be pruned so as not to spoil the symmetrical outline of the tree.

The above directions are applicable to pyramids strictly kept, and of the smallest dimensions ; and any one that can rear such can easily manage those of larger size. In some cases Pear-trees are allowed to form pyramids as much as 15 feet high, the side branches extending in proportion ; but for these it is only necessary to allow greater extension to the terminal shoots of the branches, and to the upright stem ; in all other respects the directions already given should be followed.

Espalier Training.—Of all modes of training the Pear-tree in the open ground the espalier, if well managed, is the most economical as regards space. If the espalier is only 6 feet high, there may be six horizontal branches on each side, and each branch extending, say, 10 feet, the aggregate length of the branches will then be 120 feet. The same extent of branches, trained as an open dwarf, would occupy a space of 10 feet square, or an area of 100 feet.

The mode of rearing a central stem, and that of obtaining branches from it where required, have already been explained ; and when the horizontals are started no one can be in any doubt in training them—as far as the correct form of the tree is concerned—all he has to attend to is simply to train them right along ; whilst in the fan and other modes of training, many considerations are sometimes necessary with respect to the position and direction of the branches. The espalier mode gives good command over the growth of the tree and the equal distribution of the sap ; at the same time the branches are all equally exposed to light.

Equality of vegetation is conducive not only to the health of the tree, but also to its productiveness ; and, accordingly, well-managed espalier trees are very productive, and generally bear larger and better-formed fruit than can be obtained from standards. In the latter form, it is true, many of the large kinds of Pears succeed ; yet from their weight they are apt to be blown down and spoiled when almost fit for gathering, whilst on espaliers all fruits are nearly secure from this danger. The quality of fruit grown in this way is often superior to that produced on east-and-west walls.

The advantages of this mode of training are many, whilst the only drawback is the expense of the espalier rail. This, however, will be amply compensated by the produce which can be obtained from well-managed trees. In all gardens, wherever they can be afforded, rails of a substantial character should be employed.

The distance between the Pear-trees intended to be trained should be about 20 feet ; and the espaliers, if there be two or more parallel rows, should be 15 feet apart. When placed along the sides of walks, the line of rail ought to be 2½ feet from the edge of the walk, and the trees should be planted 3 inches from the rail, otherwise the latter would be pressed out by the stem when it becomes thick. The trees should be planted on the side of the espalier rail next to the walk. There may be some objection to this as regards the trees on the south side of a walk running east and west ; it would, it is true, be advisable to plant them on the south side of the rail, but a much better effect is produced when they face the walk on both sides.

The branches of a horizontally-trained espalier Pear-tree should be about 1 foot apart. The mode of cutting down the upright stem to obtain these is the same as in the case of the Apple. The lower one should be started a little below the line along which they are intended to be trained ; the upper courses ought to proceed very nearly at right angles from the stem, and the highest one quite so.

In order that the young tree may speedily acquire strength, the shoots should not be much pinched or otherwise shortened in the early part of the summer at least. Those near the extremities of the horizontals ought, however, to be checked, so as not to compete with the terminal shoots or leaders of these branches. In order to throw more strength into the branches, the upright leader should be pinched when it presents the appearance of becoming too strong. By these means the sap will be diverted into the bases of the branches, natural fruit-spurs will soon begin to form upon them, and in four years from the time of planting, the tree will most probably commence bearing. In order to have well-formed fruit, the fruit-spurs should not be nearer each other than 6 inches ; therefore, at the winter pruning, shoots that have started growing along the branches nearer to each other than that distance should be cut off quite close. All others should be shortened back to within 1 inch of their base. Fig. 94 represents a

Fig. 94.—Pruned horizontally-trained Pear-trees.

portion of the horizontal branch of a Pear-tree. In the course of the season it will either produce shoots, as at b, or natural fruit-spurs, as d. At the autumn or winter pruning the shoot b, and others similar to it, should be cut back to about 1 inch from their base, as at $c\,c$. In the following spring a shoot e will start below c, from the part left of the shoot b, or two may appear, as $f\,g$. If more than two grow, all but that number should be rubbed off, or cut very close, so as not to be apt to start again. When the single shoot e has made six leaves, it should be pinched or cut closely under the sixth leaf, as represented at e. With regard to the shoots f and g, one of them should be cut like the shoot e, under the sixth leaf, as at g, when so many have been formed, the other under the fifth leaf, as at f. This is done with the view of giving more strength to one of the two, in order that it may take the lead, and one shoot of a fruit-spur is much more easily managed than when numerous small twiggy shoots, too weak for forming fruit-buds, are formed. In all probability the shoots which were shortened, as at $e\,f\,g$, will produce shoots from the buds in the axil of the leaf below the respective sections, as at e. When this

second shoot has grown several inches, it may be pinched or cut off below the fourth leaf, as at h, and likewise those that proceed from below $f\,h$, and others similar. At the autumn pruning, the shoot h should be cut back to within 1 inch of its origin. Buds for spurs may have commenced to grow during the summer from the base of the preceding summer's shoot below c; if not, one or two will probably appear in the following summer. At the same time a bud or buds of this description may also form on the base of the younger shoot, at a point below i; but more likely a shoot will start if the tree is young and vigorous, and if so it must be managed like its predecessor.

Fig. 95.—Pinching and Spur-pruning a vigorous Shoot.

Fig. 95 represents a shoot which has been stopped at a, the terminal eye has produced a shoot, b, which was pinched ; this pinching has caused the development of the spurs e and f, and also the small branch d, which bears a fruit-bud, and the bud c, which should be stopped in August, in order to concentrate the sap on the buds at the lower part of the shoot. Should the upper portion of the shoot prove weak, then it would be advisable to cut it back to g.

If any branch is weaker than the rest the summer shoots upon it, or at least a considerable portion of them, should be allowed to grow without stopping till September, when a few inches may be cut off from the extremity of each. If the whole tree is weak the shoots on all the branches should be treated in a similar manner. In that case the summer shoots ought to be cut back in winter to about 1 inch from their base. From the stubs left, shoots will generally proceed in the following season ; part of them may be pinched, as in fig. 94, at regular distances along the stem, others may be allowed to grow till September, when they may be stopped and cut back to about 1 inch from their base as before. There will then be about 1 inch long of the base of the first year's shoot, now two years old, and as much of the second year's shoot, which is only one year old ; from this a shoot may be allowed to grow till September, when it should be stopped ; but instead of cutting it back to 1 inch, it should be cut off entirely, together with the former year's wood on which it took its rise. By so doing, there will be left a stub consisting of about 1 inch of wood, now three years old, ter-minating in a portion only two years old. On such portions fruit-spurs will generally form.

Espaliers will bear well if not so closely pruned as above indicated, provided means are taken to ensure an equal distribution of the sap in all the branches. If this is neglected, no system of management will ensure fruit in that perfection which would be the case if the above principle were duly carried out. The means of doing so have been already fully explained in treating on pruning. Whether the trees are worked upon the Pear stock or upon the Quince they will generally soon become fruitful, and continue healthy and productive for a long period, if over-luxuriance in one portion be prevented by timely checking, whilst more than an average liberty is allowed the weaker portions till the balance is re-established.

Cordon Training. — Trained as a single lateral or bilateral cordon (fig. 96), the Pear does not usually succeed so well as the Apple, but this mode of culture is interesting, and a few trees may be tried. They will not form fruiting spurs so freely as the Apple, so that free-bearing sorts, of which Louise Bonne of Jersey is the type, should be selected ; worked on the Quince stock this variety of Pear is adapted for all forms of training, and produces finer fruit than it does on the Pear stock. For all varieties of Pears that succeed on the Quince it is the best stock to employ for trees intended to be trained as cordons. Trees of this descrip-tion are also useful for filling vacant spaces at the base of walls, but they will do no good amongst old trees unless the ground is prepared for them. The old exhausted material should be entirely removed and the roots placed in turfy loam ; indeed this is the best medium for the roots of all fresh-planted fruit-trees when the natural soil is unsuitable.

Training and summer treatment may be summed up in a few words. Always bear in mind that the less pruning necessary in winter the sooner will the trees come into bearing, and the more fruitful will they be. The experienced cultivator studies the habit of his trees, and his future proceedings are regulated by the variety he has in hand. Whatever form of cordon is intended— be it horizontal, upright, or oblique—the cultivator's aim is to obtain a regular and uniform disposition of fruiting spurs from the base to the apex of the cordon. The Jargonelle, for instance, though a very free-bearing variety even in a young state, requires persistent pinching in of the side-shoots, as well as frequent stopping of the leading shoot, in order that a regular forma-tion of fruiting spurs may be secured ; Louise Bonne of Jersey, on the other hand, will form spurs regularly if the leading shoot is pinched only once in the season. In all cases let the side-shoots be closely pinched in.

One advantage derived from training Pear-trees as horizontal cordons is that the trees, when in blossom, can be readily protected from early spring frosts, which are so destructive to our crops of choice Pears. Various methods suggest them-selves to accomplish this object, such as hoops bent over the trees and covered with mats, Hessian canvas, or some similar protecting material ; glass ridges have also been used.

The remaining forms of cordon are more adapted for covering wall surfaces, but in all cases the summer treatment already described is necessary. One of the best is the double oblique (fig. 96). The trees

Fig. 96.—Double Oblique Cordons.

are worked on the Quince stock, and in the illustration both shoots are trained from the place of union, that is, close to the surface of the ground. The shoots ought also to be of equal strength, as if one is weak and the other strong satisfactory results will not be obtained. If the trees be trained at an angle of 45°, and the leading shoot of each be stopped once, twice, or thrice, according to the habit and the tendency to produce fruit-buds, they will come into bearing in the second year after planting, and in a few seasons cover the walls with healthy bearing wood. In rich and somewhat light soils, notwithstanding persistent summer pinching, sometimes a few of the more vigorous trees will not bear ; in this case lift the tree in the autumn and replant it in fresh loam to induce fruitfulness.

The double vertical cordon, trained in the form of the letter U, requires much

about by the autumnal winds when it is fit for gathering. The training and general management of the trees is similar to that recommended for the Apple. The branches must be sufficiently far apart not to rub against each other and injure the fruit, and the centre of the tree must be kept open, so that air and light may have free access to it. This is necessary to secure the proper ripening of the fruit.

Pruning and Training Trees against Walls. —The modes of training usually adopted are the *Horizontal* (fig. 97) and the *Fan* (fig. 98). The former is to be preferred for walls of ordinary height ; but in the

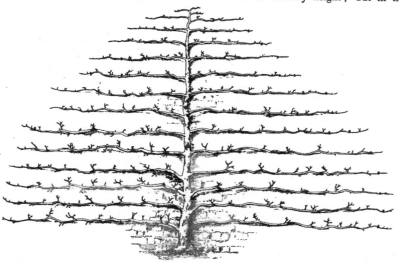

Fig. 97.—Horizontally-trained Pear.

care in training. The leading shoots grow rapidly and draw the sap past the side-shoots ; attention must therefore be paid to this tendency and the leading shoot stopped, in order that the trees may be well and uniformly furnished. Either the above or a single upright cordon may be planted as a division-line between the usual fan or horizontal-trained wall-trees, and if a careful selection of varieties be made a good supply of fruit may be obtained.

Dwarf Bushes.—For some sorts of Pears, especially those with large fruits, such as Beurré Diel, Beurré d'Amanlis, Triomphe de Jodoigne, and Beurré Rance, the bush form is better adapted than the pyramid. The fruit is not so liable to be scattered

case of trees planted against the ends of houses and other walls which are much higher than those of gardens usually are, fan-training is the more advantageous, for by it the upper part of the wall can be much sooner covered. Ample instructions for obtaining the requisite number of branches at the proper distances from each other have been already given in the chapters on pruning and training, as regards both horizontal and fan-trained trees.

The branches of a Pear-tree intended to be trained horizontally against a wall should be the distance of four courses of bricks apart. At this distance the tree will sooner reach the top of the wall than if the branches were trained at three courses or 9 inches apart ; but it may be said that, although the wall is sooner covered, it will not be covered thickly and efficiently. There will be a greater extent of uncovered wall between the branches, but this is a great advantage, especially in the colder parts of the country ; for, where a wall is almost completely shaded with foliage, it receives but little heat from the sun's rays, and consequently but little can be radiated for the benefit of the tree. For this important reason a distance of 12 inches between the branches is recommended, and more especially as it is well known that branches, even at that time the laterals on the first pair should be cut to within about an inch of their base. In the second season the shoots on the horizontals should still be allowed to grow without check, except in the case of any likely to be too strong for the leaders of the horizontals, and wherever this is seen to be the case they must be pinched. The others may also be pinched if they grow long and shade the buds on the horizontals.

When several courses of horizontals have been obtained, the highest should be subjected to a closer system of summer pruning. They ought, for the most part,

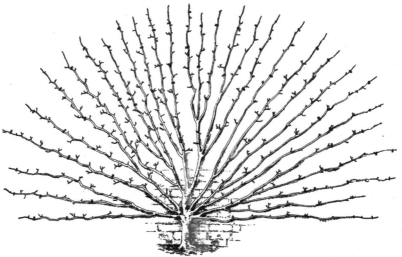

Fig. 98.—Fan-shaped trained Pear.

distance, if well managed, will bear as much fruit as a tree can bring to perfection.

The first pair of horizontals should be at least 1 foot from the ground ; but we consider 15 inches preferable, because the fruit will be better flavoured than when nearer the ground. The lower horizontals should be trained at an angle of about 45°, in order to strengthen them, for they cannot be too strong, and in fact every means should be taken to encourage them to make vigorous growth. With this view, lateral shoots, if any are produced, ought to be allowed to grow freely during the summer, and their points should be taken off in September. Before winter, the upright leaders ought to be cut so as to originate a second pair of horizontals, and at the same to be pinched as directed for espaliers ; after an interval of five or six days the next lower tier should be pinched, and so on to the lowest. When more horizontals are formed, six courses for example, the two upper may be pinched first ; after several days the next lower two, and after another similar interval the lowest two. In short, by commencing summer pruning at the upper part of the tree, and working gradually downwards at intervals, so as not to deprive the tree of too many shoots or too much foliage at one time, the trees will form abundance of fruit-spurs, and bear regularly from the stem to the extremities of the branches. The spurs will most likely be too numerous, and will require to be thinned and shortened at the winter pruning.

Pruning the Spurs.—A spur is a branch the buds of which are either blossom-buds, which do not push into regular shoots, or imperfectly-formed blossom-buds, in which case they elongate, although but slowly as compared with the growths made by the proper shoots.

Spurs are either simple, as represented at 1, fig. 99, or compound, as at 2. They require to be pruned, otherwise they would extend too far from the wall, and would lose the benefit of its warmth. It is therefore desirable to have a sufficient number of fruit-spurs as near the branch as possible, and when that is obtained the spurs should be more or less cut back at the winter pruning.

Fig. 99.—Spur-pruning.

The simple spur 1 requires no pruning. Such a one is likely to bear fruit, and in that case its terminal growth will be arrested, and one or two fruit-buds will most probably form near its base. The spur 2 is an older production. It may be cut off at *a*, or if there are plenty of others near, it may be cut back a little above the bud *b*, which will form a fresh spur. All buds similar to *b* are blossom-buds ; but spur-buds, like *c*, may retain their slender form for years without assuming that plumpness which indicates a fruiting state. It is frequently the case that nearly all the spur-buds on a tree are of this description, and are very numerous, abundance of foliage being produced, and every year more and more of these slender unfruitful spurs. The best way of dealing with them is to cut back those on the upper part of the tree to the lowest bud or the lowest two buds, to thin and shorten considerably those situated about the middle of the tree, and to do this more sparingly in the case of those on the lower part. By these means the lower branches, which are usually weak as compared with the upper, will become equal in vigour to the latter, and elongated barren spurs will become plump and fruitful. The spurs on the middle and lower parts of the tree will require to be gradually reduced, and whilst this reduction is being effected, the upper part of the tree must not acquire excessive vigour.

VOL. II

Fig. 100 represents the branch *a*, on which the shoots *b c d* have been produced, and also a fruit-bud *e*, and two terminal buds *f f* ; these two buds must be kept in check by stopping or pinching, in order that the sap may be concentrated on those at the base.

Fig. 100.—Spur-pruning.

Fertility and Sterility.—The object of the cultivator of Pears and other hardy fruits is first to secure good trees, and secondly to obtain regular crops of the best fruit. As regards the subject of these remarks, the first object is sometimes much more easily attained than the second, because apart from climatal and seasonal adverse influences, other causes occasionally interfere with the production of fruit. The two principal causes of infertility in Pears are defects in the flowers and excessive luxuriance of growth.

Recorded observations prove that some Pears are frequently self-sterile, while others are as commonly self-fertile, and it is necessary to pay attention to this matter when making a plantation. To provide against unfruitfulness arising from self-sterility it is advisable to plant self-fertile Pears alternately with the doubtful sorts.

Usually Self-Fertile.	Usually Self-Sterile.
Belle Julie.	Bellissime d'Hiver.
Beurré Bosc.	Beurré Alexandre Lucas.
Beurré Giffard.	Beurré d'Amanlis.
Beurré Hardy.	Beurré Superfin.
Colmar d'Été.	Catillac.
Conference.	Citron des Carmes.
Doyenné d'Alençon.	Clapp's Favourite.
Doyenné d'Été.	Doyenné du Comice.
Duchesse d'Angoulême.	Dr. Jules Guyot.
Durondeau.	Easter Beurré.
Fertility.	Emile d'Heyst.
Flemish Beauty.	General Todleben.
Forelle.	Joséphine de Malines.
Hessle.	Louise Bonne of Jersey.
Le Lectier.	Marguerite Marillat.
Madame Treyve.	Marie Louise.
Marie Louise d'Uccle.	Olivier de Serres.
Seckle.	Pitmaston Duchess.
Vicar of Winkfield.	Souvenir du Congrès.
White Doyenné.	Uvedale's St. Germain.
Windsor.	Williams' Bon Chrétien.

The pollination of pomaceous fruits has been studied by Mr. M. B. Waite in the United States, and his conclusions are summarized as follows :

1. Many of the common varieties of Pears require cross-pollination, being partially or wholly incapable of setting fruit when limited to their own pollen.

2. Some varieties are capable of self-fertilization.

3. Cross-pollination consists in applying pollen from a distinct horticultural variety, that is, one which has grown from a distinct

Fig. 101.—Flowers of Pear (Beurré d'Amanlis).

seed, and not in using pollen from another tree or the same grafted variety, which is no better than that from the same tree.

4. Self-pollination takes place no matter whether foreign pollen is present or not. The failure to fruit with self-pollination is due to sterility of the pollen and not to mechanical causes, the impotency being due to lack of affinity between the pollen and the ovules of the same variety.

5. Varieties that are absolutely self-sterile may be perfectly cross-fertile.

6. The condition of nutrition and the general environment affect the ability of the tree to set fruit either with its own pollen or with that from another variety.

7. Pollen is transported from tree to tree by bees and other insects and not by the wind.

8. Bad weather during flowering-time has a decidedly injurious influence on fruitage by keeping away insect visitors and affecting the fecundation of the flowers, and, conversely, fine weather favours cross-pollination and the setting of the fruit.

9. Pears resulting from self-fertilization are very uniform in shape. They differ from crosses not only in size and shape, but also, in some cases, in time of ripening, and in flavour.

10. Among the crosses the differences were slight or variable, so that the variations cannot be ascribed with certainty to differences in pollen.

11. Self-fecundated Pears are deficient in seeds, and the seeds produced are usually abortive. The crosses are well supplied with sound seeds.

12. Even with those varieties which are capable of self-fecundation the pollen of another variety is prepotent, and unless the entrance of foreign pollen is prevented the greater number of fruits will be affected by it.

13. The normal typical fruits, and in most cases the largest and finest specimens from both the so-called self-sterile and self-fertile varieties are crosses.

Times of Flowering.—The following Pears are named in the approximate order of flowering as a guide to planters :

Early.—Beurré Clairgeau, Duchesse d'Angou-lême, Louise Bonne of Jersey, Beurré Diel, Marguerite Marillat, Jargonelle, Williams' Bon Chrétien.

Mid-season.—Beurré Hardy, Doyenné Boussoch, Beurré Giffard, Catillac, Pitmaston Duchess, Dr. Jules Guyot.

Late.—Clapp's Favourite, Triomphe de Vienne, Souvenir du Congrès, Doyenné du Comice, Marie Louise d'Uccle, Durondeau.

When failure to fruit is due to early or too frequent overcropping, to a natural weakness, or to some deficiency of essential substances in the soil, liberal but judicious application of suitable manures will usually effect the desired alteration. It is in such cases that potash in some convenient form, together with superphosphate of lime, is of value as a restorative of fertility.

If undue vigour of growth, deep rooting, or rooting in unfavourable soils are the causes of the trouble, two practical remedies suggest themselves, namely, (1) lifting and replanting the trees, or (2) root-pruning. It is seldom that these operations are needed with Pears on Quince stocks ; but for those on Free stocks in some soils, root-pruning is an essential process that must be repeated periodically. Young trees for the first few years can be readily lifted, and if carefully replanted, this more effectually checks the excessive vigour of branch and root than any other means, but it soon becomes a laborious and expensive task, and recourse must then be had to root-pruning. By carefully removing the surface soil a few feet from the stem it will easily be found how far the principal roots extend, and a trench should then be formed round the tree, cutting off cleanly all the strong fibreless and downward roots, also carrying this out as far under the main ball of roots as may be possible. Preserve all fibrous roots, and when filling the trench again spread these out evenly near the surface. Render the soil firm, as if it is left loose it is apt to encourage increased root growth of the wrong character. A similar process is sometimes requisite with trees trained to walls or trellises, and if performed with judgment it speedily effects a change in the desired direction.

Routine Culture.—To ensure success with Pears, they require a good deal of attention at different times of the year, and especially in the early stages of their existence. The first season of growth after planting young trees on the Quince it is advisable to remove all flowers as soon as they show, not allowing them to expand. This must be done with care, however, to avoid injury to the young leaves and shoots. Next in importance is it to see that, if the spring and early summer prove hot and dry, the young trees do not suffer from an insufficient supply of moisture at the roots. A light mulching round the stems will aid in the preservation of a moist condition, and it is also advisable to occasionally syringe the trees in the afternoon or early evening. This is especially beneficial for trees against dry walls, fully exposed to the sun, as, until the roots are in full activity, the foliage soon suffers. The summer pinching must be moderate at first also for trees on the dwarfing stocks, as it is often difficult to induce sufficient growth to keep them well furnished with

new wood. Pears on the Free stock soon become established and grow freely, and they require more attention in stopping or regulating the growth, though there is no trouble in removing flowers in their early years.

When the dwarf trees are well rooted and can safely be allowed to bear fruit, the question of thinning should at once be considered. A young tree on the Quince will often become very prolific, and if allowed to bear without restriction it is liable to be greatly exhausted, suffering both in growth and subsequent crops. No hard and fast rule can be laid down respect-

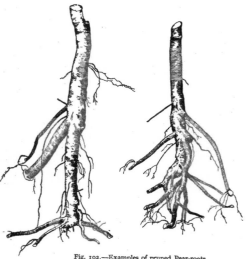

Fig. 102.—Examples of pruned Pear-roots.

ing how many fruits should be allowed to remain, this must always be a matter for the judgment of the cultivator, and should be regulated by the character of the variety and the strength of the tree. It is also wise to defer the thinning until it can be seen which fruits are taking the lead, as many will commence swelling and then fall. If the work is done immediately the petals have fallen, there is the danger of removing some that are either more fully fertilized, or, from their position or strength, are more liberally supplied with nourishment, and would develop into finer fruits if allowed to remain.

As a rule little is gained by the thinning of flowers even when these are produced in the greatest profusion. There are so many adverse influences that are calculated to prevent an excessive number of fruits setting, that it is best to make sure of the results before removing any flowers. As regards trees on walls, which may be protected when in flower from the frost injuries, this does not apply with the same force, and thinning the flowers or even the corymbs themselves may be advisable. If it is found that the fruits do not fully develop, or if a tree is flowering and fruiting with a profusion beyond its strength, a

flanged joint so that it can readily be applied without undue handling or bruising the fruit. When placed in position, suspended from the branch, the appliance is closed by clamps fixed to the edges. The material is nearly as light as muslin, and is much more durable, having been continuously exposed in all kinds of weather, fierce sun and heavy winter rains, without the least injury. It can be utilized for a variety of purposes, one of which is the protection of flowers that have been fertilized and from which it is essential to exclude insects.

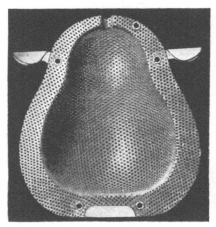

Fig. 103.—Cloister Fruit Protector (side view).

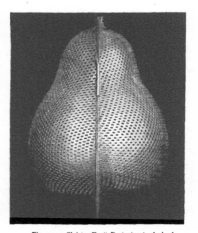

Fig. 104.—Cloister Fruit Protector (end view).

more vigorous thinning should be tried, together with the application of additional supplies of plant food to the soil.

The Cloister Fruit Protector (figs. 103, 104) is a device for protecting ripening fruit from injuries by birds, wasps, snails, &c. It is made of perforated celluloid, which is very light and neat in appearance, and is adapted for Pears, Apples, and other fruits. It is made in two halves with a

To all trained trees close attention must be given during the summer months in the pinching and reduction of superfluous shoots in accordance with the directions in previous sections of this chapter. Neglect in this matter means the crowding of the tree with useless growths, increasing the work of winter pruning, and partly defeating the object of subjecting trees to artificial training.

GATHERING AND PROPAGATION

Gathering Pears.—It was the opinion of a celebrated American pomologist, Mr. Downing, which was shared by the late Dr. Hogg and Mr. T. Rivers, that the majority of early and mid-season Pears are gathered too late. The former stated that " most varieties are much finer in flavour if picked from the tree and ripened in the house

than if allowed to become fully matured on the tree." This may be of more general application in America than it is here, but it is certainly true as regards many first-class varieties in this country. Williams' Bon Chrêtien is a notable example of the peculiarity, and the fruits of this variety imported from California and South Africa, which have been usually gathered at least a fort-night, or sometimes even three weeks, are found to possess an exquisite flavour when fully ripe. In this case the results are precisely the same in our climate, and it is true also as regards some others.

As a general rule, Pears are fit to gather when, on lifting up the fruit to a horizontal position, the stalk, without pulling, readily separates at its junction with the spur. When the stalk requires to be pulled and twisted, and will rather break than separate from where it joins the spur, the fruit has not acquired all the nourishment which it otherwise would derive from the tree. There are, however, exceptions to this very general rule. Some varieties that are apt to become mealy or too dry are better when gathered before they will part by merely lifting up. Again, some that are too musky if allowed to hang till they part very easily from the tree, should be gathered before they are in that state. The Flemish Beauty must be gathered before it has even attained its full size ; if it be allowed to hang till it become of a fine red next the sun, and thus acquire all its beauty, it is much deteriorated in quality, and instead of being melting, it becomes dry and musky. Some very early Pears must be gathered at a particular time : if removed from the tree a little too soon, they are watery and insipid ; if a little too late, their flesh becomes mealy, or their flavour proves flat. Other early kinds ripen in succession, and must be gathered accordingly. Late varieties generally require to remain on the tree as long as they can safely be allowed to hang.

The choicest Pears on walls and espaliers should be gathered by taking hold of the stalk, without touching the fruit itself, and without displacing the bloom upon its surface, for this serves as a protection from moisture. The fruit should be placed singly on shelves ; late sorts may be placed in a single layer in drawers or shallow boxes, for in such they will have a more equal temperature than on the open shelves in the room, and a steady, cool temperature is an essential condition.

Pears keep very well in clean, dry, silver sand, also when packed in kiln-dried straw, or in dried fern. Besides being employed for keeping fruit late, the two last-mentioned materials are well adapted for forwarding it, and even for ripening it. If the fruit of a variety which usually ripens in the end of December is in abundance, and if a scarcity should occur in the end of November, the later ripening sort can be brought in con-

dition to supply the deficiency by packing it closely in dry fern in a basket, and placing it in a warm situation, say near a fire, and the fruit will soon be fit for use. Many varieties that will bear well in rather cold parts of the country, in which, however, the fruit will not naturally become melting, may be greatly improved by packing them as above and keeping them warm. The proper temperature will vary according to the variety and the greater or less degree of maturity which the fruit has acquired. Some of the Pears should be kept in a very slight heat, others of the same variety in a higher temperature, and by this means the most suitable degree of heat may be ascer-tained. By the above mode the quality of the fruit will be greatly improved, much more, indeed, than any one who has not tried the process could believe possible.

The winter routine of Pear-culture should include what pruning may be needed, and the application of cleaning solutions to the stems and branches as a preventive measure against attacks of fungus disease and bark parasites. The substances to be used and the method of applying them are dealt with in other chapters of this work, and need not be detailed here. The same remark also applies to the summer spraying against attacks of insect pests.

Propagation. — The Pear is readily in-creased by cuttings, but the process is too slow to be recommended, and we only mention it as a means of securing a variety which might otherwise be lost through the failure of buds or grafts. Cuttings in such a case might be struck, so as to keep the variety alive till a favourable opportunity occurred for working from them. If it were desired to have trees on their own roots, layering might be resorted to. We are not aware, however, that there would be any advantage in this.

Budding and grafting are the modes generally adopted for the propagation of the Pear. Stocks are necessary before the propagation can take place, and these accordingly require to be first taken into consideration.

The *Pear Stock* is the most natural for the Pear ; on it, consequently, the trees possess the greatest vigour, and attain the greatest age. The stocks are reared from seeds, either of the Wild Pear or of the varieties cultivated for perry, as the seeds can be obtained in the greatest abundance from these sources. The seedlings are reared in the same way as Apple stocks. In transplanting, those of a crooked habit, or which do not exhibit a free upright mode of growth, should be rejected. In the seed-bed, some will be observed of taller growth than others ; and after the first transplantation a certain portion will again take the start of others. When about to be finally planted out in rows for grafting or budding, the best should be selected, so that all the plants in each row may be of equal height and strength. For standards, the stocks should be planted out at least two years, in order that the young shoots which they produce may possess the requisite degree of vigour. They may either be grafted near the ground, at half, or at the full intended height of the stem. In the case of such varieties as are of a weakly, spreading habit of growth, it is better that the stock should be allowed to grow up to form the stem of the tree ; but with regard to varieties that have a vigorous upright growth, and are not disposed to canker, it is preferable that the stem consist of the variety worked low and trained up, the method usually adopted.

Before the sap rises in spring the stocks should be cut back nearly to where the graft is to be placed. The scions ought likewise to be cut off before their vegetation is excited by mild weather ; they may, nevertheless, be taken and worked at any time before the leaves expand. In this case it is advisable to pick out the buds which have started growing, as they would evaporate the sap and dry the scion before it could unite with the stock so as to derive nourishment from the stock. There are usually two small buds, one on each side of the principal one, and they generally remain dormant ; but when the central bud is removed the sap flowing towards it is shared by the lateral ones, and they consequently become developed so as to contribute to the formation of a union with the stock.

Although grafting may be thus effected and advantageously practised in particular cases, yet it can only be considered as an exception to the general rule—that of cutting the scions before the buds exhibit signs of starting. The scions should be kept till the grafting season, in the same way as already directed for those of the Apple.

Quince Stocks.—The Quince is readily propagated for stocks by cutting down the plants when they are strong enough to throw vigorous shoots, and the bases of these are covered with earth in order that they may form roots. This mode is adopted in the neighbourhood of Paris, but better plants will be produced by layering at any time during the winter months, and proceeding in the following manner :—When the young shoots are laid down, there should not be more than two eyes left above ground, and when those have grown 5 or 6 inches long, one of them should be cut clean off, leaving the other to form the plant, which by the autumn will be 3 feet high. The layers must be taken off the stools as soon as the leaves are fallen, and planted out in rows at 3 feet apart from row to row, and 10 or 12 inches from plant to plant in the row. At the end of one or two years they will be fit to bud or graft.

The Quince commences growing early in spring if the weather is at all favourable. In mild springs we have seen it in leaf at the usual grafting season in March, and we have also seen the plants headed down at that period and grafted, but with very bad results. Either the grafts did not take at all, or but imperfectly, for the Quince stock, having been cut when the sap was flowing, died back to a considerable distance below the place where it was cut over, so that if the lower part of the scion did unite with the Quince the upper part of the splice could not. To the circumstance of not cutting down Quince stocks till their vegetation is too far advanced is chiefly to be attributed the want of success in grafting them with the Pear. The stocks should be cut down in January nearly to the place most eligible for grafting. It is then advisable to leave a little to be cut off at the time of grafting, because severe frost may ensue, and occasion some small splits or cracks in the exposed section of the stock.

In using the Quince as a stock we want its root, and but very little of its stem—no more of it indeed than is sufficient to receive the scion. If the scion were placed, say 9 inches or 1 foot above the surface, the Quince portion of the stem below that height would most probably not increase in thickness in the same ratio as the Pear, and thus, instead of the stem being thickest near the ground, it would be abruptly smaller. The Quince should, therefore, be worked close to the ground, so as to have no portion fully exposed to the drying influences of the sun and air. Whip-grafting is the best to adopt. After the scions are on the stocks it is a good plan to earth them up to above the junction.

As the roots of the Quince run close under the surface, and as it would not be advisable to disturb them by taking soil for earthing up from between the rows of stocks, it should be taken from the alleys or elsewhere. When these particulars are attended to, the failures are very few. Of all things, the necessity for cutting down the stocks early in January should be particularly borne in mind. It may even be done in December.

When intermediate stocks are worked on the Quince, the usual method is to allow the latter to make two years' growth; then bud or graft the intermediate variety upon that, again allowing two years' growth; then cut the second stock back to within a few inches of the Quince, and graft the desired variety upon this. By this means the roots are always four years older than the scion, which makes a material difference to the subsequent progress.

DISEASES

Canker.—The principal disease to which the Pear-tree is subject is canker. This disease attacks some varieties more than others; indeed, in both the Apple and Pear canker manifests itself in a manner so nearly alike, that what has been said of it in regard to the one fruit is also applicable to the other. Extremes of moisture and dryness at the root are to be guarded against. Where canker makes its appearance, the soil should not be made too rich, for over-luxuriance of growth seems to encourage the disease, at least in our variable and ungenial seasons. It frequently happens that for several weeks, with a warm south-west wind, vegetation is much excited in the early part of the season, and afterwards all at once checked for almost as long a period. This sudden stagnation must affect the tree injuriously, and a tendency to canker is the consequence.

Various Pears, such as the Jargonelle, in many localities are apt to suffer from canker in the open ground, but they continue healthy against a wall, all other circumstances being the same. The growth of shoots should be encouraged as much as possible in the early part of the summer, in order that the wood may be matured before frost sets in. When the trees commence growing, and shoots are being rapidly made, care should be taken that they receive no check from want of moisture; for if it is then stopped the trees are more disposed to grow late in autumn, which is not desirable. A Pear-tree that may have at one time too little moisture is badly compensated by having too much at another time. Roots that are rendered inactive from being in dry soil cannot be supposed to act so well, when abundance of moisture reaches them, as others that have never suffered from dryness. If we wished to favour canker in a tree, we should select one that had grown vigorously during some rather moist season, and in the first dry hot year, when the roots had absorbed all the moisture within their reach, and could only yield a very inadequate supply to the leaves to make up for evaporation, we should afford it no assistance. Meanwhile the leaves, deprived of their regular supply from the roots, will drain the tree, growth will be arrested or greatly checked, perhaps till autumn, and then a late growth will ensue. It is well known that shoots made under these circumstances are soft and watery, never becoming matured, consequently they are extremely liable to be affected by severe frost. All these derangements from un-seasonable and imperfect growth tend to favour attacks of canker; and as they recur more or less frequently, so will the tree be affected in a greater or less degree.

Although it has been recommended to encourage growth as soon as the weather is favourable, yet where there appears to be a disposition to canker, a rapid and over-vigorous vegetation should be guarded against. The use of rank manures must be particularly avoided; whilst, on the contrary, the application of fresh soil will prove advantageous. The special and direct treatment of this disease and other fungus attacks are dealt with in PLANT DISEASES, Vol. III.

Insects, &c.—For descriptions of insect enemies see INSECT AND OTHER PLANT ENEMIES, Vol. III., where references will be found to the following:

Bark Enemies.—Apple Mussel Scale, Pear Oyster Scale, Pear Sucker, Wœberian Tortrix. *Bud and Flower Enemy.*—Apple Blossom Weevil. *Fruit and Seed Enemies.*—Birds, Grape Moth. *Leaf Enemies.*—Figure-of-8 Moth, Garden Chafer, Lunar-spotted Pinion Moth, Pale Brindled Beauty Moth, Pear-leaf Blister Moth, Pear-leaf Mite, Red-footed Beetle, Slug-worms, Vapourer Moth, Winter Moth. *Stem Borers.*—Goat Moth, Stem-boring Weevils, Wood Leopard Moth.

PEARS FOR MARKET

Many of the details already furnished concerning the general commercial aspects of Apple culture for market are equally applicable to Pears grown with the same object. But if experience and caution are needful in the former case, they are still more important where Pears alone are to be relied upon for the returns. This, however, is rarely the way in which Pears are cultivated for profit; almost invariably they constitute a portion of a mixed plantation, though the proportion as compared with other fruits will vary in accordance with many circumstances.

Difficulties and Defects.—Except in the most favourable situations, there is considerable risk in planting Pears largely in open plantations when profitable results are essential to success. Occasional crops even of good fruits afford growers a poor chance of a satisfactory balance, and something like regularity in the annual produce is required. As far as it is possible by judgment and experience to ensure this, it must be provided for by special attention to the peculiarities of situation and aspect that may affect the results, and which have already been fully described in the chapters on Apples and Pears. The early flowering of the Pear renders it especially liable to frost injuries at that important period, therefore it is useless to attempt its culture commercially in any position that is exposed to this danger in a conspicuous degree. Further, the Pear requires abundant direct sunlight to develop its fruits to perfection of size and colour, and to ensure the maturity of the growth for continuous cropping. To secure good size there must be adequate supplies of moisture without stagnation, as, though the Pear will thrive in a moderately dry atmosphere, it will not endure an arid soil about its roots. If the trees suffer from any defect in this respect the market value of the fruit produced will be insignificant, for within certain limits size in Pears, as with other fruits, rules the selling prices to a material extent.

The best Pears always pay for careful cultivation and the greater expense needed to ensure the attainment of success, better even than Apples, as regards the actual money returns per tree and area occupied, provided the conditions enumerated are duly adjusted. But for the finest fruits at the highest prices the market is more limited, and the distribution is therefore more difficult and uncertain. Where British growers can produce and place in the markets Pears equal in quality to those imported, at an equally low price, the opportunities for increased sale are much greater. The climatal and other difficulties here must naturally restrict to comparatively few districts the possibility of competing with favoured rivals on profitable terms, though very much more could be done to improve the prospects of home growers by closer attention to our competitors' methods. As it is, the substantially profitable portion of the home Pear trade is confined to two classes—(1) the sale of small early fruits from large established trees on the Free stock, and (2) the marketing of the choicest examples, such as are obtained from the best-grown pyramids, with espaliers, cordons, or similar trees trained to walls.

With the first class very little expense or trouble is incurred. The fruit is often sold direct to the retailer, who in many cases undertakes the gathering; or it is forwarded in bulk to the more populous cities, and there immediately distributed by costermongers, &c. The prices realized are necessarily low, and will only allow of a good margin when the fruit can be sent by the ton and at the lowest rates obtainable, but where the trees are fully developed and in prolific condition the results yield a substantial profit. It must, however, be remembered that such trees cannot be raised in a few years : it requires half an average human life to bring them to their prime, and they indicate the truth of the saying : " He who plants Pears, plants for his heirs." Still, it is well to be the heir or successor to men who have had the foresight to plant such fruit-trees, and there are many who are conducting profitable market businesses at the present time who have ample reason to rejoice that their predecessors were not influenced by the same ideas as the individual who objected to provide for posterity because posterity had done nothing for him.

The second class mentioned includes not only the best Pears grown specially for market or to supply the fruiterers in the large cities, but it also comprises a quantity of private-garden produce—either the surplus from the family's requirements, or where, from reductions in income, or changes owing to deaths, the garden is let and the whole of the produce is sold. In the latter case, when there may be a large extent of wall space covered with well-grown Pear-trees and the rent is moderate, the cultivator will have a good chance to succeed. Obviously, it would never answer to rent such gardens at their residential value, or to pay interest on the outlay which had been incurred for private purposes only.

Between the two extreme classes named large quantities of British-grown Pears are include fine samples, so that if one-half of the fruits had been rejected before paying carriage upon them the prices might have been increased three- or four-fold. This has so frequently been pointed out, and the evidence is so clear to those who observe market results closely, and who have a moderate experience in the sale of fruit, that it is surprising the matter should be so persistently ignored. The cultivator's best efforts are heavily handicapped by neglect in the details referred to—in fact, what British growers have to learn in many cases, is not how to produce the finest fruit, but

Fig. 105.—Six first-quality Pears.
1. Beurré Bosc. 2. Pitmaston Duchess. 3. Doyenné du Comice. 4. Beurré Hardy. 5. Doyenné Boussoch. 6. Beurré Diel.

sent into our home markets of decidedly inferior quality, and in a condition that only serves to heighten by contrast the carefully-selected, tastefully and securely-packed samples which reach us from the Continent and America. There is scarcely a market of any importance where, during the autumn months, home-grown Pears cannot be seen just as they have been gathered into bushel or other baskets, unsorted and displaying very little more care on the part of the seller than would be bestowed upon Potatoes or Onions. Yet often the varieties are as good as, or better than, those which are commanding far higher prices for foreign growers, and in the majority of instances how to place it on the markets to the best advantage. Improvement of a most important character could be effected in this direction as regards the bulk of the Pear crop in the United Kingdom, and it is mainly by attention to this, and by reducing the cost of production to the lowest point of efficiency, that the keen competition from outside our islands can be met with a prospect of success. Commercial fruit-growing cannot be treated as a hobby or an amusement merely; if it is expected to yield the profits of a business, it must be conducted on the most exact business lines, and this is especially applicable to the culture of Pears for market at the present time.

FOREIGN AND HOME TRADE

Foreign Trade in Pears.—A brief review of the methods adopted by our chief foreign rivals, and the condition of the industry in their hands, should furnish some ideas of service to home growers. France has for many years been a formidable competitor in the production of Pears, and such quantities of well-grown, selected, and carefully-packed fruits have been placed on our leading markets, that prices and sales have been proportionately reduced for home growers. The closest attention has been paid to the production of Pears on the most economical systems, and the successful examples have been followed, modified or improved, by cultivators in other countries more readily than by our own, who have yet been chiefly concerned.

In recent years French growers have had to contend with the Californian producers, and have suffered somewhat in the contest, but substantial returns are still obtained in all the best districts. The extent to which Pears are grown in some districts of France may be judged from the statement that upwards of 700 tons of this fruit have been sent away in a season from one station (Angers) between July and January. In the same district Pears are also propagated in great numbers to supply continental growers chiefly, indeed it is placed on record· by an excellent authority, that of five varieties alone 135,000 trees are annually budded and grafted. At the head of these is Easter Beurré, of which 40,000 are produced, Duchesse d'Angoulême, Williams' Bon Chrêtien, and Louise Bonne follow with 25,000 each, and Doyenné d'Alençon with 20,000. The last-named is not in general cultivation in Great Britain, though it has occasionally been mistaken for Easter Beurré. It is principally valued in France for its productiveness, but its quality and late keeping properties are also notable, as well as its good constitution, characteristics which are prominent in the variety where it thrives in the United Kingdom. In the Angers district, which comprises a considerable area drained by the River Loire, Pears succeed to a remarkable degree, the cause, no doubt, being partly climatal suitability, and numerous examples of profitable planting could be given. One will serve as an illustration, and it is the more remarkable, as the 5 acres are planted with two varieties only, namely, Williams'

Bon Chrêtien and Beurré Giffard, and these, it is said, in a good season, yield a return of £75 to £80 per acre, a result, however, which is far surpassed in some other districts. Nearer Paris are several thriving plantations, one of which is described as producing an annual return of £150 to £200 per acre, Louise Bonne and Duchesse d'Angoulême being the varieties chiefly grown, and all in the form of dwarf trees. From the Montmorency district Pears have been exported at the rate of 100 to 130 tons per annum, valued at £20 to £40 per ton, or a total of £2000 to £5200. As a further example of the French Pear trade, Mr. W. Robinson has stated, as within his own knowledge, that one dealer every year collects and sells no less than £10,000 worth of French Pears. Many other facts bearing upon the question of returns and profits on Pear culture for market in France are enumerated by M. Charles Baltet in the *Journal of the Royal Horticultural Society*, vol. xix., part 2.

With regard to the methods adopted by French cultivators, the principal systems are similar in general practice to those prevailing in Great Britain, Pears usually taking the place of Apples. Thus market-gardening is combined with fruit-growing on both a large and small scale, the small holdings predominating, especially near Paris or other large towns, where they range from 1 to 3 acres, with a few extending to 5 acres (=2 hectares). In some cases, however, the plantations are wholly devoted to fruit, but as a rule these are rather more distant from the towns, the land being cheaper either to rent or purchase. Highly rented as land is in our own country in the proximity of towns, we by no means have a monopoly in this respect, for the best market-garden land at a convenient distance from Paris commands a rental of £10 to £20 per acre. The French grower has the advantage in three respects—1st, he does not so frequently lose his Pear crop by spring frosts as we do ; 2nd, he has a lower expenditure for labour, partly because in the smaller market holdings he performs the greater part of the work himself with the aid of his family, and partly the actual cost of hired labour is less, taking into consideration the longer days that are made by workmen ; 3rd, the best systems of selecting and packing fruits for home sale or export are more generally understood and more uniform than here ; there is also more co-operation in the shape of syndicates, enabling fruit to be forwarded to distant markets in bulk and at the lowest rates. All these points tell in favour of the producer, and especially apply to the trade in Pears.

Standard, dwarf, and trained Pear-trees are grown to furnish the supplies, but the two latter preponderate. Dwarf trees are sometimes grown, as they are here, between vegetable and salad plots ; while the trained trees, of which large numbers are grown, are commonly secured to walls, which much more frequently surround small holdings than they do here. The system of wiring walls, generally adopted, also renders this method a convenient one, as the trees are readily secured, trained, or untied when necessary.

Boxes are almost invariably used for the exportation of French Pears, the fruits being very evenly graded, and packed in one, two, or three layers, usually with paper only, either in the form of sheets or as paper shavings. In the majority of cases the boxes are stamped or labelled with the name of the variety, the grower's name, or that of the syndicate or shipper, so that the brand is recognizable as a guarantee of the quality. The number of the fruits per box may also be placed on the box. In a few districts baskets are employed that contain rather more than half a bushel (about 33 lbs.) of fruits, but these are rarely used for the best Pears.

Californian Pears.—Within recent years an enormous export trade with Pears has been developed in California, and the high quality of the fruits, together with their handsome appearance, has rendered the growers in that portion of America even more formidable rivals in the British markets than those in other states who ship such large quantities of Apples. Californian soils and climate evidently suit some varieties of Pear admirably, and they are not short-lived either, for trees are in existence there and still producing fruits which are known to have been planted for 125 years. The fruits also attain considerable size, and the samples that reach us are remarkable for their fresh clear skins and bright colour as well as rich flavour. The chief favourite is the Bartlett, our Williams' Bon Chrétien, which, owing to the varied climatal characters of the different districts in California, can be placed on the markets over a period of four or five months, namely,

from July to November, both extremes being exceptional, and the bulk of the produce would not extend beyond two or three months. Many other Pears esteemed in Britain and France are favourites in California, such as Beurré Diel, Doyenné du Comice, Glou Morçeau, Winter Nelis, Easter Beurré, Louise Bonne of Jersey, Vicar of Winkfield, Beurré Clairgeau, Beurré Bosc, Duchesse d'Angoulême Seckle, Beurré Hardy, Souvenir du Congrès, and Clapp's Favourite. There are also some that are at present mainly confined to Californian growers, namely, Dana's Hovey or Winter Seckle, Lawson or Comet, Dearborn's Seedling, Bloodgood, Harvest or Sugar Pear, Early Wilder, P. Barry, and Block's Acme. Some of these are grown for local sale chiefly, but others like the last-named—Acme—reach the London markets in excellent condition.

All the Californian Pears intended for European markets have to be gathered well in advance of their ripening period, and the greatest care is bestowed upon this, and the selection, grading, and packing. All the best Pears are shipped in wooden boxes or cases holding a few dozen fruits each ; every fruit is separately wrapped in paper, which usually bears the name of the grower in prominent letters, and the name of the variety is stamped on the boxes. The result of this superlative care and attention to details is that the Californian Pears command a sale at prices largely in excess of the inferior samples with which our markets are frequently flooded, and sufficient to pay the growers a substantial interest on their outlay, notwithstanding the long distances the fruit has to travel. The American Pomological Society has recorded an instance where a company exported Pears very extensively, and were able to pay a dividend of 50 per cent ; but how long this continued we do not know, obviously it must be quite an exceptional case.

The Colonial Pear Trade.—Apples we have received in abundance from Tasmania for some years, but the colonial Pear trade has been very limited ; now there are indications of considerable development in some directions. From South Africa Pears have been exported to Britain for several years, but lately there has been a material increase, as the trees planted some time since are coming into bearing. Boxes of Williams' Bon Chrétien, from the Hex River district in Cape Colony, were put on the London markets in 1900 and 1901 in excellent condition, and these supplies have since increased very largely, as they reach here at a time when they do not affect either the European or American trade to any great extent. In some districts of South Africa the Pear thrives remarkably, growing very quickly into finely-developed prolific trees. We have heard of plantations in which five years after planting the trees exceeded 20 feet in height.

Large consignments of Pears also reach us from Belgium and the Channel Islands, but as they display no special characteristics as apart from the French trade, they do not need particular reference here.

The Home Trade in Pears.—It is evident that the British grower who has to face foreign and colonial competition requires both skill and business acumen to give him a chance in the struggle. It is useless attempting to grow Pears for the leading markets where the conditions will not permit the production of first-rate fruit. The sorts to be grown must be selected with care, and all the other details that affect the selling value must have the closest attention.

With all the difficulties arising from our climatal variability, there are situations where, by taking an average of several years, Pears can be made to pay satisfactorily, and there is room for extension. Ample evidence of this is afforded by the official Report on Flower and Fruit Farming in England, prepared by Mr. William E. Bear, under the direction of the Royal Agricultural Society a few years ago. This review indicates some of the most successful growers and plantations throughout the best districts of England, which, as regards Pears, are chiefly confined to the southern and western counties. In the metropolitan market-gardens, especially those west of London, Pears have been largely grown for many years, and profitable results have been secured wherever the situation has been well chosen, and the greatest care has been bestowed upon the culture and marketing. As the density of the population increases, and the smoke area extends, the market-gardener is being driven farther out, and there are now thousands of acres of market-garden and Pear-growing land already in the hands of the builders or in preparation for them.

The principal sources of the home supplies of Pears to the London markets are still Middlesex, Surrey, Kent, Sussex, and Hampshire, where an abundance of fine fruit is produced, though it is not placed in the markets in the most approved style. A few of the more energetic growers are setting good examples now, though probably they do not find it to their advantage to impress neighbours and rivals with the importance of following them. Struggling men in business cannot afford to devote time to the thankless task of pointing out the mistakes committed by other growers, who have the same chances of learning as themselves.

Within recent years there has been a material improvement, which it is to be hoped will advance even more rapidly, and this is largely due to the excellent systems of horticultural education organized in the home counties. In the south-western counties, where Pears are successfully grown, good work is being accomplished in a similar direction, Wiltshire, Somersetshire, Devonshire, and Cornwall being prominent in this respect. Again, in the west, admirable work is being performed in Herefordshire and Worcestershire, particularly in the last-named county. These are only examples of the tendency to improvement which now prevails, and which is, indeed, as essential in horticulture as in all other businesses. This must include the modernizing of methods in Pear production and sale, which may be summarized in the following hints.

ESSENTIALS.

Summary of Essentials.—Do not commence Pear-growing on a large scale in any position unless there is reliable evidence from existing trees that Pears can be satisfactorily grown with a prospect of something like regular cropping, or unless the conditions are such as to leave no reasonable doubt that this result may be expected. Commercial growers cannot indulge in much experimental work, or, if they do, it must be mainly in the direction of testing varieties in a small way before planting largely. For instance, if a large mixed plantation of fruits is being formed, and there is some uncertainty respecting the possible success of Pears, a few trees of different varieties could be tried, and their number subsequently increased in proportion to their behaviour. This is the safest method in any case, but it is a slow one, and in many districts where Pears are undoubtedly at home, it would involve an unnecessary delay.

Only those varieties should be grown that possess some well-marked characteristics that will command the attention of purchasers. Size, form, colour, and quality must be considered, and if all can be combined in one variety the ideal market Pear will be secured, provided the tree possess the two other characters of hardiness and free cropping. It must, however, be remembered that a handsome Pear of good size will sell to better advantage in the general markets than small samples of unattractive appearance though of the highest quality. For the latter, a retail trade direct with consumers who require quality only is more satisfactory than a market trade, except as regards a few salesmen who make a speciality of high-class fruits.

The season at which the fruit is to be sold must be considered in selecting varieties. The majority of market-growers now rely upon early and mid-season Pears, and very few attempt to store any, so that late Pears have been generally discarded in recent years. There is another side to this question, however. A variety in use from Christmas onwards, that has been in excellent demand of late years, is Joséphine de Malines. If it is allowed to hang on the trees as long as possible, in fact until there is danger of sharp frost, the fruit will frequently keep until early in March, and if sold then will realise a good price.

It is best to make a selection that will maintain a regular supply of fruit throughout the Pear season, and it is preferable to have sufficient trees of a variety to enable the grower to send to market a quantity of each at one time. Single baskets or boxes of Pears as samples are troublesome to the salesmen and unsatisfactory or misleading to the sender. At the same time it is not safe to rely upon one or two varieties alone, as seasonal influences will sometimes affect one sort adversely while another may escape.

Liberal cultivation must be provided for Pears that are to be grown profitably, and this includes not only manurial aid when required, but the closest attention to all the details of pruning, spraying, land-cleaning, and general routine. Where fine fruits are desired and free setting is the rule, thinning is an operation that will pay for the time expended upon it, even though it be tedious work and demanding much care. If an even crop of uniform fruits can be obtained it saves some after labour in sorting, and the trees are not unduly exhausted by partly developing a quantity of useless fruits. Should the thinning be done too early or with insufficient care, it will result in a serious loss; therefore, desirable as it is under the right conditions,

it must not be attempted in a reckless or haphazard manner.

Gathering is another operation demanding both care and judgment, as carelessness may easily take a heavy percentage off the value of Pears, however fine they may be. For all the best fruits padded baskets should be used, and the Pears being gathered by the stalk, not roughly clutched in the hand and pulled, as is too often done, must be placed in the basket, which should be preferably wide and shallow. If it is necessary to put in more than one layer, separate them by sheets of soft paper, and never throw or drop the fruits on to those already gathered. If they will not pay for this extra care, they certainly will not for the rough-and-ready methods by which a few shillings may be saved in labour and as many pounds lost in the prices. The slightest bruise or injury to the delicate skin of a Pear becomes a serious disfigurement when a package is opened after a long journey, and such defects are even more conspicuous in fine samples than in those of average merit. If a heavy weight of fruits is piled up in one basket, or if they are simply turned or rolled out where they are to be sorted, instead of being taken out by hand, injury often results, and by a smart careful man the work can be done quite as expeditiously in the right way.

The importance of grading has been repeatedly referred to, but it cannot be too frequently impressed upon those engaged in the keen competition of the times. Few salesmen have had a better opportunity than Mr. G. Monro of Covent Garden Market of judging the defects or merits of British growers' methods of marketing, and this is what he says about Apples and Pears: " They are sent in bushels and half-bushels; I cannot say packed, as the bulk are simply thrown in, without any grading or packing being taken into consideration at all, in some cases only a sheet of very thin paper being placed on the top, and nothing else whatever to prevent the fruit being bruised by the basket. A customer of mine suggested the other day that a sample looked as if they had been ' gathered with a clothes-prop and packed with a rake.' These fruits are certainly packed worse now, on the whole, than they were twenty years ago, and as the competition from abroad is keener every year, it is very important that we should consider whether we cannot improve matters somewhat."

As with Apples, it seldom pays to market more than the first and second qualities of

Pears when they are sorted into three grades. It is impossible to fix a gauge for the different grades, as this would vary not only with the varieties, but in successive seasons and in proportion to the grower's success as a cultivator. The standard must therefore be chiefly a matter of judgment, but the fruits of each grade should be as even in size as possible. Some knowledge of the capabilities of the varieties is essential, the grower should familiarize himself with the finest samples in the markets and at horticultural shows, because he then gains a correct idea of what he may accomplish and of the actual value of his own produce. It may save some expense, and certainly some disappointment, if he is aware that his best fruits are only second-rate of their variety ; or, on the other hand, should he have an exceptionally handsome sample of a variety, he will be better able to form an approximate estimate of its sale value.

The care advised in gathering and grading is equally needed in the packing of Pears, or all other good work will be nullified. The fruits must be firmly packed without being crushed, and they should be protected from direct contact with the basket or box by means of paper shavings, fine wood-wool, or cotton-wool, with soft paper over this next to the Pears. The system adopted by the Californian and other growers of wrapping each fruit separately in a small square of stamped paper is undoubtedly an excellent one where the fruit has to be sent long distances or to remain in the packages for a considerable time, but how far it would pay here is a question for each grower to settle for himself. We are inclined to think that for the finest samples it would be found both satisfactory to the customer and profitable to seller, just as the largest retail fruiterers find it to their advantage to display their best fruit with the aid of a little coloured paper.

If boxes were more generally employed for the finest British Pears, it would be much easier to develop that direct communication between the producer and consumer that must be to their mutual benefit. The use of boxes also, strong but cheap, that can be given with the fruit, avoiding all the trouble and expense of returned empties, would facilitate the extension of the market trade as well as the direct retail business. The majority of salesmen would gladly be relieved of the responsibility and expenditure involved in providing baskets, which constitute a serious item in the business. The boxes provided by some of the railway companies are cheap, and as regards the smaller sizes, are strong enough for the safe conveyance of Pears with good packing and ordinary care in transit.

Suitable boxes can be readily constructed as a means of utilizing labour in the winter or bad weather. It is convenient to furnish the box-lids with simple wire hinges and a fastening in front, so that nailing may be avoided, but cording is a safeguard that adds somewhat to the expense. The sides and lids may be branded with the senders' name and that of the variety, together with the number or weight of the fruits, but preferably the former.

Owing to the great productiveness of Pears, they yield a large return for the space they occupy when the prices are not excessively low, and in suitable localities afford a better return than Apples, but except under special circumstances they are a less reliable source of income to the general grower. Still, with the requisite attention to the details here set out, British cultivators might command a larger and more profitable share of the home trade than they do at present.

SELECT PEARS

The following descriptive list is intended for reference as regards the principal characters of a Pear with which a cultivator is concerned, and respecting which he most frequently requires information. Only varieties which possess some recommendations have been included, but those of variable quality have not been entirely excluded, because under the right conditions some of these are excellent. The newer sorts of Pears are still under trial, and more experience with them is needed before they can be generally depended upon, but several now in trade lists are of very promising character.

In the descriptions the average character has been taken as near as possible ; thus a " large " Pear is one which under ordinary good culture would be not less than 4 inches in its largest diameter, a " medium-sized " Pear would be about 3 inches, and a " small " Pear about 2 inches in diameter. With special culture, particularly as cordons or espaliers, the last two sizes are often materially increased, but as regards the small highly-flavoured Pears an undue increase in size usually means a corresponding loss of quality.

The other terms used scarcely require an explanation ; " pyriform " indicates that the natural form of the fruit is conical and tapering ; " oblong " indicates that the fruit is nearly of equal breadth at the apex and base ; " obovate " that it is much broader at the eye than at the stalk, and " oval " or " ovoid " that it is nearly equally rounded at both ends.

ALEXANDRE LAMBRÉ.—November–December. Sometimes excellent, but variable ; requires a warm position. Tree compact in habit on Quince, very prolific. Fruit medium, roundish, green and yellow, melting and of good flavour.

ALTHORP CRASSANE.—October–December. A variety of high quality where it succeeds, in some places only second-rate. Tree hardy, of free growth, and prolific, suitable either for pyramid or standard. Fruit medium, roundish, green and brown, juicy and rich.

ASPASIE AUCOURT.—Early August. A useful garden Pear. Tree of moderate growth and forms a compact pyramid ; very prolific in good seasons. Fruit of medium size, pale-yellow, flesh melting and sweet.

ASTON TOWN.—October–November. Usually a first-rate Pear. Tree of strong habit and fertile on the Quince as a pyramid ; it also makes a fine standard on the Free stock. Fruit small to medium, roundish, green and yellow with russet, melting, of a fine aromatic flavour.

AUTUMN BERGAMOT.—October. An old variety, still good under the best conditions, otherwise apt to be disappointing. Tree of free growth and prolific on the Quince ; also forms a vigorous fertile standard. Fruit small, greenish-yellow and brown, melting, and finely flavoured.

BARON LEROY.—December–January. This fine dessert Pear has some resemblance to both Chaumontel and Bergamotte Esperen in general appearance. Tree hardy and fairly prolific. Fruit large with a slightly rough skin, pale-green with bronze on one side, and some russet. Flesh white, melting, sweet, and rich.

BEACON.—August. A handsome Pear for exhibition or market. Tree vigorous and free in habit on the Free stock, succeeds best in gardens double-grafted on the Quince. Prolific. Fruit large, well-formed, brightly coloured, melting and sweet.

BELLE JULIE.—October. Excellent and extremely prolific ; useful for gardens or market. Tree of moderate growth on the Quince, erect, and hardy. Fruit medium, even, rather tapering, brown or reddish-russet, juicy, sweet and aromatic.

BELLISSIME D'HIVER (fig. 106). — November–April. One of the best for stewing. Tree of strong growth, and forms a large pyramid on the Quince, or a good standard on the Pear. Fruit very large, roundish, green and brown, sweet and well-flavoured.

BERGAMOTTE CADETTE.—October–January. Of fine quality, suited for gardens or orchards. Tree very strong on the Free stock, prolific. Fruit medium, yellowish, with an abundant, rich, sweet, musk-flavoured juice.

BERGAMOTTE DE MILLEPIEDS.—October. A high quality variety for gardens. Tree of compact habit on the Quince, healthy, and fairly prolific.

Fruit medium, round or turbinate, yellow with a little red, juicy and rich.

BERGAMOTTE ESPEREN. — January – April. An excellent variety for general garden use ; needs the protection of a wall in cold positions. Tree of moderate growth as a pyramid on the Quince, fairly prolific. Fruit medium, roundish, uneven, melting, and richly flavoured.

BEURRÉ ALEXANDRE LUCAS.—December. Handsome, good for general use and exhibition. Tree very strong and erect, forming a fine standard or strong pyramid on the Quince. Fruit medium, well-proportioned and even, melting, juicy, and refreshing.

BEURRÉ BACHELIER.—December. A hardy and prolific variety, of moderate merit. Tree vigorous, forming a fine pyramid on the Pear and succeeding fairly well on the Quince. Fruit large and un-

Fig. 106.—Pear. Bellissime d'Hiver. (⅓.)

even, melting and rich at its best, but sometimes only second- or third-rate.

BEURRÉ BALTET PÈRE (fig. 107).—November. A fine exhibition Pear. Tree of moderate growth, thrives on the Quince, and forms good pyramids, espaliers, and cordons. Fruit large, turbinate, brightly coloured, juicy and rich.

BEURRÉ BOSC.—October–November. Of high quality for garden use or exhibition. Tree of medium growth, and best fitted for the Quince when double-grafted. It then forms useful prolific pyramids or trained trees for walls. Fruit large, yellowish with russet, juicy and aromatic.

BEURRÉ CADÉLIEN.—October. A useful Pear only recently brought into notice, but worthy of attention. Tree very vigorous, yet it has proved to be generally prolific in all forms, but especially on the Quince. Fruit rounded and elongated, yellow with a little russet. Flesh melting and sweet.

BEURRÉ CLAIRGEAU.—November. A handsome exhibition or market Pear of moderate quality. Tree vigorous, forming a fine standard or large prolific pyramid on the Quince. Fruit large and long, curved, yellow with bright-red, juicy with a slight aroma.

BEURRÉ D'AMANLIS.—September. One of the most prolific and useful of the early varieties. Tree of vigorous, healthy, somewhat spreading growth, succeeding equally well on both Free and

Fig. 107.—Pear. Beurré Baltet Père.

Dwarfing stocks, but coming into bearing earlier as a pyramid on the latter. Fruit large, pyriform, green and reddish-brown. Juicy, sweet, and perfumed.

BEURRÉ D'ANJOU.—October–December. A fine exhibition Pear of good constitution, often succeeds where many others fail. Tree of healthy growth, admirably adapted for the Quince as a pyramid, espalier, or cordon. Fruit large, roundish, yellowish with russet, juicy with a slight aroma.

BEURRÉ DE JONGHE.—December–February. Of the highest quality, excellent for gardens, especially on walls. Tree of moderate growth on the Quince, but usually fertile if double-grafted on a good intermediate stock. Fruit medium to large, pyriform, yellowish, with an abundant richly aromatic juice.

BEURRÉ DE L'ASSOMPTION.—August. Chiefly valued for its earliness, but sometimes disappointing in quality. Tree of moderate but rather irregular growth, best suited for the Quince as a bush pyramid or trained tree. Fruit large, pale-yellowish, rich and musky at its best, otherwise rather tasteless.

BEURRÉ DE NAGHAN.—January–March. Though known for many years, this has only been recently introduced to general cultivation. Tree of moderate growth, best suited for the Quince stock. Fruit large and rounded, greenish-yellow, flesh melting, very juicy, of rich flavour. An excellent Pear.

BEURRÉ DIEL (fig. 108).—October–November. An excellent all-round Pear. Tree very strong, and prolific in all forms on the Quince; well-adapted for walls in cold districts; also fine as a standard in the warmer counties. Fruit large, green or yellow with russet, melting, of aromatic flavour. Largely imported from France under the name of Beurré Magnifique.

BEURRÉ DUBUISSON.—December–January. A fine quality late Pear worth general cultivation, and in cold districts it should be grown against a wall. The tree is of moderate and rather slow growth, but prolific. Fruit of medium size, yellow and russet, flesh melting, juicy, sweet, and richly aromatic.

BEURRÉ DUMONT.—October. A handsome Pear for garden use or exhibition. Tree of moderate growth, best suited for the Quince stock either as pyramid, espalier, or cordon. Fruit large, round or obovate, greenish with russet, melting, sweet and rich.

BEURRÉ FOUQUERAY.—October. A useful and handsome exhibition Pear. Tree hardy, vigorous, and prolific on the Quince, cropping regularly in any form; also forms a good tree on the Pear stock. Fruit large, obovate, yellowish with russet, of moderately good flavour.

BEURRÉ GIFFARD.—August. Useful, early, and

Fig. 108.—Pear. Beurré Diel.

of good quality. Tree of somewhat loose and spreading habit, very prolific on the Quince; well-adapted for the bush form of growth. Fruit medium, turbinate, yellowish, melting, with a pleasant aroma.

BEURRÉ GOUBAULT.—September. Prolific, early,

PEARS

(From left to right): Durondeau, Doyenné du Comice, Beurré Alexandre Lucas (also shown in background)

of good quality if gathered early and used at once. Tree of moderate growth, most useful on the Quince stock. Fruit small to medium, roundish, melting and slightly aromatic at its best.

BEURRÉ HARDY.—October. Excellent in constitution and quality. Tree of free growth, forming fine pyramids on the Free stock, or strong and fertile bushes on the Quince. Fruit large, obovate, yellowish with russet, juice abundant and rich, very distinct and refreshing.

BEURRÉ JEAN VAN GEERT.—October–November. This is the name adopted by Dr. R. Hogg, but it appears in some recent lists as Beurré Van Geert. The tree is of compact, healthy growth, and fertile as a pyramid. Fruit large, yellow with some russet, but notable for the brilliant yellow cheek. Flesh white, juicy, sweet and aromatic.

BEURRÉ LANGELIER.—Somewhat delicate, but of high quality, generally best when grown on a wall. Tree of moderate growth when double-grafted on the Quince as a pyramid, espalier, or cordon, and fairly prolific. Fruit medium, pyriform, uneven, yellowish and bright-red, buttery, and peculiarly rich when fully matured.

BEURRÉ MORTILLET. — September–October.— Handsome, of good quality, suitable for general use or exhibition. Tree free and vigorous on the Pear stock, not satisfactory on the Quince unless double-grafted, when excellent pyramids, bushes, espaliers, and cordons can be formed. Fruit large, richly coloured, yellow and red, melting with an agreeable flavour. It must be gathered before fully ripe.

BEURRÉ PERRAN.—Although the Royal Horticultural Society gave an award of merit to a Pear under the above name, Messrs. Bunyard state that they find it to be identical with Duchesse de Bordeaux.

BEURRÉ RANCE. — January–March. Of high quality, late, and of good constitution. Tree free, vigorous, forming large prolific standards on the Pear stock ; but usually grown in gardens double-grafted on the Quince either as a pyramid or as a wall tree. Fruit large, even, pyriform, greenish-brown, buttery and juicy, peculiarly rich.

BEURRÉ SIX.—October–November. Variable, of fine quality in some situations. Tree of strong growth both on Pear and Quince, more reliable on the latter. Fruit large, pyriform, irregular, green and russet, with abundant juice, sweet and pleasant at its best.

BEURRÉ STERCKMANS. — December – January. Useful, handsome, and of fine quality. Tree of free growth, forming a large pyramid on the Pear, but most useful on the Quince either as espalier or cordon. Fruit medium, pyriform, green and red, melting, sweet, richly aromatic when in perfection.

BEURRÉ SUPERFIN.—September–October. Excellent, of hardy constitution, prolific, and of high quality. Tree of robust but moderate growth, best on the Quince stock, forming a fertile well-shaped pyramid, espalier, or cordon for a wall. Fruit medium to large, obovate, yellow with much russet, melting, rich, with a distinct aroma.

BLACK WORCESTER.—November–February. A useful culinary variety, one of the oldest ; it is the Warden Pear of Parkinson's " Paradisus." Tree very strong, forming a large standard on the Free stock, to which it is best suited. Fruit very large, obovate, green and brown with a slight reddish tint, rather coarse, but of good flavour when cooked.

BLICKLING.—December–January. This Pear was introduced from Blickling Hall, Aylsham, Norfolk, but it is believed to have come originally from the continent. Tree of good habit and fertile. Fruit large, green and russet, melting and very rich.

BONNE D'EZÉE.—October–November. Handsome at its best, a favourite exhibition Pear ; also known as Brockworth Park. Tree of moderate growth, prolific on the Quince ; forms useful cordons for walls. Fruit large, pyriform, yellow russet, melting and pleasantly flavoured at its best, but it does not succeed in cold or wet situations.

BRITISH QUEEN.—October. Uncertain and variable, occasionally of high quality. Tree of moderate growth on the Quince, forming a useful pyramid or cordon. Fruit medium to large, pyriform, yellow and red, richly and briskly flavoured when at its best.

BROWN BEURRÉ.—October. An old variety of good constitution and excellent quality ; has been grown in England for over 200 years. Tree of moderate growth, very hardy, forms a well-developed pyramid or standard on the Free stock, but in gardens it generally gives more satisfaction when double-grafted on the Quince in any style for training to walls. Fruit large, obovate, green and brown, melting, sweet and richly flavoured.

CAILLAT ROSAT.—August. Early and good when well grown. Tree very prolific on the Quince, of moderate growth. Fruit medium, pyriform, yellowish tinted with red, juice abundant and aromatic.

CALEBASSE BOSC. — October. Second-rate ; sometimes thrives where few other Pears can be grown, and is then useful. Tree hardy and succeeding on both stocks, prolific. Fruit medium or large, long, pyriform, yellow russet, juicy and sweet with a slight aroma under the best conditions.

CALEBASSE GROSSE. — October. Grown for exhibition and stewing. The tree is vigorous, hardy and prolific. The fruit is very large, often six inches long, yellow with reddish russet, flesh somewhat coarse grained, but crisp, juicy and sweet.

CAROLINE HOGG.—November–December. Excellent in warm soils. Tree of free growth, best on the Quince. Fruit small to medium, roundish, yellow and abundant russet, melting and richly aromatic.

CATILLAC (fig. 109).—December–April. One of the best culinary Pears. Tree strong and very hardy, thriving on the Pear, and usually fairly prolific. Fruit very large, roundish, green with red, crisp, and slightly perfumed with musk.

CHARLES ERNEST.—November–December. A handsome and useful Pear which has been rather neglected until recently. The tree is of good growth, hardy and prolific. The fruit is pyriform and very large, pale yellow, often with a rich red flush on one side. Flesh white, melting, richly and distinctly flavoured.

CHAUMONTEL. — November – March. An old variety, rather uncertain ; should be grown in warm, rich soils, when it is excellent. Tree of strong growth and prolific, forming a large standard on the Pear ; good on the Quince for espalier, and cordon for a wall. Fruit medium to large, uneven, yellow, melting, and richly aromatic.

CITRON DES CARMES.—July–August. Valuable in the south for its earliness, quality, and fertility, but in Scotland it is surpassed by Crawford. Tree hardy, and especially prolific on the Quince when double-grafted, though it forms only a small tree; standards of moderate size can be had on the Free stock. Fruit small to medium,

Fig. 109.—Pear. Catillac. (½.)

roundish or obovate, yellowish, with a plentiful sugary juice.

CLAPP'S FAVOURITE. — August. A favourite for market and exhibition; of American origin. Tree of vigorous growth on the Free stock; seldom succeeds on the Quince unless double-grafted, when it is very fertile. Fruit medium, rather long, green, yellow and bright crimson, juicy and briskly flavoured; must be gathered for sale before it is quite ripe, or for use direct from the tree.

COLMAR.—November–February. An old but excellent variety worthy of the best attention. Tree of vigorous growth on the Pear stock; most satisfactory in the form of an espalier or cordon on a wall. Fruit medium, green and russet, melting, and richly aromatic.

COLMAR D'ÉTÉ.—September. Excellent, of good constitution and prolific in warm soils. Tree of strong growth, hardy; thrives on both Free and Dwarfing stocks; especially fine in the pyramidal form. Fruit small, roundish, yellow, with red spots, juicy, sweet, and aromatic.

COMTE DE FLANDRE.—November–December. Of high quality, but requires special treatment. Tree of free healthy growth on the Pear, but slow in bearing; should be double-grafted on the Quince, and treated generously to ensure the best results. Fruit large, long, yellowish with russet, juicy, and rich.

COMTE DE LAMY.—October. Excellent in warm soils and on the right stocks. Tree of free growth, and prolific if double-grafted on the Quince; also good as a standard on the Pear, but the fruit is not so fine or rich. Fruit small to medium, roundish, yellowish with russet, melting, sweet, and aromatic.

CONFERENCE. — November. Valuable either

for garden or orchard, a favourite for exhibition and market. Tree vigorous and hardy, forming a strong standard or pyramid. Prolific in different forms on the Quince. Fruit large, pyriform, green with russet, melting, and richly flavoured in its best condition.

CONSEILLER DE LA COUR (fig. 110).—October–November. Excellent in quality, hardiness, and fertility. Tree of vigorous growth well suited for the Pear stock as a standard or pyramid: equally good and more prolific on the Quince. Fruit large, pyriform, yellow with abundant bright russet, buttery, and richly flavoured.

CRASSANE.—November–December. Good in warm soils, unreliable in cold situations. Tree hardy and healthy on the Free stock, but best when double-grafted on the Quince and trained to a wall, though rarely very prolific. Fruit medium, rounded, yellow with some russet, sweet, and aromatic.

CRAWFORD.—August. Useful and early in Scotland. Tree of free healthy growth and prolific. Fruit small, rounded, yellow and reddish, melting, and of pleasant flavour.

DANA'S HOVEY. — November – January. An American Pear, very satisfactory in England on warm soils and in sunny situations. Tree of moderate growth, preferably double-grafted on the Quince. Fruit small, rounded or obovate, yellowish-green with russet, melting, and aromatic; in its perfection it is delicious.

DÉLICES D'HARDENPONT.—November. Of high

Fig. 110.—Pear. Conseiller de la Cour

quality, tender; should only be grown in the most favoured situations. Tree of moderate growth, forming a compact standard; best on the Quince, and trained to a wall. Fruit medium to large, oblong, pale-yellow, melting, and finely flavoured.

DE MARAISE.—October. Of high quality, but little known in England. Tree of moderate growth on both stocks. Fruit medium, rounded, even, yellow and flushed-red, very juicy, sweet, and rich.

DÉSIRÉ CORNÉLIS.—August–September. Excellent; by some preferred to Williams' Bon Chrêtien, but is less fertile. Tree healthy and free on both Pear and Quince. Fruit medium to large, oblong, greenish - yellow with russet, flavour rich and wine-like.

DEUX SŒURS.—October–November. One of the best in warm soils. Tree very strong and healthy, forms a handsome pyramid on either stock, extremely prolific on the Quince. Fruit large, pyriform, and irregular, yellowish or green with a little russet, juicy, and with a richly vinous flavour.

DIRECTEUR ALPHAND.—February–May. A fine Pear for baking, valued also for exhibition. Tree moderate in growth, forming a compact pyramid on either Pear or Quince. Fruit very large, long, green with a little russet, sweet, and aromatic, but needs full exposure to the sun to ripen it properly.

DIRECTEUR HARDY. — October – November. Handsome, of good quality. Tree vigorous, hardy; remarkably prolific on the Quince in pyramid or cordon form. Fruit large and even, melting, juicy, and richly flavoured.

DR. JULES GUYOT.—September. Handsome, reliable, and prolific, of the Williams' Bon Chrêtien type; serviceable for market. Tree hardy and vigorous as a standard, forms a compact pyramid or bush on the Quince. Fruit large, yellowish, with slight colour, melting, and sweet.

DOUBLE DE GUERRE. — December – February. A useful culinary Pear that has been known sometime, but not generally grown until recently. The tree is very hardy, and prolific in an unusual degree, it is also vigorous on most soils. The fruit is large, of even shape, and rich brownish russet in colour. The flesh is devoid of the grittiness so common in culinary Pears, and the flavour when cooked is exceptionally rich and aromatic.

DOYENNÉ BOUSSOCH. — October – November. Handsome, prolific, variable, a favourite for

autumn exhibitions. Tree rather loose in habit, strong, forming a large standard; better as a bush on the Quince in favourable soils. Fruit very large, obovate, yellow with russet, juicy when fresh, but soon loses all merit.

DOYENNÉ D'ALENÇON. — December–February. A useful winter Pear of light quality. Tree of strong growth, well adapted for the pyramidal form on either stock, especially prolific on the

Fig. 111.—Pear. Doyenné du Comice. (¼.)

Quince, attains perfection against a wall. Fruit medium, ovoid, green and yellow with russet, melting, and richly aromatic.

DOYENNÉ DEFAYS. — October–November. Of high quality and reliable character. Tree hardy, free in growth, and fertile on the Quince. Fruit small to medium, yellow with russet, rich, sugary, and finely aromatic.

DOYENNÉ D'ÉTÉ.—July. One of the first to ripen in England; the fruit is of good quality if

Fig. 112.—Pear Tree. Doyenné du Comice. Fan-trained. Grown at Madresfield Court.

gathered before it changes colour. Tree of hardy and free growth, requires to be double-grafted on the Quince when it forms a fertile pyramid. Fruit small, rounded, pale-yellow with slight-red tint, juicy and refreshing.

DOYENNÉ DU COMICE (figs. 111, 112).—November – December. Rightly described as " the best Pear," for in constitution, fertility, and quality it is unsurpassed, and it is valuable to growers of all classes. Tree healthy and free in growth, forming a handsome pyramid on either stock ; prolific as an espalier or cordon on the Quince for a wall. Fruit large, pyriform, yellowish-green with little russet, richly flavoured, melting, and juicy.

DUCHESSE D'ANGOULÊME.—October–November. A general favourite, being of excellent quality in suitable positions. Tree strong and healthy in growth, forming a handsome pyramid on either stock. Fruit large to very large, broadly obovate, yellow with some russet, buttery, and finely flavoured.

DUCHESSE DE BORDEAUX. — December–February. A good variety, of excellent flavour, keeps well. Tree strong, grows well on either stock as a pyramid, bearing well and regularly if double-grafted on the Quince. Fruit small, somewhat rounded but irregular, pale yellow and russet, with an extremely rich aromatic flavour.

DUCHESSE DE MOUCHY. — February. Second-rate but good in constitution and habit. Tree vigorous, succeeding well as a pyramid on the Quince, prolific and constant. Fruit large, rounded, or oblate and even, yellow with russet, half melting, sweet, and slightly perfumed.

DURONDEAU. — October – November. Handsome, prolific, and useful either for exhibition or market. Tree strong, thrives either on the Free stock or the Quince, remarkably fertile and beautiful on the latter. Fruit large, long, even, smooth, russet and rich-red, tender, juicy, and rich.

EASTER BEURRÉ (fig. 113).—January–March. An excellent variety of the highest quality in warm rich soils and sunny situations. Tree of free growth, hardy, and prolific as an espalier or cordon on a wall when double-grafted on the Quince. Fruit large, obovate, yellowish with russet, buttery, and richly aromatic.

EMILE D'HEYST. — October–November. Prolific, useful, and of good quality ; the fruit must be gathered early, and does not keep many days after it is ripe. Tree very fertile on the Quince, but much stronger on the Pear. Fruit medium, pyriform, yellowish with abundant bright russet, melting, briskly flavoured and slightly perfumed.

EYEWOOD.—October–November. Variable in quality, but under the best conditions of exceptional merit. Tree of moderate growth, very hardy, and prolific when double-grafted on the Quince ; useful for market. Fruit small, rounded, yellowish with russet, briskly aromatic or slightly acid, the juice abundant.

FERTILITY.—September – October. Noted for the character expressed in its name, very useful for market and orchards. Tree of free, healthy, hardy growth on either stock, more compact on the Quince, and extremely prolific, cropping with great regularity. Fruit medium, obovate, or oblong, bright reddish-brown, russet, juicy, sweet and aromatic at its best but always pleasant and refreshing.

FLEMISH BEAUTY. — September – October. Handsome, of fine quality, good for exhibition. Tree hardy, of moderate strength, fairly free on

the Pear stock, more fertile and useful when double-grafted on the Quince. Fruit medium to large, obovate, yellow with russet and crimson, melting and rich if gathered before it is fully matured.

FLEMISH BON CHRÉTIEN.—November–March. A first-rate culinary variety. Tree vigorous and prolific on the Quince. Fruit medium, obovate, yellow with russet, sweet and pleasantly-flavoured, keeps its character well until late in the season.

FONDANTE D'AUTOMNE.—September–October. Of the best quality and reliable. Tree vigorous on the Free stock, forming a good standard ; it also succeeds well on the Quince as a pyramid or trained as an espalier or cordon for a wall. Fruit large, obovate, even, pale-yellow with a little russet, juicy, sweet, and refreshing, with a delicate perfume.

FONDANTE DE CUERNE. — September. Considered superior to Beurré Giffard, but is uncertain, and in some soils and seasons is only second-rate. Tree of moderate strength, forming a good pyramid on either stock. Fruit medium

Fig. 113.—Pear. Easter Beurré. (¼.)

to large, obovate, yellow, almost white, juicy, and slightly aromatic, sometimes rather dry and acid. Should be gathered early.

FONDANTE DE MALINES.—November–December. Excellent when at its best, but unreliable except in the warmest situations. Tree of good habit, moderately strong, adapted for both stocks, fairly prolific on the Quince. Fruit large, rounded, obovate, even, and handsome, much yellow with some crimson, melting, and with a sugary aromatic flavour. It must be gathered early as it soon decays.

FONDANTE DE THIRIOTT (fig. 88).—November–December. Fine in quality and of good constitution. Tree of free growth, well suited for the Quince, on which it is prolific and reliable. Fruit large, obovate, melting, sweet, and aromatic.

FORELLE. — November–February. Handsome and excellent, distinct in flavour, a great favourite with many. Tree moderately vigorous, requires to be double-grafted on the Quince to secure the best results. Fruit medium, even, and pyriform, greenish-yellow with dark crimson dots, buttery, sweet, and richly vinous. Commonly known as the " Trout Pear."

FRANC RÉAL D'HIVER. — January – March. A late culinary Pear. Tree very strong and prolific,

Fig. 114.—Pear. Gansel's Bergamot. (⅓.)

making a good standard on the Free stock, or a pyramid on the Quince. Fruit medium, pyriform, uneven, sweet, and aromatic, the flesh becoming richly coloured in cooking.

GANSEL'S BERGAMOT (fig. 114).—October– November. Of the highest quality when grown under the best conditions. Tree of moderate habit, an uncertain cropper as a pyramid, should be double-grafted on the Quince, and trained as an espalier or cordon on a wall. Fruit medium to large, rounded, yellow with a reddish tint, buttery, with a rich musky aroma. The flowers do not set freely unless other profuse flowering varieties are near.

GANSEL-SECKLE.—October–November. Usually of high quality, sometimes uncertain and second-rate. Tree of moderate growth, best on the Quince or double-grafted. Fruit small to medium, round, yellow with a slight crimson tint, richly aromatic in the way of Seckle, from which it was derived by a cross with Gansel's Bergamot.

GENERAL TODLEBEN. — December – February. A fine old distinct variety when the fruit can be fully matured ; good for culinary use or for exhibition. Tree of medium strength, but prolific on the Quince. Fruit very large, long, and pyriform, yellow with russet, sweet, and with a pleasant aroma.

GLASTONBURY. — October – November. Although known in the Glastonbury district of Somerset for a long period, this Pear has only of late years been brought into general notice. Tree hardy and healthy, grows freely on the Pear stock, but is rather slow on the Quince. Fruit large, of russet tint, flesh melting, and aromatic.

GLOU MORCEAU (fig. 115). — November– January. Excellent in warm situations and good soils. Tree of free growth on either stock ; succeeds best on the Quince as a pyramid or bush, or as an espalier or cordon against the wall.

Fruit medium to large, roundish or obovate, yellowish with a little russet, buttery, and richly aromatic.

GRÉGOIRE BORDILLON.—September. Useful, early, and of fine quality. Tree strong and very prolific as a pyramid on the Quince. Fruit large, rounded, rich yellow with a little red, sweet, rich, and aromatic. This is one of the few varieties which the late Mr. R. D. Blackmore found thoroughly satisfactory where so many failed.

HACON'S INCOMPARABLE.—November – December. Excellent and of good constitution, prolific and reliable in all favourable situations. Tree of fine habit, free and healthy as a standard or as a pyramid on the Quince when double-grafted. Fruit medium, rounded, yellowish with russet, melting, musky, and rich at its best.

HESSLE.—October. One of the best for orchards and market, hardy and reliable throughout Great Britain. Tree of strong growth, forming a large and prolific standard on the free stock ; can also be grown with profit as a pyramid on the Quince. Fruit small, pyriform, yellowish-green with russet, juicy, and possessing a sugary aromatic flavour.

HUYSHE'S PRINCE CONSORT.—October–November. In warm soils and on a suitable stock this is an excellent variety, but in unfavourable positions it is not worth growing. Tree of moderate strength, must be double-grafted on the Quince to ensure the best results. Fruit large, oblong, green or yellowish, sweet, and of distinct vinous flavour.

HUYSHE'S PRINCE OF WALES. — October– November. A high-quality variety under favour-

Fig. 115.—Pear. Glou Morceau. (⅓.)

able conditions, but uncertain. Tree of moderate growth, irregular in cropping unless double-grafted on the Quince and trained as an espalier or cordon on a wall. Fruit large, yellow with abundant russet, melting, with a rich Bergamot aroma.

JALOUSIE DE FONTENAY.—November. Useful and of good quality. Tree moderately strong, well-proportioned, fairly prolific as a pyramid on the Quince. Fruit medium, pyriform, yellow with a red tint, melting, and rich.

JARGONELLE.—August. A useful orchard Pear, hardy in all districts. Tree of free and slightly pendulous growth, forming a large prolific standard on the Free stock ; does not usually succeed on the Quince unless double-grafted. Fruit medium to large, long, pyriform.

JEAN DE WITTE.—January–March. Useful and of good quality. Tree of strong and healthy habit, forming a fine fertile standard ; well suited for the Quince in pyramidal form if double-grafted ; gives good results trained on a wall. Fruit small to medium, rounded or obovate, yellow with a little russet, buttery, and richly aromatic.

JERSEY GRATIOLI.—October. Excellent. Tree of moderate growth, good either as a standard on the Free stock or as a pyramid or espalier on the Quince ; is usually prolific. Fruit medium, roundish, yellow and brown with russet ; of wine-like flavour.

JOSÉPHINE DE MALINES.—December–March. Late, of high quality. Tree of good habit, healthy and free, does well on the Pear stock as a standard or pyramid, also as a bush on the Quince, especially when double-grafted, being then both prolific and excellent. Fruit medium, pyriform, yellowish-green tinged with red, sweet, rich, and perfumed.

KING EDWARD'S. — September – November. Remarkable for the great size of the fruit and its hardiness. Tree of free hardy growth as a standard on the Pear stock ; requires to be double-grafted to succeed on the Quince. Fruit extremely large, pyriform, green or yellow with a reddish tint, juicy and slightly aromatic, but not of high quality.

LAMMAS.—August. Though discarded by many growers on account of the small size of the fruit, yet this Pear is useful for market purposes, owing to its earliness and reliable fertility ; it ranks with Crawford in this respect. Tree hardy and vigorous. The fruit is below medium size, yellow shaded with red ; the flesh juicy and of good flavour.

LE BRUN.—October. A finely flavoured Pear which originated at Troyes in France about the middle of the nineteenth century. Tree vigorous, and very prolific. Fruit rather long, greenish yellow with russet ; flesh white, melting, and of rich flavour.

LE LECTIER (fig. 116).—January–March. A late variety of recent introduction, very promising. Tree of moderate vigour, does well as a bush or pyramid on the Quince, being fairly prolific but not a heavy cropper. Fruit large, pyriform, juicy, and richly flavoured.

LÉON LECLERC DE LAVAL. — January–May. A late culinary variety, sometimes suitable for dessert. Tree of very strong growth, forming a vigorous pyramid on the Quince, and usually prolific. Fruit large, long, pyriform yellowish with slight russet, sweet and pleasantly flavoured.

LOUISE BONNE OF JERSEY.—October. A very valuable and popular Pear for gardens and market. Tree of free growth on the Quince forming a well-developed and pro'ific pyramid. Fruit medium, pyriform, yellowish with crimson dots

and tints, melting and richly vinous, very distinct and excellent.

MADAME LYE BALTET.—December–February. A useful variety from the same district in France as Le Brun and Charles Ernest. Tree moderately vigorous making a good pyramid, and is very prolific. Fruit greenish yellow, with some russet ; flesh white, juicy, and aromatic.

MADAME MILLET.—March–May. A late and deliciously melting variety of handsome appearance. It succeeds well on the Quince, and is improved by being grown against a wall. Does well as a pyramid, and is good as a cordon.

MADAME TREYVE.—September. Prolific and of high quality. Tree of moderate growth on the Quince in bush form. Fruit large, pyriform, yellow with slight russet and crimson tint, melting, and finely flavoured.

MAGNATE.—October–November. One of the

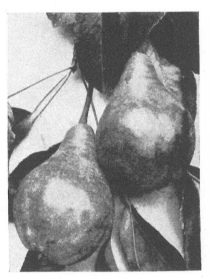

Fig. 116.—Pear, Le Lectier.

Sawbridgeworth seedlings of good quality. Tree of free healthy growth, forming a good pyramid on the Quince. Fruit large, pyriform, rich brown russet, handsome, melting, and with a rose-water aroma.

MARCH BERGAMOT.—February–March. Late, of high quality. Tree vigorous and hardy ; should be grown as a standard on the Free stock, as an espalier for a wall on the Quince. Fruit small to medium, rounded, brown with russet, of exceptionally rich aromatic flavour.

MARGUERITE MARILLAT.—Septembe . A new variety of considerable merit for garden and exhibition, prolific and hardy. Tree erect and compact, forming a shapely bush or pyramid on the Quince. Fruit large, pyriform, even, brightly coloured, and richly aromatic.

MARIE BENOIST. — November – January. A popular late garden and exhibition variety. Tree of free growth on the Pear, more fertile and useful when double-grafted on the Quince and grown

Fig. 117.—Pear. Marie Louise.

as a pyramid, espalier, or cordon. Except in the best situations it should be grown against a wall. Fruit large, rounded, yellowish with much russet, melting, and highly flavoured.

MARIE LOUISE (fig. 117).—October–November. One of the best. Tree of strong growth as a standard on the Free stock, productive when well established, more useful in gardens, when double-grafted on the Quince and trained as pyramid, espalier, or cordon. The protection of a wall is essential in some districts. Fruit medium to large, pyriform, even, yellow and slight russet, buttery, and richly vinous.

MARIE LOUISE D'UCCLE.—October. Prolific and hardy, suitable for the orchard, a good market Pear. Tree extremely vigorous, forming a fertile pyramid on the Quince. Fruit large, pyriform, covered with bright russet, juicy and sweet, but seldom highly flavoured, often insipid.

MARIETTE DE MILLEPIEDS.—March–April. A first-rate late variety in some seasons. Fruit medium, roundish-obovate, green-yellow with brown russet ; flesh white, melting, sweet, and juicy. Does best on the Quince and against a south wall.

MARQUIS.—November–December. One of Messrs. Rivers' seedlings remarkable alike for its high quality and long keeping properties. Tree of free growth, moderate on the Quince, and fertile. Fruit of medium size, bright green, with bronze and russet on one side. Flesh creamy, melting, juicy, with a rich aromatic flavour.

MICHAELMAS. — September – October. This valuable Pear was raised from a seed of Winter Nelis in a cottage garden near Gravesend, and was introduced by Messrs. Bunyard, and was first listed as Michaelmas Nelis. Tree of free growth, and prolific. Fruit medium, yellowish-green, flesh white, juicy, and excellent in flavour.

MUIRFOWL'S EGG.—October. A useful and popular Scottish variety. Tree strong and hardy, developing into a fine standard or pyramid on the Free stock. Fruit medium, rounded, yellowish-green with russet, sweet and slightly aromatic.

Fig. 118.—Pear. Passe Colmar.

NEC PLUS MEURIS.—January–March. Of high quality, late, moderately fertile. Tree very strong in habit on the Free stock, healthy and compact when double-grafted on the Quince ; requires the shelter of a wall in many districts. Fruit medium, rounded, irregular, yellow and russet, buttery, and richly vinous in flavour.

NOUVEAU POITEAU.—November. A good Pear usually, but variable in merit in cold districts. Tree of moderate vigour on either stock, forming a handsome pyramid. Fruit large, oval or obovate, yellow with bright russet, very sweet and fragrant.

NOUVELLE FULVIE. — November – February. Excellent in good soils and a warm situation, otherwise variable. Tree of moderate growth, thriving on the Quince, good as an espalier on a wall. Fruit medium, pyriform, ye low covered with russet and tinted red, richly aromatic at its best.

OLIVIER DE SERRES.—February–March. Of excellent quality when in perfection. Tree of vigorous growth on either stock, forming a large standard or pyramid. Trained against a wall it gives good results. Fruit medium, rounded, yellowish with bright russet, buttery, and richly vinous.

PASSE COLMAR (fig. 118).—November–December. Valuable on good soil in a warm district. Tree very strong, forming a large prolific standard ; on the Quince it forms a compact pyramid, also useful as an espalier or cordon on a wall. Fruit medium, obovate, pale-yellow and reddish, melting, and rich, with a vinous aroma.

PASSE CRASSANE.—January–March. Variable, excellent in the best districts. Tree of moderate strength, succeeding on either stock, forming a compact pyramid on the Quince. Fruit medium, rounded, yellow covered with russet, rich and vinous.

PITMASTON DUCHESS (fig. 119).—October–November. One of the most handsome Pears grown, valuable for gardens and the best markets. Tree of vigorous free growth, forming a prolific pyramid or bush on the Quince. Fruit large, long, even, yellow with a little russet, melting and richly flavoured when well ripened.

PRÉSIDENT BARABÉ.—December–February. A recently-introduced late variety of distinct merit. Tree of moderate growth, forming a useful, hardy, and prolific pyramid on the Quince ; suitable for training as an espalier or cordon for a wall. Fruit medium to large, pale-yellow, melting, and aromatic.

PRÉSIDENT DROUARD.—January. A seedling found by chance in France, but it has been proved to possess several good qualities under cultivation in England. Tree of moderate growth. Fruit large, yellow and russet ; flesh white, juicy, and richly flavoured.

PRINCESS. — October – December. A seedling from Louise Bonne of Jersey, an excellent, handsome, and favourite Pear. Tree of free growth and erect in habit, forming a fine pyramid on the Pear stock, prolific on the Quince. Fruit large, pyriform, yellow with the colouring of the parent, melting, sweet and pleasantly flavoured.

RED DOYENNÉ.—October–November. Useful and of fine quality. Tree of moderate growth, succeeding on either stock. Fertile on the Quince as a pyramid, or trained against a wall. Fruit medium, obovate, yellow with some russet, melting, and richly flavoured if gathered early.

RED OCTOBER.—October. A seedling regarded as superior to Beurré Capiaumont. Tree of good habit, very fertile. Fruit of medium size, brown with an orange-red tint on one side ; flesh tender, and possessing a richly aromatic flavour.

ROOSEVELT.—October. Another of the French Pears from Troyes which was introduced a few years ago and has been honoured by the Royal Horticultural Society. Tree of erect and free growth, prolific. Fruit of great size, round, green with slight red on one side. Flesh white, juicy and of good flavour. A fine exhibition Pear.

ST. LUKE.—October. A seedling raised by Messrs. Rivers at Sawbridgeworth. Tree of free growth in suitable situations, and very prolific in most seasons on the Quince stock. Fruit large, and handsome in form, covered with

Fig. 119.—Pear. Pitmaston Duchess.

rough russet. Flesh melting, mellow, and of rich flavour.

SANTA CLAUS.—December–January. An excellent late Pear, in fine condition at Christmas, and it has gained much favour with private and commercial growers. Tree of erect vigorous habit, very prolific. Fruit large, dark brownish russet, very handsome. Flesh melting, mellow, and remarkably rich. Originally from France.

SECKLE.—October. One of the oldest of American Pears, excellent in all respects. Tree vigorous, forming a handsome standard or pyramid on the Free stock ; requires to be double-grafted on the Quince. Fruit small, rounded, and even, brownish with rich-red colouring, juicy, and with an exceptionally fine aroma.

SOUVENIR DU CONGRÈS (fig. 120).—August–September. A favourite exhibition Pear, being of handsome appearance and good quality. Tree fairly strong as a standard on the Free stock ;

does not succeed on the Quince unless double-grafted. Fruit long, obovate, yellow with brown russet and crimson streaks, melting, and richly aromatic.

SUFFOLK THORN.—October. A seedling from

Fig. 120.—Pear. Souvenir du Congrès.

Gansel's Bergamot; of fine quality under the best conditions, but variable. Tree of robust growth on the Pear stock; must be double-grafted to succeed on the Quince. Fruit medium, roundish, yellow with a little russet, melting, and finely flavoured like its parent when in true character.

SUMMER BEURRÉ D'AREMBERG.—September. Of excellent quality, early. Tree of moderate growth, forming a compact and shapely pyramid on the Quince. Fruit small, roundish or pyriform, juicy and melting, with a rich flavour of musk.

SWAN'S EGG.—October. An old but prolific, excellent variety when at its best. Tree healthy, of free growth; very fertile on the Quince. Fruit small or medium, round, yellow with much russet and some red colouring, juicy, with a distinct and pleasing flavour.

THOMPSON'S.—November. Excellent, and of good constitution. Tree of vigorous growth; good as a standard or pyramid on the Pear stock; is frequently double-grafted on the Quince, as it thus comes into bearing soon, and the fruit develops its best qualities. Fruit medium, obovate, yellow with a few russet dots, melting, and finely aromatic.

TRIOMPHE DE JODOIGNE.—November–December. A handsome winter variety, usually of good quality. Tree of vigorous but loose growth on

the Free stock; very prolific on the Quince in any form. Fruit large, obovate, yellow or russet, melting, and highly flavoured with musk.

TRIOMPHE DE VIENNE.—September. Handsome, early, of good quality, useful for gardens and exhibition. Tree of vigorous habit, very prolific when double-grafted on the Quince. Fruit large, even, and pyriform, yellow with some russet, juicy, and richly flavoured.

URBANISTE.—October. Excellent in good soils and on the right stocks. Tree moderately strong, developing into a fine pyramid on the Pear stock; more satisfactory as regards cropping on the Quince. Fruit medium, obovate, yellow with russet and a red tint, melting, and richly sweet with a pleasant aroma.

UVEDALE'S ST. GERMAIN.—January–April. A remarkable culinary Pear, one of the largest grown; frequently seen of enormous size in the London markets as Belle de Jersey and Belle Angevine. Tree vigorous as a pyramid on the Free stock, but it also succeeds well double-grafted on the Quince. Fruit of great size, often exceeding 2 lb., pyriform, yellowish with a slight-red tinge, juicy, and pleasantly flavoured.

VAN MONS LÉON LECLERC.—November. A handsome and excellent Pear. Tree vigorous, forming a large and useful standard; requires to be double-grafted on the Quince, and grown as a pyramid or against a wall. Fruit large, long,

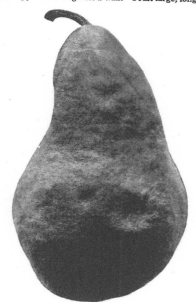

Fig. 121.—Pear. Verulam. (¾.)

pyriform, green and yellow with russet, juicy, and richly vinous.

VERULAM.—January–March (fig. 121). One of the best culinary Pears. Tree vigorous, good as a standard or pyramid on the Free stock; also very prolific on the Quince. Fruit large, green and russet, distinct in appearance, being of a dull dark tint ; it is of a fine colour and flavour when baked or stewed.

VICAR OF WINKFIELD.—November–January. Principally used for culinary purposes, but good enough in some seasons for dessert. Tree strong, does well on the Free stock as a pyramid ; also in any form on the Quince, being much used as an intermediate stock. Fruit large, long, yellow tinted with red, juicy, and aromatic.

WHITE DOYENNÉ. — September – October. Early, of good constitution, and very fertile in any form. Tree vigorous, does well on either stock ; but the largest and best coloured fruits are obtained from pyramids or wall-trees on the Quince. Fruit medium, roundish, even, green or yellowish occasionally tinted with red, of a sweet vinous flavour at its best, but sometimes rather acid or insipid.

WILLIAMS' BON CHRÊTIEN (fig. 122).—August–September. A most popular and useful Pear, more largely grown than any other variety in Europe, America, and South Africa. Tree of free but rather loose growth, forming a large pyramid on the Free stock, but does not crop

Fig. 122.—Pear. Williams' Bon Chrêtien. (⅓.)

regularly ; on the Quince it is straggling but prolific. Fruit large, pyriform, uneven, yellow with red streaks, juicy, and richly flavoured. Should be gathered before it is ripe.

WINDSOR (fig. 123).—August. An old and handsome Pear, but of such short duration that it is little grown. Tree of vigorous symmetrical growth, forming a handsome standard tree on the Free stock. Fruit large, even, and pyriform, yellow and green with bright-red streaks, melting, and of pleasant flavour if gathered before it changes colour.

WINTER NELIS.—December–February. Excellent where it succeeds. Tree of moderate growth, forming a compact pyramid on the Quince, and does well when trained on a wall. Fruit small, roundish, green and yellow with russet, remarkably rich, aromatic, and sweet.

Fig. 123.—Pear. Windsor. (⅓.)

WINTER ORANGE. — December – March. An excellent stewing Pear which has been kept quite sound until April. Tree vigorous and prolific. Fruit large, round, flattened, yellow and russet. Flavour very good for a culinary variety.

ZÉPHIRIN GRÉGOIRE.—December–January. Of high quality. Tree of free growth, developing into a fine pyramid on the Pear stock ; much more prolific and reliable when double-grafted on the Quince. Fruit of medium size, round, yellow with russet, juicy, and vinous.

LIST OF SYNONYMS

The following are the synonyms under which the Pears in the foregoing list most frequently appear :

Albertine, see Doyenné Boussoch.
Alexandrine Hélie, see Belle Julie.
Arbre Superbe, see Fondante d'Automne.
Bartlett, see Williams' Bon Chrêtien.
Beau Présent, see Jargonelle.
Belle Alliance, see Beurré Sterckmans.
Belle Angevine, see Uvedale's St. Germain.
Belle de Berri, see Vicar of Winkfield.
Belle de Flandres, see Flemish Beauty.
Belle de Jersey, see Uvedale's St. Germain.
Belle Lucrative, see Fondante d'Automne.
Belle Magnifique, see Beurré Diel.
Bell Pear, see Catillac.
Benedictine, see Brown Beurré.
Bergamot, see Autumn Bergamot.
Bergamotte Tardive, see Colmar.
Beurré d'Anglaise, see Easter Beurré.
Beurré d'Apremont, see Beurré Bosc.
Beurré d'Avalon, see Glastonbury.
Beurré d'Avranches, see Louise Bonne of Jersey.
Beurré de Cambron, see Glou Morceau.
Beurré d'Esperen, see Émile d'Heyst.
Beurré d'Hardenpont, see Glou Morceau.
Beurré d'Hiver, see Chaumontel.
Beurré de la Pentecôte, see Easter Beurré.

Beurré de Malines, see Winter Nelis.
Beurré de Mérode, see Doyenné Boussoch.
Beurré Gris, see Brown Beurré.
Beurré Magnifique, see Beurré Diel.
Beurré Quetelet, see Comte de Lamy.
Beurré Royal, see Beurré Diel.
Bon Chrétien de Rans, see Beurré Rance.
Bonne Rouge, see Gansel's Bergamot.
Bon Papa, see Vicar of Winkfield.
Brockworth Park, see Bonne d'Ezée.
Burgess's Pear, see Glastonbury.
Cadette, see Bergamotte Cadette.
Chalk, see Crawford.
Chartreuse, see Catillac.
Chopine, see Jargonelle.
Colmar Gris, see Passe Colmar.
Common Bergamot, see Autumn Bergamot.
Curé, see Vicar of Winkfield.
D'Auch, see Colmar.
De Fosse, see Jargonelle.
De Tongre, see Durondeau.
Dingier, see Comte de Lamy.
Doyenné Blanc, see White Doyenné.
Doyenné d'Automne, see Red Doyenné.

Doyenné Esterhmans (or Sterckmans), see Beurré Sterckmans.
Doyenné Gris, see Red Doyenné.
Epargne, see Jargonelle.
Grand Monarque, see Catillac.
Hazel, see Hessle.
Huntingdon, see Lammas.
Huyshe's Bergamot, see Huyshe's Prince of Wales.
Lammas (America), see Seckle.
Lammas (Scotland), see Crawford.
Louise d'Avranches, see Louise Bonne of Jersey.
Louise d'Orléans, see Urbaniste.
Madeleine, see Citron des Carmes.
Porch's Beurré, see Glastonbury.
Pound Pear, see Catillac.
Roi de Wurtemberg, see Glou Morceau.
St. Jean Baptiste, see Comte de Flandre.
Summer Doyenné, see Doyenné d'Eté.
Suprême, see Windsor.
Téton de Vénus, see Bellissime d'Hiver.
Trout Pear, see Forelle.
Winter Franc Réal, see Franc Réal d'Hiver.
York Bergamot, see Autumn Bergamot.

SELECT LISTS

In the following lists selections of Pears have been made for various purposes, to guide those who wish to grow useful varieties. It is impossible to make a selection that would be equally good in all districts and soils—experience with this fruit is more varied than with any other—but an effort has been made to include only those that are satisfactory under the greatest range of conditions.

Sixty Useful Pears

(The varieties are arranged in dozens, which are placed approximately in the order of merit as regards quality and general experience of their reliability, but each dozen constitutes a selection in itself and adapted for different requirements.)

(1)	
Beurré Diel.	Oct.–Nov.
Beurré Superfin.	Sept.–Oct.
Doyenné d'Eté.	July.
Doyenné du Comice.	
	Nov.–Dec.
Easter Beurré.	Jan.–Mar.
Forelle.	Nov.–Feb.
Gansel's Bergamot.	Oct.–Nov.
Glou Morceau.	Nov.–Jan.
Louise Bonne of Jersey.	Oct.
Marie Louise.	Oct.–Nov.
Seckle.	Oct.
Williams' Bon Chrétien.	
	Aug.–Sept.

(2)	
Beurré Dubuisson.	Dec.–Jan.
Beurré Rance.	Jan.–Mar.
Charles Ernest.	Nov.–Dec.
Conseiller de la Cour.	
	Oct.–Nov.
Dr. Jules Guyot.	Sept.
Emile d'Heyst.	Oct.–Nov.
Joséphine de Malines.	
	Dec.–Mar.
Madame Treyve.	Sept.
Pitmaston Duchess.	Oct.–Nov.
Santa Claus.	Dec.–Jan.
Souvenir du Congrès.	
	Aug.–Sept.
Winter Nelis.	Dec.–Feb.

(3)	
Beurré d'Amanlis.	Sept.
Beurré Hardy.	Oct.
Citron des Carmes.	July–Aug.
Clapp's Favourite.	Aug.
Comte de Lamy.	Oct.

Durondeau.	Oct.–Nov.
Fertility.	Sept.–Oct.
Michaelmas.	Sept.–Oct.
Neo Plus Meuris.	Jan.–Mar.
Nouvelle Fulvie.	Nov.–Feb.
Olivier de Serres.	Feb.–Mar.
Triomphe de Vienne.	Sept.

(4)	
Autumn Nelis.	Oct.
Bergamotte Esperen.	
	Jan.–April.
Beurré d'Anjou.	Oct.–Dec.
Beurré de Jonghe.	Dec.–Feb.
Beurré Giffard.	Aug.
Colmar.	Nov.–Feb.
Fondante d'Automne.	
	Sept.–Oct.
Glastonbury.	Oct.–Nov.
Jersey Gratioli.	Oct.
Nouveau Poiteau.	Nov.
Passe Colmar.	Nov.–Dec.
Red Doyenné.	Oct.–Nov.

(5)	
Beurré Bosc.	Oct.–Nov.
Beurré Clairgeau.	Nov.
Beurré Mortillet.	Sept.–Oct.
Duchesse de Bordeaux.	
	Dec.–Feb.
Flemish Beauty.	Sept.–Oct.
Madame Lye Baltet.	
	Dec.–Feb.
Marguerite Marillat.	Sept.
Marie Benoist.	Nov.–Jan.
Marie Louise d'Uccle.	Oct.
Passe Crassane.	Jan.–Mar.
Van Mons Léon Leclerc.	Nov.
Zéphirin Grégoire.	Dec.–Jan.

High-quality Pears

(Arranged in dozens, placed approximately in the order of merit, the varieties being selected with regard to their special flavours and general good quality.)

THIRTY-SIX LARGE PEARS

(1)	
Beurré Diel.	Oct.–Nov.
Beurré Rance.	Jan.–Mar.
Beurré Superfin.	Sept.–Oct.
Charles Ernest.	Nov.–Dec.
Conseiller de la Cour.	
	Oct.–Nov.
Doyenné du Comice.	
	Nov.–Dec.
Easter Beurré.	Jan.–Mar.
Glou Morceau.	Nov.–Jan.
Madame Treyve.	Sept.
Marie Louise.	Oct.–Nov.
Pitmaston Duchess.	
	Oct.–Nov.
Williams' Bon Chrétien.	
	Aug.–Sept.

(2)	
Beurré Hardy.	Oct.
Blickling.	Dec.–Jan.
Durondeau.	Oct.–Nov.
Emile d'Heyst.	Oct.–Nov.
Flemish Beauty.	Sept.–Oct.
Fondante d'Automne.	
	Sept.–Oct.

Fondante de Thiriott.	
	Nov.–Dec.
Jersey Gratioli.	Oct.
Joséphine de Malines.	
	Dec.–Mar.
Le Brun.	Oct.
Marie Benoist.	Nov.–Jan.
Souvenir du Congrès.	
	Aug.–Sept.

(3)	
Baron Leroy.	Dec.–Jan.
Beurré de Jonghe.	Dec.–Feb.
Beurré Fouqueray.	
Beurré de Naghan.	
	Jan.–Feb.
Chaumontel.	Nov.–Mar.
Comte de Flandre.	Nov.–Dec.
Délices d'Hardenpont.	Nov.
Désiré Cornélis.	Aug.–Sept.
Duc de Nemours.	
Magnate.	Oct.–Nov.
Nouveau Poiteau.	Nov.
Princess.	Oct.–Nov.

THIRTY-SIX SMALL OR MEDIUM-SIZED PEARS OF HIGH QUALITY

(1)	
Autumn Bergamot.	Oct.
Belle Julie.	Oct.
Citron des Carmes.	July–Aug.
Forelle.	Nov.–Feb.
Gansel's Bergamot.	Oct.–Nov.
Louise Bonne of Jersey.	Oct.
Madame Lye Baltet.	Dec.–Feb.
Neo Plus Meuris.	Jan.–Mar.
Olivier de Serres.	Feb.–Mar.
Seckle.	Oct.
Winter Nelis.	Dec.–Feb.
Zéphirin Grégoire.	Dec.–Jan.

Hacon's Incomparable.	
	Nov.–Dec.
Hessle.	Oct.
March Bergamot.	Feb.–Mar.
Nouvelle Fulvie.	Nov.–Feb.
Passe Colmar.	Nov.–Dec.
Suffolk Thorn.	Oct.
Urbaniste.	Oct.

(2)	
Althorp Crassane.	Oct.–Dec.
Bergamotte Esperen.	
	Jan.–April.
Beurré Giffard.	Aug.
Doyenné d'Alençon.	
	Dec.–Feb.
Duchesse de Bordeaux.	
	Dec.–Feb.

(3)	
Aspasie Aucourt.	Aug.
Bergamotte de Millepieds.	
	Oct.
Colmar d'Été.	Sept.
Dana's Hovey.	Nov.–Jan.
De Maraise.	Oct.
Doyenné Defays.	Oct.–Nov.
Fondante de Cuerne.	Sept.
Jean de Witte.	Jan.–Mar.
Lammas.	Aug.
Michaelmas.	Sept.–Oct.
Red Doyenné.	Oct.–Nov.
Red October.	Oct.

Thirty-six Handsome Pears for Exhibition and Use

Baron Leroy.	Dec.–Jan.	Emile d'Heyst.	Oct.–Nov.
Beurré Alexandre Lucas.	Dec.	Flemish Beauty.	Sept.–Oct.
Beurré Bosc.	Oct.–Nov.	Fondante de Thiriott.	
Beurré Clairgeau.	Nov.		Nov.–Dec.
Beurré Diel.	Oct.–Nov.	Glastonbury.	Oct.–Nov.
Beurré Dubuisson.	Dec.–Jan.	Glou Morceau.	Nov.–Jan.
Beurré Hardy.	Oct.	Grégoire Bordillon.	Sept.
Beurré Superfin.	Sept.–Oct.	King Edward's.	Sept.–Nov.
Charles Ernest.	Nov.–Dec.	Louise Bonne of Jersey.	Oct.
Clapp's Favourite.	Aug.	Marguerite Marillat.	Sept.
Conference.	Nov.	Marie Benoist.	Nov.–Jan.
Conseiller de la Cour.		Marie Louise.	Oct.–Nov.
	Oct.–Nov.	Marie Louise D'Uccle.	Oct.
Dr. Jules Guyot.	Sept.	Marquis.	Nov.–Dec.
Doyenné Boussoch.	Oct.–Nov.	Pitmaston Duchess.	
Doyenné du Comice.			Oct.–Nov.
	Nov.–Dec.	Président Drouard.	Jan.
Duchesse d'Angoulême.		Roosevelt.	Oct.
	Oct.–Nov.	St. Luke.	Oct.
Duchesse de Bordeaux.		Souvenir du Congrès.	
	Dec.–Feb.		Aug.–Sept.
Durondeau.	Oct.–Nov.		

Popular Pears

(The following list of Pears gives an approximate indication of the relative popularity of varieties for exhibition and general culture. The figures in brackets after each name represent the number of times each has been well shown in four of the largest fruit exhibitions held in Great Britain. The total number of exhibitors was 300. Only the varieties shown ten times and over are included.)

Bergamotte Esperen (60).	Easter Beurré (157).
Beurré Alexandre Lucas (11).	Emile d'Heyst (16).
Beurré d'Amanlis (129).	Fondante d'Automne (47).
Beurré d'Anjou (12).	Gansel's Bergamot (29).
Beurré Bachelier (49).	General Todleben (36).
Beurré Bosc (54).	Glou Morceau (147).
Beurré Clairgeau (36).	Hacon's Incomparable (58).
Beurré Diel (144).	Jargonelle (88).
Beurré Giffard (29).	Jersey Gratioli (21).
Beurré Hardy (55).	Joséphine de Malines (23).
Beurré Rance (115).	Louise Bonne of Jersey (229).
Beurré Sterckmans (17).	Madame Treyve (33).
Beurré Superfin (130).	Marguerite Marillat (20).
Bonne d'Ezée (40).	Marie Benoist (22).
Brown Beurré (25).	Marie Louise (226).
Catillac (10).	Marie Louise d'Uccle (20).
Chaumontel (29).	Nec Plus Meuris (35).
Citron des Carmes (34).	Olivier de Serres (12).
Clapp's Favourite (11).	Passe Colmar (42).
Comte de Lamy (25).	Pitmaston Duchess (136).
Conference (24).	Souvenir du Congrès (43).
Conseiller de la Cour (23).	Thompson's (45).
Doyenné Boussoch (28).	Triomphe de Vienne (23).
Doyenné du Comice (145).	Van Mons Léon Leclerc (24).
Doyenné d'Été (52).	Williams' Bon Chrétien (185).
Duchesse d'Angoulême (65).	Winter Nelis (82).
Durondeau (47).	

Pears for Large Pyramid or Orchard Standard Trees

Aston Town.	Emile d'Heyst.
Beacon.	Eyewood.
Belle Julie.	Fertility.
Bellissime d'Hiver.	Hessle.
Beurré Bosc.	Jargonelle.
Beurré Capiaumont.	Joséphine de Malines.
Beurré Clairgeau.	Louise Bonne of Jersey.
Beurré Hardy.	Marie Louise.
Clapp's Favourite.	Princess.
Doyenné Boussoch.	Vicar of Winkfield.
Doyenné d'Été.	Williams' Bon Chrétien.
Durondeau.	

Prolific Pears for Market or General Use. Pyramids on Quince (or double-grafted)

Althorp Crassane.	Oct.–Dec.	Beurré d'Amanlis.	Sept.
Belle Julie.	Oct.–Nov.	Beurré de l'Assomption.	Aug.
Bergamotte Esperen.		Beurré Giffard.	Aug.
	Jan.–April.	Beurré Hardy.	Oct.
Beurré Bachelier.	Dec.	Beurré J. Van Geert.	
Beurré Bosc.	Oct.–Nov.		Oct.–Nov.
Beurré Clairgeau	Nov.	Beurré Superfin.	Sept.–Oct.

Clapp's Favourite.	Aug.–Sept.	Hessle.	Oct.
Conference.	Nov.	Louise Bonne of Jersey.	Oct.
Dr. Jules Guyot.	Sept.	Madame Treyve.	Sept.
Doyenné du Comice.		Marie Louise.	Oct.–Nov.
	Nov.–Dec.	Marie Louise d'Uccle.	Oct.
Durondeau.	Oct.–Nov.	Pitmaston Duchess.	
Easter Beurré.	Jan.–Mar.		Oct.–Nov.
Emile d'Heyst.	Oct.–Nov.	Seckle.	Oct.
Fondante d'Automne.		Vicar of Winkfield.	
	Sept.–Oct.		Nov.–Jan.
Fondante de Thiriott.		Williams' Bon Chrétien.	
	Nov.–Dec.		Aug.–Sept.
Glou Morceau.	Nov.–Jan.	Winter Nelis.	Dec.–Feb.

Pears for Training to Walls

EIGHTEEN FOR SOUTHERLY ASPECTS

Bergamotte Esperen.		Gansel's Bergamot.	Oct.–Nov.
	Jan.–April.	Glou Morceau.	Nov.–Jan.
Beurré d'Anjou.	Oct.–Dec.	Le Lectier.	Dec.–Jan.
Beurré de Jonghe.	Dec.–Feb.	Magnate.	Oct.–Nov.
Beurré Rance.	Jan.–Mar.	Marie Benoist.	Nov.–Jan.
Beurré Sterckmans.		Marie Louise.	Oct.–Nov.
	Dec.–Jan.	Nouvelle Fulvie.	Dec.–Feb.
Beurré Superfin.	Sept.–Oct.	Olivier de Serres.	Feb.–Mar.
Brown Beurré.	Oct.	Pitmaston Duchess.	
Chaumontel.	Nov.–Mar.		Oct.–Nov.
Doyenné du Comice.			
	Nov.–Dec.		

EIGHTEEN FOR EASTERLY AND WESTERLY ASPECTS

Bergamotte Esperen.		Fondante d'Automne.	
	Jan.–April.		Sept.–Oct.
Beurré Giffard.	Aug.	Glou Morceau.	Nov.–Jan.
Beurré Superfin.	Sept.–Oct.	Joséphine de Malines.	
Clapp's Favourite.	Aug.		Dec.–Mar.
Conseiller de la Cour.		Louise Bonne of Jersey.	Oct.
	Oct.–Nov.	Marie Louise.	Oct.–Nov.
Doyenné du Comice.		Nec Plus Meuris.	Jan.–Mar.
	Nov.–Dec.	Passe Colmar.	Nov.–Dec.
Durondeau.	Oct.–Nov.	Thompson's.	Nov.
Emile d'Heyst.	Oct.–Nov.	Triomphe de Vienne.	Sept.
		Winter Nelis.	Dec.–Feb.

Pears for Small Gardens

SIX USEFUL VARIETIES

Belle Julie.	Oct.	Joséphine de Malines.	
Doyenné du Comice.			Dec.–Mar.
	Nov.–Dec.	Williams' Bon Chrétien.	
Fertility.	Sept.–Oct.		Aug.–Sept.
Louise Bonne of Jersey.	Oct.		

THREE FOR WALLS

Beurré Superfin.	Sept.–Oct.	Joséphine de Malines	
Doyenné du Comice.			Dec.–Mar.
	Nov.–Dec.		

Culinary (Stewing or Baking) Pears

Bellissime d'Hiver		Léon Leclerc de Laval.	
	Nov.–April.		Jan.–May.
Calebasse Grosse.	Oct.	Uvedale's St. Germain.	
Catillac.	Dec.–April.		Jan.–April.
Double de Guerre.	Dec.–Feb.	Verulam.	Jan.–Mar.
Flemish Bon Chrétien.		Winter Orange.	Dec.–Mar.
	Nov.–Mar.		

THE BEST THREE VARIETIES

Bellissime d'Hiver.	November–April.
Catillac.	December–April.
Winter Orange.	December–March.

THE BEST VARIETY

Catillac.	December–April.

Twelve Hardy Pears for Northern Districts

Beurré d'Amanlis.	Jargonelle.
Beurré de Capiaumont.	Louise Bonne of Jersey.
Comte de Lamy.	Red Doyenné.
Crawford.	Swan's Egg.
Doyenné d'Été.	Thompson's.
Hessle.	Williams' Bon Chrétien.

Pears for Scotland

(The following list is condensed from the returns obtained at the Royal Caledonian Horticultural Society's Pear Congress at Edinburgh some years ago, the numbers following the names indicating by how many cultivators the variety was recommended as satisfactory. The months indicate the times when the varieties are fit for use in the north, which differ slightly from the maturing periods in more southern districts. The majority of the best Pears in the northern counties of England and in Scotland cannot be grown with success except as trained trees against suitable walls.)

DESSERT PEARS

Beurré d'Amanlis (28).	Oct.	Louise Bonne of Jersey (32).	
Beurré Rance (24).	May.		Nov.
Easter Beurré (40).	April.	Marie Louise (55).	Dec.
Glou Morceau (27).	Mar.	Williams' Bon Chrétien (44).	
Hacon's Incomparable (22).			Sept.
	Feb.	Winter Nelis (20).	Jan.
Jargonelle (56).	Aug.		

DESSERT PEARS FOR BUSHES

Beurré Capiaumont (10).	Jargonelle (27).
Beurré d'Amanlis (28).	Louise Bonne of Jersey (36).
Beurré d'Aremberg (17).	Marie Louise (21).
Beurré Diel (19).	Muirfowl's Egg (22).
Easter Beurré (16).	Swan's Egg (12).
Hacon's Incomparable (22).	Williams' Bon Chrétien (35).

PEARS FOR ORCHARDS

Autumn Bergamot (12).	Louise Bonne of Jersey (13).
Crawford (17).	Muirfowl's Egg (27).
Hessle (43).	Swan's Egg (13).

STEWING PEARS

Catillac (45).
Uvedale's St. Germain (19).
Verulam (16).

Perry Pears

(The best varieties of Pear grown for the production of Perry in Herefordshire are the following, of which Mr. C. W. Radclyffe Cooke, M.P., gives full descriptions in his work on Cider and Perry.)

EARLY VARIETIES

Barland.	Taynton Squash.
Moorcroft.	Thorn Pear.
Red Pear.	

MIDSUMMER VARIETIES

Langland.	Yellow and Black Huffcap.

LATE VARIETIES

Blakeney Red.	Pine Pear.
Butt Pear.	Rock Pear.
Oldfield.	

Pears that should be Double-grafted on the Quince

Beacon.	Forelle.
Belle Julie.	Gansel's Bergamot.
Bellissime d'Hiver.	Huyshe's Prince Consort.
Beurré Berckmans.	Jargonelle.
Beurré Bosc.	Jean de Witte.
Beurré Clairgeau.	Joséphine de Malines.
Beurré de Jonghe.	King Edward's.
Beurré Langelier.	Marie Louise.
Beurré Mortillet.	Nec Plus Meuris.
British Queen.	Passe Crassane.
Brown Beurré.	Saint Germain.
Citron des Carmes.	Seckle.
Clapp's Favourite.	Souvenir du Congrès.
Comte de Flandre.	Suffolk Thorn.
Comte de Lamy.	Thompson's.
Crassane.	Triomphe de Vienne
Dana's Hovey.	Urbaniste.
Doyenné d'Été.	Uvedale's St. Germain.
Duchesse de Bordeaux.	Van Mons Léon Leclerc.
Eyewood.	Zéphirin Grégoire.
Flemish Beauty.	

PLUMS AND DAMSONS

ORIGIN

According to the highest botanical authority,[1] the Plum, the Damson, the Sloe, and the Bullace are all forms of *Prunus communis* (fig. 125), which is common in hedges, thickets, and open woods in Europe and in Russian and Central Asia. The Bullace has also been recognized as a distinct species, under the name of *P. insititia*; the Damson and numerous varieties of Plums grown in gardens, although growing into thornless trees, are believed to be varieties of *P. communis*, produced by long cultivation; they are occasionally self-sown, and may be found apparently wild in the neighbourhood of gardens and orchards, retaining their arborescent character. Some botanists, however, distinguish them as a species under the name of *P. domestica*.

"It is very doubtful if *P. domestica* is indigenous in Europe. In the south, where it is given, it grows chiefly in hedgerows near dwellings, with all the appearance of a tree scarcely naturalized, and maintained here and there by means of seeds brought from plantations. . . . In spite of the abundance of Plums cultivated formerly by the Romans, no kind is found represented in the frescoes at Pompeii. Neither has *P. domestica* been found among the remains of the lake-dwellings of Italy, Switzerland, and Savoy, where, however, stones of the Bullace and the Sloe have been discovered. . . . The Plums cultivated at Damascus (whence Damascenes or Damsons) have a reputation which dates from the days of Pliny. . . . The Chinese have cultivated different kinds of Plums from time immemorial, but they are probably of a different species from ours" (De Candolle, *Origin of Cultivated Plants*).

There are several hundred named varieties of Plums in cultivation in the British Isles. Many are of recent origin, but with regard to others nothing appears to be known beyond that we are indebted to France for their introduction. Parkinson (1628) enumerated sixty named varieties, "all which

¹ Bentham and Hooker's *British Flora*.

sorts are to be had of my very good friend, Master John Tradescante, who hath wonderfully laboured to obtain all the rarest fruits he can hear of in any place of Christendome, Turky, yea of the whole world ".

John Gerarde stated three centuries ago: " To write of Plums particularly would require a peculiar volume. . . . Every clymate hath his owne fruit, far different from that of other countries; my selfe have threescore sorts in my garden, and all strange and rare; there be in other places many more common, and yet yearely commeth to our hands others not before knowne."

As in the case of Apples and Pears, Plums raised from seeds vary considerably. They have been favourite fruits in European gardens for so long a period that their characters have been greatly modified by cultivation and selection. Some varieties are said to come tolerably true from seeds, especially the Green Gage, Prune, Myrobalan, and Damson.

In the United States of America several native species of Prunus have been brought under cultivation, and by selection and crossing have yielded improved useful fruits. " In this way, about a hundred choice forms of the native Plum of the North-west (*Prunus Americana*) have been gathered and sorted and given names; and they are so much more hardy and reliable than the European type of Plum, that they will probably form the chief foundation from which the future orchard Plums of the northern prairie states will spring. They are already grown to an important commercial extent " (Bailey). Other American species of Prunus from which useful garden Plums have been evolved are *P. angustifolia* (Chickasaw Plum) and *P. hortulana* (Wild Goose, Miner, Wayland, &c., Plums). A form of the last-named has been successfully hybridized with the Peach.

The European Plums are largely cultivated in some parts of the United States, and some good varieties have been raised there. Among them the Jefferson holds first rank; Denniston's Superb, Huling's Superb, Smith's

Fig. 124.—The Mahaleb Plum

Orleans, Autumn Gage, and others were rated first-rate by the late Thomas Rivers.

The production of dried Prunes is an important industry in many parts of Europe chen; and in California, the " Prune d'Agen (fig. 127). The fruits of these have thicker skins than ordinary garden Plums; the pulp is greenish and rather austere unless fully

Fig. 125.—Prunus communis

and in several of the United States, particularly California. The principal varieties cultivated for this purpose are: in France, the " Prunier d'ente "; in Germany, the Quets- ripe, and it does not cling to the stone. The process of curing is a somewhat elaborate one. A full account of it is given in the *Kew Bulletin* for 1890.

CULTIVATION

Soil and Situation.—The Plum grows freely in any good open loam, neither too dry nor having a wet subsoil. In strong soils the trees make vigorous shoots when the ground begins to get warm after midsummer. The roots grow nearer the surface than those of the Apple and Pear; they do not therefore require deep soil. Vicissitudes of moisture and dryness are very prejudicial to stone fruits, frequently causing them to gum; therefore the ground ought to be trenched rather deeply, for the amount of moisture in a loose soil is far more uniform than in shallow untrenched ground. The subsoil should be drained.

Choice varieties of Plums should be accorded the protection of a wall, preferably one having an eastern or western aspect. Many varieties succeed either as standards or bushes in the open.

Planting.—The ground having been prepared, as already directed for the Apple and Pear, the distance between the trees requires to be determined. If they are to be planted in the open, the distance for standards, half-standards, and dwarfs may be from 20 to 25 feet between the rows, and about 20 feet apart. If the rows are 20 feet apart, then the trees in the row will be about 17 feet apart. If espaliers are afforded for Plums they may range from 12 to 15 feet apart from row to row, and a like distance between the trees. Small pyramids and bushes may be planted from 6 to 9 feet apart. Against walls the distance may be from 15 to 20 feet for trained trees, and 2 feet apart for single-stemmed cordons.

The trees should be planted as recommended for the Apple and Pear. Mulching, in case of dry weather, is advantageous; for, if the root fail to supply enough sap to the tree, gumming is apt to ensue. The supply of sap cannot be uniform unless the moisture of the soil about the roots is steadily maintained, and this is done by mulching.

Pruning and Training.—For standard trees, where under-cropping is intended, the height of the stem should not be less than 6 feet. By depressing early the strongest and elevating the weakest shoots on young standards, the equilibrium of the head is maintained; or the points of the strongest shoots must be pinched when about a foot long. Towards September the shoots should be so disposed as to have an equal divergence. After this, it will only be necessary to check

prepared in the same manner as recommended for standards, only with this difference in the case of pyramids, a central shoot must be preserved to extend the trees to the desired height. In regard to bushes, the central shoot should be dispensed with, the aim being to form a bush with an open centre, and with the branches widely disposed, rather than compact as in a pyramid. This admits sunlight to all parts of the tree.

These two forms of trees should always be summer pruned, i.e. to stop all young

Fig. 126.—Hybrid Plum—Greengage × Victoria

over-luxuriant shoots, and to keep the head of the tree clear of branches that would rub against each other. If the shoots grow luxuriantly, it would be well to pinch their tops about midsummer; otherwise, when very long shoots are allowed to form, nearly their whole extent may be naked in the course of a year or two.

For trees against walls the fan mode is the best; for the branches of the Plum are more apt to die off than those of the Apple and Pear, and fan-training admits of vacancies being filled up by a redistribution of the branches.

The foundation of dwarf trees, trained either as pyramids or bushes, should be

growths emanating from spurs and last season's wood, to five buds, to form spurs in the latter case, and to induce the formation of fruit-buds in the former. This is best done about the middle of August. If done earlier the buds on the shortened back shoots are apt to break and make secondary growths. Shoots on the extremities of the main branches should be left intact until winter, when they may be shortened as much as is necessary.

Cordons are formed by planting one-year or " maiden " trees. Cut back the stem to a prominent bud and train up the resulting shoot the following summer. Stop all other growths produced below this shoot to five buds, to form spurs. If all goes well, the leading shoot will make from 4 feet to 6 feet of growth by the autumn. This must in turn be shortened back, and another leader trained up the following summer, stopping all growths below to form spurs as before, and continuing in this manner until the tree reaches the top of the wall. In the autumn of the third season after planting, lift and transplant the tree to throw it into a bearing condition, and summer prune in mid-August every season afterwards.

The shoots of the Plum do not require to be shortened at the winter pruning if their

fruitfulness of the tree; and the sap can only be equally distributed by every branch being furnished with foliage. Where shoots give indications of excessive vigour, they should be kept in check. The young summer shoots in the upper part of the tree should receive their summer pruning before those in the lower part. Frequently the shoots in the central part of fan-trained trees are inclined to become excessively vigorous. As they cannot well do this without crowding those on the sides, their vigour may be checked by pinching, or cutting out the growing point with a sharp knife.

Fig. 127.—Californian Prune or Prune d'Agen (*Prunus communis*, var.).

extremities are well ripened, except where branches are required. Numerous shoots will push, more especially from the upper sides of the branches. These shoots must be pinched below the sixth leaf, when they have made as many. They should be shortened at the winter pruning, and fruit-buds will form or shoots push (fig. 128). In the latter case pinching must be resorted to.

When spurs grow too far from the wall they must be cut back; but those on the lower branches should be allowed to extend a little more than those on the upper side, in order that as much foliage may be on the lower branches as on the upper; otherwise, most of the sap would be drawn to the latter, and the lower branches would suffer. In proportion to the equal distribution of the sap, so will be the health, duration, and

For horizontal training, whether on walls or espaliers, the first course should be 1 foot from the ground, and the others 9 inches apart. Care, however, must be taken to originate the branches 4 or 5 inches below the horizontal line along which they are intended to be trained. If this be done, the branches will not be so liable to die as when they are taken at right angles from the upright stem, which in training stone-fruit trees should never be the case.

Root-lifting.—Plums, when planted in rich soil, are likely to grow over-luxuriantly, and to bear little or no fruit. To remedy this, they should be lifted and replanted about the end of October. Some lime rubble should be added to the soil, and no manure. This lifting checks rank growth and induces the formation of fruit-buds. Trees when once in a bearing condition rarely give further trouble; but, should they still be unfruitful, lift them again the following autumn and mix some more lime rubble with the soil when replanting.

The roots of the Plum run near the surface (see fig. 129), and on this account the ground must either be dug every year or not at all. Trees have been known to thrive very well where the ground was regularly dug for vegetable crops; but on its being

Fig. 128.—Plum Shoots

On the left, a two-year-old shoot, showing fruit-buds. On the right, a one-year-old shoot, showing wood-buds.

left undug for two years, the roots made rapid progress towards the surface, and on again digging the soil, for cropping, the trees suffered from the loss of these young roots. It has been suggested that the Silverleaf disease is started by this practice.

Suckers that spring from the base of Plum trees should be removed. They are more apt to push from trees that are sickly than from healthy ones. The under side of the foliage is sometimes entirely covered with aphides, and when this is the case the tree cannot long remain healthy, however well it may be circumstanced in other respects. Every possible means should therefore be

adopted to keep the foliage clean; and at the same time, in order that it may be naturally healthy, the roots must be duly supplied with moisture. Established trees in full

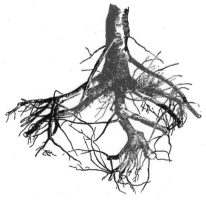

Fig. 129.—Root System of a Well-managed Plum

bearing should each season be dressed either with farmyard or artificial manure, otherwise they are apt to become exhausted and bear but indifferent crops of fruit.

GATHERING AND PRESERVING THE FRUIT

Plums should be allowed to remain on the tree as long as is safe. Choice fruit ought to be gathered by severing the stalk with a pair of grape scissors and without disturbing the bloom, especially if the fruit is of a variety intended to be kept for some time. Such kinds as Coe's Golden Drop, Ickworth Impératrice, and Reine Claude Violette, may be kept for months if gathered in dry weather, wrapped in paper, and laid in a dry airy place.

PROPAGATION

Some kinds of Plums are propagated by seed, others occasionally by suckers; but the usual mode of propagation is by budding and grafting. The stones are sown for raising stocks on which to graft Plums, Peaches, Nectarines, and Apricots. The Mussel, White Pear Plum, and St. Julien are chiefly employed for this purpose. For standards the Mussel is preferred.

The stones should be sown in a bed of rich sandy soil an inch apart, in drills 2 inches deep, and 1 foot asunder. Some recommend first drying them in the sun and keeping them in dry sand till November, and then sowing them. The French stratify the

Fig. 130.—Plum. Victor Christian

stones till spring, and then plant them out in rows. By either of these modes the seedlings will be fit for transplanting into nursery lines in autumn. When doing this the unripe extremities of the leading and side shoots should be cut off; the tap-root may also be shortened. Twelve months after this they ought to be cut down to two buds above the surface. In the following spring both buds will likely push, but only one should be allowed to grow to a stem.

Strong-growing sorts intended for standards may be grafted or budded near the ground, and the stem formed from the scion. In the case of weaker-growing kinds, such as the Mirabelle, it is better to allow the stock to grow up, and bud or graft it standard high. Some prefer budded plants, others those which are grafted; but, if properly worked, good trees can be obtained by either mode. Nurserymen usually have less work on hand at the budding than at the grafting season, and therefore find it convenient to propagate at the former period. Besides, if buds should not take, the stocks can be grafted in the following spring. In order that the graft may form a sound union, attention to a few particulars is necessary. The scions should be taken off early in the season, say in January, or at least before the buds begin to push. At the same time the stock

should be headed down near to the point where the scion is to be put on. If either the scion or the stock, or both, are too far advanced when they are cut, success is ren-

Fig. 131.—Sizes of Plums
a, Washington, large. b, Coe's Late Red, medium.
c, Coe's Mirabelle, small

dered uncertain. Even if the graft should take, gum or canker is likely to follow. The grafts of Plums are more apt to fail than those of Apples and Pears; yet, when the stocks are early headed down and the scions taken off in good time, as directed, they generally succeed. It is a good plan to earth up the grafted plants above the clay, as the soil keeps the clay from drying.

In budding, care must be taken that wood and not blossom buds are inserted; and in grafting, it is necessary to see that there are wood-buds on the scion. Occasionally it may be desirable to propagate a particular variety, the shoots of which have scarcely any wood-buds, except terminal ones; and when such shoots must be employed for scions, the buds at the extremities should not be cut away; they must form the terminal bud of the scion.

ENEMIES

Apple Mussel Scale, Birds, Plum Sawfly, Red Grub of Plum, Wasps, Plum Aphides, Red Spider, Slug-worms, Small Ermine Moth, Winter Moth, Stem-boring Weevils, Wood Leopard Moth. See INSECT AND OTHER PLANT ENEMIES, Vol. III.

SELECT LIST OF VARIETIES

PLUMS

Those marked with an asterisk are good for forcing in pots

ANGELINA BURDETT.—Dessert. August–September. A Plum of the finest quality. Fruit medium, round, dark-purple, marked with a suture; skin thick, mottled with brown; flesh

BELGIAN PURPLE.—Culinary and dessert. Mid-August. Fruit medium to large, roundish, violet-purple, with a copious bloom; flesh greenish, juicy, sweet and rich when thoroughly ripe. The tree has a hardy vigorous constitution, and is a great bearer. A first-rate market variety.

BELLE DE LOUVAIN. — Culinary. August-September. Fruit large, oval, deep-purple, with

Fig. 132.—Plum. Coe's Golden Drop

yellowish, juicy, and richly flavoured. A good grower and bearer either on a wall or as a bush.

ARCHDUKE.—Culinary. October. Fruit large oval, purple. An immense cropper and a good grower on walls or fences, or as a bush. Raised by Mr. Rivers.

AUTUMN COMPOTE. — Culinary. September. Fruit handsome, very large, bright-red; skin thin; flesh yellow, tender, and juicy. A hardy and productive variety, best grown on a wall, as the skin is apt to split on trees in the open in a wet season.

a thin bloom; flesh firm, yellowish, juicy, and richly flavoured. A heavy cropper, hardy, succeeds either on a wall or as a standard or bush.

BELLE DE SEPTEMBRE.—Culinary. October. Fruit large, roundish, oval, reddish-purple, with light-brown dots and thin bloom; flesh yellowish, firm, juicy, and fairly sweet. Should be grown against a wall, as the fruits are inclined to burst if grown in the open.

BONNE BOUCHE.—Dessert. September. A hardy Gage, suitable either for a wall or the open; very fertile as a cordon. Fruit medium, greenish-yellow; flesh golden-yellow, tender, juicy.

BOULOUF.—Dessert. September. Fruit large, roundish, red, heavily dotted and blotched with russet; heavy bloom; flesh yellowish, tender, juicy, with a rich Gage-like flavour. Tree hardy, a good bearer as a cordon on an eastern aspect.

BRAHY'S GREEN GAGE.—Dessert. Late September. Fruit very large, roundish, and sutured, greenish-yellow, with greyish bloom; flesh yellow, tender, juicy, flavoured like the old Green Gage, ripening a fortnight earlier. Best when grown against a wall.

BRYANSTON GAGE. — Dessert. September. Hardier than Brahy's Gage; very prolific, either when grown as a bush in the open or against a wall or fence. Fruit like a Green Gage but larger, more golden in colour, richly flavoured and juicy. Is the result of crossing Green Gage and Coe's Golden Drop at Bryanston Park.

*COE'S GOLDEN DROP (fig. 132).—Dessert and culinary. Late September. Fruit large, oval, greenish-yellow, freckled with dull-red on the side exposed to the sun; flesh greenish-yellow, adhering to the stone; very sweet, and deliciously flavoured when fully ripe. The fruits will keep long after they are gathered, either on the shelves of a fruit-room or suspended by the stalk inside a window facing the sun, or wrapped in paper and kept in a dry room. The tree is a shy bearer when young, but is productive later. May be grown as a standard in the south and west, but in the north of England and in Scotland it requires an east or west wall, and one inclining to south-west is still better. Raised about a century ago by Mr. Coe, a market-gardener, near Bury St. Edmunds.

COE'S LATE RED.—Dessert. October or November. Fruit medium, roundish, depressed at both ends, purplish-red, with yellow dots and azure bloom; flesh pale-amber, separating from the stone, crisp and juicy, with a rich vinous flavour when the autumn is fine. One of the latest to ripen. An excellent bearer as a standard in the warmer parts of the kingdom; elsewhere it requires the protection of a wall.

*COUNT ALTHAN'S GAGE.—Dessert. September. Fruit large, handsome, of same shape as the Green Gage, greenish-yellow, mottled and dotted with red; flesh yellow, tender, juicy, exquisitely flavoured. Succeeds either as a cordon or trained on a wall, or as a bush in the open.

CZAR.—Dessert and Culinary. Early August. Excellent either for private or market supply. Fruit medium to large, roundish, oval, sutured; skin fairly thick, blue-black, with a copious bloom; flesh yellowish, tender, juicy, and sweet. May be grown either against a wall or as a bush or standard. Raised by Mr. Rivers from Prince Engelbert and Early Prolific.

DENBIGH (Cox's Emperor) (fig. 133).—Culinary. Mid-September. Fruit very large, resembling Orleans, dark-red, with grey spots and bluish bloom, darkest on the side exposed to the sun; flesh yellow, firm, juicy, and sweet. Is a great bearer, and makes a good cordon for a wall.

DENNISTON'S SUPERB.—Dessert. Mid-August. Fruit large, roundish, sutured, bright golden-yellow when fully exposed to the sun, and ripened on a wall or fence; flesh yellow, firm, juicy, with a rich Gage-like flavour. Does well in any form, and is particularly prolific as a bush or cordon.

DENYER'S VICTORIA. — Culinary and dessert.

Late September. Fruit large, oval, red, with a thin light bloom; flesh yellowish, parting freely from the stone, moderately juicy, flavour agreeable. An excellent all-round Plum; most prolific bearer as a standard, the branches often requiring support.

DIAMOND.—Culinary. Mid-September. Fruit very large, oval, deep-purple; flesh yellowish, coarse, juicy, and acid. A very vigorous grower and a good bearer. Does well as a bush.

EARLY ORLEANS (Wilmot's).—Culinary. Mid-August. Fruit similar to Orleans, but of a somewhat deeper violet colour, and ripening a fortnight earlier. An excellent bearer.

Fig. 133.—Plum. Denbigh (Cox's Emperor)

EARLY PROLIFIC (Rivers') (fig. 134).—Dessert and culinary. Late July. Fruit medium, roundish, dark-purple, with a thin bloom; flesh yellow, juicy, sweet, agreeably flavoured. The best early Plum, largely grown for market. The tree is hardy, and bears most profusely either as a standard, bush, or trained against a wall.

*EARLY TRANSPARENT GAGE.—Dessert. Early August. Fruit large, roundish and flattened, yellow, mottled with red; flesh firm, juicy, and as richly flavoured as the Green Gage. A seedling from Transparent Gage, and is one of the most delicious of early Plums. Does best against a wall.

*GOLDEN ESPEREN (Drap d'Or d'Esperen). Dessert. Late August or September. Fruit large, roundish, oval, yellow, with crimson spots on one side; flesh yellowish, separating easily from the stone, juicy, with a rich sugary flavour.

*GOLDEN TRANSPARENT.—Dessert. Late September. Fruit large, roundish-oval, bright golden yellow when fully ripe; flesh rich, juicy, and deliciously flavoured. Should be trained against a wall. One of the best.

GOLIATH.—Culinary. September. Fruit large, handsome, roundish-oblong, depressed at both ends, purple, bloom azure; flesh firm, greenish-yellow, coarse, adhering to the stone.

*GRAND DUKE (fig. 135).—Culinary. Mid-October. Fruit large, oval, deep-purple in colour, covered with a dense blue bloom; flesh yellowish, firm, and sweet. A variety of great excellence,

flesh yellowish-green, firm, rich, juicy, and excellent. A valuable late Gage, a good grower and bearer, fully deserving the protection afforded by a wall.

HERON.—Culinary. Early August. Fruit large, reddish-purple, of the free-stone section. Being

Fig. 134.—Plums. Early Prolific (Rivers'). Nat. size

raised by Mr. Rivers from Autumn Compote. Is worthy of a place against a wall.

GREEN GAGE.—Culinary and dessert. Mid-August. Fruit medium, round, with a small suture, pale-green, faintly tinged with yellow, sometimes russet-red, and speckled on the side exposed to the sun; flesh pale-green, melting,

Fig. 135.—Plum. Grand Duke

juicy. Generally an abundant bearer, either as a standard or trained against a wall. It has also been called Isleworth Green Gage, Wilmot's Green Gage, Bradford Gage, Ahicot Vert, Damas Vert, Dauphine, Grosse Reine, Grosse Reine Claude, Reine Claude, Sucrin Vert, Verte Bonne.

GUTHRIE'S LATE GREEN.—Dessert. Late September. Fruit medium, roundish-oval, sutured skin, greenish-yellow, with a thin grey bloom;

a very heavy cropper of great excellence, this is highly recommended both for garden and market culture.

HULING'S SUPERB.—Dessert. Mid-September. Fruit as large as the Washington, roundish-ovate, greenish-yellow; flesh pale greenish-yellow, parting from the stone, rich, juicy, and of excellent flavour.

ICKWORTH IMPÉRATRICE. — Dessert. Early October. Fruit medium, obovate, purple, with golden lines radiating from the stalk or disposed in a circle, bloom bright-purple; flesh greenish-amber, partly adhering to the stone, juicy and very rich. Will keep several months if wrapped in paper and placed on a dry shelf. It also makes a good preserve. Raised by Mr. Knight, and named after Ickworth Park near Bury St. Edmunds.

*JEFFERSON.—Dessert. Late September. Fruit large, roundish-oval, dark-yellow, speckled with purple and red, bloom thin; flesh deep orange, juicy, exceedingly rich and sugary. Tree a good grower and excellent bearer, either in the open as a standard or bush in warm localities, or against a wall in colder parts. Of American origin.

JULY GREEN GAGE.—An early variety of the Green Gage, with golden-yellow fruit, not so rich in flavour as Green Gage. Is very prolific when grown against a wall.

*KIRKE'S.—Dessert. Early September. Fruit very large and round, dark-purple, with small golden specks; flesh greenish-yellow, parting from the stone, firm, juicy, very rich, and Gage-like. Tree a good bearer, either as a standard or bush. Succeeds well on a north-western aspect in the West Midlands.

LARGE BLACK IMPERIAL. — Culinary. Mid-September. Fruit very large, purplish-black, sutured; flesh yellow, firm, juicy, sweet. Tree hardy; heavy regular cropper, either as a standard or bush.

LATE ORANGE.—Dessert. Late October. Fruit large, roundish, orange-yellow, with a heavy bloom; flesh juicy and rich, parting freely from the stone. A variety of great merit.

LATE RIVERS.—Culinary. October–November. Fruit small to medium, roundish, dark-purple; flesh yellowish, adhering to the stone, juicy, sweet,

Fig. 136.—Plum. Monarch (Rivers').

and richly flavoured. A valuable late Plum and a great bearer.

*LATE TRANSPARENT.—Dessert. Late September. Fruit large, round, greenish-yellow, with patches of red and purple, and a thin white bloom; flesh greenish-amber, firm and tender, juicy, and quite equal to Green Gage in flavour. A favourite late Gage of the highest quality. Tree hardy, and a good bearer as a bush or standard, or when trained against a wall.

LAWSON'S GOLDEN GAGE.—Dessert. Early September. Fruit small to medium, oval, sutured on one side only, deep-yellow, speckled with crimson; flesh yellow, tender, juicy and richly flavoured. Tree hardy, bears well as a pyramid.

M'LAUGHLIN'S GAGE.—Dessert. Mid-August. Fruit large, roundish, yellow, speckled with red; flesh greenish-yellow, tender, juicy, not equal in flavour to Green Gage. Tree hardy and prolific.

MITCHELSON'S.—Culinary. Early September. Fruit medium, oval, black; flesh yellow, parting from the stone, very juicy and sweet. A first-rate preserving Plum, and, being an extraordinary bearer, is largely grown for market.

*MONARCH (fig. 136).—Culinary. Late Sep-

tember. Fruit large, roundish-oval, dark-purple; flesh very firm and juicy. Tree quite hardy, very prolific, succeeding either as a standard, cordon, or bush. A first-rate market kind. Raised by Mr. Rivers from Autumn Compote.

NECTARINE PLUM. — Dessert and culinary. August. Fruit large, roundish, when not too thick on the tree, otherwise oval, reddish-purple, bloom thin; flesh tolerably rich, greenish-yellow, partially adhering to the stone. Tree a great bearer, frequently so much so that unless the crop is thinned the branches break down with the weight of fruit. Also known as Caledonian, Howell's Large, Jenkins' Imperial, Louis Philippe, Peach, Prune Pêche of some.

ORLEANS.—Culinary. Late August. Fruit large, roundish, depressed on the summit, purplish-red, with pale-red specks, bloom close, giving it a handsome Prussian-blue colour; flesh yellowish-green, firm, parting freely from the stone, fairly rich and juicy. Also known as Old Orleans, Red Damask, Monsieur.

*OULLIN'S GOLDEN.—Dessert. Early August. Fruit large, roundish-oval, rich yellow with crimson dots; flesh yellow, slightly adhering to the stone, tender, rich, and juicy. A beautiful and first-rate Plum, and an abundant bearer. Also known as Reine Claude d'Oullins, Reine Claude Précoce.

PERSHORE.—Culinary. Mid-August. Fruit medium, obovate, yellow; flesh tender, with a slightly acid flavour. Largely cultivated in the Evesham district for the markets of Birmingham and other large towns.

POND'S SEEDLING (fig. 137).—Culinary. Mid-September. Fruit very large, handsome, oval, dark-red speckled with grey, with a thin bluish bloom; flesh amber, juicy, with a brisk flavour. A valuable kitchen Plum, much grown for market. A hardy and prolific variety in the open.

PRIMATE.—Culinary. Late October. Fruit large, purplish-red, with thin bloom; flesh sweet,

Fig. 137.—Plum. Pond's Seedling

juicy, parting from the stone. The fruit hangs well after attaining maturity. A new variety of excellent quality.

PRINCE ENGLEBERT. — Dessert and culinary. Late August–September. Fruit very large and oval, deep-purple, with minute reddish dots and a dense-grey bloom; flesh yellow, juicy, rich, and sweet. A hardy variety, very prolific when grown as a standard.

PRINCE OF WALES.—Culinary. Late August–September. Fruit resembling Orleans, but differs in having smooth instead of downy shoots. The tree is vigorous and a great bearer, but so tender and liable to die off in an unaccountable manner that it is not much grown.

RED MAGNUM BONUM (Red Egg Plum, Red Imperial).—Culinary. Mid-September. Fruit large, oval, distinctly sutured, of irregular shape, deep-red, paler where shaded, with small brown dots and thin bloom; flesh greenish, firm, juicy, and agreeably flavoured. Tree hardy, and a great bearer either as a standard or bush.

REINE CLAUDE DE BAVAY (Monstrueuse de Bavay, St. Claire).—Dessert. Late September–October. Fruit large, roundish, greenish-yellow with a thin white bloom; flesh yellow, very juicy, rich, and sugary, of delicious flavour, separating from the stone. A valuable late Gage of first-rate quality. Should be grown on a wall.

*REINE CLAUDE VIOLETTE (Purple Gage, Violet Gage). — Dessert. Early September. Fruit medium, roundish, violet-purple with yellow dots, and a light bloom; flesh firm, greenish-amber, parting from the stone, sugary, rich, and excellent. Will keep in dry favourable seasons till October. The tree is a good bearer as a standard, and it deserves a place against a wall.

ROYAL HÂTIVE (Miriam).—Dessert. Early August. Fruit medium, roundish, purple, netted with yellowish-brown; flesh yellowish, parting from the stone, sugary, rich, and delicious. Wasps and flies attack it in preference to other sorts. The tree is a good bearer, and should be in all large collections, on account of the great excellence and earliness of the fruit.

SULTAN.—Culinary. Mid-August. Fruit medium to large, round, deep-red, with a thick bloom; flesh greenish-yellow, juicy, agreeably flavoured. Tree a strong grower, bearing freely; considered to be an improved Prince of Wales.

*TRANSPARENT GAGE.—Dessert. September. Fruit large, round, flattened, slightly sutured, pale-yellow, mottled with red; flesh yellowish, transparent, juicy, rich, and luscious.

VICTORIA (fig. 138). — Dessert and culinary. Most popular, as it grows well almost anywhere and is a prolific bearer. August. Fruit large, ovate, vinous purple; free stone; flesh green-yellow, juicy, and sweet, rather wanting in flavour. Unfortunately it is very subject to Silverleaf.

WASHINGTON.—Dessert and culinary. Fruit very large, roundish-oval, dull-yellow, obscurely streaked with pale-green, flushed with red when well exposed to the sun; flesh yellow, parting freely from the stone, sweet and luscious. The tree is a shy bearer when young, but bears abundantly when older either as a standard or against a wall. The branches should be allowed plenty of space to expose broad foliage to the light. Raised in 1818 near New York. Also known as Bolmar, Franklin, Bolmar's Washington.

WHITE MAGNUM BONUM.—Culinary. September. Fruit large, oval, yellow, with a thin whitish bloom; flesh firm, adhering to the stone, pale-yellow, juicy, crisp, not rich. This large handsome fruit is excellent for sweetmeats and preserving whole. Tree vigorous, and bearing freely both in standard and bush form. Also

known as Yellow Magnum Bonum, Egg Plum, White Holland, Wentworth, Dame Auber, Dame Auber Blanche, Dame Auber Blanche Grosse Luisante, Impériale Blanche.

WINE SOUR (Rotherham).—Culinary. Mid-September. Fruit slightly larger than a Damson, obovate, purple; flesh greenish-yellow tinged with red, juicy and subacid. Excellent for jam. Tree a good bearer.

WYDALE.—Culinary. Late October. Fruit small, oval, purple, coated with a blue bloom; flesh greenish-yellow, juicy, briskly flavoured.

Fig. 138.—Plum. Victoria

Hangs for a long time on the tree in good condition. Tree a great bearer, either against a wall or in the open as a bush or standard. A famous old Yorkshire Plum.

List of Twenty-four First-rate Dessert Plums

Angelina Burdett, Bonne Bouche, Boulouf, Bryanston Gage, Coe's Golden Drop, Count Althem's Gage, Denniston's Superb, Early Transparent, Golden Transparent, Golden Esperen, Guthrie's Late Green, Green Gage, Ickworth Impératrice, Jefferson, July Green Gage, Kirke's, Lawson's Golden Gage, Late Orange, Late Transparent, Oullin's Golden Gage, Reine Claude de Bavay, Reine Claude Violette, Transparent, Washington.

List of Twenty-four First-rate Culinary Plums.

Archduke, Autumn Compote, Belgian Purple, Belle de Louvain, Belle de Septembre, Coe's Late Red, Czar, Diamond, Early Prolific, Goliath, Grand Duke, Large Black Imperial, Late Rivers, Mitchelson's, Monarch, Orleans, Pond's Seedling, Prince Englebert, Primate, Red Magnum

Bonum, Sultan, Victoria, White Magnum Bonum, Wydale.

DAMSONS.

BRADLEY'S KING.—Late September–October. A very fine-flavoured variety, a great bearer, succeeds well on a shallow soil. Much grown in Kent for market.

sons. Is a much heavier cropper than the Shropshire Prune, and the fruit is larger, but the growth is less robust. The branches droop as the tree attains age.

PRUNE or SHROPSHIRE.—Fruit large, obovate, black, with dense blue bloom; flesh greenish-yellow, firm, juicy, sweeter than the common Damson, sometimes sightly bitter, excellent for preserving. Much prized in Shropshire and Cheshire, where

Fig 139.—Damsons

COMMON or ROUND.—September. Fruit small, roundish-oval, blue-black, with azure bloom; flesh firm, yellowish-green, parting from the stone, acid and astringent. Much used for pies and for preserving. A great bearer.

CRITTENDEN.—Mid-September. Fruit roundish-oval, small, black; flesh greenish-yellow, sweet when thoroughly ripe. A most prolific cropper, may be grown as a bush.

HEREFORDSHIRE PRUNE.—Late September. Fruit large, obovate; flesh firm, yellowish-green, juicy, and quite the sweetest flavoured of all the Dam-

it is extensively grown. Is not such a heavy cropper as Crittenden.

BULLACES

The chief distinction between the Bullace and Damson is in the shape of the fruit, which is round instead of oval, and in the colour, which is white.

The three best varieties are White, New Large Bullace, and Shepherd's White

FORCED PLUMS

The Plum, like the Cherry, requires but a slight amount of forcing to bring the fruit to perfection. The house in which the trees are grown may be either lean-to or span-roofed; it should also be roomy, airy, and light, with sufficient hot-water pipes to exclude frost.

The trees may be either planted out or grown in pots or tubs; the latter method, perhaps, being preferable, as it admits of

their being removed to the outer air after the fruits are gathered to ripen and rest.

If planted out, the border should be 3 feet in depth, and if at all damp, or if water rises in the spring, the bottom should be concreted and a drain provided to carry off the surplus water. The border should consist of about a foot of drainage, and 2 feet of good turfy loam. Plums require a liberal quantity of water throughout the growing season.

JAPANESE PLUMS

Trees grown in pots or tubs should be well drained, and it is necessary to stand them on three or four bricks or tiles to allow the water to get away, and to prevent worms getting into the pots. A temperature of 45° at night and 50° by day will be high enough to start with. The soil in the border and in the pots should then be thoroughly watered with tepid water. After this take advantage of a calm evening to vaporize the house as a precautionary measure, as the Plum, under glass, is very liable to become infested with aphis. Ordinary tobacco-paper will suffice for fumigating, but one of the vaporizing compounds now in use is much more pleasant to handle, and certainly more effective in killing the insects. Unless aphis should put in an appearance in the interval, this one application will suffice until the flowers are about to expand, when a second fumigation is desirable. This will carry them over that stage, or until the fruit is set, when an occasional vaporizing and vigorous washing with a garden-engine should keep them clean.

When the buds begin too push, increase the temperature to 50°–55° and syringe the trees twice a day with tepid water. Previous to this a light syringing every morning suffices. Maintain a dry atmosphere whilst the trees are in flower, and set the flowers with a camel-hair brush about the middle of the day. Ventilate as freely as circumstances will permit during the forenoon, to ensure the pollen being free and dry, and if the weather is mild a chink of air may remain on at the front and top ventilators throughout the night. Resume syringing as soon as the fruit is set, and, if the set is heavy, thin the fruits with a pair of fine grape scissors. With regard to the amount of fruit to leave on each tree, this should be governed entirely by the size, age, and health of the tree, and these are matters best determined by those under whose charge the trees may be. This much may be said, always avoid over-cropping, and at the same time do not err in the opposite direction, otherwise the trees will rush to strong growth.

The growths on the spurs and branches should be stopped to about four buds, leaving leaders and terminal shoots their full length if required for extension purposes, otherwise pinch them at the fifth or sixth leaf. This pinching or stopping is best done while the shoots are young and tender. Unless the trees are aged they will require to be pinched several times during the season. A good look-out must be kept for caterpillars. After the stoning period is safely passed, a higher temperature may be maintained to hasten the fruits to maturity, or sun-heat alone may maintain the requisite temperatures if air is shut off early in the afternoon to run the heat up to 65° or 70°. When hot weather sets in, the house will need to be aired abundantly, and the trees washed either with a syringe or garden-engine twice a day.

Mulching the surface of the border and pots with rich compost must not be neglected, and the roots must not feel the want of water at any time. In addition to this, liquid or artificial manure may be administered pretty frequently, as a good crop of fruit creates a heavy demand on the roots. When the fruits begin to ripen, gradually dispense with overhead syringing, and frequently sprinkle the paths and border surfaces with water and withhold stimulants. On dull or wet days a little fire-heat will prevent moisture from disfiguring the fruits.

JAPANESE PLUMS

In the United States particular attention has been paid to the Japanese Plums, in the belief that they will prove adapted to that country and add a race of varieties with qualities different from those of what are there known as the European (domestica) race. The following is a précis of an account of some of them, which was published in the form of a *Bulletin* in 1899, under the signature of Mr. L. H. Bailey.

Japanese Plums have been the subject of careful study at Cornell, and an effort has been made to secure all the varieties. The following notes are made directly from fruits produced there. Japanese Plums are a very important addition to our orchard fruits. They will not drive other Plums from the field, but they have attributes which make them an excellent supplement to the European and native sorts. The particular merits of the Japanese Plums are their great productiveness, adaptation to a wide range of territory, beauty, earliness of many of the varieties, comparative freedom from diseases and insects, and long-keeping qualities of fruit. Most of the varieties tend to over-bear, and good fruits can be secured only by severe thinning. This is especially true of Burbank, Abundance, and Red June. There is great range in quality, the poorest of them being inferior and the best of them nearly equal to the best of the European kinds,

Fig. 140 —Japanese Plum.   Abundance

whilst all of the leading sorts are better in quality than the Lombard, if they are properly thinned and ripened.

A great merit of the Japanese Plum is the fact that it is adapted to an exceedingly wide range of territory, in this respect excelling both the domestica and native types.   There are varieties which thrive from Canada to the southern States, and apparently from ocean to ocean. Japanese Plums are less seriously attacked by insects and fungi than the European or domestica type.

Most of them are worked on Peach stocks; and on these they seem to thrive. They also do remarkably well when topworked on Lombard stocks. These Plums are now so extensively planted that the time cannot be far distant when seed can be obtained cheaply enough to warrant the raising of Japanese Plum stocks. It remains to be demonstrated, however, whether the Japanese Plum stocks are actually better than the Peach or the domestica Plum stocks.

As a guide in the choice of varieties, those kinds are here named which seem to be worthy of general planting.   They are given in the order in which they ripened at Ithaca in 1899: Engre, Lutts, Red June, Abundance, Burbank, Chabot, Satsuma.

This order is not uniform year by year. It is characteristic of most Japanese Plums, that even though they are uncoloured when picked, they ripen if kept in a cool and dry place.

VARIETIES

ABUNDANCE (fig. 140).—Fruit medium to large when thinned, round-oblong, the suture more or less prominent; colour pink-coppery-red; flesh firm, juicy, sweet.   Ripe early in August.   An excellent Plum, and one which most people delight to eat.

BURBANK.—Fruit medium, round-oblong; colour orange-yellow, becoming more or less uniformly red on the cheek; flesh firm and meaty, yellow, sweet and rich, clinging.   Ripe mid-August. Heretofore we have regarded Burbank as the best all-round Japanese Plum, but we are now inclined to give that place to Abundance.

CHABOT (fig. 141).—Fruit medium to large, oblong-conical, the suture usually pronounced; colour deep-orange, red on the sunny side; flesh soft to firm, yellow, sweet, of excellent quality, clinging.   Ripe early September.   One of the best.

ENGRE.—Fruit small, somewhat flattened endwise, the suture usually prominent; colour red; flesh soft and yellow, clinging, sour, and the skin

Fig. 141.—Japanese Plum.   Chabot

tough. Ripe mid-July. A prolific bearer, and the fruits are attractive.   Its quality is not as good as that of Burbank and Abundance, but its great earliness commends it.

LUTTS.—An excellent early Plum. Fruit round-oblate, in general form and appearance very like the Burbank, but running smaller; colour dark red; flesh light-yellow and soft, clinging, with only a tinge of Almond flavour; skin rather tough. Ripe mid-July. This is the largest and best of the very early varieties. The tree is a good grower and productive.

SANTA ROSA (fig. 142).—Fruit large, round, with a deep suture; colour purplish-crimson; flesh crimson and yellow; stone small, free; very sweet, juicy, and fragrant; ripens early. Said to be one of the best.

Fig. 142.—Santa Rosa Plum

RED JUNE.—Fruit medium to large, cordate-oblong, distinctly pointed, often lop-sided; colour deep vermilion-red; flesh light-yellow, clinging or partially so, firm and moderately juicy, slightly acid to sweetish, of good quality though not very rich, the skin slightly sour. One of the very best of the Japanese Plums, being very handsome and productive. A bushy-topped, upright grower.

SATSUMA.—Fruit medium to large, round-oblong, with a deep suture; colour dark brown-red; flesh hard and blood-red, clinging, rich and pleasant when fully ripe. Ripe early September. A very long keeper. One of the coming Japanese Plums. An excellent Plum for culinary purposes. Tree moderately spreading.

PEACHES AND NECTARINES

ORIGIN

The origin of the garden races of Peaches and Nectarines is now generally admitted to be Chinese. They are both forms of *Prunus* (*Amygdalus*) *persica*, the Peach having a downy and the Nectarine a smooth skin. They have been cultivated from a remote period. According to De Candolle,[1] the Peach spreads easily in the countries in which it is cultivated, so that it is hard to say whether a given tree is of natural origin and anterior to cultivation, or whether it is naturalized. But it certainly was first cultivated in China; it was recorded there two thousand years before its introduction into the Greco-Roman world, a thousand years, perhaps, before its introduction into the lands of the Sanskrit-speaking race.

The facility with which Peach trees are multiplied from seeds in America, and have produced fine fleshy fruits, indicates that little change has been wrought by long cultivation or hybridization. The varieties of recent origin are either seedling sports or the result of crossing.

The late Mr. Rivers, who raised many seedlings of both Peaches and Nectarines, found that some of the varieties came true from seeds, viz.: Royal George " reproduces itself from seeds with rare exceptions "; Noblesse, " very rare to find the least deviation "; Grosse Mignonne, " out of twenty seedlings it is rare to find much deviation from the parent stock "; Walburton Admirable, " reproduces itself from seeds ". There are recorded instances of a Nectarine originating from the seed of a Peach, and vice versa. Also of the same tree bearing both Peaches and Nectarines, as well as fruit in part Nectarine and in part Peach.

The Peach is extensively grown between latitudes 30° and 40°, in Asia, Europe, Africa, and America. Under circumstances particularly favourable it will succeed considerably beyond these limits, but, its deciduous nature requiring a period of rest, it is not fitted for a tropical climate. On the other hand, beyond lat. 48° the ground is too cold for its roots, and it will not long continue to thrive unless budded on some hardier species; the tree, also, requires the shelter of a wall or other artificial means of protection. If the summer is hot enough to ripen the wood, it will stand a severe winter uninjured; but this is not found to be the case with trees in the open ground, if the young shoots have been grown under too low a temperature. In localities where the mean temperature of February is 40°, and that of March 44°, the Peach tree will be in full flower against a south wall in the last week in March; and if the mean temperature of April is 49°, that of May 55°, June 61°, July 64°, and August 63°, the season may be considered a favourable one. The general crop in that case will be ripe in late-August or first week in September, and the fruit be of a high degree of perfection.

By artificial means, or in a warmer climate, the above period of five months from the time of flowering to that of ripening may be reduced to four, but not advantageously to a shorter period, except in the case of very early varieties. From the above it will be seen that the Peach flowers at a comparatively cool period. The blossoms may be destroyed by too much heat, but not by cold, unless actually frozen; therefore no warmer coverings than are just sufficient to keep out frost are necessary.

OPEN-AIR CULTURE OF THE PEACH

Soil and Situation.—In the British Islands the Peach requires a wall. In the southern parts of the kingdom it will succeed on an east or west aspect, if the locality is not too elevated and exposed to cold winds, nor, on the other hand, too low and subject to damp and fogs, which prevent the wood from

[1] *Origin of Cultivated Plants.*

142

ripening. But the most favourable situation is a wall with a southern aspect. As the Peach requires to be trained against a wall, it follows that its roots must occupy a border in front. This should be made as recommended in the chapters on the formation of fruit progress favourably; therefore draining must be effected to remedy this. If this is impossible, for want of fall or outlet, then the level above which drainage may be carried out should be ascertained, and the depth of soil raised above that level; for it is better to

Fig. 143.—Peach. Peregrine

the fruit and kitchen garden. In old gardens, in which the borders have been formed, some improvements ought to be made before young trees are planted.

The subsoil should be examined as to its condition with regard to moisture. If it is too wet, trees cannot thrive, neither will the raise the border at the expense of losing, say, 1 foot of height of wall, than to plunge the roots to that depth in unsuitable soil conditions.

Where the soil is shallow, and resting on a subsoil that is dry and gravelly, it often happens that the tree suffers from want of moisture in dry weather. Exposed to the heat of the sun, often above 100°, the leaves evaporate an astonishing amount of moisture as long as the roots can supply it; but when all is exhausted the condition of the tree must undergo a change for the worse. Although the supply of moisture from the roots may have ceased, evaporation will still continue, drawing, to a considerable extent, from the juices of the tree; then comes red spider, and this, if not arrested, would ruin the tree in one season. In order to prevent this, much labour must be employed, large quantities of water must be wheeled about, the engine must be kept at work, and, after all, the trees will not be so healthy as those in properly made borders. In many cases

Fig. 144.—Fruit, part Peach, part Nectarine

one year's expenditure in watering and syringing, if laid out in thoroughly preparing the border before planting, would effect a saving.

The dry gravelly subsoil ought to be dug out to the depth of 2½ or 3 feet. Although the bottom may be dry, yet, with a good depth of soil, the trees will not suffer readily from drought. When soil of the depth of 2½ or 3 feet is well moistened, either by rain or watering, it takes a considerable time before the trees can suffer from drought.

If the ground is old and worn out, or if trees have long been grown in it, it should be changed or refreshed with other soil. If there is a stratum of loam below, let a considerable portion of it be brought up to the surface, and as much of the top soil turned down to the bottom, there to be dug over, mixing it at the same time with a portion of the loam and some broken limestone, or mortar rubbish, in order to ensure thorough

drainage and to supply the tree with lime, required when the fruit is stoning. The proportion of mortar rubbish to be added will depend on the character of the soil, and will vary from one to two ordinary barrowloads to each cart-load, the former for light sandy loam, the latter quantity for more retentive soils. These should also have one-eighth part of burnt earth added. This helps to keep the border open and sweet, and supplies potash and other fertilizers.

If the soil is poor and sandy, the trees will not find nourishment to enable them to support a good crop; yet, as it can afterwards be enriched, it is preferable to soil that is too adhesive. Stiff clays are most unfavourable, and the most difficult of any to deal with; in fact, the Peach ought not to be planted in such. The best plan is to remove the whole, and replace with soil of more friable nature.

At Montreuil, where the Peach is extensively cultivated, the soil is by no means rich; it appears to be a calcareous sandy loam, of a yellowish-brown colour, too poor for corn crops. In the grounds of M. Lepère, one of the most skilful cultivators, the borders are prepared, to the distance of 5 or 6 feet from the wall, by trenching 2 feet deep, and mixing manure with the soil. Afterwards, when the trees bear heavy crops, a little manure is forked into the border. The success of the Montreuil cultivators is, no doubt, largely owing to the sun-heat being greater there.

Although a border 6 feet wide will answer for Peaches, yet a greater width will answer better. Peaches grown in pots, with the advantage of rich soil, may produce a dozen fruits of fair size; but a well-grown tree against a wall may bear as many as forty dozens, and to obtain nourishment to support such an effort the roots must have considerable scope. As space on a south border is required for various early crops, the breadth may be 12, 15, or 18 feet, according to the size of the garden, and the made portion of the border should not be less than 6 feet, but 8 feet would be better. It should be made and kept firm, and no digging should be practised about the roots.

Planting.—The border having been prepared, the next consideration is the distance apart at which the trees should be planted. In good soil and a warm situation this may be 20 feet; where the soil is not rich, or where the climate is rather cold, 18 feet, or it may be 15 feet, would suffice; but less than this must be considered too limited for fan-training.

The best season for planting is the autumn,

for the growth of the Peach commences early. If planting cannot be done before spring, the trees should be taken up early in February, and healed in a cool, shaded place,

Fig. 145.—Peach. Crimson Galande. (⅔)

till the planting can be performed. When the plants are cut back before they are taken up they should not. be cut so low as they would require to be when planted against the wall, in order to leave a choice of well-

Fig. 146.—Nectarine. Pine Apple. (⅔)

situated buds, to which they can then be cut.

The trees should be planted at the same depth as they were before removal, and about 6 inches from the wall. Some recommend the tree to be planted with the

budded scar outward, but this is immaterial; indeed, if there is any wound, it will heal sooner on the south side than on the opposite one, especially if shaded from the sun's rays, because on the former thicker layers of wood are deposited. The mode of planting detailed for the Plum may be followed for the Peach. When planted it is well to mulch as far as the roots extend with stable litter.

Production of Fruit.—As the young shoot grows, leaves are produced singly, in twos, or in threes, at every node, and in the axil of each leaf either flower-buds or leaf-buds are formed. In the following spring the blossom-buds expand before the leaf-buds. Fruit is occasionally borne on short shoots resembling spurs, and terminated by a cluster of blossom-buds, with a leaf-bud in the middle, which remains almost stationary. Spurs of this sort, however, should not be encouraged on trees trained to walls or

Fig. 147.—Peach. Double Eyes

Fig. 148.—Peach. Triple Eyes

trellises, as they are apt to snap off when the fruit gets heavy.

Fig. 147 represents part of a branch with double eyes, that is, a leaf-bud *a*, and a flower-bud *b*. Triple eyes are represented in fig. 148, and consist of a leaf-bud *a* between two flower-buds *b b*.

It is necessary to be able readily to distinguish leaf-buds from flower-buds; for if, in pruning, a shoot is cut back to a flower-bud, no young shoot can proceed from it, and it will die back to the nearest leaf-bud below the section.

Leaf-buds are of a conical, pointed form, and consist of scales surrounding a growing point, which, under favourable circumstances, pushes and becomes a shoot; but many of them remain dormant, especially if the shoot is weak and left at full length. When, however, the shoot is shortened to a leaf-bud, that bud is almost sure to push.

Flower-buds are ovate, and gradually become globose, assuming then a hoary appearance, from the scales opening and exposing

24

their downy integuments. They are likewise much plumper than leaf-buds.

It will be observed, on referring to the
accompanying figures, that some buds are
single leaf-buds, others are single flower-
buds. Frequently the buds are double—

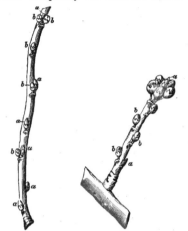

Fig. 149.—Peach.   Fig. 150.—Peach.
a, Wood; b, flower-buds.   a, Leaf, and b, flower-buds.

one being a flower-bud, the other a leaf-bud,
or both may be flower-buds; and, lastly,
some are triple buds. These generally consist of two flower-buds with a leaf-bud between them. As there must be wood before
there can be fruit, it is natural for a young
tree to produce chiefly barren or leaf buds;
but when the tree has attained a considerable size it is more disposed to produce
flower-buds, and pruning becomes necessary
in order that flower-buds may not too much
predominate, for in that case a deficiency of
young shoots would be the consequence.

Pruning and Training.—The Peach tree
requires either winter-pruning in January or
February, before the flowers begin to open,
or for trees under glass as soon as the leaves
fall; or summer-pruning, performed during
the growing season. Training may be done
any time after the trees are pruned in
autumn or winter, and before they start into
active growth in spring. The summer-
training of the young shoots ought to be
attended to throughout the growing season.

The Peach tree is trained in a variety of
ways, the fan-method being the best. Commencing with a maiden plant, consisting of
a simple shoot, as at *a*, fig. 151, let that be

cut back, as at 1, above two eligible buds,
situated one on each side, and about 9 inches
from the surface of the ground. Two shoots
will likely push from these buds in the course
of the summer, and they should be encouraged to grow as much as possible during the
early part of the season by training them
rather upright, as in the direction *b c*; but
in August they should be lowered by degrees
to the position *d e*. They are thus brought
nearly to a horizontal position, with the exceptions of their extremities, which are
turned upwards in order still to encourage
growth, and so long as they continue to grow
it matters not whether they are straight or
otherwise, for they will be cut off at the
winter-pruning.

The dotted lines, fig. 152, corresponding
with those in fig. 151, represent the state of
the tree, as regards its shoots, at the end of
the first summer's growth, reckoning from
the time when the maiden plant was headed
back. At the ensuing winter-pruning, the
shoots *d e* are cut back, as at 2, fig. 152, and
in the course of the summer four shoots,
f, g, h, i, are the result. Here it should be
observed that the extremities of the two
lower branches *f g* are turned upwards during
the growing season; whilst the two upper
ones *h i* are not so favoured, otherwise, from
being situated on the upper side, they would
grow much stronger than the two lower
branches, an occurrence which should be

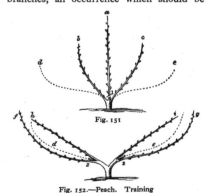

Fig. 151

Fig. 152.—Peach. Training

carefully guarded against. By the first
cutting the plant is provided with two
branches; and by the second, performed
twelve months later, it is provided with four.
At the third cutting, which takes place after
the second summer's growth, each of the four
shoots is shortened, as at 3, 3, 3, 3, fig. 153.

During the ensuing summer two shoots and a leader are trained from each of these branches, which eventually form the branches marked *b c f g m n q r*. The young shoots which are to form *f* and *g* should start almost close together from *a*, and the same applies to the corresponding branches on the other side of the tree. When the branches are trained in the following season, the spaces between *d* and *f*, also between *p* and *n*, are widened so as to leave room for another branch on each side, *e o*. All young growths are shortened back to firm wood as before, and shoots are left when disbudding to form leaders, for bearing wood whenever there is room, for the two new branches, *e* and *o*, and for four more in the centre, *h i k l*. Thus at the end of the season there will be eighteen principal branches, which

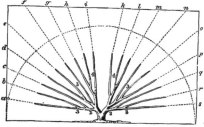

Fig. 153.—Peach. Training. (¼ inch to 1 foot)

are to be trained as the dotted lines show. These will be quite sufficient to furnish the whole tree.

Other modes of training are practised, but they are open to the objection of encouraging one or two leaders on each side which serve as bases for the other branches. In a properly-trained fan-shaped tree all the branches should be of equal strength, and disposed so as to divide the sap equally over all portions of the tree. They are also conveniently placed for removal should a branch die, as the others can be lowered to fill its place, and the centre refilled with young branches.

In training the Peach an equality of vigour amongst all the branches should be aimed at. The branches should be frequently examined in detail; a comparative inspection ought to be made of every three, of the lowest three with the next three, and so on; and again, every three on the one side with the three opposite on the other side. If one side of the tree is found to be weaker than the other, the branches of the weaker side should in

general be elevated above their assigned position, and, on the contrary, three of the stronger side should be depressed. The latter ought also to be disbudded, and their summer shoots nailed in before those on the weaker side of the tree; over-vigorous shoots should be checked at an early stage of their growth. All superfluous shoots ought to be cut away. Whilst a sufficient supply of shoots for succession must be encouraged, none beyond these should be allowed to exist, with the exception of those necessary for leaders. If, in the early part of the season, it is seen that a succession shoot will unquestionably become too strong, it should be stopped.

With regard to the weak side, an opposite mode of proceeding should be adopted. Shoots not absolutely required for succession may very properly be allowed to grow. The succession shoots generally should be trained at full length, and, where there is space, the shoots at the extremities of the bearing shoots may also be left unshortened. If a few over-strong shoots should start on the weak side, they had better be checked; but all others on that side encouraged.

Supposing the trees to be planted 20 feet apart, and the wall to be 12 feet high, the space which a tree like that represented in the figure might occupy would be 240 square feet; but if limited within the semicircle it would only cover 166 square feet, leaving nearly one-third of the space unoccupied. Rather than this should be the case, it would be almost better to put up with the loss of the three lower branches on each side. But, in order to guard against this, something may be done; allowing the radius of the semicircle to be 10 feet, then the distance between the branches where they intersect the dotted arc line—that is to say, when they have extended 10 feet from the centre—will be very nearly 21 inches, which would be wider than necessary. To fill that space, branches may be originated from the upper side of *a, b, c*, at about 5 feet from the stem. There will then be six branches in connection with the base *a, b, c*, and they may be distributed over the space of wall from *a* to *d*, the latter being trained closer to *e*, so that between these two an intermediate branch may not be required; then, if *e* and *f* be subdivided, there will only be five branches in connection with the base *d, e, f*, instead of six, as in the case of the base *a, b, c*. This will give the latter considerable advantage; and, with the other means already detailed, an equality of vigour as regards the first two subdivisions of the tree may be maintained, whilst the symmetry of the whole is also preserved. What has been said of the branches on the one side of the tree applies, of course, to those on the other side.

From the principal branches shoots for bearing should be allowed to proceed, and also for subsidiary branches, where space admits of such. In order to maintain a symmetrical tree, these smaller shoots and branches should start from the upper side of the main branches. In our climate the extremities of the shoots do not usually become perfectly ripened, and this is one reason why they should generally be more or less shortened back. In doing this it is best to cut to a bud situated at the back of the branch, or nearly so; for if cut to one at either side the young shoot forms a bend from where it proceeds, and if cut to a bud in front it curves outwards; but when cut to a bud on the side next the wall the branch grows quite straight.

Pruning.—The directions for pruning the Peach tree will be easily comprehended on reference to figs. 149 and 150. In fig. 150 the buds marked *a* are leaf-buds, and all the others flower-buds. In fig. 149 we have two single leaf-buds near the base of the shoot; then a twin bud, consisting of a leaf-bud and a flower-bud; next a single leaf-bud; then a triple bud, composed of two flower-buds and a leaf-bud in the centre; then a single flower-bud; and, finally, two flower-buds, with a leaf-bud between them, above which the shoot is cut. It would be wrong to cut to the next lower joint, or immediately above the single flower-bud *a*, for that bud would not produce a shoot, and the branch would ultimately die back to the next leaf-bud. In fig. 150 there are only two leaf-buds; one, which forms the growing point or apex, situated in the midst of a cluster of flower-buds, the other near the base of the shoot. In such cases the entire shoot must be left or cut back above the leaf-bud at the base. The latter is generally preferable, as a succession shoot would be obtained.

In the Peach tree all wood that is more than one year old serves only to support shoots that do or may bear fruit; but enough of main branches, and others subsidiary to them, should be provided for, in order that a sufficiency of bearing shoots in every part of the tree may be ensured.

The management of the bearing shoots, and of those intended to form a succession to them, remains to be considered.

In fig. 154, *a* represents a portion of a branch before the winter-pruning; *b* and *c* are bearing shoots, which were shortened at the previous winter-pruning, bore fruit in the following summer, and also produced the shoots *d* and *e* for succession. The shoots *b* and *c*, having once borne, will do so no more, and therefore they are cut off close to the origin of the succession shoots *d* and *e*. These succession shoots are shortened at the winter-pruning, in order that, whilst they bear fruit in the ensuing season, they may

Fig. 154.—Peach. Pruning

also produce, in their turn, shoots for succession. In general, every bearing shoot throughout the tree should do this, and the nearer the young shoot springs from the base of the bearing shoot the better. It may be encouraged from the side of the bearing shoot next the branch, as at *e*, or from the opposite side, as at *d*. This should be arranged when disbudding, so as to prevent the shoot from getting too far away from the main branch. If at any time a bud starts closer to the branch than where *d* and *e*

Fig. 155.—Peach. Pruning for Succession Shoot

originated, it should be encouraged, and the stub, which results from repeatedly shortening back to near the base of the bearing shoots, can then be reduced. In fact, wherever there is an opportunity of obtaining a succession shoot from the old branch, it should not be neglected, provided there is room for it.

Fig. 155 represents a branch with two shoots, one of which, *b*, is intended for succession, and is pruned at *e*, whilst the shoot *a* is stopped at *c*, and at the next pruning is cut off at *d*. A number of other succession shoots may be allowed to grow to the length of 10 inches or 1 foot, and then be stopped. Several summer laterals will result; but they will push mostly just below where the shoot was stopped; whilst, lower down, enough of flower-buds will in most instances be formed. By these means the amount of foliage will be much less than would otherwise be the case.

Fig. 156 represents a branch with two shoots, one of which is pruned at *a*, whilst the other is cut close to the base at *c*, thus leaving the leaf-bud *b* to form a succession shoot.

From this it appears that the pruning and training of the Peach tree, when it is once formed, is reduced to three very simple proceedings:

1. Shortening the intended bearing shoot at the winter-pruning, if the tree is growing

Fig. 156.—Peach. Pruning

outside. For all indoor culture this shortening is rarely required, as the shoots get well ripened and may be laid in full length.

2. Training a succession one in summer.

3. The removal of the shoots that have borne fruit, except such of them as are leading shoots of branches.

The length to which the bearing shoots ought to be shortened depends on their vigour, and occasionally the position of the leaf-buds; for in order to cut immediately above one of them, the shoot may have to be cut much shorter, or left at greater length than would otherwise be advisable.

The distance along the branches, from one bearing shoot to the other, may be 12 or 14 inches. On a branch that is weaker than it ought to be, more succession shoots should be encouraged than on the adjoining stronger ones, and more space should be allowed them, by training those from the stronger branch in a limited space; but all young branches of the previous year's growth, when trained in at the spring-pruning, should have a clear space between them of not less than 4 inches.

Stopping or Pinching.—This is in many respects the same as disbudding, and is practised during growth. Its object is to accelerate the formation of flower-buds, and to prevent confusion with respect to the branches. If not done with judgment, stopping may produce the very opposite effect, hindering the formation of buds, or causing them to be developed before the proper time; but when the operation is well done it is one of the most useful in the art of developing trees.

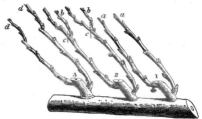

Fig. 157.—Peach. Stopping or Pinching

Fig. 157 represents a branch the shoots on which have been shortened. No. 1 shows two shoots which have been stopped above the eighth leaf, at *a a*. The flow of sap occasioned by this operation has had the effect of swelling the fruit, at the same time avoiding bursting the eyes made below. At the end of eight or ten days the two or three terminal eyes are developed as shown in No. 2; when these shoots have acquired sufficient length the second pinching is per-

Fig. 158.—Peach. Stopping before the Fruit is set

formed, which takes place on the lowest shoots *b*, *b*, a little above the fifth leaf; the two remaining shoots are pruned at *c*, *c*. No. 3 shows the shoots after the last operation has been performed.

Fig. 158, *e*, gives an example of stopping where the fruit has not set. The upper branch *a* is cut back, as well as the lower branch *b*, in order to give vent to the sap and promote the growth of the eyes near the base, which ought to yield fruit; *f* shows the effects of the first stopping. Then the first shoot is cut back to *c*, and the second is stopped at *d*; *g* gives the result of the second stopping, a feeble result, as the sap is not in full flow.

Fig. 159 represents a branch which has been pruned above the fifth bud from the base. In this example the pinching ought to be short because the sap is most divided.

Fig. 159.—Peach. Stopping for Succession Shoot

The terminal shoot has been pinched, and afterwards cut back to *a*, which has had the effect of causing the sap to flow back on fruit at the base. The two shoots *b* and *c* have been pinched twice, which has caused the fruit to swell and promoted the growth of the succession shoot *d*.

Disbudding.—This consists in the removal of buds, or rather shoots in a very young state. It is evident that if all the young shoots were allowed to grow, they would soon become excessively crowded; it is therefore necessary that all should be removed except those for which there is sufficient space. The operation ought to be commenced by the removal of those situated in front of the strongest branches, especially if these are in connection with branches too strong for the others. Then in a day or two those in front of branches or shoots lower down should be removed, but care must be taken to preserve the lowest side shoots on each for succession. Those having fruit at their bases should also be left untouched.

The process of disbudding should be regulated by the weather and the condition of the tree. If the weather proves ungenial, and vegetation is languid, it is not advisable to disbud much; if, on the contrary, the days and nights are warm, disbudding should be thorough. Vegetation may commence with a considerable degree of activity, but frequently cold weather ensues, and the slightly developed leaves linger or remain in a stationary condition. When they are in this state it is better to refrain from disbudding till vegetation again becomes active. Every bud that is being developed maintains a circulation of sap in its vicinity, but when a bud, or the young shoot resulting from it, is pinched or cut off, circulation must cease or find other channels.

In order that the disbudded shoots may continue healthy, the disbudding should be performed by degrees. The forerights, in the first place, and then the others, should be gradually thinned away, till no more shoots and foliage are left than there is light for.

The leading young shoot intended for extension should be trained at full length. The terminal young shoot of bearing branches ought to be allowed to grow till its lower leaves are nearly full-sized, and then it should be shortened to 3 inches. Other young shoots having fruit at their bases should also be cut or pinched back to three or four leaves; and when the fruit is thinned, many of such shoots, from the bases of which the fruit is removed, may be dispensed with. It will sometimes happen that on shoots laid in for bearing there will be no fruit. When

Fig. 160.—Nectarine. Humboldt. (⅜)

this is found to be the case, they may be cut off at the base, and the succession shoots trained in their place. When any of the succession shoots appear likely to become too vigorous, their tops must be pinched off, but it would be desirable that this should be done not lower than 1 foot or 15 inches from the base.

After the fruit is gathered, all wood that is not required for the following year's fruiting, or for extending the size of the tree, must be removed, so as to give the shoots

Fig. 161.—Peach Tree on Wall Outdoors. Shoots not yet nailed in

Fig. 162.—Peach Tree on Wall Outdoors. Shoots nailed in to expose fruits

left the full benefit of the food supplied by the roots, and of air and sunshine.

Thinning the Fruit.—To what extent thinning should be carried depends on the vigour of the tree and size of the fruit. If the tree is weakly, its fruit should be left thin as compared with that on a tree that is vigorous; and on weak branches fewer fruit should be left than on the more vigorous branches of the same tree. If the tree is healthy the fruit will set in abundance, and few will drop when young unless injured by frost. Large-fruited varieties require more thinning than small. Nectarines, being generally smaller, need not be much thinned.

A large vigorous tree may be allowed to mature as many as twenty dozen fruits, and these, if the foliage is healthy, ought to be large and fine. Trees are sometimes allowed to bear so many fruits that they are weakened, and the fruits, though numerous, are small, thin-fleshed, and sour.

The first thinning should take place when the fruit is scarcely the size of a Hazel-nut. The smallest, of course, should be dispensed with. In removing them, care should be taken not to tear the bark off the shoots, as is likely to be the case if the fruit is pulled backwards towards the base of the shoot. It should be a little twisted and pressed in the opposite direction, or it may be cut or clipped off. For medium-sized sorts one fruit per square foot of trellis is quite enough, in order to secure perfection in size and quality. Small sorts, such as Alexander Peach and Elruge Nectarine, may be left 9 inches apart each way; large varieties, such as Sea Eagle and The Nectarine Peach, should be twice that distance apart.

Other Cultural Matters.—After the operations of pruning and training, one of the most important points is the soil with respect to moisture. In one week the roots may have just enough moisture, and if the weather is hot the tree will make shoots and foliage with great rapidity; in the second week rain may not fall in sufficient quantity to get down to the roots, which have then to meet an increased demand from a diminished supply; and in the third week the tree exhibits symptoms of disease. The leaves droop and lose colour; and although this appearance may have the effect of causing the watering tubs to be employed, yet when full-grown

leaves have once been allowed to droop and assume a yellowish sickly tinge, they cannot again be brought to their former healthy condition, whilst the attacks of insects, induced by dryness, must also be taken into account.

It is easier to keep a tree healthy than to restore it after it has become sickly. Let the border therefore be frequently inspected, and whenever water is applied give enough to thoroughly soak the soil to the full depth of the roots. If the crop is heavy and the fruit has stoned, give weak liquid manure or a moderate dressing of Thomson's Vine Manure, forking it under the surface and putting some short litter over before watering with clear water. If necessary, let the soil be forked over in ridges, and let the hollows be filled and refilled with water till the border is thoroughly moistened to the bottom. When the top soil has dried, so as to be in working condition, it should be levelled, and a good mulching of stable litter given, to keep the ground moist longer and assist the swelling of the fruit.

When the trees are moist at the roots less syringing is necessary. It is a good plan to syringe not only the trees, but the whole wall, with Gishurst Compound, 2 oz. to the gallon of water; or a mixture of soft soap 12 oz., tobacco juice ½ pint, water 3 gallons, before the buds expand in the spring. If the weather is cold this should be done early in the day, so that the trees may get dry and escape getting frozen at night. Syringing should be discontinued after this until the blossoms fall, but after the fruit is set it should again be daily resorted to at about 4 p.m., using clear water. This helps to keep off red spider.

Attention to these matters ensures healthy foliage, and consequently healthy shoots.

As the fruit ripens it should be exposed to the direct rays of the sun by putting aside any leaves that shade it. If the foliage cannot be removed entire without weakening the tree, take away half of each leaf which obstructs the light. In the case of succession shoots, whole leaves should never be removed, as it destroys the buds at their base. When the fruit has almost reached its full size, a pad of cotton-wool should be used if it is likely to bruise against the branches.

GATHERING THE FRUIT

The usual method is by carefully taking the fruit in the hand so as not to bruise it, then by a gentle twist it will usually separate from the stem, so easily, indeed, that when the whole pressure is divided among the parts brought in contact with it, no part is bruised. Another excellent plan, but one little in practice, is to separate the fruit at the stalk by means of a pair of vine scissors. The fruit is often well coloured next the sun before it is ripe, the part next the wall being still green; but afterwards the green acquires a yellow tinge, by which the ripening can be known. Peaches may be gathered in the heat of the day. The better time, however, is in the morning, when the fruit are firmer and not so susceptible to bruising. They may be kept for a week or more by placing them in a cool, dry room or cellar. The flavour is easily spoiled if they are placed near anything with a strong smell, such as deal boards, damp hay, or moss. Clean paper shavings are best for laying them on.

DISEASES

Gumming is sometimes a troublesome malady, and is difficult to cure; indeed, if the tree is affected to any considerable extent, the sooner it is removed and replaced by a healthy one the better. If the symptoms are but slight, the bark should be frequently well washed with a brush and water in moist weather. The disease is apt to occur on trees planted in soil too richly manured, and when strong shoots are allowed to grow as much as they will and are then cut back. It is not well to use any manure below the surface when planting the tree, but if that has been done, and the tree is inclined to over-luxuriance, the greater care must be taken over summer-pruning, so that there may be no large pieces to cut out at the winter-pruning. It is also advisable to lift the whole of the roots as soon as the foliage commences to decay in the autumn, preserving all the fibres possible, and pruning away any long straight pieces which are devoid of fibre, also all that strike downwards into the subsoil. See that the drainage is perfect before replanting, and supply fresh soil if needed. Large wounds on the branches of Peach trees are apt to give rise to gumming.

Mildew may be got rid of by sulphur vaporizing.

Blistered leaves are occasioned by cold, particularly when this occurs after a spell of warm weather. The growth of the midrib is arrested, and, the circulation of the sap being obstructed, the leaves, or part of them, become swollen inert masses. There is no cure. The preventive is, of course, warm covering. The leaves that are most affected should be taken off at once, if they can be spared without injuring the growth of the tree. If the disease is very prevalent, remove only the worst, and leave the others until later.

Sun-burning.—The bark of Peach trees may be scorched by the exposure to hot sunshine, which has most effect on the stem and thick naked branches; they should be protected with tiles, slates, or any other suitable material, or by training some of the young shoots over them.

PEACH CULTURE UNDER GLASS

With the exception of the Grape-vine no kinds of fruit-trees have been so generally grown under glass in this country as the Peach and Nectarine. In the northern parts of the kingdom the fruit cannot be brought to full perfection on the open wall, but under glass, with more or less artificial heat, according to the climate and period of the season, fruit both large and excellent can be obtained in the extreme north. The tree requires a good soil, maintained in a proper state as regards moisture, abundance of light—that of the solar rays as direct as circumstances will permit—and a full command of heat sufficient for the growth of the trees and maturation of the fruit, even when the house is not closely shut up. A free circulation of air is essential for dispelling the moisture, which would otherwise lodge too long upon the foliage, or upon the blossoms and the fruit; for although the foliage must be washed, and the air of the house rendered moist at times, yet a moist stagnant atmosphere is injurious.

The border in which the trees are intended to be planted should be well drained, as already detailed under Open-air Culture (p. 142), and care must be taken that by no possibility the roots can come in contact with water percolating through the substratum, or stagnant there. If a test-hole were dug to the depth of 3 or 4 feet from the surface, and if in this water should stand for some weeks at any period of the season, then means must be adopted to prevent the roots from ever going down so far. Draining is the best, provided there be enough fall; if not, concrete or paving ought to be resorted to, if the expense can be afforded. If the bottom of the whole border cannot be concreted or paved, a portion may be done below, and to some distance from the place where the tree is planted, to prevent the growth of tap-roots;

Fig. 163.—Nectarine. Violette Hâtive. (⅝)

and, if this be done, the horizontal roots can always be enticed to the surface.

It may be safest to build Peach and other forcing-houses on a terrace. The bottom having been put in a satisfactory condition,

the soil may be laid on to a depth of not less than 2½ feet, a mass of this thickness retaining a steadier supply of moisture than a shallow border.

The soil ought to consist of good mellow turfy loam, which is substantial but not of a binding nature. If the loam is rich, manure will not be required in the first instance. If the soil is rather strong and adhesive, add mortar rubbish and burnt earth; some ½-inch bone manure will afford nourishment even after the trees come into bearing, when of course they require it more than at first. For very early forcing the border should be made so that the roots will be inside, and safe from chill caused by cold rains or melted snow.

The choice of trees partly depends on the position which they are intended to occupy in the structure. The best mode is to plant dwarfs in front, and train on wires from 12 to 15 inches below the glass. In order that forced Peaches and Nectarines may be well flavoured they must not be grown far from the glass. Some train dwarfs planted in front of the house on trellises, curved so as

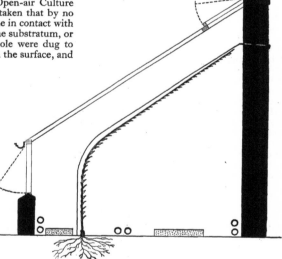

Fig. 166.—Early Peach House (Scale ¼ inch to 1 foot)

not to intercept the sun's rays from the trees which are trained against the back wall. We have known trees which were trained on a trellis at considerable distance from the glass; but they did not yield good crops till

Fig. 164.—Peach Case, Royal Gardens, Frogmore

Fig. 165.—Specimen Tree of Downton Nectarine under Glass, Royal Gardens, Frogmore

their branches were raised and trained near the glass; excellent crops were then obtained. It is not the greatest quantity of shoots and foliage that can possibly be grown under a certain extent of glass that should be the aim, but the greatest amount that the sun can shine upon with the fullest effect.

If curved trellis-work were constructed there would be a greater surface for training, but the amount of the action of the light on the foliage would on the whole be diminished. A distance of from 12 to 15 inches, as already stated, between roof and trellis, answers very well; farther would prove disadvantageous so far as light is concerned; on the other hand, the trees would be liable to injury from frost and cold wind if they were nearer the glass.

Fig. 166 shows the form of house for early forcing. Succession houses may be span-roofed, or if lean-to houses are preferred they should be built with flatter roofs than the above, in order that they may be cooler when the fruit is ripening.

The trees may be planted after they have been trained for several years with a view to the position they are intended to occupy. The length of the stem must depend on the height of the trellis from the ground at the place where the trees are to be planted.

The late Mr. Errington, one of the most skilful gardeners in the country, selected the largest, cleanest, and best-formed tree on the open wall, where it covered 480 square feet, removed it to a Peach-house, of course with due care, and the tree ripened in the same year about eight dozen of very good fruits. In the succeeding seven years it produced at least 2300 large and fine fruit. This is proof that trees of considerable size may be planted in a Peach-house. The time for planting is any time after the leaves have fallen in autumn, but not later than January, unless in cases of necessity.

The pruning of the tree should be conducted as for trees on the open wall. If the summer-pruning is properly attended to, very little wood will require to be taken away in the winter; but as soon as the leaves fall all the trees under glass must be examined, and any superfluous wood removed. No large branches should be cut away unless absolutely necessary, as the Peach and Nectarine will not stand severe pruning, nor do they break readily from thick branches if headed back. It is not advisable to shorten the young shoots of trees growing under glass if they have ripened to their full length, except in the case of young trees to make them

break more regularly. Strong shoots, if not thoroughly ripened, should be removed entirely.

If ripe Peaches are required by the middle of May, the trees ought to shed their leaves during the second or third week in October at the latest; but if they do not fall so early it is better to start forcing with a few of them still hanging than to strip them off. The house should be closed at night after the middle of November, and no fire-heat should be used if the weather is mild. Plenty of air should be given by day, the object being to get the trees to start very gradually, or the buds will drop without expanding at this season of the year. After the house has been closed at night for a fortnight fire-heat may be applied, but cautiously, less air being given during the day-time. The pipes should be only slightly warmed at first, or the air will be dried too much, and the trees excited. A minimum temperature of 45°, or even 40° if it be frosty, is quite sufficient, but this must depend on the outside temperature. The trees should have a light syringing when the air is dry, though the frequency of this will depend very much on the state of the weather outside. A little sun-heat should be closed in early in the afternoon.

In summer, care must be taken to maintain as far as possible an equal growth by checking over-luxuriant shoots in good time, and encouraging those that are weak. As soon as pruning is finished, the whole of the glass and woodwork should be thoroughly cleaned with hot water and soft soap. After this the trees must be cleaned with soft soap or Gishurst Compound, using 4 oz. to the gallon of water. Scrub all the old branches thoroughly, as the large brown scale may often be found on them, and if left undisturbed will rapidly increase the following season. The young wood for next year's fruiting must be carefully sponged, drawing the sponge upwards from the base so as not to injure the buds. All walls must be lime-washed. The surface-soil of the border should be removed to the depth of an inch, and replaced with fresh, sweet loam. The house will then be ready for starting.

Fire-heat must be sparingly applied whilst the flowers are expanding, and until the fruit is set. When the Peach is in flower on the open wall the nights are usually cold, but if not so severe as to freeze the blossoms they set well.

There is less danger in a low temperature during the blossoming period, provided it is not so low as freezing, than from a high one.

The latter has often caused the total failure of a crop, the blossoms dropping prematurely after the house has been kept close and too warm by fire-heat at night. It is not, however, necessary that the temperature should be so low as 34°. As time is an important object in forcing, it is desirable, where fuel can be afforded, that as much heat be applied as can be done with safety to the health of the tree and the crop. It has been proved that 50° is a safe temperature at flowering-time. The day temperature may be allowed to rise by sun-heat to 60° or 65°, with plenty of air; but any sudden influx of cold air should be avoided. Ventilation may

Fig. 167.—Nectarine. Spenser. (⅔)

be necessary to prevent the temperature from rising. Independent of sun-heat the range between the minimum at night and maximum by day may be 5°. For example, if at a certain stage of growth (as when the trees are in flower) the maximum temperature with sun-heat in January is 65°, and the minimum temperature at night is 50°, a little air should be given at the top when the thermometer rises to 53°, to be increased when it has risen 5° more, and a chink of front air should be put on when it reaches 60°, and increased afterwards if the temperature is likely to rise above 65°.

After the blossoms drop, the condition of the expanding foliage should be watched, and if it be tender compared with that in a similar stage on Peach trees on the open wall, less heat and more air must be given, till by a slower growth the proper firmness of texture is produced.

When the young fruit are the size of small marbles the heat may be gradually increased to 60° at night, and 65° by day or 70° with sun-heat. After the fruit is stoned the temperature may be raised to 65° minimum, 70° fire-heat on dull days, and 80° or 85° by sun-heat. When the fruit has stoned, a higher temperature can be safely allowed, provided the trees are duly supplied with moisture, and are in a vigorous healthy condition.

A good washing occasionally with water from a hose-pipe, judiciously applied before closing the house in the afternoon, is the best means of keeping the trees healthy and free from red spider and other insects. Care must be used not to get the surface of the border soddened, or the fruit will not swell evenly. The border will require water at intervals of two to three weeks, and must have enough each time to give it a thorough soaking. After stoning is complete, weak liquid manure may be applied with advantage; when the fruit is about half grown, and commences to colour, more water will be required.

Air must be admitted cautiously during windy weather, so as to avoid cold draughts, which favour the attacks of mildew and aphis. When the fruit commences to ripen, a little air should be left on throughout the night; this will greatly improve its flavour; syringing must then be discontinued until all the fruit is gathered.

The fruit must be kept exposed to the sun and light by removing all growths which are not required for furnishing the tree, tying the others to the trellis whenever it is required. The sun will not burn the fruit of Peaches under glass in this country, if they are kept fully exposed during the whole of their growth, and the structure is properly ventilated. Some kinds of Nectarines, however, are apt to be damaged on exceptionally bright days, as they have not a downy coat like the Peach to protect them. Lord Napier is especially liable to damage from this cause; a light shading of tiffany is therefore advisable on very bright days when it is ripening. Syringing should also be discontinued earlier with this variety, especially in the morning, the time when the sun is most likely to be harmful.

Before the fruit is half grown, and soon after stoning is completed, the trees should be carefully looked over to see that no more fruit is left on than can be properly ripened; they must also be exposed to the sun as much as possible by trussing up all that have fallen on their sides, by means of a new and clean deal plant label, taking away leaves or parts of leaves from those on the top of the trellis, and doing all that is possible to afford the maximum of sunshine to every fruit. This will require periodical attention until the fruit commences to get soft and syringing is discontinued.

Directions for gathering the fruit are given elsewhere. The summer-pruning should be done as soon as possible after the fruit is gathered.

Water will now be required less frequently but at no period of the year should the roots be allowed to get dry, this being the cause of bud-dropping in the spring. Little else remains to be done before the leaves fall, beyond giving abundance of air day and night. Red spider and other insects must be watched for, and dealt with as directed. If lateral growths start they must be cut back to the first leaf, or they will rob the bearing wood for the next season.

Manures.— Peach and Nectarine trees planted out under glass are apt to grow too strongly after a few years, producing gross shoots which do not ripen, and therefore fail to form flower-buds; or those which are formed are not properly matured, and they drop instead of opening. This is sometimes caused by too liberal feeding, especially if manures rich in nitrogen are used; the only time during the life of the Peach tree when an application of nitrogenous manure is beneficial is after stoning is completed, and only then if the tree has a full crop of fruit. A quick manure, such as nitrate of soda, is therefore required, or drainings from the

farm-yard. If the former is applied, phosphoric acid and potash must be given at the same time, or a strong leaf growth will be induced, to the disadvantage of the fruit.

Thomson's Vine Manure, or a similar preparation, if used with discretion, is safe and effectual for Peaches and Nectarines. The question of manuring, however, depends on the nature of the soil in which the trees are growing. Trees in poor stony soil, when the crop is good, should be liberally fed, so also should trees growing in pots and tubs. A light mulching of short litter is helpful to trees in borders during hot weather, both under glass and outside; but if the trees are growing freely this mulching must not be of rich manure, and whatever is applied should be removed as soon as the fruit is gathered, when all feeding with liquid and other manures must be discontinued.

Treatment during the Resting Period.— While the wood is maturing, and after the leaves fall, the houses must be well ventilated. Cold will not hurt the trees if they are dry and the wood is well ripened. A close atmosphere must always be avoided, even if it is cold, as it will cause the buds to fall; air must therefore be given every day. If fire-heat is applied to keep frost from other things that may be in the house, the night temperature should be kept below 40°. Care is necessary in such cases to ensure that the borders are never dry near the roots of the trees. Water is not required so abundantly as when the trees are in active growth, but enough must be given to thoroughly soak the border.

POT CULTURE

Peach and Nectarine trees may be cultivated in tubs or pots under glass, either alone or mixed with other fruits, but preferably alone, and, by a judicious selection of varieties, a supply of fruit may be had lasting for six months.

The form of tree best adapted for this purpose is the pyramid (fig. 168). For large houses the half-standard form is sometimes preferred (fig. 169). Early Alexander and its near allies are difficult to keep in pyramid form owing to their shyness in forming woodbuds. They are also notorious bud-droppers.

Nurserymen now grow and train trees specially for pot culture, and by purchasing these two or three years old much time is saved.

Repotting.—This should be done when the

leaves turn yellow, shaking the old soil away as much as possible without injuring the principal roots. Remove all suckers and root-buds. Many of the young fibrous roots may be taken away from pot trees in the autumn without affecting the next season's crop of fruit. In repotting, drain thoroughly, and put a handful of soot over the crocks to keep out worms. Care must be taken that the old ball is not dry when replaced in the pots; if there is any doubt about it, soak it well in a tub of water for fifteen minutes. The soil used should consist of good turfy loam, adding a little old Mushroom - bed manure, and one-twelfth chalk or lime-rubble broken and put through a ½-inch sieve. Pot very firmly, and leave a space of an inch below the rim for water

Storing the Plants for the Winter.—One advantage of pot culture is that the plants may be removed elsewhere and stood close together, the house being used for other purposes during the winter; but, wherever the trees are placed, they must be protected from severe frost, which would crack the pots. They require to be kept cool and well

Fig. 168.—Pyramid Peach

and top-dressing. Water the plants well soon after repotting. It is a good plan to

Fig. 169.—Half-standard Peach

syringe the trees for a few weeks after the repotting is finished. In a dry autumn the wood may occasionally shrivel.

Fig. 170.—Peach Tree in Pot, 16 years old

ventilated. A sudden rise of temperature must be carefully guarded against, as it would excite the buds and cause them to start into growth prematurely, with subsequent loss through their falling off instead of expanding their flowers. They must not be allowed to get dry at the root; at the same time they do not require so much water as when in active growth. Should the roots get frozen they will take no harm if allowed to thaw gradually.

The Flowering Period.—If the trees are to

be grown without fire-heat they should be in their places by the first week of February. When the flowers commence to open, which will be a fortnight later, the house should be fumigated on two successive evenings to destroy insects. Abundance of air must be given on every favourable occasion, and a

Fig. 171.—Peach in a Perforated Pot

small quantity should remain on at all times if the weather is mild. Keep the temperatures at all times as near as possible to those recommended for Peaches grown in borders under glass, and thin the fruits when they are set after the same manner. Owing to the limited space in which pot trees have to grow they must not be cropped heavily, or the fruits will be small and deficient in flavour. Four to six fruits are sufficient for a tree in a 9-inch pot. Those in tubs or pots 20 inches in diameter will mature from twenty to twenty-five fruits.

Disbudding and stopping will require attention during active growth, as recommended for fan-trained trees, allowing for the change of shape in the tree, also for the fact that trees in pots do not grow so freely as those planted in borders, and therefore form short natural spurs without any assistance.

Top-dressing.—When the fruits are an inch in diameter the trees should have a top-dressing of manure. Horse manure is suitable for this purpose, as it is favourable to root growth. It should be collected fresh, the straw removed, and then turned every second day for a week. About one-third part of turfy loam chopped small should be added to it before the first turning, and if some kiln-dust from the malthouse (not malt culms) is added also, and some liquid manure thrown on at each turning, the mixture will be improved. It should not be thrown into a large heap or it will heat violently. Care is necessary in applying this manure, as it sometimes burns the roots if not well mixed and sweetened.

After top-dressing the trees require to be carefully watered, as the state of the roots beneath the manure is not so easily ascertained. In bright sunny weather fruit-trees in pots, when in active growth, may require water three or four times per day. Sometimes this may be modified by using perforated pots, and plunging them in the borders (fig. 171). The borders in which they are plunged must be porous and properly drained, and be occasionally watered near the pots; a mulching of manure will prove beneficial after the roots have taken possession of the border and the fruit is swelling. Trees thus grown must be lifted in the autumn and their outside roots cut off close to the pots after the fruit is gathered and the leaves have turned yellow. The surface soil should also be removed to the depth of 3 or 4 inches; this will destroy many surface roots, but that is of no consequence, as others soon form again in the spring. If the drainage of the pots is perfect the trees will need repotting at least every other year, but preferably every year. After the foliage is off, the trees and house will require cleaning in the same way as recommended for fan-trained trees.

PROPAGATION

The Peach and Nectarine are propagated from seeds by budding, and sometimes by grafting.

Propagation from seeds is employed to obtain new varieties, for continuing some of the old ones, and for stocks. The method of raising plants from seeds is described in the chapter on propagation. The plants will frequently be fit for budding in the same season, much depending on circumstances of soil and climate, whether natural or artificial, with which they may be favoured. Downing states that in America a Peach stone planted in autumn will germinate in the ensuing spring, and the stem be fit to be budded in August or September. It is convenient to have a few young seedling Peaches for the purpose of budding them with any scarce variety that might fail on the Almond or Plum stock.

The Peach stock is of course the most natural, but experience has proved that in temperate countries the tree does not long succeed on its own roots. At all events, the leaves, after several years, acquire partial tinges of yellow; and this goes on every year increasing, whilst the leaves are produced narrower and narrower annually, till at last the tree becomes useless.

The stock next in value, as regards natural adaptation for the Peach, is the Almond. Of this, as a stock, the French have had long experience, and they prefer the hard-shelled sweet Almond (*Amandier doux à coque dure*). All the varieties of the Peach take readily and thrive on the Almond in soils that are not cold and wet. Some varieties that do not thrive on the Plum stock are better worked on the Almond for cultivation in the southern parts of the kingdom, provided proper borders have been formed.

Plum stocks are nearly always employed in this country for Peaches and Nectarines, usually the Mussel and the Brompton Plums. The Mussel is the stronger grower, and is the best for those kinds that take well on it. The Brompton Plum is employed for those which nurserymen term French Peaches. Although many of the finer kinds of Peaches take readily on this stock, it has the disadvantage of not increasing in thickness with the scion. The obstruction to the flow of sap which this disparity occasions tends to throw the tree into a bearing state, but the tree dies off sooner than on a stock which permits a freer circulation of the sap. The French employ the varieties called Saint-Julien, Damas Noir, and Myrobolan. M. Lepère of Montreuil states that preference is to be given to Damas Noir or Black Damask—which the gardeners near Paris get from Fontenay-aux-Roses—that they are cut down nearly to the level of the ground on planting, which is best done in November, and that they are budded when they have made fresh shoots fit for being worked at the proper season. We have seen trees worked upon Saint-Julien stock, that, even after a number of years, showed no inequality in stem thickness. Peaches and Nectarines succeed well when budded on White Magnum Bonum Plum.

The Peach and Nectarine may also be grafted, if care is taken to use as scions firm short-jointed shoots with about 1 inch of two-year-old wood at the base. Such should be taken off early in spring, and kept half-buried in moist sand till grafting-time. When worked, the successful taking of the grafts is promoted by earthing up to the top of the clay. The following mode of grafting has proved satisfactory. Kernels of Peaches, Nectarines, or Apricots are sown in autumn at the foot of a wall where they are to remain. Each will make a vigorous shoot the following spring, and this may either be budded in August of the same year or grafted in March of the year following. Grafting is preferred, and the scion should have ¼ inch of two-year-old wood at its lower extremity. The stock is cut with a dove-tail notch for the scion to rest on, and tied in the usual manner. The buds of the scion at back and front are removed, leaving two on each side and a leader; when these have grown 6 or 8 inches, their extremities are pinched off, which causes each shoot to throw out two others, and thus produce in autumn a fan-shaped tree with ten branches. They generally bear two or three fruit the second year from the graft.

ENEMIES

Peach Scale, Aphis, Figure-of-8 Moth, Garden Chafer, Red-legged Garden Weevil, Thrips, Red Spider, Cockchafer, Ants, Birds, Earwigs, Wasps. See INSECT AND OTHER PLANT ENEMIES, Vol. III.

VARIETIES—PEACHES

Varieties of Peach are difficult to distinguish by the fruit alone. The following arrangement is founded on the fruit having either melting flesh which parts readily from the stone, or firm flesh clinging to the stone; the leaves being serrated, without glands, or having either globose or reniform glands at their base; and the flowers being either large or small.

CLASS I.—MELTING PEACHES
Flesh parting from the stone

Division 1.—*Leaves serrate, glandless*

Subdivision 1.—Flowers large.	Subdivision 2.—Flowers small.
Goshawk.	Dymond.
Noblesse.	Royal George.
Rivers' Early York.	

Division 2.—*Leaves serrate, with globose glands.*
Flowers small
Crawford's Early.

Division 3.—*Leaves crenate, with globose glands.*

Subdivision 1.—Flowers large.	Subdivision 2.—Flowers small.
A'bec.	Bellegarde.
Alexandra Noblesse.	Crimson Galande.
Barrington.	Late Admiral.
Belle Bauce.	Stirling Castle.
Early Grosse Mignonne.	Violette Hâtive.
Hales' Early.	Walburton Admirable.
Princess of Wales.	
Sea Eagle.	

Division 4.—*Leaves crenate, with reniform glands*

Subdivision 1.—Flowers large.	Subdivision 2.—Flowers small.
Dr. Hogg.	Dagmar.
Early Beatrice.	Early Alfred.
The Nectarine Peach.	Golden Eagle.
	Prince of Wales.
	Salway.

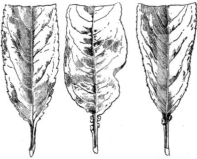

Fig 172.—Leaves of Peaches, showing position and form of glands

CLASS II.—CLING-STONE PEACHES
Flesh firm, adhering to the stone

The divisions and subdivisions in this class are the same as in the preceding one, but few of the varieties are worthy of cultivation in this country.

Fig. 173.—Peaches. Alexandra Noblesse

Division 3.—*Leaves crenate, with globose glands*

Flowers large.
Alexander

Division 4.—*Leaves crenate, with reniform glands*

Flowers small.
Early Louise

DESCRIPTION OF VARIETIES.

A'BEC.—Fruit large, round, yellowish-green on shaded side, deep-red where exposed to the sun;

Fig. 174.—Peach. Bellegarde. (⅓)

flesh melting, juicy, sweet, and richly flavoured. Ripening mid-August; a first-rate variety. Tree tender; one of the best for second early house.

ALEXANDER.—Fruit large, round, somewhat flattened, greenish-white on shaded side, very dark-red where exposed to the sun; flesh greenish-white, clinging slightly, tender, juicy, and of good flavour. One of the very early varieties, but difficult to manage under warm treatment under glass, owing to premature development of the buds in the autumn, which causes them to fall in the spring; good for a cold house. Also ripens on a south wall about 19th July. It is similar to Amsden June, and Waterloo, and was introduced from Illinois, U.S.A., in 1874.

ALEXANDRA NOBLESSE (fig. 173).—Fruit very large, round; skin pale, with the exception of some red dots on the side next the sun; flesh white, pale at the stone, from which it parts freely, juicy, melting, rich, and vinous. A seedling from the old Noblesse, but, unlike that variety, the tree is not subject to mildew. It ripens in the middle of August.

BARRINGTON.—Fruit large, somewhat elongated; skin downy, deep-red next the sun, pale yellowish-green on the shaded side; flesh whitish-green, slightly rayed with red at the stone, from which it parts freely, very juicy, melting, rich, and of high flavour. The tree is vigorous and less subject to mildew than most others. Mid-September.

BELLE BAUCE.—Fruit large, round, somewhat depressed and hollowed at the summit; skin thin,

downy, of a fine clear colour, the greater portion of the fruit, however, being profusely covered with deep-red; flesh white, red next the stone, very tender, juicy, melting, and rich. A very handsome and delicious Peach. Ripe in the middle of September.

BELLEGARDE (fig. 174).—Fruit large, globular, skin dark-red, streaked with dark-purple or violet next the sun, pale-green, slightly tinged with yellow on the shaded side; flesh pale-yellow, parting freely from the stone, at which it is slightly rayed with red; melting, juicy, rich, and excellent. Ripens mid-September. The tree is very healthy, and is not subject to mildew.

CRIMSON GALANDE (fig. 145).—Fruit medium, round, somewhat flattened, and often indented at the apex; skin thin, pale, speckled with red, very dark red on the sunny side; flesh white, marked with red next the stone, very tender, melting, juicy, and of excellent flavour. One of the very best. The tree has a good constitution, bears freely, and stands forcing well. Late August.

DAGMAR.—Fruit large, handsome, somewhat elongated, dotted and shaded with red, highly coloured next the sun; flesh white, very tender, melting, juicy, sweet, and of good flavour; skin thin. A first-rate cropper. Early August.

DR. HOGG (fig. 175).—Fruit large, round; skin very pale yellow, with a slight tinge of crimson next the sun; flesh yellowish-white, red at the stone, from which it parts freely, firm, melting, with a sweet rich flavour. Ripens about the first week in August. The tree is a strong, vigorous grower, and bears abundantly.

DYMOND.—Fruit large, round and even in outline; skin greenish-yellow with red dots, bright-red next the sun; flesh white, juicy, melting, sweet, and of good flavour. A first-class variety. Unsurpassed for exhibition. It bears well outside. Is rarely attacked by mildew.

EARLY ALFRED.—Fruit large, elongated, often bearing a nipple at the apex, yellowish-green

Fig. 175.—Peach. Dr. Hogg (⅓)

dotted with red, bright-red where exposed to the sun; flesh white, very tender, melting, juicy, and of good flavour. A very useful variety for forcing. Tree hardy, robust, and a great bearer. Early August.

EARLY BEATRICE.—Fruit of medium size, roundish; skin thin, downy, of a marbled-red colour on the exposed side; flesh white, moderately rich, and juicy. One of the earliest Peaches. The fruit is much larger if the tree is worked on the Brompton stock. Raised by Mr. Rivers from a seedling White Nectarine. Mid-July.

GOLDEN EAGLE.—Fruit round, very large and handsome, deep-yellow, highly coloured with red next the sun; flesh yellow, tender, juicy, and of rich piquant flavour. The best of the yellow-fleshed varieties. Early October.

GOSHAWK.—Fruit large, round, green, striped and flushed with dull-red next the sun; flesh white, very tender, melting, and of exceptionally rich flavour. The tree is vigorous and a good cropper. Of American origin. One of the finest mid-season varieties.

GROSSE MIGNONNE (Early).—Fruit large, round, somewhat depressed, hollowed at the summit, furnished with a deep suture; skin slightly downy, pale-yellow mottled with red towards the sunny side, which is of a dark-red colour; flesh pale-yellow, rayed with red at the stone, from which it parts freely, melting, juicy, very rich, and vinous. The fruit does not bear carriage well. The tree is a good bearer, forces well, and is not subject to mildew. Late August, early September.

HALES' EARLY.—Fruit large, round, green flushed with red, dark-crimson where exposed to the sun; flesh white, tender, juicy, and of moderately good flavour. A very useful variety, ripening about the end of July.

KESTREL.—A very fine introduction, fruit highly coloured and large, ripens a week earlier than Peregrine; flesh firm and of good flavour; colours early and hangs well. Raised by Mr. Rivers from Early Rivers Nectarine × Hales' Early Peach. Good for pot culture. End of July.

LATE ADMIRABLE.—Fruit large, roundish, somewhat oblong, with a slight depression at the summit, in which there is commonly a small nipple; skin downy, dull-crimson with dark streaks next the sun, pale-green on the shaded side, slightly mottled at the junction of the two colours; flesh pale yellowish-green, red at the stone, from which it parts freely, melting, and very juicy. One of the best late Peaches either for the open ground or forcing. Mid- or late-September.

NECTARINE PEACH.—Fruit very large, somewhat elongated, often with a prominent nipple at the apex, greenish-yellow, blotched and shaded with red next the sun; flesh white, tender, juicy, and of good flavour when grown under glass. A very fine autumn variety for a cool house. A fruit grown at Ketton Hall measured 12 inches in circumference and weighed 14 oz. Late September.

NOBLESSE.—Fruit large, globular, depressed on the summit, sometimes rather pointed; skin slightly downy, pale yellowish-green, streaked and blotched red on the side next the sun; flesh white to the stone, from which it parts freely, melting, very juicy, rich, and excellent. Constitution not so good as Alexandra Noblesse. Early September.

PEREGRINE (fig. 143).—One of the very best of the newer Peaches. Fruits large, with brilliant crimson skin, melting and excellent, flesh firm, hence it travels well; robust constitution. Early August.

PRINCE OF WALES.—Fruit varying much in shape, especially if forced, when it resembles Bar-rington, but grown in a cool house it is round and even in outline; skin green, shaded with very bright red where exposed to the sun; flesh greenish-white, very tender, juicy, and of good flavour. Bears abundantly. One of the best autumn kinds. Mid-September.

PRINCESS OF WALES.—Fruit very large, round, and pointed; skin pale-cream with a rosy cheek, very clear and beautiful; flesh melting, juicy, rich, and excellent, having a tinge of red at the stone. A very fine and handsome late Peach. Very excellent for late supply. A fruit grown at Ketton Hall measured 12 inches in circumference and weighed 14 oz. Late October.

RIVERS' EARLY YORK (fig. 176).—Fruit medium, ovate; skin downy, greenish-white, deep-red on the side next the sun, and frequently much spotted and mottled on the shaded side; flesh white, melt-

Fig. 176.—Peach. Rivers' Early York. (⅓)

ing, juicy, and tolerably richly flavoured. A fine early Peach of good constitution; an improvement on the old early York. Early- or mid-August.

ROYAL GEORGE.—Fruit large, globular; skin very downy, deep-red next the sun, pale greenish-white dotted with red on the shaded side; flesh pale-yellow, rayed with red at the stone, from which it parts freely, very juicy, melting, rich, and vinous. The tree is a good bearer and forces well, but is subject to mildew. Late August.

SEA EAGLE.—Fruit very large, somewhat elongated; skin very downy, greenish-white, bright-red where exposed to the sun; flesh white, marked with red next the stone, sweet, juicy, and of good flavour. An excellent Peach for a cool house, but not suitable for outside culture north of London. It has produced fruit at Ketton Hall which were over 12 inches in circumference and weighed 16 oz. Late September.

STIRLING CASTLE.—Fruit medium, roundish; skin light, with a marbled-red cheek; flesh white, free, melting, rich, and excellent. A fine hardy-constitutioned Peach, and one that should be in every collection ripening in the beginning of September. A tree of this variety should be grown in a pot for forcing purposes because of its profusion of pollen.

VIOLETTE HÂTIVE (fig. 177). — Fruit medium, round and even in outline; skin greenish-white, dark-red where exposed to the sun; flesh white, juicy, sweet, and of good flavour, not so soft as some varieties, and therefore travels well. One

Fig. 177.—Peach. Violette Hâtive. (½)

of the best and hardiest varieties. It bears forcing well.

WALBURTON ADMIRABLE.—Fruit large, round; skin pale yellowish-green, crimson next the sun, mottled and clouded with darker colour; flesh yellowish-white, melting, juicy, rich, and high-flavoured. Ripens end of September or beginning of October. The tree is very hardy, and a good bearer. A most excellent late variety.

Six Best Varieties for Early Forcing, in order of ripening.

Duchess of Cornwall.	Peregrine.
Duke of York.	Royal George.
Kestrel.	Stirling Castle

Twelve Best Varieties for a Cool House, in order of ripening.

Duchess of Cornwall.	Goshawk.
Kestrel.	Bellegarde.
Peregrine.	Prince of Wales.
Rivers' Early York.	Princess of Wales.
Royal George.	Sea Eagle.
Crimson Galande.	Nectarine Peach.

Twelve Best Varieties for Outside Culture.

Alexander.	Alexandra
Kestrel.	Noblesse.
Peregrine.	Bellegarde.
Rivers' Early York	Princess of Wales.
Crimson Galande.	Sea Eagle.
Dymond.	Nectarine Peach.
Stirling Castle.	

Twelve Best Varieties for Exhibition, in order of merit.

Peregrine.	Barrington.
Royal George.	Bellegarde.
Kestrel.	Princess of Wales.
Crimson Galande.	Sea Eagle.
Early Grosse	Nectarine Peach.
Mignonne.	Golden Eagle.
Stirling Castle.	

NECTARINES.

The same method of classification for the varieties of the Peach is adopted for Nectarines.

FLESH MELTING, PARTING FROM THE STONE.

Division 1.—*Leaves crenate, with globose glands.*

Subdivision 1.—Flowers large.	Subdivision 2.—Flowers small.
Humboldt.	Elruge.
Pine Apple.	Stanwick Elruge.

Division 2.—*Leaves crenate with reniform glands*

Subdivision 1.—Flowers large.

Byron.	Pitmaston Orange.
Cardinal.	Rivers' Orange.
Early Rivers.	Spenser.
Goldoni.	White.
Lord Napier.	

Subdivision 2.—Flowers small.

Balgowan.	Victoria.
Downton.	Violette Hâtive.
Dryden.	

BALGOWAN.—Fruit considerably larger than Violette Hâtive, roundish oval, broadest at the

Fig. 178.—Nectarine. Elruge. (¾)

base; skin greenish-yellow, mottled with dull-red, dark-red next the sun; flesh yellowish, flaked with red at the stone, from which it parts freely, rich, melting, and excellent. Early September. Tree remarkably vigorous; ought to be in every collection.

BYRON.—Fruit large, inclined to conical, deep-yellow, dark-red where exposed to the sun; flesh orange-yellow, melting, juicy, and of good flavour. A good grower. September.

Fig 179.—Nectarine. Pitmaston Orange. (⅔)

CARDINAL.—Fruit medium, pale-green, bright-red on the side exposed to the sun, flavour excellent. The earliest of all Nectarines, ripening ten days sooner than Early Rivers. It forces well and bears abundantly, but is not recommended for a cool house or outside.

DOWNTON.—Fruit much resembling the Violette Hâtive, but somewhat larger; flesh melting, rich, and high flavoured. Tree a good bearer and of a good constitution, more vigorous than Elruge, between which and Violette Hâtive it appears to be a cross. Late August.

DRYDEN.—Fruit large, green, dotted with red, dark-red on the sunny side; flesh greenish-white, melting, juicy, sweet, and of good flavour. The tree is a sure bearer. One of the very best, pays for extra care in cultivation. Fruits of it grown at Ketton Hall weighed 8 oz. and measured 10 inches in circumference. Mid-September.

EARLY RIVERS.—Fruit extra large, greenish-white, bright-red where exposed to the sun; flesh white, very tender, sweet, melting, and of excellent flavour. Tree vigorous and bears well. Is not unlike Lord Napier, but ripens three weeks earlier. One of the best for market purposes. Early August.

ELRUGE (fig. 178).—Fruit middle-sized, roundish, inclining to oval; skin pale-green, dark violet-red next the sun; flesh whitish, tinged with red at the stone, from which it parts freely, melting, juicy, rich, perfumed, and delicious. An abundant bearer and forces well. One of the best. Late August.

GOLDONI.—Fruit medium to small, round, bright-yellow, streaked and shaded with red where exposed to the sun; flesh yellow, very tender, juicy, and of very pleasant flavour. A delicious Nectarine. A healthy grower and an abundant bearer.

HUMBOLDT (fig. 160).—Fruit very large, round, or inclined to be conical; yellowish-green, dark-red where exposed to the sun; flesh yellow, juicy, and of good flavour. Ripens Mid-September. Bears abundantly, and the fruit hangs well.

LORD NAPIER.—Fruit extra large, round; skin pale-green, bright-red where exposed to the sun; flesh white, very tender, juicy, sweet, and of excellent flavour. One of the very best Nectarines. Late August. The fruit is easily burnt by the sun when ripening, especially if it is wet; it should therefore be shaded in very hot weather. Fruits grown at Ketton Hall measured 9½ inches in circumference, and weighed 8 oz.

PINEAPPLE (fig. 146).—Fruit large, roundish, inclined to conical; skin yellow, dark-red where exposed to the sun; flesh deep-yellow, red near the stone, sweet, juicy, and of excellent Pineapple flavour. One of the best. Late September.

PITMASTON ORANGE (fig. 179).—Fruit large, globular or almost heart-shaped, terminating in a small point or nipple; skin deep-purple, spotted with brown next the sun, orange on the shaded side; flesh rich-yellow, red about stone, from which it parts freely, melting, juicy, sweet, and of good flavour. Late August. The tree is hardy, and an abundant bearer.

RIVERS' ORANGE.—Fruit medium, round; skin yellow, dark-red where fully exposed; flesh yellow, very tender, juicy, sweet, and of good flavour. Early September.

SPENSER (fig. 167).—Fruit of the largest size, roundish, somewhat elongated; skin green, dull-

Fig. 180.—Nectarine. Stanwick Elruge. (⅔)

red where exposed to the sun; flesh greenish-white, tender, melting, and juicy. Mid-September. One of the best for exhibition.

STANWICK ELRUGE (fig. 180).—Fruit large, roundish, often elongated; skin pale-green, bright-red on sunny side; flesh white, flecked with red next the stone, exceptionally tender and melting, juicy, sweet, and of good flavour. A great improvement on the old Elruge for size and colour. Mid-August.

VICTORIA (fig. 181). — Fruit similar in every respect to Stanwick, but does not crack, and consequently preferable to it. One of the highest

Fig. 181.—Nectarine. Victoria. (⅗)

flavoured and the best of all late Nectarines. Raised by Mr. Rivers from Stanwick. August.

VIOLETTE HÂTIVE (fig. 163). — Fruit medium, roundish; skin yellowish-green, dark purplish-red, mottled with pale-brown dots next the sun; flesh whitish, much rayed with red to some distance from the stone, from which it parts freely,

melting, juicy, very rich, and excellent. A good forcer. Late August or early September.

WHITE.—Fruit large, roundish, depressed on the summit; skin yellowish-green, tinged with red next the sun; flesh greenish-white, parting freely from the stone, very juicy, rich, and vinous. Late August.

Six Best Varieties for Early Forcing.

Cardinal.	Stanwick Elruge.
Early Rivers.	Pineapple.
Lord Napier.	Humboldt.

Twelve Best for Orchard-house Culture, in their order of ripening.

Early Rivers.	Pitmaston Orange.
Lord Napier.	Humboldt.
Stanwick Elruge.	Pineapple.
Balgowan.	Spenser.
Dryden.	Newton.
Goldoni.	Victoria.

Nine Best for outside Culture.

Early Rivers.	Pineapple.
Lord Napier.	Spenser.
Stanwick Elruge.	Humboldt.
Dryden.	Victoria.
Pitmaston Orange.	

Twelve Best for Exhibition, in order of merit.

Early Rivers.	Stanwick Elruge.
Lord Napier.	Spenser.
Pineapple.	Byron.
Dryden.	Pitmaston Orange.
Newton.	Humboldt.
Balgowan.	Victoria.

APRICOTS

ORIGIN

The Apricot (*Prunus Armeniaca*) is now regarded as indigenous in Armenia, Mongolia, Manchuria, and Northern China. It is said to have been cultivated by the Chinese two or three thousand years before the Christian era, at the beginning of which the Greeks and Romans are supposed to have first received it. It has long been cultivated in the north of India and Thibet, and in these and other regions it has become more or less naturalized, hence the statement that it is a native of the temperate parts of Central Asia. Dr. Bretschneider found it wild in the mountains of Pekin, where it grew in abundance, and produced red and yellow fruit $1\frac{1}{4}$ inches in diameter, with salmon-coloured, sour, but edible flesh. This may therefore be accepted as the wild progenitor of our garden Apricots, which show a considerable range of variation and yet are reproduced true from seeds.

The Apricot is very distinct in foliage and wood from all the other species of Prunus, and the granular pulp of the fruit is another distinction. Its leaves resemble those of the Lombardy Poplar. It succeeds perfectly when grafted on the Mussel or common Plum, and either Peaches, Almonds, or Nectarines may be grafted on it.

Apricots appear to have been first introduced into England from Italy in 1524 by Wolff, gardener to Henry VIII.

CULTIVATION OUT-OF-DOORS

The Apricot will succeed in any good free garden soil or calcareous loam that is rather sandy than otherwise; strong clay soils do not suit it, neither does it thrive so well in heavy, close loams as it does in those that are friable. In any case the soil ought to be well drained. The tree will grow rapidly in moist seasons; but when it has attained a considerable size it is apt to suffer from dryness at the roots; the leaves then become weak for want of sap, mildew ensues, and the tree is soon ruined. The soil should be trenched; and in so doing, if the soil, or part of it, is clayey and rather adhesive, it should be turned up to the top, where it will be rendered permeable by the weather. Turf which contains much fibre is excellent for mixing with heavy soils; lime rubble, brick rubbish, old plaster, road sidings, turf parings, burnt soil, and wood ashes also may be added to the soil.

Borders for Apricots should be from 8 to 10 feet wide, 2 feet 6 inches deep, and with 9 inches of drainage. If the locality is damp and low-lying, the bottom of the border had better be concreted. It should also slope outwards from the wall.

In the south of England some kinds of Apricots, such as the Breda, bear well as standards if the spring weather is favourable; and although the fruit is not so large as from trees on walls, yet it is more juicy and of richer flavour. The trees may be planted as standards at from 20 to 25 feet apart. The Apricot, however, is chiefly cultivated against walls. In the warmer parts of the country east and west aspects are suitable; but an aspect inclined to south-west or south-east is to be preferred; whilst in the northern parts of England, and in Scotland, a south aspect is generally necessary to give the fruit its full flavour.

The distance between trees against walls should be from 15 to 20 feet. Planting should be done about the middle of October, for the buds on the lower part of the shoots are matured early in the season, and growth stops in August, or at least the elongation of the shoots is almost entirely arrested at that period for a short time. The shoots then make a fresh start, and a marked difference may be observed between the portion of the shoot produced before and that after the stoppage.

When the tree is about to be taken up, the older leaves should be on the point of dropping. Those on the second growth will be

Fig. 182.—Standard Fan-trained Apricot, on south wall, outside

Fig. 183.—Apricot, Fan-trained, on south wall, outdoors

sufficient to draw sap and maintain circulation until fresh roots are formed; and having done this before winter, the tree will be ready to push new growth in spring. If the weather should be hot, and the soil dry at the time of planting, settle it about the roots with copious supplies of water. If the borders cannot be prepared in the autumn, planting may be performed any time during mild weather in the months of December and January, but not later than the middle of February. As already observed,¹ the Apricot vegetates early, and the trees do not grow so vigorously if transplanted after they have commenced to grow. It is a good plan to plant a few maidens each year, so that there

to 10 inches from the ground, and from the buds immediately below the section let three shoots be encouraged, one to be trained upright, and one on each side for the lowest pair of branches. It is of the utmost importance to manage these three shoots so that the two side ones may be as strong as, or even rather stronger than, the upright one, which, if left to themselves, would not likely be the case. The central one should be checked early in June, when the wood will be firm as far up from the base as the place to which it will have to be cut back in autumn, at which time the two side-shoots ought to be of equal thickness and vigour, and stronger than the central one.

Fig. 184.—Apricot.   Frogmore Early

may be a stock of nice healthy trees ready to hand for making good deficiencies as they occur. This is preferable to purchasing trained trees, as they can be lifted in good time and with a good ball of soil attached to the roots, so that they may be partly established before winter sets in.

Lifting to check Growth.—When an Apricot is growing too rampantly it should be lifted and the stronger roots pruned back. Some growers make a practice of lifting their trees periodically.

Pruning and Training.—Fan-training is the best for the Apricot, because the branches are apt to die off, and, as explained in treating of the Plum, vacancies can be most readily filled up. Besides, the tree is one of those which do not admit of horizontal branches being trained from an upright stem without risk.

Commencing the training with a maiden plant, consisting of one upright vigorous shoot, let the latter be cut down in autumn

The trees should be frequently inspected during the growing season, and if the side-branches are evidently not keeping pace with the central upright, means must be taken to check its progress, and the sooner such means are taken the better. The flow of sap is easily diverted in greater force to any shoot that is on an equality, or nearly so, with those towards which the flow is intended to be in a diminished ratio; but when any shoot or shoots have been drawing an undue share, it is not an easy matter to divert the sap into less vigorous shoots. A strong shoot may, however, be checked by bending it somewhere about where it will ultimately be pruned; this may be done, not so as to break it, but to check the growth.

The main branches ought to diverge equally; when they extend so as to be 15 inches apart, each branch should be formed into two; and when the branches resulting have extended so as to be again at the above distance apart, they should be again subdivided. In this way the principal branches will be produced with regularity, and there will be space for laying in young wood for fruiting.

When the Apricot arrives at a bearing state, it produces its fruit on the shoots of the preceding year's growth, and also on spurs on wood that is two, three, or more years old. The finest fruit is, however, produced on wood one and two years old; therefore a proper supply of such ought to be encouraged in all parts of the tree. Young shoots should be laid in between the principal branches, rather thinly, for it is an error to crowd the tree with more shoots than there is space for, when on half the number of

branches. In the second summer, from the base of each of these shoots another should be trained. When the shoot first laid in is in its second year, a young shoot to replace it will be growing. If considered advisable to retain both of these for another summer, no young shoot for succession will require to be grown in that summer; but if only one be retained, then a succession shoot must be encouraged.

A good number of spurs should be permitted to form on all the main branches, which would otherwise remain naked and unfruitful. From these spurs, however, long shoots ought not to be allowed to grow. The young shoots should be pinched or cut back

Fig. 185.—Apricot. Hemskerk

shoots much more fruit would set than the tree could possibly bring to perfection. Young shoots should therefore be laid in at every 10 or 12 inches, and shortened to about 1 foot in length, a little longer if they are strong, and shorter if weak. If they fail to bear when they are one year old, they may be allowed to remain another year.

The young shoot, after having been pruned in autumn, should in winter be nailed pretty close to the old branch, in order to afford room for a succession shoot in the following summer. If the shoot first laid in has borne fruit, and if at the autumn-pruning the young shoot is seen to be furnished with blossom-buds, the one that has borne should then be cut away; but if not, both ought to remain another season. In the autumn the older of the two should be cut out and the younger trained in its place. Thus there will be single shoots, originating at about 10 or 12 inches apart, laid in between the principal

to three or four buds when only a few inches long.

Disbudding consists in removing shoots when they are quite young, chiefly those in front of the branches, where they would otherwise form useless breast-wood. The operation should be first performed in the upper and more vigorous parts of the tree, and after a short interval another portion should be treated. The finger and thumb only ought to be used when the shoot is young; but as soon as it becomes somewhat woody the knife must be used, otherwise the bark is apt to be torn, and gumming will result.

The foreright shoots having been gradually removed, superfluous shoots situated elsewhere should either be cut clean out or shortened for spurs. If all the branches are in a proper degree of vigour the sap will be equally distributed, and, as a consequence, the tree will be healthy and fruitful, other circumstances being favourable.

Thinning the fruit should be done, to a certain extent, when it is very young, in which state the thinnings may be used for tarts. The final thinning, that is, the reduction of the crop to safe limits, is best deferred until the fruits have stoned. Large kinds should be allowed twice the space afforded to those which are only half their size. On vigorous branches, or on shoots that proceed from such, more should be left than on parts that are weak.

General Treatment.—About the beginning of February, and again in March, the soil and subsoil on which Apricots are growing should be examined, and, if dry, watered. At this season the surface soil is usually moist enough; but loamy subsoils, that have not been thoroughly trenched and rendered porous by an admixture of suitable materials, are not readily moistened throughout either by rain or by mere surface watering. The surface soil should be ridged as deeply as can be done without interfering with the roots, the ridges running parallel with the wall. The hollows between the ridges should then be filled with water again and again until the subsoil is thoroughly soaked; the ridges may then be levelled.

If only the surface roots are supplied with moisture, whilst to those more deeply situated the supply is deficient, mildew is apt to attack the foliage; and although this most destructive disease may be checked to a considerable extent by flowers of sulphur, yet the health of the trees cannot be restored whilst the cause of the disease is allowed to exist. Apricot trees which were nearly killed by mildew, notwithstanding the repeated application of sulphur and frequent syringing, have been cured in the following manner. They were taken up in autumn, and, after the border had been deeply trenched, and the loamy subsoil broken up, replanted. In the following season they produced healthy foliage, quite free from mildew. Where a border has not been properly prepared, and where the trees are severely attacked by mildew, it is advisable to take them up, if not too old, and replant them after the border has undergone due preparation; for although watering as we have recommended will be effectual in many cases, yet there may be others in which it would be difficult to ensure the uniform moistening of all parts of the soil. If summer-watering be necessary, rain- or pond-water is best.

A mulch of long litter spread 4 inches in thickness on the surface of the alleys early in June prevents rapid evaporation of moisture and encourages the formation of feeding roots just under the surface. Established, healthy trees in full bearing, after the fruit has stoned, will need assistance from stimulants in the form of liquid or artificial manure (preferably the latter) each time water is given, sprinkling the latter on the surface before the water is applied.

To add rotten manure to the soil when planting Apricots is a mistake. When trees make rank, sappy growth, and fruit indifferently, the cause may generally be traced to their having been planted in a too rich compost.

Protection.—The flowers of the Apricot appear so early in the season as to be liable to injury from frost. Even the swelling buds will succumb if exposed to severe frost. They should therefore be afforded protection as soon as the buds are on the point of bursting. Wide coping-boards are good, as they shed rain-water clear of the trees, and sometimes are sufficient protection. Generally, however, something more than this is needed. Among the materials used for this purpose are " Frigi Domo ", and woollen netting, constructed so as to form a blind. Another plan is to fix securely some new netting with the mesh made to hang square, not diagonally. Long stakes or poles, 2 yards apart, should be fixed in front of the wall, for the purpose of keeping the blinds and nets from damaging the blossoms. The trees should be covered every evening and uncovered again next morning, unless the weather be unfavourable.

In hot, sunny weather the fruit of the Apricot is apt to become ripe and soft on the exposed side, while it is yet hard and green on the side next the wall. By partially shading the fruit either with netting or by drawing the leaves partly over them, the ripening process, though retarded, will be more regular.

FORCING THE APRICOT

The Apricot forces well provided it is not subjected to much heat until the fruits have stoned, after which, if necessary, a fairly high temperature will do no harm. In the open air it is the most precocious of all fruit-trees; therefore when given the protection of glass but little warmth is requisite to excite it into growth. Such being the case, the structure in which it is grown need only be heated to 40° in severe weather. A lean-to structure is, on the whole, the best for the purpose, and the trees should be trained on a trellis 18 inches from the roof-glass.

The border should be made as directed for Peaches under glass. Until the trees flower and set, a temperature of 45° to 50° will be ample, and on very cold nights it may descend to 40°. A rise of 5° may be allowed after the fruits begin to mature, and as far as artificial heat is concerned it is not advisable to exceed these temperatures. With sun-heat the temperature of the house may rise to 60° before admitting air, but it should be closed early enough to secure a temperature of 65°.

As the season advances, more air will be required, until the ventilators may ultimately remain wide open both day and night. The house may be closed for a few hours in the afternoon after the stoning period has been safely passed if early fruits are required;

the fruits begin to swell, in the forenoon only, or early morning, until the season is more advanced and sun-heat becomes more powerful, when it should be performed copiously twice daily, and continued until the time that the fruits begin to colour and soften, when it should be discontinued until after the fruit has been gathered.

When the trees are started into growth, the borders should receive a good soaking of tepid water, so that the soil is moistened down to the drainage. During the winter months the borders may have a good soaking with liquid manure, but after this it is questionable whether stimulants are not better withheld until the fruits begin to

Fig. 186.—Apricot. Large Early

otherwise it is much better to leave them to ripen under more natural conditions.

The flowers require to be fertilized by hand. It is best to allow a little air on the house for an hour or two before operating upon the flowers with a camel-hair pencil, thereby ensuring that the pollen is ripe and dry. Until the flowers are set, it is necessary to keep the atmosphere in the house dry and buoyant; but when the petals have fallen, a light dewing with tepid water will prove very beneficial.

Should a heavy set result, thinning should be done as soon as the fruits are large enough to distinguish the best of them, but the final thinning must be left until the stoning stage is passed. If fruits are required for dessert, they should be left a trifle closer on the trees than would be advisable for Peaches, but if for culinary and preserving purposes leave about one-third more than for Nectarines.

Syringing may be resorted to so soon as

make their final swelling, when manure may be applied with every watering. Should the trees be in a weak condition and need a stimulus when started, a mixture of 1 lb. of muriate of potash, 1½ lb. of dissolved bones, and 2½ lb. of bone-meal may be applied at the rate of 2 oz. to each square yard, just before affording water.

Pinching the shoots to form spurs, and the laying-in of young growths where they are required for filling blank spaces, must be attended to, and it is at this time that the caterpillar of the Apricot moth puts in an appearance. This must therefore be watched for, its presence being revealed by the insect drawing the young leaves together, which gives them a rolled and twisted appearance. A sharp pressure of these rolled-up leaves between the thumb and finger is sufficient to dispatch the insect, and the trees should be carefully examined every few days so long as any of these insects are to be found. Red spider puts in an appearance either when the internal atmosphere is kept too dry and hot or when the border is not kept in a uniformly moist condition. If care be taken to afford the trees an abundance of air, to give them a daily syringing, and to keep up a good supply of water at the roots, red spider will not give any trouble.

In the autumn all necessary pruning should be performed, this being a much better time to do it than the winter, as the wounds heal so much quicker while there are yet leaves on the trees. Keep the ventilators and doors wide open, and above all things see that the border never feels the want of water. A dry border in the winter will cause the trees to shed their buds in precisely the same manner that forced Peach trees do. When the trees are quite dormant, give them a thorough cleansing with an insecticide, wash the woodwork and glass, and whitewash the brickwork, so that all will be clean and in readiness for starting-time in spring.

It is not advisable to force the Apricot as forcing is usually understood. It may, however, be grown under glass with the most satisfactory result, as at Welbeck Abbey and Strathfieldsaye, where Apricots are grown in what are known as wall cases.

ENEMIES

Insects, &c. (see INSECT AND OTHER PLANT ENEMIES, Vol. III). *Bark Enemies.*— Wœberian Tortrix. *Fruit and Seed Enemies.* —Ants, Wasps. *Leaf Enemies.*—Red-legged Garden Weevil, Red Spider.

PROPAGATION

Propagation.—The Apricot is propagated by seeds, by budding, and occasionally by grafting.

There are, however, some sorts which reproduce themselves with considerable exactitude from the stone, and are accordingly propagated in that way. Moor Park is one of these; and although the original variety should not be lost sight of, it is certain that very good seedlings might be raised from it in abundance. This variety and several others are frequently raised from seeds by the French. They select the stones from the finest ripe fruit, and stratify them till autumn. They are then planted in rich soil, covered 2 inches deep, and in case of severe frost a covering of leaves or of litter is afforded. The seedlings are transplanted in the following autumn, when the tap-root is shortened.

Budding is the general mode of propagation, the Mussel and common Plums being the stocks employed. The Brussels stock is also employed for standards to cover the upper parts of high walls, as its shoots are tall and vigorous, and soon form the required height of stem. Budding is done as early as the middle of June, but later than this is preferable, so long as the buds run freely. Care should be taken not to choose blossom-buds instead of wood-buds.

Grafting is seldom resorted to, except where buds of any particular variety have failed. Success greatly depends on the selection of scions. They should be cut off in January, and laid in to half their length in moist sandy soil, or in sand kept moderately moist, but not saturated; and they should be grafted as soon as the sap becomes active in the stocks. The grafts ought to be immediately afterwards earthed up as high as the top of the clay.

LIST OF VARIETIES

BREDA.—Fruit small, roundish, or somewhat obtusely four-sided at the base, the summit slightly depressed; skin brownish-orange; flesh orange, parting freely from the stone, juicy and rich. Ripe about the beginning of August on a wall; its season is considerably prolonged on standards.

EARLY MOOR PARK.—Fruit round, inclined to oval, sutured on one side only; skin yellow, blotched with crimson on the sunny side; flesh reddish-orange, juicy, and of luscious flavour, separating from the stone. Early August, or three weeks in advance of Moor Park.

FROGMORE EARLY (fig. 184). — Fruit small, roundish, sometimes oblate, and sutured; skin pale-yellow when shaded, deep-yellow when exposed to the sun, mottled with red; flesh orange. tender, juicy, richly flavoured. A free-stone variety, and worthy of extended cultivation for early supply. Tree hardy and a good cropper. Was raised in the Royal Gardens, Frogmore.

HEMSKERK (fig. 185).—Fruit as large as in Moor Park, roundish, with the sides flattened and sutured; skin yellow, darker on the exposed side; flesh deep-yellow, tender, juicy, and equal to Moor Park in flavour. Late July. Tree hardier than Moor Park, a good grower, and a heavy cropper.

KAISHA.—Fruit medium, roundish, ovate, slightly depressed on the summit; skin slightly downy, pale-citron coloured, orange tinged and marbled with red next the sun; flesh citron-coloured, somewhat transparent, parting freely from the stone, tender, juicy, sugary, and delicious. Ripens early. From Aleppo, where it is stated there exist thirteen varieties with sweet kernels.

LARGE EARLY (fig. 186).—Fruit large, somewhat oblong, flattened on the sides; skin pale-orange, bright with reddish-russet spots next the sun; flesh orange, juicy, and rich. Valuable on account of its earliness.

LARGE RED.—A variety of the Peach Apricot, resembling Large Early in shape and size, but having a much deeper coloured skin, which is most

Fig. 187.—Apricot. Moor Park

handsome when the fruits have had full exposure; flesh free, juicy, and rich. Tree hardy and a good cropper. Late August to early September.

MOOR PARK (fig. 187).—Fruit large, roundish, compressed, flattened on the summit; skin brownish-orange with brownish-red specks; flesh, dull-orange, juicy, peculiarly rich and excellent. Is not liable to become mealy; but in some unfavourable seasons and situations it occasionally does not ripen thoroughly on the side next the wall, and in wet seasons it sometimes cracks. Extensively cultivated, and deservedly so. It is said to have been imported from the Continent by Lord Anson, and planted at Moor Park, near Rickmansworth.

MUSCH-MUSCH. — Fruit small, roundish, 1¾ inches in diameter; skin slightly downy, lemon-yellow, deep-orange tinged with red next the sun; flesh somewhat transparent, parting from the stone, tender, and rich. Bears abundantly; fruit excellent for preserving. Said to be cultivated in Egypt.

NEW LARGE EARLY.—In appearance this resembles Large Early, but is richer in flavour, and ripens a fortnight earlier. The mentioning of these two important facts will alone suffice to commend this variety to the notice of cultivators, and a place for one or more trees should be found in every garden where the Apricot will succeed.

OULLIN'S EARLY.—A variety of the Peach Apricot, equal to it in size, surpassing it in flavour. A first-rate grower and a free bearer; the bark is conspicuously shining. Early August. Should be planted on a southern aspect to supply very early fruits.

PEACH.—Fruit large after the style of Large Early, oval and flattened, sutured; skin yellow, darker when exposed; flesh deep-yellow, juicy, and very richly flavoured, parting freely from the stone. Early September.

POWELL'S LATE.—Resembles Moor Park, and is quite as free a cropper, but is of hardier constitution. Fruits medium, richly coloured; flesh juicy, and highly flavoured. Mid-September.

ROMAN.—Fruit above the middle size, oval, compressed; skin pale-orange, dotted with red next the sun; flesh pale-yellow, parting readily from the stone, soft, and soon becoming mealy, especially if not gathered a little before it is fully ripe. Tree vigorous and a great bearer.

ROYAL.—Fruit about the size of Moor Park, roundish oval, slightly compressed; skin dull-yellow, tinged with red next the sun; flesh pale-orange, juicy, and rich. Ripens about ten days earlier than Moor Park, to which it bears much resemblance. Raised in the garden of the Luxembourg.

ST. AMBROISE.—A large-fruited early variety, the fruit being fit for use by the middle of August. It has a juicy rich flesh, and is of similar flavour to Moor Park. Tree hardy, and a great bearer.

SHIPLEY'S (Blenheim).—Fruit large, oval ; skin yellow; flesh juicy, not so rich as Moor Park. A good sort for culinary purposes. Ripe mid-August. Allied to Large Early.

TURKEY.—Fruit large, spherical, deep-yellow, with a number of brownish-orange spots and blotches on the exposed side; flesh pale-yellow, firm, juicy, sweet, with a little acid, very rich and excellent, stone separating freely. Ripens on a south wall about mid-August.

SELECTION OF SORTS SUITABLE FOR GROWING UNDER GLASS

Frogmore Early, Hemskerk, Large Early, Moor Park, Oullin's Early, Shipley, Powell's Late.

CHERRIES

The cultivated varieties of Cherries have been derived from two species of Prunus which grow wild in Britain, namely, *P. Cerasus*, the wild Cherry, and *P. Avium*, the Gean. The former is the origin of the Morello, Duke, and Kentish varieties, and the latter of the Gean, Heart, and Bigarreau varieties. The cultivation of the Cherry in this country is said to have been started in the time of Henry VIII, when several varieties were introduced from Italy into Kent. There are now more than one hundred named varieties grown in England, and some of the best of them were raised by Mr. Rivers of Sawbridgeworth. The Cherry Orchards of Kent have long been famous for the quantity and quality of the fruit produced in them. In some parts of Germany, Belgium, and Italy they are common as roadside trees, where they afford shade and yield copious crops of fruit.

The fruit of the Cherry is ripe earlier than that of any other hardy fruit-tree. The sweet kinds are highly valued for dessert, the acid or sub-acid varieties being used for pies, tarts, and in confectionery. The Morello is excellent for bottling, or preserving in brandy; and from a small black variety, largely grown in the district of the Upper Rhine, the Germans make the well-known Kirschwasser. Griotte de Ratafia, a small Morello, is employed for making the cordial ratafia; and a small, black, wild Cherry is used in the distillation of the Italian liqueur maraschino. It may, however, be well to remark that in the manufacture of the above liquors the stones and kernels are pounded and fermented with the pulp; and, as the kernels contain prussic acid, due caution should be exercised in their use. The Kentish, Flemish, and Montmorency varieties have the stalk so firmly attached to the stone that the latter may be drawn out by it, so that the fruit may then be dried like raisins, in the sun, or in an oven.

The varieties of the Cherry are divided by the French into three groups, namely, *Merisiers* and *Guigniers*; *Bigarreautiers*; *Cerisiers* and *Griottiers*.

Merisiers are the wild Cherries of the woods; the tree is tall and pyramidal, the branches horizontal, the fruit red, black, or white, with some degree of bitterness. *Guigniers* are considered to be improved varieties of these, the fruit being larger, heart-shaped, with a soft, very sweet flesh.

Bigarreautiers do not naturally assume a pyramidal form, and the extremities of the shoots are rather inclined to become pendulous, whilst the fruit differs from that of the Guignier in the flesh being crisp and firm. This division includes the Bigarreau, and many of the Heart Cherries.

Cerisiers are not so strong-growing as the preceding, and the fruit is more or less acid, the pulp being tender and juicy. *Griottiers* are scarcely distinguishable from them, except by a bitterness which is combined with the acidity of the fruit. The May Duke, Kentish, and Flemish Cherries belong to the Cerisiers; the Morello to the Griottiers.

Another and perhaps simpler classification of Cherries was proposed in the *Horticultural Transactions*, 2nd series, vol. i, p. 251, and is as follows:—

The first class consists of Cherries of which Bigarreau and Black Heart may be instanced as typical of the better kinds. The leaves are generally large, pendant, coarsely serrated, undulated, the veins prominent beneath, of thinner texture and of a more yellowish green than those of the second class; buds pointed; flowers large, produced on wood not less than two years old; petals loosely set, not forming a well-expanded cup-shaped flower, like those of May Duke, Kentish, &c.; stamens slender, and irregular in length, some being longer and others shorter than the style.

The second class is composed of aqueous Cherries, such as May Duke, Kentish, and Morello. The leaves are generally smaller than those of the first class, and are not toothed or undulated; the veins are less prominent, whilst the texture is thicker. The petioles are thicker, and keep the leaves from hanging loosely and pendent. The flowers expand widely, and the petals form

CHERRIES

Early Rivers (black): Emperor Francis (red): Bigarreau (white)

-a regular cup-shaped flower, with strong stamens, generally shorter than the style.

The subdivisions of the first class are taken from the form and colour of the fruit, and require no further explanation.

In the second class, as all the varieties are coloured nearly alike, no white nor white-and-red fruit having yet been met with among them, the form of the fruit, the sweetness or acidity of its flesh, and the colour of the juice constitute the distinctions of the sections.

CLASS I.—*Geans.*—LEAVES UNDULATED

Division 1.—*Fruit heart-shaped or oval.*
A, Colour uniform, dark-red or black.
B, Colour pale-yellow and red.
C, Colour uniform, pale-yellow.

Division 2.—*Fruit round or oblate.*
A, Colour uniform, dark-red or black.
B, Colour pale-yellow and red.
C, Colour uniform, pale-yellow.

CLASS II.—*Griottes.*—LEAVES NOT UNDULATED

Division 1.—*Fruit roundish heart-shaped.*
A, Flesh sweet.
  a, Juice pale.
  b, Juice purple.
B, Flesh acid.
  a, Juice pale.
  b, Juice purple.

Division 2.—*Fruit round or oblate.*
A, Flesh sweet.
  a, Juice pale.
  b, Juice purple.
B, Flesh acid.
  a, Juice pale.
  b, Juice purple.

Dr. Hogg, in his *Fruit Manual*, divides the above two classes into Geans and Griottes respectively, a very simple classification that finds favour with most fruit-growers.

CULTIVATION IN THE OPEN AIR

Soil and Situation.—The best soil for the Cherry is a moderately rich, free, rather sandy loam, with a well-drained subsoil. Stiff moist soils are unsuitable; and so, on the other hand, are dry gravelly subsoils. The trees require a large amount of moisture, particularly the sorts with large leaves, such as the Bigarreau and Heart Cherries. In free soils the roots can more easily travel after moisture; but in clayey or stiff loamy soils, when this is exhausted, they are fixed, as it were, in a compact, hard-baked mass, from which they can draw no moisture. In dry loose soil, on the contrary, there is considerable circulation of air, which, being charged with moisture at night, will afford a supply of that necessary element to the roots, not in abundance, it is true, but to a beneficial extent.

A southern exposure is best for the Cherry; but the Morello and Kentish varieties will bear fruit useful for kitchen purposes on a wall with a north aspect. An east wall can also be utilized for the production of a good succession of sweet Cherries.

Planting.—The soil must be well prepared and in good condition, but not freshly manured. It should be trenched 2 or 3 feet deep, and if there is a stratum of light sandy loam below the surface soil, the latter ought to be placed in the bottom of the trench, and the loam brought to the top. The border should be made firm before planting is done. The holes must be made large, and the tree

should be planted, not amongst heavy clayey loam, but in tolerably rich free soil, and if the latter is mixed with turfy loam so much the better. The method of planting is the same as for the Apple, Pear, and Plum.

The distance should vary according to the size which the variety usually attains, and according to the breadth of its foliage, for if it have large leaves it will evaporate much, and will require a larger space for its roots to travel in quest of moisture, to make good that evaporation which in dry weather will be more than the amount of rain which falls upon the surface overhung by the branches. As standards the Bigarreau tribe may be planted 30 feet apart, or even more in rich soil; the May Duke, Morello, and similar varieties at 20 and 25 feet apart. Bushes and pyramids of the vigorous Bigarreau varieties should be 12 feet apart; the Duke family 9 feet apart. Single cordons may be 18 inches apart, and the two-branched vertical-trained trees 30 inches to 3 feet apart. Against walls and espaliers from 20 to 24 feet should be allowed for the Bigarreau, Elton, and Florence Cherries, and from 15 to 20 feet for the May Duke and Morello. Riders or tall trained standards may be disposed between the dwarf trained trees with a view to utilizing all the wall space till the dwarf trees want the room, when they may either be gradually cut out or transplanted to another position.

Pruning and Training.—The Cherry, as a

Fig. 188.—Standard Cherry (May Duke)

The head should be formed as directed for the Apple and Pear, with this exception, that the first three shoots of the Bigarreau kinds may be shortened to 15 inches; two shoots from each should be encouraged, one situated at the end, the other 3 inches nearer the stem, so that there may be room for the branches to increase in thickness without pressing against each other, as this gives rise to gumming, as is also sometimes the case when two large limbs originate from two adjoining buds. After the principal branches of the head have been started, very little pruning will be required. It will be well, however, to see that the principal branches are maintained of as nearly equal strength as possible for a few years, and then the tree may be allowed to take its natural development, with the exception of cutting out shoots that would otherwise form cross branches.

The Morello succeeds well as a low standard, and all the Duke family, together with the sturdy-growing Early Rivers, Elton, and Governor Wood, may be grown either pyramidal, bush, or cordon form. In either case they can be framed out from maidens, much as advised for Apples and Pears thus trained. Birds are the greatest hindrances to success with these forms of trees, but if grouped they might be permanently protected

standard, requires but little pruning after the stem has been reared and the six principal branches of the head formed. The stem ought to be grown so as to ensure its tapering; and on this account it is necessary that it should not be stripped of shoots and foliage. The temporary side-shoots left should not, however, be allowed to retain too great a length; they ought not to be permitted to compete with the leader, but must be checked when likely to do so. Further, these shoots should not be more than two years old when they are cut close to the stem, in order that the wounds may heal the more readily, and with less risk of gumming. As the leaves on the shoots of a young tree are usually large, a few shoots will deposit a considerable quantity of alburnum on the stem below them; consequently, in proportion to that amount, the stem will be thickened more beneath such shoots than above them. Hence the requisite taper form will soon be obtained, and the side-shoots dispensed with when one, or at most two years old.

Fig. 189.—Cherry, half standard (Morello)

with galvanized wire-netting, cordons often being employed for clothing the support of wire-netting-covered structures, principally devoted to Gooseberry culture.

In training against espaliers the branches should be 1 foot apart, and, like those of the Plum, they ought to spring from the stem with an upward course, and afterwards be trained horizontally. In summer pruning, whilst the tree is young and requires foliage to assist in making roots, the summer shoots may be allowed to grow to 1 foot or 15 inches

In training the Cherry against walls, the horizontal mode may be adopted for those that are under 7 feet high, but those above that height will be sooner covered by the fan method. Whatever mode be adopted, care should be taken that the lower branches are vigorous. It is difficult to render a branch vigorous if it has originated in a weak shoot. A weakly stem cannot produce a strong shoot; therefore the young tree must be well established, and in a vigorous state, before shoots to commence the lower branches are started.

Fig. 190.—Dwarf Bush Cherry (Morello)

in length, and then be shortened to 3 inches. But the shoots on the upper branches must be shortened at least a week before those on the lower ones. The leading shoots, those at the extremities of the horizontals, need not be shortened. After the tree has been planted a few years, clusters of fruit-buds will generally form round the bases of the shoots, and likewise on spurs along the branches. With regard to the winter-pruning, very little will be required, presuming that the summer-pruning has been well performed. The stubs left in shortening back the summer laterals should be cut back to a length of 2 or 3 inches, or to the first wood-bud beyond the fruit-buds above alluded to as likely to form at the bases of the shoots.

The directions given for espalier training will apply to horizontal training against a wall, only the summer shoots ought to be shortened more, in order that the fruit may be produced near the wall.

The distance between the branches may be 9 inches for the Duke, and 1 foot for the Bigarreau kinds, their leaves being not only much larger than those of the Duke, but also more pendulous.

The Morello Cherry requires different pruning and training from other kinds, owing to its mode of growth and bearing. Its shoots are slender, and it fruits on those of the previous summer's growth; sometimes all the buds along the shoot are blossom-buds, the terminal bud only being a wood-bud; therefore at the winter pruning such shoots ought not to be shortened. Further, as the fruit is borne chiefly on the young wood, a succession of such must be kept up. There ought, of course, to be a certain quantity of old wood to bear the young, in fact the shoots should be treated somewhat like those of the Peach; they must be trained in summer to bear fruit in the following season, after which they should be cut away; but, whilst bearing fruit, a young shoot ought to be trained to replace them. It is frequently the case that branches and shoots of Morello trees are overcrowded, but this should be avoided, otherwise large and fine fruit cannot be obtained.

Manures.—Cherry trees arrived at a large, heavy-cropping stage soon exhaust the soil of much of its fertility, in particular lime, potash, and phosphoric acid.

These elements must annually be returned to the soil, otherwise the trees will not remain in a profitable condition. Farmyard and horse-stall manure freely applied is apt to promote a too rank growth, but may safely be applied in the form of a top-dressing during the winter—not digging it in for fear of injury to the roots—when the trees show signs of exhaustion. Artificial manures, as a rule, are most easily applied. A mixture that answers well for Cherry trees is as follows: Superphosphate of lime, 5 lb.; sulphate of potash, 2 lb.; sulphate of magnesia, $\frac{1}{2}$ lb.; chloride of soda, $\frac{1}{2}$ lb. Apply this during mild weather in February at the rate of 4 oz. to the square yard, or the full quantity (8 lb.) per rod.

Protection.—Birds, and particularly the blackbird and thrush, are the greatest enemies to the Cherry crop, and the only effectual means of protecting the fruit is by enclosing them in netting. This should be put over the trees so as not to confine the foliage. Although in the case of wall-trees it is necessary that the net should be well closed, so as to prevent ingress at top, bottom, and sides, yet when in doing so the leaves are crowded against each other, the appearance and the effects are bad. The net should hang clear of the leaves; and this may be easily done by running a wire through hooks below the coping, and having another sup-ported about 12 inches from the wall. If the netting be fixed to the former, and drawn over the latter, the object will be so far attained. The netting will hang tolerably clear of the foliage, but it has yet to be fastened at bottom, and this should be done so that it may be readily loosened at any time

when fruit requires to be gathered. Small stakes may be driven in to a uniform height, a stout wire fastened along their tops, and to this the net can be easily hooked. When nets touch the ground they are liable to be damaged by rain and damp; it would therefore be better to fix wire-netting to the stakes close to the ground.

For espalier trees wire-netting, if only 1 foot in width, should also be used next the soil, and joined to such other kind of netting as can be afforded for protecting the rest of the tree. If wire-netting be run along to the height of 1 foot, and so that its lower edge may touch the ground, a light netting, such as that used by fishermen, may be thrown over the tree, and attached to the wire on both sides; for the material alluded to is so light that it will not press so as to crowd the foliage.

By adopting some efficient means of protection, good crops of the sweet kinds of Cherries may be obtained from walls; and this is more than can be said of standard trees, for from these it is scarcely possible to obtain a crop of perfectly ripened fruit on account of the birds. If the trees be not too large, some fruit may be saved by the use of black cotton; this should be got in reels and the reel thrown over the tree repeatedly from side to side. If a supply can be obtained from espaliers, it is certainly better to grow the trees against these, and thus render the space they would otherwise have occupied on walls available for other fruits. It is, however, in most gardens quite worth while to devote some wall-space to Cherries.

Propagation.—For stocks and for obtaining new varieties the Cherry is raised from seeds. Those of the small black or red Cherries are the kinds usually sown for stocks. For trees intended to be planted against a wall or espalier, stocks raised from the stones of the Duke, or Morello, have been recommended. For very dwarf trees the Mahaleb has long been employed in France, and to some extent in this country, as a stock on which to graft or bud May Duke, Kentish, Morello, and such like sorts, but it is not adapted for large-leaved strong-growing varieties like the Bigarreau. The stones may be stratified till early in spring, when those beginning to germinate should be planted in drills, and covered to a depth of $1\frac{1}{2}$ inches; or they may be sown at that depth in light sandy soil immediately after they have been taken from the fruit. In two years the seedlings intended for stocks will be fit to plant out in nursery rows.

Budding and Grafting.—Propagation by these means is the same as for the Plum. The operation must be performed early, and, if properly done, there is little danger of failure. If left until the buds have considerably advanced, the grafts frequently do not resist the effects of dry weather. We have seen vigorous shoots with large pith cut off for scions and stuck in the ground in January; and though in March, when grafted, the pith was discoloured, being of a dark instead of a light colour, yet the grafts all succeeded, whilst scions cut off and grafted fresh failed to a considerable extent, although treated with the same care in every other respect. Sometimes, in old trees of the May Duke class, every bud on the scions is a blossom-bud with the exception of the terminal one; this should therefore be preserved, otherwise failure is certain.

CHERRIES UNDER GLASS

The following directions for the cultivation of Cherries under glass are taken, with the author's permission, from a paper by Mr. H. Somers Rivers, Sawbridgeworth.

The most convenient house for Cherries is a span roof 24 feet wide, 4½ feet high at the eaves, and 12 feet to the ridge. Ventilators 18 inches wide, hinged at the bottom, run round the sides; the top ventilators are 3 feet wide by 15 inches, 7½ feet apart, on alternate sides of the ridge. We used to fruit our Cherries in a smaller house, 14 feet wide and 9 feet to the ridge. This scarcely allowed sufficient head room for the trees, many of them fifteen years old. Certainly they seem grateful for the increased breathing-space.

As soon as their crops are finished, the trees are taken out of the house and plunged nearly up to the pot-rims in a border outside. The reason for plunging is twofold: first, the earth which envelops them keeps the pots and their contents moist and renders the labour of watering less heavy; and, secondly, the somewhat top-heavy trees are thus in no danger of being blown over. Water must be given to the trees during dry weather, and an occasional good syringing will keep them clean and healthy. In October the trees should again be brought into the orchard-house for repotting, before which process they must be under cover for a time, so that the earth in the pots shall not be sodden. This also applies to the mixture to be used for repotting: a good loam with rotten manure in the proportion of one load to two, and broken-up mortar-rubble, a barrow-load to a load.

In repotting, the outer soil, filled with fibrous rootlets, is scraped away, leaving a ball of earth containing the larger roots; the tree is replaced in the pot, and the new soil rammed in firmly and evenly nearly up to the rim. The surface is at the same level round the trunk as before. Thorough repotting need only be done in alternate years. In intermediate years the outer soil can be removed nearly down to the bottom of the pot and replaced by fresh without taking out the tree. A good drainage, very necessary with Cherries, is provided for by a layer of crocks at the bottom of the pot. In repotting, the tree must not be moved into too large a pot: an 11-inch pot is ample for a three-year-old tree, which may be given one size larger at each repotting if necessary; an 18-inch pot will contain the largest tree.

When this operation is finished, the trees are stood as close together as possible, in single rows, in the house, in one end of which is heaped sufficient barley-straw to pack round and over the pots, making a layer of about a foot deep, when there is severe frost, and the trees are snug for the winter. Water must be given until the leaves are all fallen; from about the middle of November to the end of December the trees will require none at all. If January be mild they should have some water again, and from then onwards occasionally when necessary.

Towards the end of February the trees must be pruned—an operation rendered quite unnecessary in some cases, where the older trees in full bearing make no new shoots. The last year's growths must be cut back to about five eyes; with very strong shoots, or in the case of strong growers, eight to ten eyes may be left. Water will now be wanted about once a week. The pruning finished, the house should be set out, i.e. the trees placed in their permanent positions for the summer; and this should be done symmetrically and carefully, as it makes all the difference in the appearance of the house. A centre border 5½ feet wide takes two rows of trees, a path 3 feet wide runs round it, leaving side borders 5½ feet wide. The floor of the house is firm and solid, never being stirred, and the path is rammed gravel and clay. A thin layer of fine cinders over the surface of the borders gives them a neat appearance and is kept raked and clean. The pots may be plunged in the borders up to about 3 inches of their rims, a bed of large cinders being placed in the bottom of each hole to allow the water to drain efficiently. The trees should be grouped with regard to the colour of their fruit. A good smoking with tobacco paper now will lessen the

Fig. 191.—Cherry. White Heart

number of aphides hereafter, the trees being syringed thoroughly the next morning.

About the middle of March the trees are a mass of white blossom, and are wonderfully beautiful: this gives place to dinginess for a time when the flowers fade. The calyx remains round the swelling fruit for a long time and must be removed, as also the scales at the base of the fruit-stalks, which, although they fall off eventually, persist until the fruit is nearly developed, if suffered to do so, and harbour insects, &c. The thinning of the fruits should be done when stoning is finished, and all those fruits which are not going to swell can be detected. Ample room must be allowed to each berry, so that

the fruits shall not be overcrowded when ripe. The bunches will have ultimately from six to sixteen or twenty fruits.

During flowering all the ventilation possible must be given, except when there are cutting winds; a single hot-water pipe running round the house will keep out the frost if necessary. Water will not be required in large quantity, sufficient being given to prevent the earth from becoming over-dry. When the foliage is coming out, and from then onward, water must be given more frequently according to the weather. The amount of water the individual trees require may be easily ascertained by tapping the pot, which will give quite a bell-like note if the earth be dry. When watering, the borders and paths should be thoroughly damped down to ensure moisture in the air. The trees must be syringed morning and evening until the fruit begins to colour, after which it should be discontinued, or the fruit will crack.

Liquid manure or soot water should be given twice a week after stoning; and, as there is so little earth in the pot compared to the crop it ripens, additional food must be given in the shape of a top-dressing of equal parts of kiln-dust and horse-droppings mixed, making a layer of about 2 inches thick near the rim of the pot, sloping down to the stem so as to form a basin to hold the water. Two top-dressings will be necessary: the first when the fruits are stoning, the second when they are colouring, by which time the goodness of the first application will be exhausted. When the young shoots have made a dozen or so good leaves they should be pinched back to eight or ten. One pinching is sufficient, subsequent growths being left alone.

The worst insect enemy to contend with is the black fly, but it may be kept down by watchfulness. The first smoking, with tobacco paper, referred to above, will do much; subsequently the trees may be smoked at any period with the patent vaporizing compounds now sold. X L ALL may be used with perfect safety, even during flowering. For Cherries the glass should be shaded by syringing with whitewash when the fruit is ripe. The direct rays of the sun are too scorching if the summer be hot.

There are many good Cherries well adapted to pot work when budded on the Mahaleb. Though it is a mistake to have too many varieties, several are needed to cover all the season.

In mid-June Belle d'Orleans and Guigne Annonay are ripe, the former light-red, the latter black, both excellent Cherries and good croppers, though the fruit is somewhat small, and that of the latter soon becomes dull after ripening. Werder's Early Black ripens next; the fruit of this sort also soon loses its lustre, and it is scarcely worth growing, since Early Rivers ripens almost at the same time. Early Rivers is an ideal pot Cherry, bearing its large black fruits abundantly; they are of excellent flavour, and hang on the tree a month after ripening, perfectly sound and bright to the last. Black Circassian, Bigarreau de Schreken, and Bedford Prolific, three good black Cherries, follow.

In July we have Bigarreau Noir de Guben; Governor Wood, an excellent pale-red Cherry, which is, however, very liable to crack if water touches the ripening fruit;

Belle de Choisy, a fine Duke; Frogmore Bigarreau, red; May Duke; Elton, a handsome bright-red Bigarreau; White Bigarreau, with waxen-yellow fruit, slightly tinged with red next the sun; Turkey Black Heart, a fine pot Cherry with firm, juicy fruit; Reine Hortense, a large Duke; Monstrueuse de Mezel, a very large dark-red Bigarreau; Bigarreau Napoléon, deep-red; Black Hawk and Emperor Francis, a very large bright-red Bigarreau.

In August ripen Late Duke; Large Black Bigarreau; Guigne de Winkler, bright-red; Late Black Bigarreau; and last, but not by any means least, Géant d'Hédelfinger, a brownish-black Cherry of immense size with very firm flesh.

DISEASES AND INSECTS

The Cherry suffers little from pest or disease when planted in a suitable soil and situation, and in other respects properly managed. The disease of most frequent occurrence is that known as gumming, and this is rarely injurious, except in cases where it prevails to a very great extent. It is caused by an exudation of the sap from a rent in the bark arising from accidental wounds, unskilful pruning, or from the breakage of a branch. It sometimes occurs in consequence of too many branches being allowed to grow very closely together on the stem, and not unfrequently results from the tree having been worked on an unsuitable stock, or planted in too rich soil. In the latter case the obvious remedy is to take up the tree and replant it in a poorer soil; but if this cannot be done, root pruning, which by limiting the supply of nourishment obtained by the roots will diminish the flow of sap, may be advantageously adopted with a view of checking the disease; but, above all, vicissitudes of dryness and moisture at the roots should be prevented.

A leaf disease of Cherries has lately been reported from several orchards in the county of Kent. In the early summer it affects the leaves and fruit simultaneously, rendering the latter unfit for market. In autumn and winter its presence is easily detected. The diseased leaves remain attached to the branches as if the tree had been killed in the full vigour of growth, just as the withered leaves remain on a branch that has been severed from the stem. The fall of the leaf in autumn is a normal process carried out by the living leaf, which forms at the point of

its attachment to the branch a cicatrix that secures when completed the easy severance of the leaf from the branch, leaving a clear scar. The speedy and fatal injury to the leaf caused by the fungus prevents the formation of this cicatrix, and the leaf remains attached to the tree, showing in black spots the fruits of the fungus.

A further striking characteristic of this disease is the shortening of the branches which bear the diseased leaves. The internodes or joints between the leaves of these branches have not been developed. The year's growth, which should have extended to a considerable length, measures less than an inch. The crowded leaf bases have each a healthy bud in the axil. The dwarfing of the branch is not due to any attack from a fungus, for no fungus is present in the tissues. The dwarfing is entirely due to the want of food, consequent on the early death of the leaf. That this is the case is confirmed by the fact that some of the dwarfed branches have produced in the following year vigorous normal shoots.

The disease has been spreading rapidly in Kent during the last few years. The varieties of Cherry trees that have been reported as specially liable are Waterloo, Bigarreau, Frogmore, Napoléon, Black Hearts, Clusters, and Eltons. Turks and Governor Woods have not as yet suffered much, and English and Flemish Reds and May Dukes have not been attacked, though odd trees of other varieties, such as Bigarreau, growing among them have been diseased. In one orchard the disease attacked Waterloo first, soon spreading to other kinds, while at another place this variety had not been affected until later, and then only the leaves had suffered, the fruit had not been damaged.

Professor Frank has described a serious injury to Cherry trees in Germany which, there is little doubt, is the same as the disease that has attacked the Cherry orchards in Kent. The malady was first observed in the Cherry orchards of the Altenland on the lower Elbe in Germany about the year 1880. The diseased leaves remain on the tree all winter, and are intermixed with the new foliage of the following season. In spring he found on the dead leaves a fungus fruit that had not been present on them in autumn, a perithecium round at the base, about one-twelfth of an inch in diameter, tapering up into a pointed beak that projects from the under surface of the leaf. These perithecia contain the spores that re-infect the young leaves and fruit. The fungus had already been described by Auerswald under the name of *Gnomonia erythrostoma*. Frank traces the rapid spread of the disease in the Altenland to the overcrowding of fruit-trees and to the presence of open ditches in the neighbourhood of the orchards causing too much moisture, and so presenting conditions favouring the growth of parasitic fungi. While such adverse conditions should be remedied, he recommends, as the only method of stamping out the disease, the gathering and burning of all diseased leaves, which, he considers, need not be attended with more difficulty than the yearly harvesting of the fruit. It is very important that Cherry-growers should at once be made acquainted with the cause of the injury to the orchards and the remedy recommended by Frank, which is the destruction of the dead leaves. To be efficient, this collecting and burning of the dead leaves must not be done in a solitary orchard here and there, but must be carried out throughout Kent.

Enemies.—Tortrix, Birds, Cherry Aphis, Pear-leaf Blister Moth, Slug-worms, Vapourer Moth, Winter Moth, Goat Moth, Stem-boring Weevils. See INSECT ENEMIES, Vol. III. *Fungi.*—Black knot, Shot hole, Leaf scald, Leaf rust. See PLANT DISEASES, Vol. III.

LIST OF VARIETIES

GEANS

BELLE D'ORLEANS.—Tree strong grower, but tender; free-bearing. Fruit medium to large, roundish, somewhat heart-shaped, yellowish-white, pale-red on sunny side; flesh juicy and rich in flavour. Ripens middle of June. Excellent for forcing in a cool house, south wall, also garden and orchard in warm positions.

BIGARREAU (fig. 192).— Fruit large, roundish heart-shaped, slightly flattened on the side and at the apex, white on the shaded side, bright-red mottled with amber next the sun; flesh firm, nearly white, sweet, and rich. Tree vigorous, an abundant bearer, succeeds well as a standard in the south of England; requires a wall in the northern parts of the kingdom. It ripens in late-July to mid-August, according to the season and situation.

BIGARREAU DE SCHREKEN.—Tree strong-growing, branching freely. Fruit extra large, roundish, shining black; flesh firm, juicy, rich, and pleasing. Ripens end of June. Good for cool house and walls.

BIGARREAU NAPOLEON.—Resembles Bigarreau, the fruit being about the same size, the flesh equally firm, and the flavour similar; but it is rather longer in shape, darker in colour, and ripens later. A most abundant bearer, and is well deserving of cultivation either as a standard or upon a wall.

BIGARREAU NOIR DE GUBEN. — Very prolific, large and good, lustrous brownish-red. Good garden variety. July.

BLACK EAGLE.—Tree forms a roundish spreading head. Fruit roundish heart-shaped, black when well exposed and fully ripe; flesh tender, with a rich, dark-purplish juice. Ripens soon

after May Duke. Deserves cultivation as an orchard tree. Was raised at Downton Castle

Fig. 192.—Cherry. Bigarreau

about 1806, by Miss Elizabeth Knight, from Bigarreau, fertilized with pollen of May Duke.

BLACK HEART. — Branches spreading. Fruit tolerably large, blunt, heart-shaped, somewhat compressed, nearly black; flesh deep-claret, tender, tolerably juicy and rich. Stone large roundish ovate.

BLACK TARTARIAN. — Tree upright, vigorous grower, spreading with age, rather tender, an abundant bearer. Fruit very large, blackish-brown, black when full ripe; flesh rather tender than firm, juicy and richly flavoured, keeping well. Ripens early in July. One of the best for forcing, good for walls and in warm positions; succeeds well in an orchard.

BÜTTNER'S BLACK HEART. — A good bearer, scarcely distinguishable from Black Heart. It has, however, a more vigorous constitution, and does better in orchards.

EARLY JABOULAY (Early Lyons). — Tree a strong grower and spreading in habit, but tender, bearing abundantly. Fruit large, obtuse, heart-shaped, light-red; flesh juicy, coloured, rich, and delicious. Ripens end of June. Good for forcing, cool house and wall.

EARLY PURPLE GUIGNE. — Flowers early. Fruit above the middle size, heart-shaped, shining dark-purple; flesh purplish, juicy, tender, and rich. Is of moderately strong growth, and a medium bearer, its principal merit being its earliness. It ripens, in the south of England, on an east or west wall, in early June, or about a fortnight earlier than May Duke.

EARLY RIVERS (fig. 193).—Tree vigorous, healthy, hardy, and an abundant bearer. Fruit large, heart-shaped, shining black, borne in clusters often ten or twelve, two to four being on one peduncle; flesh juicy, sweet, and richly flavoured. Ripens middle to end of June. Considered by many practical growers as the best black Cherry in cultivation. A fine Cherry, good for forcing, walls, pyramids, or standards.

ELTON.—This very excellent variety was raised by Mr. Knight in 1806, probably from Bigarreau crossed with White Heart. Tree very strong and spreading. Fruit large, heart-shaped, pale waxy-yellow on the shaded side, mottled with red next the sun; flesh whitish, rather firm, sugary, and very rich. Ripens in the beginning, middle, or end of July, according to climate and situation.

It is a good bearer, and highly deserving of cultivation either as a standard or against a wall.

EMPEROR FRANCIS. — Tree strong-growing, branching, and free-bearing. Fruit very large, bright-red, very handsome; flesh firm, juicy, rich, and delicious. Ripens middle of August, afterwards hanging well.

FLORENCE.—Tree vigorous, resembling Bigarreau. Fruit very large, obtusely heart-shaped, pale-amber, mottled with red; flesh firm, juicy,

Fig. 193.—Cherry. Early Rivers

rich, and sweet. Ripens so as to succeed Bigarreau, but requires a west or south-west wall, except in warm parts of the kingdom.

FROGMORE EARLY.—Tree free-growing, healthy, and an abundant bearer. Fruit large, obtuse, heart-shaped, pale-yellow, marbled with red; flesh very juicy, sweet, and rich. Ripens early in June. Good for wall and garden culture. Forces well.

GOVERNOR WOOD.—Tree attains a large size, and bears abundantly. Fruit large, yellow, washed and mottled with light-red; flesh more tender than firm, juicy, sweet, and rich. Ripens early in July. Excellent for forcing, walls, pyramids, or standards.

GUIGNE D'ANNONAY.—The earliest Cherry to ripen on a south wall. Fruit blackish-brown, small, but of good flavour. Excellent for early forcing in pots.

KNIGHT'S EARLY BLACK.—Fruit large, heart-shaped, shining black; flesh deep-purple, firm, juicy, and rich; differs from Black Tartarian in being more blunt at the apex, and it is also earlier. Has ripened on a south wall about the middle of June, even before May Duke. This excellent sort was raised by Mr. Knight, about the year 1810, from Bigarreau crossed with May Duke. The tree is similar in growth and foliage to Black Tartarian. It fruits freely either as a standard or against a wall. Good also for pot culture.

LUDWIG'S BIGARREAU.—Tree strong-growing and spreading, an abundant bearer. Fruit large, heart-shaped, handsome, shining bright-red; flesh tender, melting, sweet, and rich. Good for garden culture.

MONSTRUEUSE DE MEZEL.—A very large and fine Bigarreau. Fruit dark-red. August. Good for pot culture.

NOBLE.—Tree robust and hardy. Fruit resembling Black Tartarian, but larger and firmer when ripe. Of excellent quality. Ripe in July, keeping well into August. A comparatively new variety of great merit.

TRADESCANT'S BLACK HEART.—An old variety, said to have been raised by John Tradescant, gardener to Charles I. It differs from Black Heart in having leaves not so deeply serrated. The fruit is about the same size, blackish, with stripes of dark-red; flesh firm, with a similar flavour to that of Black Heart, and ripening about a week later. Rather a shy bearer.

WATERLOO.—Tree of vigorous growth, bearing abundantly in most localities. Fruit large, obtuse heart-shaped, dark-purple and brownish-red, black when fully ripe; flesh rich and delicious. Ripens end of June. Good for gardens and orchards.

GRIOTTES

ARCHDUKE.—Tree vigorous, pendulous, and free-bearing. Fruit large, nearly an inch in diameter, inclining to heart-shape, dark-red, becoming almost black if allowed to hang; flesh very tender, rich, and briskly flavoured. Ripens middle to end of July. Good for walls and as a low standard.

BELLE DE MAGNIFIQUE.—Tree semi-erect, forming a good pyramid, and very prolific. Fruit very large, handsome, clear bright-red; flesh tender, juicy, and sub-acid. Ripens middle to end of August.

BÜTTNER'S OCTOBER MORELLO.—Fruit medium, roundish or oblate, dark brown-red; flesh pale-red, tender, acid. Ripens in October. Tree hardy, and a good bearer, and is deserving of cultivation as the latest Cherry which may be used for pies and for preserving.

EMPRESS EUGENIE.—Tree a moderately strong grower and a very free bearer. Fruit large, roundish, bright-red, purplish when fully ripe; flesh rather firm, but melting, very juicy, sugary, and refreshing. Ripens end of July. Forces well, and is also good for wall and garden trees. A serious defect is its liability to gumming.

KENTISH (Common Red, Pie Cherry, Sussex).— Fruit medium, round or oblate, bright-red, some-

times darker; flesh pale, very juicy, and acid. Ripens end of July. An abundant bearer, much cultivated as a standard, sometimes on a north wall.

LATE DUKE.—Tree vigorous, with spreading habit. Fruit large, roundish heart-shaped, shining-red; flesh amber-coloured, tender, juicy, and rich, more acid than May Duke. Ripens in August, when most tender-fleshed Cherries are over. A most abundant bearer as a standard, and deserves a place upon a wall, where it can be netted when in fruit.

MAY DUKE.—Tree erect. Fruit large, roundish, dark-red when well exposed; flesh red, tender, juicy, and rich. Ripe on standards in July, or in late June on walls. A good bearer, well adapted for forcing.

MORELLO.—Tree round-headed, with spreading or pendulous branches. Fruit large, obtusely heart-shaped, somewhat compressed, dark-red, becoming nearly black if allowed too hang; flesh deep purplish-red, tender, juicy, and acid. Ripens in July or August, but may be preserved on a tree against a wall till October. One of the most useful for preserving; bears well on a north wall.

NOUVELLE ROYAL.—Tree sturdy, compact, and a free bearer. Fruit larger than May Duke, dark-red, changing to black; flesh tender, juicy, brisk in flavour. Ripens end of July.

REINE HORTENSE.—Tree vigorous and very productive. Fruit large, long, and handsome; skin thin, bright-red, changing to dark brilliant-red by hanging; flesh tender, juicy, and somewhat acidulous.

ROYAL DUKE.—Tree similar to May Duke. Fruit large and handsome, oblate, shining dark-red when fully ripe; flesh reddish, tender, juicy, and very rich. Ripens middle or end of July, after May Duke and before Late Duke.

Twelve Sorts suitable for Cultivation as Standards

Bigarreau Napoléon.	Knight's Early Black.
Black Eagle.	Late Duke.
Büttner's Black Heart.	May Duke.
Early Rivers.	Morello.
Elton.	Royal Duke.
Governor Wood.	Waterloo.

Six Sorts suitable for a South Wall.

Bigarreau de Schreken	Elton.
Guigne d'Annonay.	May Duke.
Governor Wood.	Bigarreau Napoléon.

Six Sorts suitable for an East Wall.

Early Rivers.	Frogmore Early Bigarreau.
Emperor Francis.	
Florence.	Noble.
	Tradescant's Heart.

Three Sorts for a North Wall.

Kentish, Late Duke, and Morello.

Sorts suitable for a Cottage Garden.

Early Rivers.	May Duke.
Elton.	Morello.

GOOSEBERRIES

The cultivated varieties of the Gooseberry are all the progeny of *Ribes grossularia*, a native of N. Africa, N. W. Himalaya, and Europe, including the British Islands. The name Gooseberry most probably had its origin in the use of the fruits, which were made into a sauce to be eaten with young or green geese, instead of the apple sauce usually preferred now. It is especially in Germany, Holland, and England that the Gooseberry has been cultivated for its fruits, from about the sixteenth century.

"The Gooseberry is not alluded to by writers of the classical period. Turner mentions it in 1573, and Parkinson, in 1692, specifies eight varieties. The catalogue of the Horticultural Society for 1842 gives 149 varieties and the lists of Lancashire nurserymen are said to include above 300 names.

"The most interesting point in the history of the Gooseberry is the steady increase in the size of the fruit. Manchester is the metropolis of the fanciers, and prizes of from five shillings to five or ten pounds are yearly given for the heaviest fruit. The *Gooseberry Growers' Register* is published annually; the earliest known copy is dated 1786. The *Register* for 1845 gives an account of 171 Gooseberry shows held in different places during that year; and this fact shows on how large a scale the culture has been car-

ried on. The fruit of the wild Gooseberry weighs about a quarter of an ounce, or 5 dwt.; in 1786 Gooseberries were exhibited weighing 10 dwt.; in 1817, 26 dwt.; in 1825, 31 dwt.; in 1852, 37 dwt., that is between seven and eight times the weight of the wild fruit" (Darwin, *Animals and Plants under Domestication*).

The Gooseberry not only grows and bears well in the comparatively cool climate of Scotland and the north of England, but the fruit is also better flavoured than in the hotter parts of the south. It is not so good when brought to maturity by very hot weather as when ripened by a moderate temperature. In the northern counties the fruit acquires its full richness of flavour; but near London and farther south it is frequently overheated in ripening; the large sorts with thin skins appear as if parboiled, especially where the soil is not well manured and moist; likewise where the trees are pruned so as not to afford sufficient shade.

The large-fruited varieties are much cultivated for culinary purposes, the young fruit soon acquiring a size fit for pies, tarts, and puddings; hence they are of great importance in the neighbourhood of large towns. In this way the Gooseberry, though not the first ripe, is of all hardy fruits the earliest fit for use.

CULTIVATION

Soil and Situation.—The Gooseberry succeeds in any good garden soil that is loose and moist. It does not grow well in stiff clayey soils that become hard in hot, dry weather. To produce large fruit it should be planted in a compost of good turfy loam and rotten stable manure. The best-flavoured fruit is obtained from plants grown in an open situation.

Planting.—If planted on a large scale the distance between the plants should be 6 feet. The roots must be regularly spread out, and not buried deeper than they were before removal.

Pruning.—Bushes raised from cuttings, at

the end of the first year should have about four shoots each a foot long; these should be shortened to about half their length. From these four shortened shoots during the next summer a dozen or more new shoots will spring, and of these two of the best-placed and most vigorous on each main branch should be allowed to grow, pinching back all the others to four leaves. These summer-pinched laterals should be cut back in winter to an inch in length, but the extended new shoots will only require a few inches of the unripe tips cut off. For bushes of good size it is desirable to retain some young shoots their full length, or nearly so, to replace old, worn-out branches, which should be cut away, thus securing a supply of young shoots throughout the bush. This annual renewal of shoots will keep the bush in vigorous health. At the same time, there must be no overcrowding through neglect of summer-pruning.

A Gooseberry bush thus pruned fruits freely on the spurs formed along the entire length of the main branches, as well as on the annual new shoots. The older spurs, from their position, can only be kept vigorous and fruitful for successive years by the

young plants with three shoots, only they incline them nearly to a horizontal position. For this purpose they employ hooked sticks to pull down the shoots that are inclined to grow upright, and forked ones to support those that are inclined to grow too drooping. By next autumn these three shoots will have produced a number of lateral shoots, most of which may be cut back to one eye, and the others to half their length. The less the number of shoots, and the younger the tree, the larger will be the fruit. In November the tree is pruned so as to consist of the

Fig. 194.—Gooseberry. Leveller

free admission of air and light. A larger crop and finer fruit of better quality can be got from bushes thus pruned than from bushes in which the young shoots are all cut hard back, resulting in a thicket of shoots which smother all the lateral shoots growing inside the bush.

A model Gooseberry bush may be described as having main branches thinly disposed, furnished throughout with vigorous fruiting - spurs, and maintained so by the annual extension and addition of young wood. The largest fruit is produced on vigorous shoots of the preceding summer; and therefore, when size is the object, young shoots must be encouraged to supply the place of old wood, which must be cut away.

The Lancashire growers, who excel in growing very large Gooseberries, begin with

three primary shoots, each bearing two young shoots, which are shortened to about 7 inches in length. These last are pruned in the following autumn so as to have only two young shoots each, all the others being closely cut off. The aim is to keep up a constant supply of strong healthy young shoots, from which alone can be expected large and fine fruit; and wherever the shoots grow beyond bounds, they are cut back so as to keep the bush compact and furnished with new bearing wood; large fruit cannot be expected if the tree is crowded with shoots. Attention must be given to the roots also, which are pruned every two or three years. Trenches filled with compost or manure are formed round the bush, into which it may strike root. The bushes are mulched and regularly supplied with water; the fruit is thinned excessively, so as to leave only two or three on each branch. By these means, and by placing a saucer with water under the fruit, the latter attains an enormous size —upwards of 1¾ oz. in some cases. Under

Fig. 195.—Fruiting Shoot of Spineless Gooseberry

these circumstances richness of flavour cannot be expected.

By the mode of pruning described, the bushes assume a concave form. This is suitable for the northern and midland parts of the kingdom, but in the warmest parts of the south it exposes the fruit too much to the sun, and therefore many growers leave a few shoots in the middle. Some prune their bushes only every second year, only half their

plantation being pruned in one season, and the other half the next. In the portion not pruned the young fruit often escapes destruction from spring frosts, whilst that on the pruned trees, from being more exposed, is cut off; and again, if excessively hot weather should set in when the fruit is ripening, the unpruned bushes afford more shade.

Gooseberries may be trained against espaliers or pales, in which case the fan mode is most suitable, because it affords the greatest facility for training in a succession of young wood. They are also trained on arched trellises. For this purpose they ought to be planted 15 or 18 inches apart, and trained with a single stem, which should be shortened at the autumn pruning, in order that it may be well furnished with spurs and laterals, none of which should be allowed to grow so strong as the leading shoot.

Gooseberry plantations should be dressed in autumn, taking care in stirring the soil not to injure the roots. The surface of the soil near the stems ought to be drawn back towards the middle of the space between them. Manure should be plentifully supplied as mulchings on the surface, and no digging allowed near the roots. It answers well to give a light dressing of a well-proven artificial manure when the ground is lightly forked over in the early spring. This will supply to the bushes the necessary elements for fruitfulness rather than strong growth.

The best-quality Gooseberries, both as to size and flavour, are obtained from plants grown on what is known as the cordon system; each little bush is restricted to four branches, and trained to a V-shaped post and wire trellis, 6 feet high, running north and south for preference. These trellises form an excellent screen or dividing-fence. Their erection is very simple, and may be done by any handy labourer. Oak posts, 6 inches thick and 6 feet out of ground, should be used for the two ends. Across the top of each post a piece, 2 feet long and 3 inches square, should be fixed, the ends projecting equally sideways; stretch tightly a stout wire from end to end of row, and fix with staples to the outsides of the cross-pieces. Then run a single bottom wire through holes in the posts, and quite close to the ground. If the row is long, intermediate posts will be required. Bamboo canes or sticks 6 feet long should now to be tied, 6 or more inches apart, to both bottom and top wires, thus forming the V-shaped trellis. One- or two-year-old plants, each with four shoots, should be planted 18 inches apart, two shoots to be tied to the outside of the stakes on either side of the trellis. This cordon system admits the maximum amount of sun, air, and light to the shoots and fruit. Other advantages in favour of cordons are that the depredations of bud-destroying birds are less persistent, probably because the branches are less convenient perches for them. Furthermore, the cordons can be so easily netted when the fruit is ripe. We have also found that fruit grown on cordon fences will keep better and is less but not hardened by exposure to the sun. They should then be sown in sandy loam in the open ground, or in pots filled with loam, sand, and leaf-mould, covering with about an inch of soil. Those sown in beds will be fit for transplanting into nursery rows in the following autumn. Those sown in pots may be forwarded by potting them singly, as soon as fit, into small pots, and taking care to shift again, or transplant, before the roots get in the least matted. The seedlings gener-

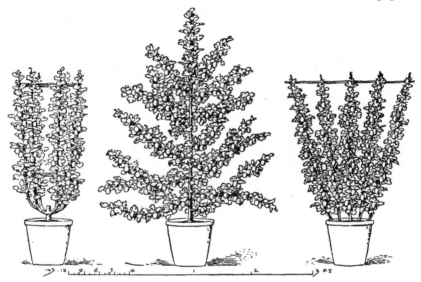

Fig. 196.—Pot-grown Gooseberries, showing three styles of training

susceptible to mildew. Any waste fence, not open to stock, or where a lining-screen is required, may be utilized for Gooseberries grown on any of the cordon forms, and more fruit can be had from a given extent of land by this method of training and good cultivation than by any other means. All the varieties do well as cordons.

Summer pinching of the laterals of these trained cordons to four leaves is essential, and the laterals should be further cut back to an inch in length in the following winter; the leaders, however, must only have their unripe tips shortened in winter.

Propagation.—The Gooseberry is propagated by seeds, cuttings, layers, and suckers. New varieties can, of course, only be obtained from seed. The seeds ought to be washed, and dried on sheets of brown paper, ally come into bearing in the third or fourth year.

Propagation by cuttings is the usual mode, and is best performed in autumn. The firmest and ripest of the one-year-old shoots are preferred and they are cut to a length of 12 inches. If the shoots are cut off close to the branch from which they spring, so much the better. Roots are emitted from any part of the cutting below ground; therefore the deeper it is inserted the more roots will be produced. Nevertheless it is found that roots produced along a great length of shoot are not so vigorous and effective as those which proceed from points nearer the leaves; at least this is the case with the Gooseberry, which is not a deep-rooted plant.

Layering is resorted to when plants of any particular sort are required to be speedily obtained without risk of failure, though the plants are not so shapely as those raised from cuttings; but the most rapid mode of obtaining well-rooted plants is by that which

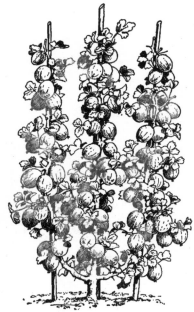

Fig. 197.—Cordon Gooseberry

has been termed layering by insertion of the growing point. In moist seasons the pendulous shoots root at the extremities if they come in contact with the soil. If towards the end of June the tips of the shoots of any variety are inserted to the depth of an inch

in soil that has been recently dug and made fine, they will form a large quantity of roots before autumn, together with a bud for a shoot. In autumn these plants will be so well-rooted that they may be taken up, and either planted where they are to remain or put in nursery rows till next autumn; but, in doing so, care must be taken not to break the bud formed at the crown of the roots.

Propagation by suckers is generally considered objectionable, as the plants so obtained are apt to produce suckers.

When Gooseberries are intended to be grown in bush form it is important that the cuttings should be properly prepared and of the best kind to produce clean, healthy bushes, each with straight clean stems about a foot high. Bushes on stems can be easily kept free of weeds and manured; the fruit is also out of the reach of splashes of soil during heavy rain, and can be easily gathered.

The last week in October is the most favourable time, and the best cuttings are those taken from short-jointed ripe growths of the current year. All the buds, except five at the top of the shoot, should be carefully cut out to prevent the growth of suckers. They should then be planted 4 inches deep and apart, in rows 18 inches apart, in sandy soil for preference, treading the soil firmly about them as the planting proceeds.

Market growers, whose Gooseberries are gathered green, do not trouble about keeping the plants to a clear stem, but allow suckers to come up thickly from the base, and do scarcely any pruning; but such bushes produce fruit of very inferior quality.

Enemies.—Birds, Wasps. Gooseberry and Currant Saw-fly, Green-fly, Magpie Moth, V - Moth. Red - legged Garden Weevil. American Gooseberry Mildew. See INSECT AND OTHER PLANT ENEMIES, Vol. III.

VARIETIES

ALLEN'S GLORY OF RATCLIFFE. — Branches spreading, somewhat pendulous. Fruit middle-sized, oblong, quite smooth, light-green, thick-skinned, very good, and sweet. Middling early, a moderate bearer.

ANTAGONIST.—Fruit very large, long, hairy, creamy-white, of good flavour. The largest white exhibition Gooseberry. An excellent bearer.

BEAUMONT'S SMILING BEAUTY. — Branches somewhat pendulous. Fruit large, oblong, quite smooth, yellowish-white, thin-skinned, somewhat transparent, sweet and good. Early, and an abundant bearer.

BERRY'S FARMER'S GLORY.—Branches somewhat pendulous. Leaves slightly pubescent above. Fruit very large, obovate, downy, red

intermixed with green, thick-skinned, well-flavoured. Middling early; an abundant bearer.

BRATHERTON'S LORD OF THE MANOR.—Branches spreading. Fruit very large, roundish, hairy, red, rather thick-skinned, very good. Late, and a good bearer.

BROOM GIRL. — Branches erect. Fruit very large, roundish, hairy, yellowish-olive, thin-skinned, and of first-rate flavour. Early, and an abundant bearer.

CARELESS. — Fruit very large, long, smooth, creamy-white, very handsome, and of good flavour. An abundant bearer.

CATHERINA.—Fruit very large, obovate, slightly hairy, bright-yellow, of excellent flavour.

CHESHIRE LADY. — Branches erect. Leaves

pubescent. Fruit middle-sized, oblong, hairy, deep-red, rich and excellent, with a clear pulp. Rather late.

CLEWORTH'S WHITE LION.—Branches somewhat pendulous. Fruit large, obovate, slightly hairy, white, thin-skinned, rich, and excellent. Very late.

Fig. 198.—Gooseberry. Cobham Seedling. (Natural size.)

COBHAM SEEDLING (fig. 198).—A variety with exceedingly large fruit, oval, slightly hairy, greenish-yellow in colour, and conspicuously veined; flavour rich and tasty; a first-rate dessert Gooseberry.

Fig. 199.—Gooseberry. Criterion

COLLIER'S JOLLY ANGLER.—Branches erect. Fruit large, oblong, downy, light-green, thin-skinned, of good flavour. Late, and a good bearer.

COOK'S WHITE EAGLE.—Branches rather erect. Fruit large, obovate, smooth, white, thick-skinned, of good flavour.

CRITERION (fig. 199).—Bush of upright habit, a robust grower. Fruit large, oval, smooth, dark-yellow. Popular in Lancashire. Mid-season.

CROWN BOB.—Branches spreading. Fruit large, thin-skinned, flavour good. Early and prolific.

DAN'S MISTAKE.—Erect growth. Fruit enormous, flavour excellent, light red, hairy, one of the very best. Mid-season.

DR. HOGG.—Branches erect. Fruit very large, slightly hairy, purplish-red, veined with a darker shade, of good flavour.

DRILL.—Branches spreading. Fruit large, long, smooth, greenish-yellow, of good flavour. Late, and an abundant bearer.

EARLY GREEN HAIRY.—Branches erect. Leaves dark-green, slightly pubescent. Fruit small, round, hairy, deep-green, thin-skinned, very sweet, and rich. Very early; a good bearer.

EARLY SULPHUR.—Branches erect, armed with numerous strong prickles, which are generally triple. Leaves light-green, pubescent above. Fruit middle-sized, roundish oblong, very hairy, bright-yellow, thin-skinned, tolerably good. Very early, and an abundant bearer. Its earliness is its principal merit. It is distinguished from the Sulphur by its earliness, and the leaves being pubescent.

EARLY WHITE.—Branches spreading. Fruit roundish oblong, slightly downy, yellowish-white, with a thin transparent skin, very sweet, and well flavoured. Early, and an abundant bearer.

EDWARD'S JOLLY TAR.—Branches somewhat pendulous. Leaves rather large, of a shining deep-green colour. Fruit very large, roundish obovate, smooth, green, veined with yellow, rather thick-skinned, rich and sweet. Middling early; a good bearer.

FANNY.—Branches erect. Fruit large, round, hairy, pale-yellow, of a rich, fine flavour. An excellent bearer.

FORESTER.—Fruit large and uniform, hairy, bright-red, and of excellent flavour. Early; an abundant bearer.

GARIBALDI.—Branches pendulous. Fruit very large, long, hairy, bright orange-yellow, of very good flavour. An abundant bearer.

GLENTON GREEN.—Branches somewhat pendulous. Leaves pubescent above. Fruit middle-sized, oblong, narrower at the base than at the opposite end, very hairy, green, with whitish veins, thick-skinned, very sweet, and good. Early.

GOLDEN GEM.—A cross between Antagonist and Whitesmith. The fruits are of a deep buff-yellow and very fine in flavour.

GREEN OVERALL.—Fruit middle-sized, round, smooth, dark-green, of first-rate flavour. An early variety, and bears abundantly.

GREEN WALNUT.—Branches spreading. Leaves adpressed to the branches. Fruit middle-sized, obovate, smooth, dull dark-green, very thin-skinned, sweet, moderately good. Early, and an abundant bearer.

GREGORY'S PERFECTION.—Branches pendulous, very prickly. Fruit middle-sized, round, slightly downy, green, veined with white, rather thick-skinned, sweet, and agreeable. Late; a moderate bearer.

HEBBURN GREEN PROLIFIC.—Branches erect. Fruit middle-sized, roundish, hairy, dull-green, rather thick-skinned, sweet, and very rich. Early, and an abundant bearer.

HENSON'S SEEDLING.—Branches erect. Fruit of medium size, roundish oblong, very hairy, deep-red, of excellent flavour. Late, and an abundant bearer.

High Sheriff. — Branches pendulous. Fruit very large, round, hairy, orange-yellow, of excellent flavour. An abundant bearer.

Ironmonger. — Branches spreading. Leaves pubescent. Fruit small, roundish, hairy, dark-red, with rather a thick skin, rich, but not so rich as the Red Champagne, with which it is often confounded. Middling early.

Keen's Seedling. — Branches somewhat pendulous. Fruit middle-sized, oblong, very hairy, bright-red, thin-skinned, rich, and excellent. A good bearer, ripening earlier than the Red Warrington.

Fig. 200.—Gooseberry. Late Emerald

Keepsake (Banks). — Branches slightly pendulous, of very strong growth. Fruit large, obovate, smooth, but sometimes hairy, greenish-yellow, thin-skinned; flavour excellent. Ripens early.

Lancashire Lad. — Growth compact and erect. Fruit large and hairy, very prolific, dark-red. A favourite market variety. Mid-season.

Langley Beauty. — A cross between Yellow Champagne and Railway. The berries are very large, of a buff-yellow colour, semi-transparent, somewhat hairy, and of delicious flavour. It combines the size of Railway, a large greenish fruit, with the fine flavour and upright growth of the little Yellow Champagne.

Langley Gage. — A cross between Pitmaston Gage and Telegraph. The berries are in size between medium and small, silvery white, transparent, and of very fine flavour; an enormous bearer.

Large Early White.—Branches erect. Fruit large, obovate, downy, greenish-white, thin-skinned, and of rich flavour. Very early.

Late Emerald (fig. 200).—A favourite sort in the United States. It crops well, and is an excellent dessert fruit. It has a tendency to mildew in damp weather.

Leigh's Rifleman.—Branches somewhat erect. Fruit very large, roundish oblong, hairy, red intermixed with green, thick-skinned, sharp, rich, and agreeable. Late, and a good bearer.

Leveller (fig. 194). — Fruit large, long and tapering, smooth, greenish-yellow, of good flavour. An excellent bearer.

Lomas' Victory.—Branches somewhat pendulous. Fruit rather large, roundish oblong, hairy, light-red, thin-skinned, of moderately good flavour. The unripe berries are esteemed for cooking.

London (Banks).—Branches pendulous. Fruit very large, of a roundish ovate shape; skin smooth, of a dark-red colour. Quality rather inferior; a somewhat tender and uncertain bearer, but the largest Gooseberry grown.

Magnet.—Branches spreading. Fruit large, very long, hairy, light-red, flavour very good. Early; an excellent bearer.

Massey's Heart of Oak.—Branches pendulous. Fruit large, oblong, with a thick footstalk tapering in to the fruit, smooth, green, with pale-yellowish veins, thin-skinned, rich, and excellent. Middling early; an abundant bearer.

May Duke.—Erect growth. Fruit medium, bright-red, a good grower and heavy cropper. One of the very earliest sorts to gather green.

Monarch.—Fruit very large, oblong, hairy, deep-red; of good quality. A very heavy and sure bearer.

Mount Pleasant.—Fruit large, long, hairy, deep-yellow, of very good flavour. Late, and an abundant bearer.

Parkinson's Laurel.—Branches erect. Fruit large, obovate, very downy, pale-green, nearly white, thin-skinned, very sweet. Rather late, and an abundant bearer.

Peer's Queen Charlotte.—Branches somewhat erect. Fruit middle-sized, oblong, smooth, yellowish-white, thin-skinned, flavour very good. Early, a moderate bearer.

Peru.—Branches spreading, somewhat pendulous. Fruit large, long, and tapering, slightly hairy, pale-yellow, of a very good flavour.

Pitmaston Green Gage. — Branches erect. Fruit small, obovate, smooth, green, rather thick-skinned, rich, very sugary, and excellent. Late, and an abundant bearer. The fruit will hang till it shrivels without deteriorating in flavour like that of most other varieties.

Porcupine.—Fruit small, roundish oval, extremely hispid and downy. Flavour rich and honeyed.

Princess Royal.—Branches pendulous. Fruit large, obovate, hairy, greenish-white, of excellent flavour. A very good bearer.

Raspberry. — Branches spreading, somewhat pendulous. Fruit small, roundish oblong, hairy, dark-red, thick-skinned, rich and sweet, with a Raspberry flavour. Very early, and a good bearer.

Red Champagne.—Branches remarkably erect. Fruit small, roundish oblong, hairy, light-red, rather thick-skinned, very rich and excellent, with a clear vinous pulp. Middling early, and a good bearer.

RED TURKEY.—Branches somewhat erect. Fruit small, obovate, smooth, shining, dark-red, thick-skinned, of an agreeable sweet flavour. Late, and a good bearer.

RED WARRINGTON.—Branches pendulous, armed with strong prickles, which are generally triple. Fruit roundish oblong, hairy, red, thick-skinned, with a clear, rich, vinous pulp. Late, and an abundant bearer. One of the best.

ROB ROY. — Branches erect. Fruit middle-sized, obovate, hairy, pale-red, of rich flavour. Very early.

ROUGH RED.—Branches spreading, rather upright. Leaves smooth. Fruit small, roundish, very hairy, dark-red, rather thick-skinned, of good flavour. Early, and an abundant bearer. A favourite for preserving.

ROYAL WHITE.—Branches erect. Leaves pubescent. Fruit small, round, downy, and slightly hairy, white, thin-skinned, very rich, and good.

RUMBULLION. — Branches erect. Fruit small, roundish, oblong, very downy, pale-yellow, rather thick-skinned, of moderately good flavour. Middling early, and a very abundant bearer. Much cultivated for bottling.

SAUNDERS' CHESHIRE LASS.—Branches erect. Fruit large, oblong, downy, white, thin-skinned, rich, and sweet. Very early, and a good bearer.

SCOTCH BEST JAM. — Branches erect. Leaves pubescent above. Fruit small, roundish, slightly hairy, dark-red, thick-skinned, brisk, and rich. Middling early, and a good bearer.

SHINER (fig. 201).—Branches spreading. Fruit large, round, smooth, green flushed with red, of very good flavour. A free bearer, and one of the heaviest Gooseberries. Late.

SMALL DARK ROUGH RED.—Branches spreading, rather upright. Leaves pubescent. Fruit small, round, very hairy, dark-red, nearly black when fully ripe, rather thick-skinned, of good flavour. Early, and an abundant bearer.

SNOWDROP (Bratherton).—Fruit very large, roundish, hairy, white, veined with green, thin-skinned, and of excellent flavour. An abundant bearer.

STRINGER'S MAID OF THE MILL.—Branches erect. Fruit large, roundish oblong, or somewhat ovate, very downy, white, thin-skinned, excellent. Early, and an abundant bearer.

SULPHUR. — Branches erect. Fruit small, roundish, hairy, yellow, moderately thick-skinned, of rich flavour. Rather late; a good bearer.

TAYLOR'S BRIGHT VENUS. — Branches erect. Fruit middle-sized, obovate, very slightly hairy, white, sugary, rich, and excellent, hanging till it shrivels. Middling early; a good bearer.

THUNDER.—Fruit large, roundish, hairy, green, of excellent flavour. Early, and an abundant bearer.

VICTORIA.—Vigorous grower and hardy constitution. Fruit red, large, a sure cropper, being a late bloomer. Somewhat new. After Crown Bob, but with larger berries.

WHINHAM'S INDUSTRY.—Branches partly erect. Fruit large if ripened, the best variety for picking green for tarts, attaining size early, a great improvement on older varieties, both habit and constitution good.

WHITE CHAMPAGNE. — Branches very erect. Leaves pubescent above. Fruit small, roundish oblong, hairy, slightly downy, white, rather thick-skinned, sweet, and rich. Middling early; a moderate bearer.

WHITE DAMSON.—Branches erect. Fruit small, roundish, smooth, greenish-white, thin-skinned, excellent. Very early, and a good bearer.

WHITE FIG.—Branches erect. Fruit small, obovate, tapering to the stalk, smooth, white, rather thick-skinned, rich, and excellent. It will hang and shrivel on the plant like a raisin. The bush is not vigorous.

WHITE HONEY.—Branches erect. Fruit small or middle-sized, roundish oval, generally smooth, white, rather thick-skinned, and of excellent flavour.

WOODWARD'S WHITESMITH.—Branches erect. Fruit large, roundish oblong, very downy, white, thin-skinned, excellent. A variety rarely equalled,

Fig. 201.—Gooseberry Shiner

scarcely ever excelled. Middling early; an abundant bearer.

YELLOW BALL.—Branches erect. Fruit middle-sized, roundish, smooth, yellow, thick-skinned, of good flavour. Deserving of cultivation on account of its lateness.

YELLOW CHAMPAGNE.—Branches erect. Fruit small, roundish, oblong, hairy, yellow, thin-skinned, rich and excellent. Rather late; an abundant bearer. The best yellow-fruited variety.

The earliest to ripen is Early Sulphur, the richest flavour Red Champagne, and the best varieties for picking green for bottling or for tarts are Keepsake, Whinham's Industry, and Lancashire Lad. New varieties that show any marked improvement on existing varieties, or that possess sufficient merit when tested by a severe standard, have not been very numerous until quite recently, when Messrs. Veitch, of Chelsea, were successful in raising three very fine-flavoured seedling varieties—namely Golden Gem, Langley Beauty, and Langley Gage. When these varieties become better known, doubtless they will become universally grown.

CURRANTS

ORIGIN

There are three principal sorts of Currants: the Red (*Ribes rubrum*); the White, a pale-fruited variety of the same species; and the Black (*R. nigrum*). They are natives of Europe, including the British Islands, and also of other temperate regions, including North America. They are, as garden fruits, comparatively a modern development, probably since the sixteenth century. Compared with their relation, the Gooseberry, the cultivated forms show little difference from the wild types.

The Red Currant is extensively used for pies, tarts, and jellies; and both it and the White are employed for making Currant wine. The White, being less acid than the Red, is preferred for dessert, although it is not unusual to use both for the sake of colour.

The skin of the Black Currant contains an oil of a powerful and peculiar odour, which is disagreeable to many persons. The fruit is, however, in much request for preserving and for making wine. On the whole, Currants are important objects of cultivation, especially in the neighbourhood of towns, where the fruit is always in demand.

CULTIVATION

Soil and Situation.—A deep, loamy soil is best adapted for Currants, and the fruit acquires the richest flavour in a situation open to the sun. They are frequently planted against north walls, on which they succeed with certainty when other kinds of fruit-trees often fail. The fruit attains a good size and acquires a fine colour, but it is not so rich in flavour as that grown in sunshine. It can be kept in good condition on the plants, and will thus afford a late supply.

The soil should be prepared as for the Gooseberry; and, as with it, the planting is best performed in autumn. The distance apart, when planted in quarters, should be 5 or 6 feet each way.

Pruning and Training.—Plants consisting of a clean stem of 9 inches, and having three shoots, should, when transplanted, have these shortened back to about 4 inches, and to a bud pointing upwards. In the following spring two shoots should be encouraged from each of the shoots so cut back, so that in autumn the plant will consist of six shoots. These should all be cut back at the winter-pruning, so as to leave them from 4 to 6 inches long. The terminal shoots of the six branches should be cut at every winter-prun-

ing, and when they have nearly attained the intended height, which need not exceed 3 feet, the terminals should be shortened every autumn to within two or three buds from the base.

In soil that is naturally favourable to the growth of the Currant, the plants may be allowed to grow to the height of 4 or 5 feet, and in that case nine or even twelve branches may be allowed. The laterals should be shortened in winter to about half an inch in length. The base of the shoot consists of nearly solid wood, but farther up the shoot is pithy, and by exposure to the air the pith wastes, leaving the shoot hollow below the cut, and it usually dies back. It is therefore better to cut back nearly close to the old wood, or to the origin of the shoots, in order that the buds, whether for young wood or for fruit, may have a solid basis. It is a mistake to allow too much crowding of young shoots in summer. When this is likely to be the case, they should be moderately thinned early, by removing some of the weakest shoots, or any that cross each other. Besides this, the tops of the strongest shoots may be cut off in June, taking care, however, that no extensive removal of foliage takes place at any one time.

Currants are trained in some gardens with a single upright stem, and when well managed they bear well. There is also an advantage as regards the fruit being kept free

Fig. 202.—Currant—Red Dutch

from soil, by which those grown as dwarfs are frequently injured after heavy rains. When grown as standards, the principal aim should be, in the first place, to grow the stem as straight and as strong as possible. It is necessary to keep the leading stem trained to a rod or stake. Shoots must be allowed to grow along the stem; and if the latter is intended to be ultimately naked, the lower shoots and spurs should be gradually taken off as others are produced higher up.

When intended to be trained against a wall or espalier, Currants should be planted 3 feet apart, and one strong upright shoot encouraged for a stem. The plants should be well established before the formation of the primary branches is attempted; therefore, if the plants are not strong and well rooted when planted, it is better to merely shorten the shoot a little, and allow the plant to grow at freedom till the following

autumn, and then cut down the upright to 3 inches from the ground. Train one shoot, the strongest of course, upright, cut it back in autumn to 6 inches from the ground, and in the following summer, from the base of the last year's shoot, train one young shoot horizontally to the right, and another to the left. From these horizontals four upright shoots should be trained, at the distance of 9 inches from each other. These perpendicular shoots ought to be allowed to grow at full length, and should be shortened back in autumn to 9 or 12 inches. A leader from each must be trained upright every summer, and shortened to the above height every autumn; the laterals from the upright branches should be cut very closely, as directed for the laterals of the branches grown in the open ground.

Red and White Currants succeed admirably grown as cordons on V trellises, either on the one-, two-, or four-branch system, as described for Gooseberries.

The soil should every year be drawn from

Fig. 203.—Summer-pruning of Red Currants. The marks on the branches show how much should be cut off.

around the trees with a hoe, and buried in the middle of the intervals, for which purpose a spade is best; but in stirring the ground near the trees, a fork should be employed. Plenty of manure should be given. Manure water increases the size of the fruit, but does not improve the flavour; therefore it is better to apply an artificial compound before the ground is stirred in the spring.

is long enough to admit of these being at the proper height from the ground. If the cutting is short, the strongest and most upright

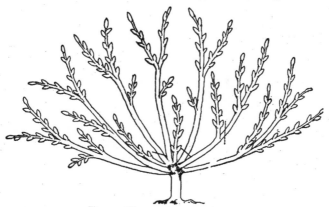

Fig. 204.—Winter-pruning of Black Currants
The marks on the branches show how much should be cut off.

The fruit should not be gathered when it is wet, and, if intended for preserving, not immediately after a wet period.

Propagation. — The Currant, like the Gooseberry, may be propagated by seed, cuttings, suckers, and layers; also, as we have seen in particular cases, by budding and grafting. The best mode, and that which is generally practised, is by cuttings. These may be taken soon after the fruit is gathered, that is, when the young shoots are mature; but any time from the beginning of autumn till March will do; those struck in autumn being best, inasmuch as they are prepared to start in spring, and shoots are produced at the same time, so that nearly a year is gained.

The cuttings should consist of well-ripened vigorous young shoots. If taken off close to the old wood so much the better. The end should be cut smooth, and the buds removed, leaving only three or four at the top.

A Currant bush ought to have a clean stem of 5 inches above the ground. If cuttings sufficiently long can be obtained, 6 inches may be allowed for insertion in the ground, 5 inches for the stem, and 3 inches for shoots to form the head, thus making the whole length 14 inches. When prepared, the cuttings should be inserted as for the Gooseberry. When the shoots begin to push, three should be encouraged, if the cutting

shoot ought to be allowed to take the lead, and should be trained as straight as possible

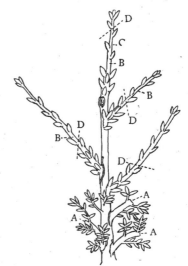

Fig. 205.—Winter-pruning of Red Currants
A, Spurs; B, current year's growth; C, leader, stopped at D;
D, shortening of lateral shoots.

at least to 8 inches above the surface. If other shoots push they may be allowed to

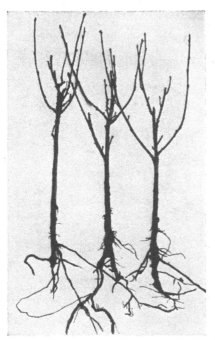

Fig. 206.—Two-year-old Currant bushes struck from cuttings, suitable for transplanting

Transplanting Old Stools.—It is not generally known that Red and White Currants and Gooseberries may be successfully transplanted when of full fruiting size. If lifted with all the fibrous roots possible, and carefully replanted, the ground being made firm, they will succeed. By a little harder pruning the first season, and by taking a lighter crop, they are quite re-established in one season. The first season after lifting them the ground should be mulched with manure in early spring.

ENEMIES

RED AND WHITE CURRANTS: Apple Mussel Scale. Currant Aphis, Gooseberry and Currant Saw-fly, Green-fly, Magpie Moth, V-Moth. Red-legged Garden Weevil. Currant Clear-wing Moth, Currant Shoot Moth. Birds.

BLACK CURRANT: Currant Gall Mite. Currant Aphis.

See INSECT AND OTHER PLANT ENEMIES, Vol. III.

SELECTION OF VARIETIES

BLACK NAPLES.—Bunches abundant; berries large. A good black-fruited variety for general cultivation, and hangs well when ripe. It comes into leaf early.

BOSKOOP GIANT.—A strong-growing variety, bearing long bunches of enormous berries, and ripens early, skin thin.

CARTER'S CHAMPION.—Fruit in long clusters,

grow, as their foliage will assist in forming roots; but they should be kept subordinate to the one trained upright. They will require to be cut off close in autumn, and the upright one shortened back so that the third bud below the cut shall be 5 inches above the ground. The plants should be fit for planting out in autumn, but if not strong they had better remain another year.

Red and White Currants may be advantageously grown as standards. First strike and then grow on from cuttings, keeping to a single stem until the required height has been attained. This may vary from 3 to 4 feet. Under this system there is a distinct advantage, in that the birds cannot so easily steal the fruit. The head should be supported with a stout stake. Another plan is to graft the Currant upon *Ribes aureum* at the required height. Gooseberries also may be cultivated as standards in a similar way, using the same stock. It is an advantage to grow dessert Gooseberries in this fashion.

Fig. 207.—Currant—White Grape

large, black, juicy, and palatable; a very prolific bearer.

COMET.—An exceptionally free Red, remarkable for length of bunch and size of berry. The fruits will hang on the bushes till September if netted.

FAY'S PROLIFIC.—Fruit large, red, and of agreeable flavour; often used for dessert and for flavouring ices.

KNIGHT'S SWEET RED.—Bunches large; berries medium, of a fine deep-red. An abundant bearer, not so early as Red Dutch.

LA VERSAILLAISE.—Strong grower and heavy cropper. Good bunches, the berries large.

LEE'S PROLIFIC.—An excellent black; bunches large, very abundant; berries larger than Black Naples, very sweet and pleasant when ripe; hangs long after ripening.

RABY CASTLE.—A great bearer. Bunches long; berries large, with a sharp acidity; ripening late and hanging well. Vigorous and suitable for growing as a standard or large bush. This variety is synonymous with May's Victoria, Houghton Castle, Goliath, and Walker's New Red.

RED DUTCH (fig. 202).—Surpassed by none in size of bunch, quality, and abundant bearing; ripens early, and the berries are large, juicy, and bright-red.

WHITE DUTCH.—Habit and appearance of Red Dutch; bunches large and abundant, berries large, transparent, yellowish-white, with a mild sweet juice. The best White.

WHITE GRAPE (fig. 207).—Larger than White Dutch, marvellously productive, in crowded clusters. Bush somewhat straggling, and requires to be carefully pruned.

RASPBERRIES

ORIGIN

The parent of the Raspberry, *Rubus Idæus*, a deciduous shrub, is found wild in the cooler parts of Europe, including the British Islands, where it is not uncommon in woods. The cane-like biennial stems are more or less been raised in gardens, but some of the so-called hybrids between the Raspberry and others are seedling forms of *R. Idæus* simply. " Seedling Raspberries from the Yellow Antwerp produce, for the most part, yellow fruit

Fig. 208.—Hybrid Raspberry—Mahdi. (½)

prickly; the leaves consist of from three to five leaflets, which are ovate, white and hoary beneath; the flowers are borne in drooping cymes; and the fruits, which are red or yellow, are covered with a hoary down. These characters are found in all the cultivated forms, including some that are said to be hybrids between the Raspberry and the Blackberry. Numerous hybrid Rubi have with but little variation, except that a few will give red fruit. It is rare to find any variety worth perpetuating among them. Seedlings from the Red Antwerp and Fastolf also vary but little. The latter is said to have produced both the Yellow and Red October Raspberries, which reproduce themselves from seeds with but little variation " (T. Rivers, 1863).

CULTIVATION

Soil and Situation.—Raspberries succeed in any garden soil that is not too stiff, but preferably in one that is rich and rather moist. They grow well in sandy alluvial ground, also in peat and soils that are mixed with peat; but those which are heavy and compact, becoming hard in dry weather, are not suitable. The ground should be trenched at least 2 feet deep and a good

able distances; or the rows may be 8 feet apart, so that other crops may be grown between. Care should be taken that the soil is kept well manured and sufficiently moist.

Raspberries are sometimes planted for arched training, in rows 4 feet asunder, and the same distance between the plants in the row (fig. 209). When planted to be

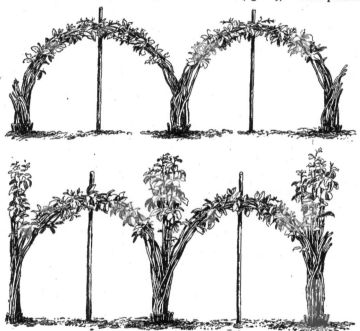

Fig. 209.—Raspberry—Arched training

dressing of manure added, placing it between the spits of soil as the trenching proceeds. An annual mulch of farmyard manure should also be given. As an alternative an application of an artificial manure has been found most efficacious.

Planting.—Raspberries are usually planted in rows, and their canes tied to stakes. In this way the distance allowed between the rows may be 5 feet, and that between the plants in the row 3 feet. In very rich soil, 6 feet between the rows, and 3 or 4 feet between the plants in the row, would be suit-

trained against an espalier, they may be 2 feet apart (fig. 210). The best time to plant is October or early in November. If one-cane suckers are used they should be planted in triangular groups of three about 9 inches apart. They should be planted firmly. The canes should be cut to within 6 inches of the ground as soon as they show signs of growth.

The Raspberry sends up shoots or canes in spring which lose their leaves in autumn, and from these canes branchlets push in the following spring, on which fruit is produced in the course of the summer and autumn. The branchlets diverge in all directions, so that in the natural state they cannot be over-crowded. Whilst these are bearing the fruit new canes spring from the base, and suckers frequently spring from the roots, at a distance from the plant. These bear in the following season, forming a succession to those which are bearing, and which die back to the ground before winter.

Pruning and Training.—When the plants are intended to be fastened to stakes in the usual way, the pruning and training are very simple; especially with a new plantation, where one, two, or three canes have been planted to be tied to a single stake. Stakes are not necessary the first season, as the canes require to be cut down as advised,

remain. These should be shortened where they exhibit signs of weakness and begin to twist or bend. If there are more canes than the number here stated, they should be cut away. The stakes should be driven in correctly in line, and their tops cut to a regular height. The canes should then be tied to the stakes with osier twigs, than which nothing is better, or tar-twine may be substituted. This operation completes the first year's pruning and training.

Objection has been made to this mode of training, as it brings the canes close together; but as they do not require much light, whilst the buds do, the shoots from the latter extend outwards and are fully exposed to sunlight. There is therefore less danger of the fruit-bearing branchlets crowding each other than

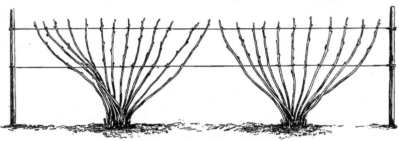

Fig 210.—Raspberry—Espalier training

although, if strong, and fruit be desired the first season, they should be shortened more than the bearing shoots of an established plantation. The object of cutting back the year-old canes is to invigorate the young ones. When these push, three, four, or five of the strongest of them should be left, and the others rubbed off, or destroyed by means of the suckering-iron.

In October or November the plantation should be pruned, in order that the ground may be surface-manured, leaving it there to be washed in by rain, as it is not wise to fork over the surface or dig the manure in, lest by so doing the best fibrous surface-feeding roots be injured. Some think that the canes are injured by frost and rain when pruned before winter; but this is very unlikely, except so far as the pith may get too much soaked with wet, which will be only a little way, especially if the canes are cut slanting.

In pruning, the two-year-old canes, now dead, should be cleared, and three or four of the strongest young canes selected to

of the interference of the young shoots which spring from the root.

In the second season the tied-up canes will require no further attention. Lateral shoots will push from them; and these, as already remarked, bear the fruit. At the same time shoots for succession spring up, and frequently in too great abundance. When such is the case they must be thinned out more or less, as in the preceding season; only, as the plants are now established, from four to six shoots may be allowed to grow. In autumn three, or if strong enough four, from each stool should be pruned and tied as already directed.

When Raspberries are intended to be trained to a rail, the latter may be constructed of stakes and strips of deal about 1 inch thick. The stakes should be driven in line 5 or 6 feet apart, and the strips of deal nailed along their tops, which may be 3 or 4 feet from the ground, according to the length of the canes; other strips may run along at 18 inches or 2 feet from the surface, or a wire may be stretched at that height. To these horizontals the canes should be trained, so as to leave room for a succession shoot between each. The weak

points of the bearing canes ought to be cut off, and superfluous shoots removed at an early stage of their growth. Perhaps the best support is obtained by fastening the points of the shoots to a slight horizontal rail or bar, about 4 feet high, and placed 1½ feet on the south side of the rows. By this means the bearing shoots are deflected to the sunny side of the row, and are not shaded by the annual wood.

Raspberries are sometimes trained by arching, and for this mode they are planted about 4 feet apart in the rows. A stake is driven in midway between the plants; half the canes belonging to one plant and half of those of the adjoining plant are bent towards each other, and their ends tied together so as to form an arch, which is secured to the stake.

Some varieties of Raspberry naturally produce fruit late in autumn; these should be cut down close to the ground in February, just before any signs of growth are noted. The object is to secure as strong a growth as possible. The fruits of true autumnal Raspberries are produced in the upper half of these young growths. Others may be induced to do so by cutting down the canes to within 1 foot of the ground. The shoots which push from these shortened canes grow vigorously, and usually produce fruit late in the season. Another

mode is to shorten the canes rather more than usual; then, when the laterals push, and before they flower, they are cut back

Fig. 211.—Raspberry—Belle de Fontenay, an autumn-fruiting kind

nearly to the base, and fresh shoots push which bear fruit late in the season. In order to obtain large fruit, so far as this depends on pruning and training, few bearing shoots should be left to each plant, or in particular cases some plants, or a row or two, may be sacrificed by permitting no suckers to grow. Of course no fruit can be obtained in the following season from plants so treated, the formation of shoots for future bearing being prevented; but in consequence of this the fruiting canes will be better nourished and the fruit larger.

Fig. 212.—Raspberry—Golden Queen. (⅔)

Summer Management. — This consists chiefly in an occasional hoeing to keep down weeds, and the timely thinning of the suckers to prevent waste of vigour; from four to six of the strongest suckers should be left on each stool. The next season's crop depends entirely upon the management of, and the encouragement given to, these new growths. The summer management of autumn fruiters consists in taking care of the young canes. About the end of July the flowers will be opening at the points and downwards a little

later on. These canes that do not show any flowers should then be cut out, and the rest tied in an upright manner by the use of a wire or thin stake fixed in a horizontal fashion just above the extreme length of the shoots.

In autumn, as soon as the crop is gathered, all the old canes that have borne fruit should be removed, so as to allow air and light to the young canes.

In winter there is little to be done beyond cutting off the unripe tips of the canes.

Raspberries may be grown as advised for Gooseberries on the four-to-six-shoot cordons on the V-trellis system, and they will produce heavy crops of large, good-quality fruit. Thus trained, the canes and leaves are well exposed to sunshine, and more and better fruit is got in consequence.

On large fruit farms, where the labour and cost of stakes and tying have to be considered, it is advisable to select one of the dwarf, sturdy, self-supporting varieties, such as Carter's Prolific, which is in every way adapted for field cultivation. The canes are cut back to various lengths up to 3 feet.

Forcing.—The Raspberry is seldom forced, but plants in pots may be brought on in the orchard-house along with the Gooseberry and Currant, or they may be planted along the front of a pit, and trained to a trellis under the glass. They bear very well in pots, which can be removed to the open air when the crop is gathered. For this purpose plants should be taken up in autumn, and potted in 12-inch pots. All buds on the roots likely to produce suckers ought to be picked off. The soil should be a mixture of turfy loam, peat or leaf-mould, and sand. The canes may be shortened to 3 or 4 feet in length. The pots should be placed where they can be protected from frost and snow till they can be introduced into the house. If this be done in January, ripe fruit may be obtained in the beginning of April. Or if introduced into gentle heat in February, with a little assistance in dull or severe weather, well-flavoured fruit may be obtained in May. The plants should be duly attended to with water, of which they will require a good deal when in full growth, and until the fruit begins to colour. Suckers must be removed as soon as they make their appearance.

Plants established in the pots in the course of the summer will stand forcing better than those lifted and potted in October. Suckers ought to be planted in large pots in autumn or early in spring; at the same time the bearing wood should be cut away, in order that the canes intended to bear when forced may have every advantage.

Red Antwerp is one of the best sorts for forcing.

Propagation.—The Raspberry is propagated by seeds, and occasionally by cuttings, but the usual mode is by suckers or offsets.

The seeds should be taken from ripe fruit, washed from the pulp, and sown in sandy

Fig. 213.—Parsley-leaved Bramble

Fig. 214.—Spineless Blackberry (*R. ulmifolius inermis*). (½)

soil, in pans. They will vegetate in the spring, and in autumn the seedlings will be fit for transplanting, the first shoot being then shortened to a few eyes.

In propagating by suckers or offsets, care should be taken not to injure the plants from which they are separated. The best time to remove them is October, which is likewise the best time for making the plantation. Root suckers are often thrown up at a considerable distance from the plant, but usually the suckers come out almost like offsets. When this is the case, they ought to be detached with a sharp suckering-iron, and at the same time care should be taken not to injure the bud or buds which will be found on the part of the root just below-ground, at the base of the shoots made in the course of the current season; for these buds give rise to the shoots which become the canes for bearing in the following year.

INSECTS, &c.—See INSECT ENEMIES, Vol. III. *Bud and Flower Enemies*—Raspberry Beetle, Red-bud Caterpillar. *Fruit and Seed*

Enemies — Birds. *Leaf Enemies* — Clay-coloured Vine Weevil. *Root Enemies*—Daddy Long-legs, Red-legged Garden Weevil.

VARIETIES

SUMMER FRUITING

BAUMFORTH'S SEEDLING.—A medium grower and cropper, with almost spineless canes. Fruit large, of a deep-red colour and good flavour.

CARTER'S PROLIFIC.—Sturdy in habit, dwarf, a

atus. The foliage is in three divisions instead of five, as in the true Raspberry, and the stems are as spinous as in the Bramble. The fruit is large, rich-yellow, of delicious flavour, and borne in great clusters. Distributed in 1900 by Messrs. J. Veitch & Sons.

HORNET.—A strong grower, of good constitution, very prolific. Fruit in great clusters, round, large, deep-crimson, exceptionally sweet.

LAXTON BERRY.—Another hybrid, said to be from the Logan Berry crossed with Superlative Raspberry. It has the habit of the Logan Berry and Raspberry-like fruits, the core separating

Fig. 215.—American Blackberry

easily from the berry proper. They are juicy and sweet, soft when ripe, and red in colour. The plant requires a wet soil.

LOGAN BERRY.—Of American origin and stated to be a cross between a Raspberry and a Blackberry. Growth extremely vigorous. Should not be planted in rows, but as a division between other crops. Requires a trellis quite 7 feet high. Valuable for tarts, bottling, and preserving. Fruit long, dark-red in colour, and very prolific. A valuable fruit.

LOW BERRY.—Of English origin, and more nearly allied to the Blackberry than to the Raspberry. Growth also very robust. Fruits long and jet black in colour, the flavour excellent. Requires the same treatment as the preceding.

MAHDI (fig. 208).—Said to be a hybrid between Raspberry Belle de Fontenay and the common Blackberry. The fruit in appearance resembles a large red-purple Blackberry, and the leaves are intermediate between the two parents. The plant bears freely, the fruits ripening after Raspberries are over and before Blackberries are ripe. Distributed by Messrs. J. Veitch & Sons in 1900.

heavy cropper. Fruit in big clusters, large, deep-red, sweet; carries well.

CUTBUSH'S PRINCE OF WALES.—Canes strong and long, slightly glaucous, nearly smooth. Fruit large, globular, or inclining to conical, of a bright-red colour and good flavour. An early and most abundant bearer; not disposed to sucker freely.

FASTOLF.—Canes very strong, of a light-brown colour, nearly smooth. Fruit large, globular, of a bright-red colour, and of good flavour. A most abundant bearer, and a generally useful sort.

GOLDEN QUEEN (fig. 212).—Said to be a hybrid between Raspberry Superlative and the North American Parsley-leaved Bramble *Rubus lacini-*

PHENOMENAL BERRY. — Best described as a stronger grower than the Logan Berry, a heavier bearer and with larger fruits.

RED ANTWERP.—Canes strong, yellowish-green, slightly glaucous, occasionally tinged with purple, covered with dark-brown bristles, especially towards the base. Fruit large, conical, dull-red, sweet, and rich in flavour. It bears carriage well, and is therefore much cultivated by market-gardeners. A second crop is sometimes borne in autumn, but the fruit is both scanty and small.

SUPERLATIVE. — Canes tall and strong. Fruit crimson, extra large and luscious, firm in texture, and carries well. Probably the best Raspberry grown.

YELLOW ANTWERP.—Canes with numerous small prickles. Fruit medium, ovate, pale-yellow, rich, and sweet. A good bearer, not so strong-growing as Red Antwerp.

YELLOW SUPERLATIVE.—A seedling raised by J. Veitch & Sons from Superlative and Yellow Antwerp. Fruit as large as Superlative, clear-yellow, with a crisp sub-acid flavour especially agreeable for preserves. The canes are strong and robust, bearing enormously and continuously.

AUTUMN FRUITING.

ALEXANDRA.—Fruit large, conical, deep-red, rich flavour, vigorous in growth and prolific. Height about 5 feet.

BELLE DE FONTENAY (Merveille Rouge).—Fruit of medium size, large pips, round in form and deep-red in colour. A sturdy and somewhat dwarf grower (fig. 211).

HAILSHAM.—Fruit enormous, round, dark-red, the most prolific of any autumn kind; growth vigorous; leaves very large, thus sheltering the fruit in wet weather. A most distinct variety.

NOVEMBER ABUNDANCE.—Fruit very large, deep-red, borne in clusters, canes very strong. Fruits up to end of November when the weather is mild.

SURPRISE D'AUTOMNE.—The most prolific of all; yellow-fruited, sweet in flavour. The colour, however, is against it in the autumn, as it is easily tarnished by weather.

A spineless Blackberry (fig. 214) is grown at Kew under the name of *R. ulmifolius inermis*. It is vigorous in growth, fruits freely, the fruits are of good size and palatable, and as it has no prickles on either stems or leaves it ought to find favour as a breeder.

The Blackberry has been improved either by accident or by design more than is generally known. The varieties are cultivated in the United States more than they are here, where they have been neglected by gardeners no doubt because they are so abundant everywhere as wild plants.

STRAWBERRIES

ORIGIN

The Garden Strawberry is comparatively a modern creation. It does not appear to have been cultivated by the ancients, although the fruits are said to have been gathered from the woods where it grew wild. " It was probably during the Middle Ages, or perhaps only at the beginning of modern times, that the custom of growing Strawberries in the garden became established, with the result that new and improved strains originated owing to the plants being more amply fed and carefully cultivated " (De Candolle).

Three species of Fragaria appear to have been concerned in the origination of the Strawberries now grown, namely, *F. vesca*, a native of temperate Europe, Asia, and North America; *F. virginiana*, also North American; and *F. chiloensis*, a native of South America. From these, three distinct races have been bred, namely, the large-fruited or English, the Alpine, and the Perpetual Strawberries.

The English or large-fruited varieties are by far the most important. They are supposed to have originated in England about a hundred and fifty years ago from a chance cross between *F. virginiana* and *F. chiloensis*, which produced the variety known, and still grown, as the Old Pine Strawberry (*Fraisier Ananas*). " It was only in the earlier part of the present century that skilful horticulturists began to originate named varieties of this large-fruited Strawberry. Keens', Myatt's, Rivers's, and Turner's novelties were successively sent out, several of which still hold a prominent place among esteemed varieties " (De Candolle).

Among the most successful breeders of new Strawberries in recent years are Messrs. J. Veitch & Sons, Laxton Brothers, Carmichael, and Allan. There is a marked tendency to breed for size and form of fruit only, consequently, whilst some of the new sorts are in these characters superior to older favourites, they are inferior to them in the real test of a good Strawberry, viz. firmness of flesh and richness of flavour.

CULTIVATION

Soil and Situation.—The Strawberry will grow in any good garden soil. Some kinds prefer a rich sandy loam; but the Pine varieties, and especially the Old Pine, succeed well in rather strong loam, provided it is enriched by manure and kept moist. Tenacious soils do not suit them, unless ameliorated by such means as have been pointed out in the chapter on soils. Ground that is apt to get very dry from the effects of only ten days' or a fortnight's drought is not suitable, on account of the enormous quantity of water that will be necessary; and if once the plants begin to flag for want of moisture, the crop will suffer. A soil that is naturally somewhat moist, but not too wet, answers well; and where the land admits of irrigation, heavy crops may be produced every year on even light soils.

If the nature of the ground permit, it should be trenched to the depth of at least 2 feet, supplying, at the same time, plenty of manure, most of which should lie at 1 foot from the surface. If the surface consists of old garden soil that has been long manured, and if there is any yellow loam below, it will be very desirable, in trenching, to turn up some of the latter to the top, and then, after trenching, to spread a layer of dung on the surface, mixing it well with the fresh loam in digging it in. The loam will tend to prevent the plants from growing too much to leaf, instead of forming flower-stems. For stiff soils, good peat, if at command, may be added; leaf-mould is also an excellent mulch for Strawberries.

Planting.—The best time for this operation is as soon as the plants are well rooted.

If the ground is not available for planting in summer, then it should be done early in autumn, whilst the ground is warm enough to encourage the plants to root before winter; or, if this cannot be done, the operation had better be deferred till the plants are about to start into fresh growth in spring, say February or March, according to the season and state of the weather. When it is foreseen that the plantation cannot be made in autumn it is a very good plan to take up the runners when well rooted, and plant them at 6 inches

at Deptford planted in rows 18 inches apart, and the same distance from plant to plant in the rows, but left a space of 30 inches for an alley between every three rows, and after the fruit was gathered in the first year the middle row was cleared away. Another successful grower, near Bath, planted in rows 2½ feet apart, the plants being 2 feet from each other in the rows.

Young plants that are early rooted and well grown may be planted doubly close for bearing in the following season, and after the

Fig. 216.—Planting Strawberries
On the left a plant showing roots properly placed; on the right a plant showing roots wrongly placed.

apart each way, in 4-feet beds, with 1-foot alleys between them, which will afford convenient space for weeding and watering. In this way 4 or 5 rods will hold sufficient for planting ¼ acre. When the ground is ready for planting, furrows should be drawn with a hoe, as if for sowing Peas.

The plants ought to be carefully taken up with balls, laid on a hand-barrow, and planted with a trowel. The proper distance between the rows varies according to the nature of the soil and the variety. In very rich soil the varieties with large foliage may be allowed as much as 2½ feet between the rows, and 18 inches from plant to plant in the row. For such large growers as Royal Sovereign 2½ feet apart each way is not too much, if the room can be spared. A celebrated grower

fruit is gathered every other plant can be removed, care being taken in doing so not to injure the roots of the plants intended to be left. In planting, the roots with the ball of earth should be placed as deep as they can be without covering the heart of the plant. Water must be plentifully given at first, but afterwards sparingly, until the plants have taken root. Plants that have been forced, and are still healthy and strong, may be planted outside. These will bear a good crop the first season after planting and frequently a small crop the same autumn. Both Vicomtesse H. de Thury and Royal Sovereign are varieties from which a second crop may often be taken. Some growers follow this plan every year, planting out about the end of May at the usual distances.

Cultivation.—After the planting has been completed, the ground should be kept clear of weeds, and the surface stirred. Runners should not be cut off on their first appearance, otherwise a superabundance of foliage is induced; but when the runner has formed a second joint or bud, it may be cut off near to the plant from which it springs, unless wanted for propagation. After August all runners should be taken off as they make their appearance.

With regard to the removal of the foliage before it has faded, much has been said both for and against this proceeding. We believe it to be advantageous or the contrary according to the time and manner in which the operation is performed. To mow down the foliage, young and old indiscriminately, is doubtless injurious; but the removal of the old leaves at the proper time must prove beneficial, inasmuch as more light is in consequence admitted to the young and active portion of the foliage. The practice is adopted by the Bath growers, so celebrated for their magnificent Strawberries, some of which have measured fully 7 inches in circumference, and who, as soon as the fruit is gathered, cut off all the old leaves with a knife. This is certainly preferable to mowing them with a scythe, for with the knife the old foliage can be removed and the young spared.

These young and vigorous leaves are in a condition to elaborate sap to form equally vigorous roots for supplying abundant nourishment to the ensuing crop. After it is gathered, the knife is again immediately employed to remove all old leaves, in order to give space and light for new ones. And inasmuch as the large amount of fresh foliage thus annually encouraged produces a corresponding amount of new tissue, the plants are so far annually regenerated.

Mulching between the rows of Strawberries is very advantageous. Before this is done, however, it is essential to surface-dress the soil close up to the plants with freshly-slaked lime to keep in check both slugs and wireworms. It serves to keep the ground moist and the fruit clean, as well as to afford nourishment to the plants. This mulch should consist of stable litter, put on in spring as soon as the fruit is set. It helps to keep the fruit clean and the soil moist. In poor soils the mulch may consist of horse-droppings, covered with at least 1 inch thick of clean straw, laid on just when the plants are coming into flower; and by watering frequently in dry weather the manure is washed down amongst the roots by the time the fruit is ripe, and when they are most in need of it, leaving the straw clean.

Various other materials are recommended as a mulch, but, on the whole, nothing serves the purpose better than stable litter. Tiles have been employed in order to hasten the ripening process of the earliest kinds, but they are apt to get heated by the sun and spoil the flavour of the fruit which rests upon them; they also afford shelter to insects injurious to the crop.

From the time the blossoms appear, until the fruit is ripe, the ground should never be allowed to become dry. Plants in full foliage and active growth evaporate a large amount of moisture in dry weather. Watering over the tops is not sufficient. In some soils it is necessary to flood the whole surface of the ground repeatedly, so that the water may reach the lowest roots. The leaves should never be allowed to flag, or they will never perfectly recover, even if afterwards supplied with abundance of moisture, and the fruit will consequently be poor in flavour.

RENEWING AND GATHERING

Renewing the Plantations.— Whilst some growers recommend the plantations to be renewed every year, others prefer every second or third year. Some of the celebrated growers near Bath allow a plantation to run for six or ten years without renewal. Much depends on the way the plants are managed, and equally as much upon the soil itself; if kept free of runners and divested of the old leaves after fruiting, the plantation may be allowed to remain longer than when these matters are neglected.

The system of planting annually, i.e. de-stroying the plants after the first crop and thus treating them as annuals, is only to be recommended for early kinds, such as Royal Sovereign, and then only upon warm, sheltered borders and the most favourable open spots in the garden. Such late kinds as Latest of All crop better upon two-year-old plants.

If the stem of any strong-growing sort be taken and the lower leaves stripped off, it will be seen that there are a number of white eyes ready to push when circumstances are favourable. They do not push through the coatings formed by the bases of the leaves above-ground; but if the stems are buried in soil, or in a good top-dressing of rotten dung, leaf-mould, or even leaves, they will strike root, in consequence of which the plants will be greatly invigorated, and will bear well for many years. The Old Pine has been known to produce excellent crops for twelve years when so treated.

A covering of leaves suits the Strawberry remarkably well. Some have been known

Fig. 217.—Strawberry—Royal Sovereign

to bear good crops under a large Bigarreau Cherry tree, the leaves of which were allowed to remain, as they fell, upon the plants. The Strawberry will push through a considerable thickness of leaves, or any light substance. A top-dressing of loam is beneficial, if applied before the plants begin to grow in spring, after which they should not be disturbed either at root or top.

Digging between the rows with the spade is often injurious. The object can only be to loosen the soil, in order that fresh roots may push freely; but many of those formed the previous season will be cut off in the operation, and they are the roots which contribute most to the support of the crop. If the soil is stirred with a fork with care, the plants generally derive benefit from the operation.

Strawberry plants sometimes produce a great number of leaves and flowers from the same stock. When it is desired to have the fruit large and fine, about four of the strongest flower-scapes should be retained, and the others, as well as all superfluous leaves, cut out. The lowest blossoms on the scape produce the largest, earliest, and best fruit, and these are ripe whilst those higher up are still green or only bearing flowers. The fruit from the latter never acquires the perfection of that formed lower down. In forcing, it is found advantageous to remove all except a few of the young fruits, which attain a larger size than would otherwise be the case. The same operation might be advantageously performed on plants in the open ground.

Strawberries are occasionally grown on banks, ridges, and terraces; but it is unnecessary to enter into details respecting these modes, for the plant will grow in almost any situation where it can be supplied with moisture and sufficient nourishment, and where, at the same time, the foliage is exposed to light. There are, however, advantages in the terraced ridge formed to run east and west, the plants on the south side ripening fruit earlier than those on the level ground, whilst those on the north side afford a later supply.

Gathering.—Strawberries should be gathered when dry, but not when heated by the sun. For dessert, they ought to be gathered with the calyx and just as much of the stalk below it as is sufficient to lay hold of. It is better to pick early in the day in every instance for dessert. Gathered thus early, the fruits will be better. To obviate handling the fruits again before they are placed on the table, they should be picked into clean punnets, and these go on to the table. Those intended for preserving are picked without the calyx.

The flowers of Strawberries often prove abortive, either from the effects of late spring frost or from abnormal growth. In the former case there is neither stigma nor style to be seen, only stamens, the styles having been killed. Sterility has, however, been known to affect a whole plantation of Hautbois, although the plants were not injured by frost. These plants, however, had been taken from bearing beds the year previous, and planted in a rich, well-manured border, in which they started rapidly into luxuriant growth, the growth being to leaves rather than to fruit. The plants, however, were not removed, nor were others introduced, nevertheless they bore an abundant crop the following season.

FORCING

Strawberry runners intended to form plants to be forced should be selected from the first or earliest rooted. The earlier in the summer the runners are established the longer the period of growth, and consequently the stronger and more matured the plants will be by the end of the growing season.

It is necessary to observe that although

over a small spongy centre. By degrees they take on the forms of calyx, corolla, stamens, and pistil. They form successively in the order in which they are named, the calyx first, the pistil last. The calyx and corolla are the most simple, grow the quickest, and most easily bear to be hastened; stamens require more time for growth,

Fig. 218.—Pot-grown Strawberry—Fillbasket. (⅓)

the plants may be vigorous, with large well-formed buds, capable of producing blossoms that would set their fruit well, yet, without a knowledge of the mode of growth, the whole or greater part of the blossoms may be rendered abortive. " Those who would understand the philosophy of Strawberry-forcing should begin from the beginning, and first determine what it is which they have to deal with. This can only be ascertained by examining the young flower-buds as they exist in the plant when it makes its first move towards growth. At that time they are collections of tiny scales, placed

the pistil most of all. When a high temperature, night and day, with abundance of moisture, and as much light as February yields, are suddenly applied to the Strawberry, it is compelled to grow; the predetermined parts advance, and, obedient to the influences which their nature cannot disregard, they by degrees unfold. But how? The oldest parts, namely, the calyx and corolla, simple in structure, and already advanced in their formation, suffer no injury, but appear in their usual state, arraying the blossom in gay apparel of white and green. The next, however, the stamens, having less time to form, acquire perhaps their yellow colour, but are powerless for their allotted office; while the pistil, the most complicated of all the parts—that which demands the longest period for its perfect formation, but which is the latest that the flower produces, and which is to become the fruit—is a mere tuft of abortions, incapable of quickening, and shrivelling into pitch-black threads as soon as it is fully in contact with the air " (Dr. Lindley).

It is evident, therefore, that the main points to be kept in view in forcing Strawberries are, 1st, to have strong, stocky plants, grown under the influence of plenty of sunlight; 2nd, to grow them slowly till fruit is set, in order that the parts of the flowers may have time to form, as they naturally do, in gradual succession. The first consideration ought therefore to be directed to obtaining plants with good substantial stems and well-formed heart-buds.

In dry weather the plants from which the runners are to be layered should be kept watered. Plants that have been growing one year, or not more than two, throw out stronger runners than those that are older. By the time they have pushed a joint, some good rich loamy soil should be prepared, and also a number of 3-inch pots. If moss can be easily procured, a little of it put in the bottom of each pot will serve for drainage, otherwise a few crocks or some bits of old turf may be employed. The pots should be filled with soil, the same being pressed firmly, plunged a little in the ground by means of a trowel or other tool adapted for the purpose; but in doing this care must be taken not to injure the roots of the Strawberry plants near which the pots are plunged.

The runner plant should be inserted lightly in the soil of the pot, and kept down either by a hooked twig or small stone, as explained in treating of the culture of the Strawberry in the open ground. If kept moist, the runners will soon take root. The point of the runners beyond the joint should be stopped, so that the nourishment from the mother plant may go only to the one layered.

When well rooted, the plants should be shifted into 5- or 6-inch pots, properly drained, using a good turfy loam, mixed with leaf-mould or well-rotted cow-dung. If the compost is prepared about three months previous to its being required for the purpose, so much the better. One plant in each pot will be sufficient. The plants when potted may be shaded till they recover, and then be placed in an open

space with a hard surface—either paved or covered with coal ashes, to prevent the worms from working up into the pots; quicklime may also be sprinkled over the surface with the same object. The plants may be placed tolerably close at first, but as they grow larger they should have more space allowed, so that the foliage may have plenty of light and air. To prevent the roots from growing through the bottom of the pots, which they will be apt to do in wet weather, it is a good plan to lay the pots on their sides, or to stand them on ordinary bricks. The latter method serves to keep out worms.

On the approach of winter, when the leaves mostly decay and the season of growth is over, the plants should be placed in a pit, where they can be protected from frost. Or they may be put into a heated pit close to each other, on shelves near the glass; abundance of air must here be admitted to them, and the heating apparatus only used to prevent frosts from injuring the roots. Where there is not the convenience of pits, ordinary garden frames will serve well. The lights should only be placed over them when it is either wet or frosty. The plants can then be stood closely together. Or the pots may be placed on their sides in layers, one above the other, with their bottoms against a wall, coal ashes, old tan, or leaves being interposed between the layers. Some stack them in double rows by placing a row of pots on their sides, then another row with their bottoms against those of the first, any substance that will not readily freeze being laid upon and stuffed among the pots. Before the plants are taken in to force, the pots should be cleaned, and a little of the surface mould taken off and replaced with rich soil. The crown of the plants, before they start into growth, may be covered with half-decayed leaf-mould. The plants should, wherever it be possible, be dipped in a pailful of sulphur and water—a handful of sulphur being ample. This is about the best possible preventive of mildew.

When the plants are started, the temperature should not exceed 45° or 50° by fire-heat. Air must at all times be freely admitted, but of course much less will suffice when the weather is cold than when it is warm. The temperature and air should be regulated by the appearance of the foliage. If the leaflets are observed to be broad, yet of thin substance, and if the leaf-stalks are drawing up, as if likely to be taller and more slender than those in the open ground, less fire-heat and more air must be given, but an average temperature of 55° by day may be allowed, and continued when the flower-buds begin to open, at which period forcing must be conducted very slowly, for the reasons already stated, and if this is done every flower will set, or at least as many as the plants ought to bear. The tops of the flower-stalks are inclined to continue to produce flowers; but these should be cut off, for they only rob the fruit already formed, while they themselves are worthless.

After the fruit is set the temperature should be gradually increased, and towards the ripening period it may be raised to 65°, and occasionally as high as 75° by sun-heat. An occasional watering with weak liquid manure is a great assistance. Do not, however, be led away with the too-popular notion that manure water is so essential as some think it to be. Three, or at the most four, such applications are ample. The plants should never be allowed to get dry, or the growth of the fruit will not afterwards progress so favourably, neither will the flavour be good.

When the fruit begins to colour, no more water should be given than is requisite to keep the leaves from flagging, the quantity depending upon the temperature and dryness of the air, or, in other words, upon the amount of evaporation. This must be supplied, especially in hot sunshine, even during the period of ripening, otherwise the fruit would get heated, and the flavour be spoilt. The fruit ought to be gathered in the morning, and placed in clean punnets and sent straight on to the table. If, however, the fruit has to be packed to send away, it should be placed in a single layer in square punnets. The punnets will then fit into boxes specially made for the purpose, taking two, four, six, or eight punnets in one box. A box with four punnets may be packed two upon two and larger numbers in the same way, a thin strip of wood being placed between the layers. The boxes supplied by Messrs. J. Meredith & Sons, Derby, are excellent for this purpose. This applies to all small fruits that are picked and packed to send away. In these punnets the fruit can go straight on to the table. The plants should be removed from the house as they are stripped of fruits.

Instead of layering the runners for plants to be forced in the ensuing winter and spring, runners may be planted out in August, the plants taken up just before they begin to grow in spring, potted in 4-inch pots, and

shifted into 6-inch pots towards the end of July. In this month the spring foliage begins to get too old, and the plants are disposed to start a second growth of young foliage. This is favoured by the shift into fresh soil and larger pots. Along with new foliage fresh roots are produced, and these are much better feeders, whilst the plant is being forced, than older roots would be.

Where there is not a sufficient supply of pots, or not enough labour to attend to potted plants, young plants from runners may be put in about 8 inches apart, in rows 15 or 18 inches asunder; neither fruit nor runners should be allowed to grow on these in the following summer; a portion of the oldest foliage of each plant should be cut off in July, and a top-dressing of rich soil or leaf-mould and loam ought to be given close up to the necks of the plants, to encourage fresh roots from that part. These plants may be taken up in oblong strips about 1 foot wide, and placed near the glass in a pit, on some gently-heating material, or on a platform with a hot-water pipe below. The heat from the latter should not exceed 60°.

Various other plans may be followed in forcing Strawberries. We have known patches cut out of a plantation with the spade, potted into 8-inch pots, and immediately taken in to force: the crop was very good, although the fruit was not so large as from plants prepared for the purpose.

In France, Strawberries are sometimes forced in beds in the open air, and where stable manure is plentiful this might occasionally be adopted in this country. Frames are placed over the bed, trenches 18 inches deep are dug out around the outside of these, and filled in the first instance to the level of the surface with fermenting manure, and afterwards to the height of the frames if necessary, to maintain the proper temperature. At night the sashes are covered with straw mats. In order to obtain a second crop from the beds so forced the plants are kept dry for some time after the forced crop is gathered; the old leaves are cut off, a top-dressing is given, water supplied, and in August a fair second crop is frequently obtained. The best variety for this purpose is Vicomtesse Hericart de Thury, which, if forced early, or reasonably so, will yield another crop in August and September. An open plot of ground is most desirable for this late second crop.

PROPAGATION

The Strawberry is propagated by seeds, division of the plant, and by runners. The Alpine varieties are always best raised from seeds, the others by runners.

To obtain the seeds the fruit may either be crushed on sheets of brown paper and dried by exposure to the sun and air, or it may be bruised by hand in water, and the seeds washed, those which float being rejected. If intended to be kept till spring, the seed should be well dried; but if not, it ought to be merely surface-dried and immediately sown, either in a sheltered part in the open ground or in pots. If in the open ground, the soil should be a very fine rich mould, mixed with peat, well-decomposed dung, or leaf-mould. The ground, if dry, should be watered; and when in working condition, the surface having been made smooth and even, the handle of the rake or any straight round rod should be laid across the bed at every 6 inches, moderately pressed, and in the impressions so made the seeds should be thinly sown, then pressed by again applying the rod; and they ought afterwards to be very slightly covered by sifting over them a little decayed leaf-mould. When necessary, the bed should be watered, a fine rose being used on the can.

The young plants, which should appear in less than a month, as soon as they have made four or five leaves may be transplanted to where they are to remain for fruiting. The plants may, however, be much more quickly brought forward under glass, where that is at command. The runners should be kept cut off the seedling plants, unless some are required to extend the plantation, and in that case it is a good plan to employ the first plant made by the runner from the seedling.

Runners are usually produced in abundance from most varieties. The growing point of a runner is furnished with a bud, and when the runner has extended to some distance from the stem the bud unfolds, and soon afterwards roots are emitted from its base. If in contact with moist permeable soil, these soon fix themselves, and a young plant is established. This is fed from the mother plant by means of its stolon, and until it has formed roots of its own; then a second stolon springs from the young plant, and another young plant is formed; and so on. It is evident, therefore, that if the runner be stopped after the first plant is formed, it will be better nourished than

if several were allowed to grow from the same source. Again, the earlier the young plant can be rooted, the stronger and more substantial it will become, from having the advantage of exposure to light whilst the days are long.

The first proceeding is to encourage the plants to emit runners. This they do readily in moist warm weather, or when well watered The runner makes greater progress along a moist surface than it does along one that is dry. On a large scale, the runners for propagation are allowed to root in soil adjoining the plants; it should therefore be dug or forked over and made fine for the roots to strike into, which they will soon do if it is kept moist and they are closely watered with it; and this, in many cases, can be easily secured by placing a bit of stone on the runner.

As soon as the young plant has developed a few leaves, the runner from it should be removed. On a small scale, and to obtain plants for forcing, 3-inch pots can be very advantageously employed; these to be filled with good rich soil, and then buried in the ground nearly to the brim. As soon as the bud at the first joint of the runner has developed a few leaves, it should be pressed closely upon the soil in the pot, and kept in contact with it either by means of a small hooked peg or a small stone.

The Strawberry may be propagated, in cases of emergency or in the absence of runners, by division of the plant into separate crowns; but it is neither a sure nor an expeditious method, for the plants are apt to fail, and, if they do take root, they grow but slowly compared with young plants from runners. The best time to divide them is in early spring, before the young leaves expand, or in August, whilst there is heat in the ground to encourage the growth of roots before winter. If done in August, old leaves should be mostly taken off. The plants must be protected from the direct rays of the sun till they have struck root, and the ground should be kept moderately moist. They ought to be mulched, before winter, with leaves, or any kind of litter that will afford some protection during severe frost.

ENEMIES

Birds, Slugs, and Snails. Black Vine Weevil, Red-legged Garden Weevil. Daddy Long-legs, Ghost Swift Moth, Red-legged Garden Weevil, Rose Chafer. See INSECT AND OTHER PLANT ENEMIES, Vol. III.

VARIETIES

The following descriptive list of varieties of Strawberries has been mainly supplied by Messrs. Laxton Brothers, of Bedford, whose collection of varieties is probably the largest known, and whose efforts to raise new and improved seedlings have met with exceptional success:

ABERDEEN FAVOURITE.—A fine late variety with handsome bright-crimson fruit, much grown in the north, and succeeds well in Bedford.

ADMIRAL DUNDAS.—An old and well-tried mid-season variety, of a bright-red colour, fruit inclined to be slightly furrowed, of large size, wonderfully prolific, and good flavour.

A. F. BARRON.—A large first-class mid-season fruit, varnished or glossy-scarlet in colour, raised from Sir J. Paxton crossed with Sir C. Napier. A valuable main-crop Strawberry, and good for forcing purposes.

AUGUSTE BOISSELOT.—A fine French variety, which has recently come into much prominence. A main-crop variety, large, and finely flavoured.

Fig. 219.—Strawberry—Auguste Nicaise

AUGUSTE NICAISE (fig. 219).—An excellent variety both for growing in the open and for forcing. In addition to its enormous size the fruit is very beautiful, firm of flesh, of regular size, and of good flavour. The plant is free and productive.

BEDFORD CHAMPION.—Fruits of large size, forces well, bright-scarlet in colour, robust grower.

BICTON WHITE PINE.—The true white Strawberry. Heavy cropper, rich pine flavour; worth cultivating as a novelty.

BLACK PRINCE. — A very early, small, dark-coloured, good-flavoured fruit, much grown for earliest supplies and preserving.

BRITISH QUEEN.—The richest flavoured of all Strawberries, sweet and vinous, large and bright-coloured, but not ripening regularly; plant of vigorous growth, but requires a deep and warm soil and high cultivation.

CLIMAX.—A cross between Latest of All and Waterloo. It is intermediate between its parents, partaking of the enormous cropping qualities of Latest of All with the firmness of flesh of Waterloo. Flavour rich, colour bright glossy-crimson, flesh firm and solid. A standard late variety.

COCKSCOMB.—Fruit large, ovate, occasionally cockscomb-shaped, pale-scarlet with white flesh, prominent seeds, richly flavoured; mid-season.

COMMANDER.—A distinct and fine-flavoured main-crop Strawberry; plant hardy and most prolific; will grow and succeed well where British Queen fails.

CONNOISSEUR.—A somewhat new variety, one that forces well as a second early, flavour good.

COUNT.—Colour bright-crimson, flesh white and firm with small seeds; a compact grower and very prolific. Cockscombed shape.

COUNTESS.—Large second early fruit, good colour and flavour, and of handsome cockscomb shape.

CRESCENT SEEDLING (American Scarlet, Little Gem).—An early American sort, tried and recommended by the Royal Horticultural Society as the earliest Strawberry and a free bearer suitable for market purposes; a hardy and distinct variety.

DR. HOGG.—One of the finest of all late Strawberries, of large size, quality first-rate, but does not succeed in all localities; considered by many superior to British Queen.

DR. MORÈRE.—This well-known French variety is, *par excellence*, the Strawberry grown in France for market, forcing, and for general purposes, and is as popular there as Sir J. Paxton is in this country; fruit highly coloured, quality excellent, travels well; plant is hardy and vigorous.

DR. VIEILLARD.—A recent French introduction, near Crescent Seedling; prolific, early fruits produced in clusters on a stout footstalk, and said to be a fortnight earlier than any other known variety.

DREADNOUGHT.—A new market Strawberry from the north of England, of large size and an enormous cropper.

ELTON PINE.—The true variety, very late, flavour somewhat acid, a good bearer and hardy. Useful for preserving.

EMPRESS OF INDIA.—Plant of compact habit and a fine bearer, fruit obtusely conical, bright-scarlet, flavour approaching that of British Queen; an excellent free-setting variety, and one of the best for forcing.

ENCHANTRESS. — One of the most richly-flavoured; fruit dark-coloured, cockscomb in shape; requires to be well done to be good.

EPICURE.—Of the true British Queen type, with vigorous constitution, fruits medium in size and highly flavoured.

EXCELSIOR.—Fruit medium size, of conical shape, firm flesh and of excellent flavour, for which it has received an *Award of Merit*.

FILLBASKET (fig. 218).—Raised from Royal

Sovereign and Latest of All; colour bright-scarlet, similar to Royal Sovereign; flesh white and firm with no hollowness in the centre; size between that of the two parents; flavour juicy, sweet, and luscious. The cropping qualities of this variety are most remarkable, no other variety approaching it in this respect—it carries more flower-spikes than foliage, with as many as thirty fruits on each. The habit of the plant is compact and robust, leaves thick and leathery, resisting mildew thoroughly. Ripens with Latest of All. As a second early-forcing variety it will prove equally valuable with Royal Sovereign.

FROGMORE LATE PINE.—Where this variety will succeed it is one of the most useful high-flavoured varieties to grow for a mid-season or late crop. Requires a rich soil.

GIVONS' LATE PROLIFIC.—An excellent and reliable late variety, a firm berry of brilliant scarlet colour, sub-acid in flavour, and a heavy cropper.

GUNTON PARK.—Fruit extra large, varying in shape from cockscomb to obtusely conical, dark crimson-scarlet, and of a pleasant brisk flavour, flesh firm and light-coloured; a fine early kind, very useful for forcing, and bearing in long succession.

KEENS' SEEDLING.—The well-known and much-appreciated hardy second early variety, useful for all purposes; fruit large and of good flavour; plant hardy and prolific.

KING GEORGE V.—A fine forcing and outdoor variety, as large as Royal Sovereign and superior in flavour. Similar in shape and habit to Royal Sovereign, but in every respect better. This has been well proven by practical growers.

KING OF THE EARLIES.—Now well known and largely cultivated as a most productive, early, and richly-flavoured sort.

LADY SUFFIELD.—An excellent all-round variety, cropping well in the open, and forcing as a second early most satisfactorily. Fruits long, tapering, dark-crimson, deliciously flavoured.

LA GROSSE SUCRE.—The best Strawberry of the Keens' Seedling type, unsurpassed for flavour, size, and fertility as a forcing variety, and in the open as a continuous bearer of large, fine-flavoured fruits.

LATEST OF ALL.—A cross between British Queen and Helena Gloede. Fruit larger than that of either parent, the flavour vinous, yet luscious, and quite equal to that of British Queen, but ripening several days after it. The best flavoured and largest late Strawberry yet introduced.

LAXTON'S LATEST.—Fruits very large, of conical shape, colour deep rich crimson throughout, habit robust.

LEADER.—A cross between Latest of All and Noble, of good constitution. Fruit large, wedge-shaped, bright-crimson; flesh firm, of good flavour. Very prolific. A good forcer.

LORD KITCHENER.—A cross between British Queen and Waterloo. The plant is vigorous and a most prolific cropper, ripening early in July. The fruits are large, roundish, dark-red, and very richly flavoured. A valuable addition to the mid-season varieties.

LORD SUFFIELD.—Plant of good habit and foliage, very prolific; fruit large and handsome, inclining to cockscomb shape, dark-crimson flesh, firm and richly flavoured, ripening after President and Paxton.

MENTMORE.—Raised from Noble and British Queen. A handsome main-crop Strawberry of a

rich-crimson colour with a smooth varnished appearance which adds much to its attractiveness; large, regular, flat-pyriform in shape; flesh rich-red throughout, with no hard core or hollowness in the centre, in large loose trusses; a very heavy cropper. A good forcing variety.

MONARCH.—A distinct second early variety with berries of enormous size, richly-coloured, wedge-shaped, and ripening early.

NEWTON SEEDLING. — A very hard, distinct, and free-bearing mid-season to late variety, which grows in partial shade where other sorts will not succeed.

PINE APPLE.—Flavour excellent, medium-sized fruit of conical shape.

PRESIDENT.—One of the most useful and highly-flavoured main-crop Strawberries grown. Fruit large, bright-crimson, flavour excellent; plant hardy and prolific, forces well.

PRESIDENT LOUBET.—A new variety of exceptional flavour. Fruits dark-crimson, late in ripening.

PRESTON SEEDLING.—A Strawberry largely grown under various names as a garden and market variety chiefly in northern districts. It is very productive, hardy and vigorous, the fruit large, long conical in shape, and of good flavour.

QUEEN OF DENMARK.—Raised from Frogmore Late Pine and Waterloo, new in colour, firm in flesh, and of good flavour; good for general culture.

REWARD.—Fruits very large, wedge-shaped, rich vinous flavour, deep-red flesh and firm. Mid-season.

RIVAL.—A late variety and a heavy cropper. Fruit medium size, flesh firm and white. A fine addition to the lates.

ROYAL SOVEREIGN (fig. 217).—Raised from Noble, crossed with King of the Earlies. This possesses all the qualities required in a good Strawberry, either for open-air cultivation or as a forcer. The fruit is of the largest size, conical and sometimes flattened in shape, colour bright-scarlet, flesh firm and white, flavour rich. As a forcing variety is unequalled for early work; even when hard forced it throws its flower-spike well out, setting freely and swelling quickly to a large size.

SCARLET QUEEN.—A cross between Noble and King of the Earlies, and coming in between these two fine early sorts. One of the handsomest, brightest-coloured, richest-flavoured, and best early Strawberries yet produced.

SHARPLESS.—The best of all the American Strawberries. Very large, early, and productive, and succeeds well in this country. Probably one of the parents of Noble.

SIR JOSEPH PAXTON.—The most appreciated and widely grown of all main-crop Strawberries. Fruit large, handsome, bright-scarlet, flesh firm and travels well, flavour good; plant hardy and vigorous.

SOUVENIR DE BOSSUET.—A very large new main-crop variety raised in France, with enormous fruits, of first quality and fine form, flesh firm and white.

TEUTONIA.—A large-fruited variety, credited as being the earliest sort grown in Germany, and much recommended. In an election of Strawberries, conducted in 1913 in Germany, this variety obtained the largest number of votes.

THE EARL.—Stated to be an improved Vicomtesse H. de Thury, being equal in flavour, as firm, and a better cropper. A vigorous grower.

THE LAXTON (fig. 220).—Fruit firm, large, dark-crimson, first-rate in quality, does not rot on the ground in damp weather, and is a good traveller. A very hardy and vigorous grower, retaining its foliage well in winter.

THE QUEEN.—Stated to be an improvement size, crop, and colour, and as late as Waterloo. The fruit is pointedly conical in shape, very large, flesh and skin very firm, yet sweet and luscious. A good traveller, and exceptionally good grower and cropper, and likely to supersede many of the later varieties.

Fig. 220.—Strawberry—The Laxton.   (Rather less than half natural size)

upon British Queen and of robust constitution. It will grow, and with vigour, where that old and well-known variety will not live. Fruits pale-red in colour, with pale-red flesh.

TRAFALGAR.—An exceptionally fine late variety of rich pine flavour, equalling Royal Sovereign in

VICOMTESSE HERICART DE THURY.—A most excellent early Strawberry of high quality; plant hardy and prolific.

WATERLOO.—A very distinct and popular late Strawberry. Fruit very large, dark-coloured, and of good flavour.

ALPINE STRAWBERRIES

The French growers have for some years past adopted the system of raising their stock of Alpine Strawberries from seed, treating them, in fact, as annuals or biennials, but it is only recently that English cultivators have followed their example. Plants raised from runners (the first runners from the seedling plants excepted) will not bear comparison with those raised from seed. One plant of the latter is worth a dozen of the former, not only in vigour of growth but also in the size and quality of the fruit and the extent of the crop. If raised from seeds annually the

Alpine Strawberry is bound to become popular.

Sowing the Seed.—The Continental, and particularly the French growers, recommend that the seed be sown in August and September, but we prefer March or April, in order to have strongly-rooted plants before the hot weather sets in. Sow the seed thinly in shallow boxes or seed-pans, in the same way as for Celery. The first batch should be sown early in March, and later on another, if the stock obtained in the earlier sowing be not sufficient for the purpose. The seeds germinate quickly in a gentle and moist heat. As soon as the plants are large enough to handle they must be pricked off in shallow boxes 12 inches by 24 inches. These will take fifty plants comfortably. A genial temperature will be conducive to growth without any perceptible check, shading being scarcely needed. As soon as the plants are well established, a cold pit or frame near the glass will be the better choice, and a few weeks later—say by the middle of May—they can be quite hardened off to stand outside. The best soil for the seed is a light sandy loam with leaf-mould passed through a fine sieve; this retains moisture and saves frequent waterings.

When the plants crowd each other, they should be pricked off upon prepared ground —a light sandy loam with either leaf-soil or the manure from a spent bed of Mushrooms; or, failing this, roadside scrapings form a good substitute. A heavy and retentive soil is not in any sense desirable. The position should be partially shaded, such, for instance, as at the foot of a wall with an eastern aspect, where the sun does not shine upon the plants long. In this position the plants can remain until September or October. The position now need not be a shaded one, but all the same semi-shade suits the Alpine Strawberry at all times, such, for instance, as that afforded by standard trees of Pears or Apples; not Plums, however, because of the woolly aphis, which will deposit filth upon the foliage.

The ground should be well prepared by deep digging or trenching, as the case may be, regard being had to its previous good culture. Avoid a shallow soil with a hard subsoil, which will invariably be productive of dryness. It is quite true that the Alpine Strawberry is not deep rooting; moisture, however, is essential for its successful culture. Either sloping banks or flat ground will answer. Beds made upon the flat can be watered more thoroughly than those upon sloping ground.

For the main planting, decomposed farmyard manure worked into the second spit will afford considerable assistance upon light or warm porous soils. From the time of first pricking off the seedlings until the fruiting stage the hoe should be freely worked amongst the plants to keep the surface open as well as to cut down weeds. After pricking off, and also after planting, see that the plants are thoroughly watered so as to settle the soil around the roots. Whilst still in the former stage a damping overhead in the

afternoon during hot weather will be beneficial. The plants should also be well watered when the fruit is ripening. This will need to be frequently repeated, from the fact that the same plants will remain in a continuous fruiting condition for months together. The ripe fruit does not so readily suffer as do those of the large-fruited varieties. Mulching is advisable, quite as much so as in other kinds, but it should be of a finer description. The mulch may consist first

Fig. 22 —Alpine Strawberry—Sutton's Large Red

of leaf-soil fairly well decomposed, or manure from a spent Mushroom bed with short clean litter added as the fruits begin to colour.

It is better to plant 18 inches apart each way in beds, missing out every fourth row to form an alley. If the plants have time to become well established before winter, and at the same time are vigorous, they may be allowed to bear an early crop of fruit the following summer. The better plan, however, would be to pick off all the flower trusses until the middle of July, as in the case of the runners. By this means a grand autumn crop of fine fruits will be ensured up to the time of frost supervening. The following season the plants so treated should carry the first early crop, which will ripen about the same time as Royal Sovereign; these same plants will continue to bear well until the beginning of August, when the young plantation will be ripening their crops. After the early crop has ceased to be good, it is better to destroy the plants and rely upon the younger plants alone for the autumn supply. The annual raising of a sufficient number of seedlings will recommend itself as the most satisfactory mode of cultivation.

On the approach of winter, and when a morning frost is apprehended, the plants may with advantage be netted over, preferably by straining the nets upon wires at about 4 feet or so from the ground. This will ward off a considerable amount of frost. Although birds are well known to prey upon Strawberries, they do not do much harm to the Alpine sorts.

Alpine Strawberries are grown in pots for forcing in France, but this system will scarcely find favour with us, more particularly where the claims upon the glass space are heavy. The pot system is better perhaps for extending the late supply rather than for an early crop. If movable frames can be spared, these might be placed over a portion of the plants either for the first early picking or for the latest crop. The best time for picking the fruit is in the early morning, and the time when the fruits are most appreciated is at breakfast. In gathering the fruits it is best to pick straight away into the dish, fancy basket, or punnet, so that they go straight to the table. It is not necessary to retain the stalks in picking.

SELECTION OF VARIETIES OF ALPINE STRAWBERRIES

BELLE DE MEAUX.—This is quite distinct and of excellent flavour. In form and colour it much resembles Hautbois, being of the two the darker fruit, and in shape obtuse rather than conical.

BERGER and JANUS are recommended by the French growers. The red and white varieties of F. de Gaillon do not produce runners, and are not so desirable. The plants are of dense growth, and the fruit somewhat small.

BLANC (White) is a very distinct and useful variety and is much superior to the old white form. When gathering, a mixture of this and a red-fruited kind has a pretty effect.

ROUGE AMÉLIORÉ (Improved Red).—This is a very distinct variety with slender fruits, often measuring 2 inches in length. Very prolific and hardy.

SUTTON'S LARGE RED (fig. 221).—An excellent variety with long fruits. It crops well and is of good flavour.

PERPETUAL STRAWBERRIES

These recent additions to garden Strawberries were brought into prominence a few years back on the Continent, and are now better known in this country, although their culture is not yet well understood. They are reputed to be crosses between the ordinary large-fruited or English Strawberry and the Alpine forms. The ordinary methods of cultivation for Strawberries do not answer for these.

The first Perpetual Strawberry raised was Louis Gauthier, a white-fruited variety with a slight tinge of pink upon the sunny side. As a summer-fruiting Strawberry it does not compare well with our best-known kinds. It is most prolific, and many fine fruits are produced. Its habit is robust, hence it should be planted at least 2½ feet each way —3 feet even, if room can be spared. The old crowns do not produce fruits again in the autumn, hence it is not in this respect similar to those yet to be noted.

The successional crops of fruit are produced upon the first and second runners of the current season; hence the advice to plant far apart and to encourage the production of runners as early as possible, even if it be necessary to denude the old stools of all their flower trusses. When these runners have been secured they should at once be pegged down securely, stopping the growth beyond the second one. As soon as they are well rooted the old crowns should be removed to afford room and light for the young stock. These will quickly develop flower trusses and in due course ripen fruits, if mulching and watering are attended to.

The runners can be layered into 4 to 8 inch pots, and during the months of September and October be placed in a frame or upon shelves in a cool house to ripen. There is no difficulty in securing ripe fruit up to the end of November in a Strawberry-house proper, or where a slight warmth can be maintained.

The runners for pots should be taken as early as possible, selecting the strongest only. As soon as these are well established they should be cut off in order to give room for those rooted upon the ground, these latter providing a crop oftentimes in advance of the pot-grown stock. When the pot plants are cut off they should be placed fairly close together, so that the necessary watering is an easier performance. When housed, these

Fig. 222.—Perpetual Strawberry—St. Antoine de Padoue

pot-plants should be damped over, either with a rose or syringe, both morning and evening, to supply the place of the dew then lacking. No harm will come of this practice, and if it were followed more with early forced Strawberries there would be fewer attacks from red spider. Of course when the fruits are ripening it should be discontinued, and discretion exercised if the weather be damp or foggy.

These pot-plants after fruiting make capital stock for planting in the open. Never retain the old stools of Perpetual Strawberries, not even of the more recent kinds, but treat them as annuals, renewing the stock every year.

In autumn it is an excellent plan to support the fruits with sprays from old birch brooms to keep them from touching the soil or the mulch, which of itself retains moisture in excess oftentimes of the requirements at that season. Bearing this in mind, the wisdom of planting at 3 feet apart is clear, as at least six runners from each plant may be depended upon, oftentimes more.

SELECT VARIETIES OF PERPETUAL STRAWBERRIES

JEANNE D'ARC.—Very similar to St. Joseph, and possibly an improvement upon it, possessing greater vigour.

LA PERLE.—A prolific variety, deeper in colour than Louis Gauthier. Growth small and compact.

Will thrive in a rather shaded position at times.

LOUIS GAUTHIER.—One of the oldest of the perpetual varieties. Fruits well from the runners of the same season. Colour a pale pink. Fruit large.

MERVEILLE DE FRANCE.—One of the best and most prolific of this section. Fruits of unusual size, growth very free.

OREGON.—Of supposed American origin, very similar in appearance to small fruits of Royal Sovereign, very productive upon runners, and good on the old stools.

ST. ANTOINE DE PADOUE (see Plate, and fig. 222). —All points considered, this is the best variety yet sent out in this section; it is a reputed cross— and its characteristics tend to confirm it—between Royal Sovereign and St. Joseph. Its fruits may be described as second-sized fruits of the first-named parent, which it also resembles in flavour, colour, and solidity of flesh.

ST. JOSEPH.—Distinct and most prolific, requiring to be thinned of the smaller fruits to ensure size and good quality.

The Perpetual Strawberries are much more cultivated on the Continent than in England. The essential in their culture is an open and sunny position for the ripening of their fruits in the autumn. It pays to use cloches for the latest supplies out-of-doors; they keep the fruit dry in wet weather and obviate the use of netting.

These varieties should all be tried, even if in small quantities, for it is possible that one may thrive better than another in a given district.

All that is needed is a good Strawberry soil, an open, sunny position—then propagation by runners is ample and efficient.

MISCELLANEOUS HARDY FRUITS

ALMOND (*Amygdalus communis*) (fig. 223) is a deciduous tree, growing to the height of 15 or 20 feet, a native of the warmer parts of Asia. The fruit consists of a dry or fleshy husk, and a shell of greater or less degree of hardness, containing a kernel which is sweet or bitter according to the variety. Sweet Almonds are eaten as dessert; they are also largely used in confectionery and cookery. An oil

Fig. 223.—Almond (*Amygdalus communis*)

obtained from them is employed in medicine and the arts, especially in perfumery. Bitter Almonds are used in the production of noyau and for flavouring confectionery. They contain hydrocyanic acid, which is a poison. They also yield an oil which is extensively used in flavouring, but it should be used with caution, as it is poisonous.

The Almond seldom bears any considerable quantity of fruit, even in the south of these islands; for the blossoms, appearing in March and sometimes in February, are frequently destroyed by frost; and, even if they do escape, there is rarely sufficient sun-heat to ripen the fruit as well as that imported from the south of France. The tree is therefore rarely planted in this country for any other purpose than ornament, or occasionally to serve as a stock for Peaches and Nectarines.

The Almond prefers a warm, deep soil, well drained, a sheltered situation, and a sunny aspect. Propagation is effected by seeds, or by budding. The finest nuts only should be selected for sowing. The seedlings when a year old should be planted 18 inches apart, in rows 2 feet apart, and they may be budded near the ground the same year, or standard-high when two or three years older. Generally they require the same treatment as young Plum trees, and, in respect to pruning, like the Peach. If fruits are matured, as sometimes happens, they may either be gathered whilst the shell is soft, for immediate use, or remain on the trees till they fall, spreading them out on a shelf in a fruit-room or greenhouse to dry. They may be stored in dry clean sand in a dry cool place.

Little is known respecting the comparative merits of the varieties in this country; and the following particulars as to the principal sorts are chiefly taken upon the authority of M. Vilmorin:—

BITTER ALMOND.—Differs little from Common, except in the kernel being bitter. The shell is generally hard and of a dark colour; there are several sub-varieties, differing in the size of the nut, as well as in the colour and thickness of the shell.

COMMON (Amandier Commun).—Nut about 1¼ inches in length; shell hard and smooth, terminating in a sharp point; kernel small, sweet, but inferior to that of the other kinds. It is productive, and the sort most commonly cultivated in France. According to Downing it is hardy and productive in New York. It is used as a stock for the Peach.

HARD-SHELLED SWEET (Amande douce à coque dure).—Nut about 1½ inches long, smooth; shell thick and hard; kernel small. Differs from Common in having larger fruit. Also used as a stock.

LADIES' ALMOND (Amandier des Dames).—Nut oval, about an inch in length; shell porous and easily broken, kernel sweet and rich. Better in quality, but not so hardy as Common.

PEACH ALMOND (Amandier Pêcher).—Said to

be a cross. It produces two kinds of fruit on the same tree, and sometimes on the same branch. The one is large, fleshy, and succulent, like a Peach, but bitter; the other has a dry husk like the Almond. They have a tolerably sweet kernel.

SOFT-SHELLED SWEET (Amande douce à coque tendre).—Resembles the Hard-shelled Sweet, but has a softer shell. Very productive in France.

SULTANA ALMOND (Amandier Sultane).—Nut like that of the Ladies' Almond, but smaller. Not an abundant bearer, and is peculiar to the south of France.

CHESTNUT (*Castanea sativa*) is a native of South Europe, North Africa,

and more aromatic than the ordinary Chestnut, and are the result of careful selection and cultivation, which has been going on for centuries. Marrons of the best quality are produced in France, although it is in Italy that the Chestnut is more used as an article of food than in other parts of the world " (*Sargent*).

Almost all the Italian Provinces cultivate the Chestnut, some 500,000 acres being covered with it. The total annual produce of nuts runs into millions of bushels. They are ground into flour, which is used for

Fig. 224.—Chestnut. (Natural size)

and the Orient. It was probably introduced into England by the Romans, and was cultivated for its fruits for centuries. In Italy and France careful attention has been paid to the raising of improved varieties, of which there are now many. It forms a large tree in this country, where it has become naturalized in the warmer districts.

" The cultivated Chestnuts are divided into two classes, known as Marrons and Châtaignes, the latter bearing about the same relation to the former as the Crab-Apple does to the Apple. Marrons are larger, more farinaceous, and much sweeter

cakes, soups, porridge, &c., and is considered to be good food. There are several methods of preserving the nuts, from sugaring them to slightly boiling and then drying them, or laying the newly gathered nuts in dry sand in earthenware vessels and burying the vessels in dry earth, where they will keep fresh till the following June.

In England very little attention has been given to the Chestnut as a food-producer, yet there are few forest trees which have anything like so great a value in this respect. Chestnuts are largely planted for effect, being excellent shade-trees, and suitable for screens, avenues, or groups, or as single specimens; moreover, there are few trees which thrive so well on poor sandy or gravelly soil. It prefers a deep well-drained soil and dislikes lime. In stiff clays and retentive subsoils it seldom lives for any length of time If, therefore, instead of planting the common sort, the large-fruited Marrons were planted, the crop of nuts obtained from them each year would be of considerable value.

The Chestnut of North America (*C. dentata*) and the Japanese Chestnut (*C. crenata*) are very nearly allied to the European sort, and their nuts are used as food in the same way.

Propagation is effected by grafting and budding for named varieties; and by seeds for the common sort. The latter may be sown in October or November in drills 2 feet apart, the seeds about 4 inches apart, and buried to a depth of 3 inches. Beyond keeping the ground clean, nothing further is required till the plants have attained the age of two years, when they should be taken up any time between October and March, about one-third of the tap-root cut off, and replanted 1 foot apart, in rows 2 feet asunder. A clear stem ought to be preserved by pruning off lateral branches.

The young trees should be transplanted every other year, and, according to their growth, allowed more space. When they have stems about 2 inches in diameter, they should be planted where they are to remain.

Pruning.—Stop the lateral branches where disposed to make an undue growth, with a view to forming a straight main stem. Thin out the shoots where they cross or interfere with each other, and check grossness by root-pruning.

The fruit when fully ripe naturally detaches itself from the tree, and may be collected from time to time as it falls. The nuts should be beaten out of the husks and spread out in a thin layer in the fruit-room. Those not required for immediate use, after having been exposed for some time to the air, to get rid of a portion of their moisture, may be packed in alternate layers with dry sand, and kept in any dry place secure from frost.

HAZEL-NUT or **FILBERT** (*Corylus Avellana*) (fig. 225).—A shrub or small tree with a comparatively thick trunk, a spreading head, and orbicular cordate leaves. It is a native of the British Islands and other parts of Europe, and is not uncommon in our copses and hedgerows. The size and quality of the nuts have been improved by cultivation and selection, and there are now numerous named varieties. They are extensively cultivated in the south of Europe, especially in Spain, whence come the large variety known as the Barcelona nut. They are also much grown in Kent.

The term Cob-nut is applied to those with short-tailed husks, those with longer tails being known as Filberts.

Soil and Situation.—The Hazel-nut will grow in almost any soil; but that in which it is most fruitful is a loam upon a dry sandy rock. It succeeds very well in sandy loam, or in a mixture of loam and brick rubbish. In strong, moist, loamy soils the trees are apt to grow too much to wood. In the warm parts of the Continent they are planted towards a northern exposure, but in this country a southern slope is the best.

Culture.—The distance between the trees may be 10 feet each way, and they must be kept within limits by pruning, so that they may not crowd each other. If the soil is thin, sandy, or rocky, manure of some sort should be given every year, especially if the trees bear heavy crops. Old woollen rags are found to be a good manure, and the decayed prunings and foliage of the trees themselves are likewise used as a mulch. Manure is applied by laying it on after having removed the surface soil for some distance round the tree in autumn. When the soil is removed, all suckers should be cut away, a most important point in the cultivation of the Hazel-nut, if, indeed, it is not of all others the most important.

Pruning.— The young trees should be pruned to a single stem, and topped at 18 inches from the ground. If, after planting, the stem remains weak, it is advisable to allow the plant to grow unpruned, except in respect to suckers.

When the plants have grown for one season, those that have too weak stems should be cut down to the ground, and only the strongest one of the shoots which subsequently push be permitted to grow, cutting it back in autumn to 18 inches from the ground. This constitutes the main stem, 1 foot of which should always be kept quite clear of shoots. If above this height six sufficiently strong shoots push, let them be inclined outwards and at equal distances from each other. This is easily done by means of a hoop placed in the centre. If six good shoots cannot be obtained, select three of the best, and endeavour to grow these three of equal strength during the summer, and cut them back to within 4 or 5 inches from their base. In the following summer two shoots from each of these three will become the origin of six branches for forming the head. The leading shoots of these branches require to be shortened more or less at every

exceed 6 feet in height. In consequence of the leading shoots being thus shortened, laterals are abundantly produced; they should be checked by pinching. In autumn, the laterals should be shortened back nearly close to the stem, and in consequence of this two or more shoots will push from

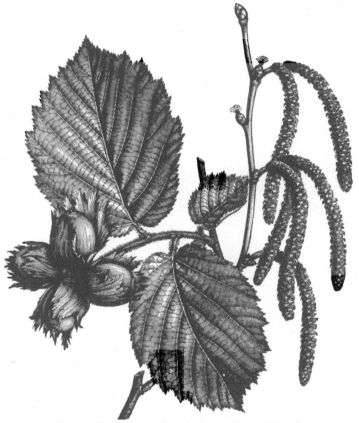

Fig. 225.—Hazel (*Corylus Avellana*) with flowers and fruits. (Reduced)

winter-pruning. How far they should be shortened back depends on the soil and climate. The object is to cause the shoot to push laterals along its whole length, instead of being naked near its base, as would otherwise be the case; and this will be ensured by cutting off two-thirds; but one-half or one-third may, under some circumstances, be found sufficient.

In Kent, the trees are not allowed to

the base. If the plant is not growing too luxuriantly, these shoots will bear fruit. If they are too numerous they should be thinned. If any shoot is allowed to push with excessive vigour in any part of the tree, the fruitfulness of the other parts will be rendered uncertain.

The Hazel is monœcious, that is, separate male and female flowers are produced on the same plant (see fig. 225). The male flowers, those long pendulous catkins, appear in January, the female flowers opening in spring. The female flower-bud is a little more plump than the wood-bud, and from its apex several deep-crimson thread-like styles are protruded in spring. It is necessary to save a good number of catkins when the trees are pruned in January, but if catkins are scarce it is advisable to delay pruning till the female blossoms have expanded; and even then, if the catkins are so situated that, in order to give the tree a symmetrical

gathered for immediate use when the husks become brown; but for keeping they should remain till ready to drop from the tree, and then be gathered when perfectly dry. Red and White Filberts are best adapted for keeping in the husk. The base of the latter is succulent, and must be thoroughly dried before the nuts are packed for keeping. When the husks become dry, they are exposed to the fumes of sulphur to prevent them from becoming mouldy. Or they may be packed in dry-ware casks, or in

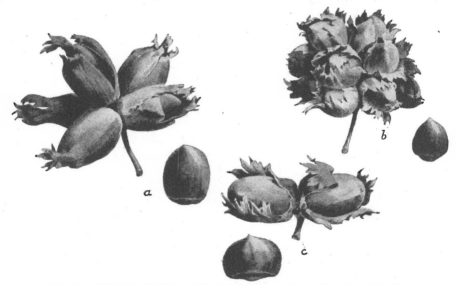

Fig 226.—*a*, Webb's Prize Cob Filbert. *b*, Spanish Prize Filbert. *c*, Downton Large Square (Atlas) Nut

form, they would have to be cut away, it is well to leave some of the shoots furnished with male blossoms for a week longer. In cases where the catkins have been injured by frost, branches furnished with them may be cut from the common Hazel and fixed among the branches of the cultivated trees for the purpose of pollination.

The lateral shoots, which generally bear the fruit, should be shortened to a female blossom-bud. Occasionally some of the shortest twigs, with a flower-bud at the extremity, may be left unpruned; but laterals that have borne should be cut back to two eyes, or within $\frac{1}{2}$ inch of the branch from which they proceed.

Gathering and Storing.—Nuts may be

new flower-pots or jars, with a sprinkling of salt to prevent mouldiness. In all cases they should be kept in a cool, dry place.

Propagation.—The Hazel may be propagated by seeds, layers, suckers, or grafts. The nuts should be ripe, and sown in October in rich light soil. Plants thus raised are rarely so good as their parents, but they are useful for planting in woods for rods and other purposes; or they may be reared with single stems and grafted with improved sorts.

Layering is performed in autumn, or at any time before spring. Some growers prefer plants from layers to those raised by any other method.

Propagation by suckers is the usual

method adopted in Kent; they are taken from the parent plant in autumn, shortened to 10 or 12 inches, and planted in nursery rows, where they remain three or four years. Grafting is not usual, but it may be very advantageously employed in some cases. The grafts take readily, and if a strong-growing sort be grafted on one that is less vigorous, fruitfulness will be induced, and over-luxuriance checked. Whip-grafting is the best mode, and the operation should be performed in February or March.

Diseases and Insects.—The tree is rarely attacked, but the crop is sometimes destroyed by the nut-weevil (*Balaninus nucum*), which pierces the tender shell of the young nut and deposits a single egg in the interior. The maggot hatched from this feeds upon the kernel until it has attained its full size, when it eats its way out either before or after the nut has fallen to the ground, and buries itself in the earth, where it pupates. All that can be done to prevent the mischief is to shake the trees in August, and, having collected the fallen nuts, to burn those which are perforated.

The most esteemed varieties are:—

COB.—Husk short, hispid. Nut large, short ovate, slightly compressed; shell very thick and hard, generally well-filled kernel of good quality. Tree of strong upright habit, and a good bearer.

COSFORD.—Husk nearly the length of the nut, deeply divided, slightly hispid at the base, expanding but not becoming reflexed when the nut is ripe. Nut large, oblong; shell light-brown, thin; kernel filling the shell, white, sweet, and very good. Tree a good bearer, ripening its fruits early.

DOWNTON LARGE SQUARE (Atlas) (fig. 226, *c*).—Husk smooth. Nut large, short, four-sided, rounded at the corners; shell thick; kernel very good.

DUKE OF EDINBURGH (Princess Royal).—Husk frequently longer than the nut; downy, coarsely fringed. Nut large, shell thick; kernel of fine flavour. Tree a good bearer.

FRIZZLED FILBERT. — Husk about twice the length of the nut, deeply divided, spreading open at the mouth, frizzled, hispid. Nuts in clusters of three or more, small, oblong, flattened; shell rather thick, well filled. Ripens rather late.

MERVEILLE DE BOLWILLER.—Husks shorter than the nut, frizzled. Nut large, shell thick; kernel large and of good flavour. Tree vigorous and productive.

PEARSON'S PROLIFIC (Dwarf Prolific, Nottingham Prolific). — Husk short and hairy. Nut medium-sized, shell thick; kernel large and sweet. Tree sturdy, productive, quite young bushes bearing freely.

RED FILBERT. — Husk long, hispid. Nut medium-sized, ovate; shell thick; skin of kernel crimson; flavour good. Tree a good bearer.

WEBB'S PRIZE COB FILBERT (fig. 226, *a*).—Husk nearly smooth, longer than the nut, which is large, over an inch long, produced in large bunches;

shell thick, brown; kernel full, covered with reddish skin, richly flavoured, a good keeper. Tree vigorous, very productive.

WHITE FILBERT.—Husk long, tubular, contracted round the apex of the nut, hispid. Nut medium-sized, ovate; shell thick; kernel covered with a white skin; flavour good. A good bearer.

Other cultivated sorts are: Brunswick Cob, Close-headed Prolific, Cosford Club, Daviana, Emperor, Kentish Cob, Louis Berger, Prize Exhibition Cob, Purple-leaved, Reigate Cob, Trebizond and Spanish Prize (fig. 226, *b*).

WALNUT (*Juglans regia*) (fig. 227).—A lofty monœcious tree, a native of Europe, Asia Minor, the Caucasus, Persia, Himalaya, China, and Japan. Introduced into Italy,

Fig. 227.—Walnut (*Juglans regia*)

France, Spain, &c. The date of its introduction into Britain is unknown, the tree not being recorded as cultivated till the year 1562. It is now extensively cultivated in France, Germany, and throughout southern Europe, both for timber and fruit as well as an ornamental tree. The fruit whilst young and tender is largely used for pickling, and when ripe, for dessert. An oil, much used in the arts, is obtained from the kernel; and the wood, being light, durable, and susceptible of a high polish, is largely used by the cabinet-maker, for gun-stocks, &c.

The Walnut succeeds in most kinds of soil so long as it is warm and not over wet. It requires plenty of room, as well as a free exposure to air and light, and is generally planted as a single specimen or to form a bold open group in a park, where its shade and wide-spreading roots will not interfere with other plants.

It may be planted either in autumn, after the fall of the leaf, or in spring. The ground should be deeply trenched, large holes having been made, the trees must be carefully lifted with balls and planted, as they have a straggling root system and do not transplant well.

The trees form their heads naturally, so that little pruning is required except to keep the branches balanced. The best time

store its plumpness and cause it to part readily from the thin pellicle with which it is covered.

Large quantities of Walnuts are imported into this country from France, Belgium, and Holland. The tree grows so well and crops so regularly and abundantly in this country that it would be worth while to plant it largely for the sake of its nuts.

Propagation is effected by seeds, budding, grafting, and inarching. The best nuts should be selected for seeds, and these, having been stratified in sand in a cool place during the winter, may be planted in February, either where the trees are in-

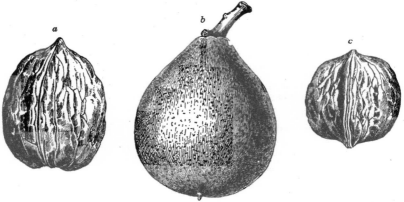

Fig. 228.—Walnuts. *a*, Parisienne. *b*, Pear-shaped (fruit). *c*, Noix Saint-Jean

for this is in autumn, before the fall of the leaf.

For pickling, the fruit should be gathered whilst the shell is so soft that it can easily be pierced with a needle. When perfectly ripe, the husk opens, and at this time it is usual to beat the tree with rods; but this is at best a barbarous practice, for the nuts, when ripe, drop, and may then be collected.

The nuts, when gathered, should be spread out in a layer about 3 inches thick, in a dry, airy place, and turned frequently till they easily part with their husk; and, after having been thoroughly dried, they may be packed in alternate layers with sand in jars or casks, or in jars and salt scattered over them as they are put in. The jars should then be kept in a cool, dry place. Before use, the Walnuts should be wiped perfectly clean with a cloth, and if the kernel is shrivelled they should be steeped for several hours in milk and water, to re-

tended to remain or in a nursery for transplantation. By the former method the tallest and best trees for timber are obtained, whilst the latter mode is generally more convenient, and affords trees which come sooner into bearing and ripen their fruit earlier in the season than those not transplanted. The ground having been trenched 2 feet deep, the nuts, if sown where they are to remain, should be placed 4 inches apart, in patches of three or four, and covered to the depth of 2 inches. In general 60 feet may be allowed between the patches, but in rich, deep soil 70 or 80 feet will not be too much. The strongest seedling in each patch should be retained.

If the plants are to be grown in a nursery, the nuts should be placed 18 inches apart, in drills 2½ feet asunder. In the autumn of the year after sowing, and as soon as the leaves have fallen, every alternate plant should be taken up with a ball, and replanted elsewhere at 1 yard apart, the extremity of the tap-root having been cut off, in order to induce the production of side roots. The next year, those not transplanted should be taken up, treated in a similar manner, and replanted. Transplantation should take place every second or third year till the trees are planted in permanent positions.

Grafting is seldom practised in this country for the Walnut, but in France it is usual where named varieties are cultivated. The trees are grafted when the stems are from 3 to 5 inches in circumference.

Insects.—The Walnut rarely suffers from insects, to which the smell and astringency of the leaves appear to be peculiarly distasteful.

The principal varieties are:—

CLUSTER.—Fruit produced in clusters of fifteen or twenty, thin-shelled, and of good flavour.

COMMON.—Fruit oval, not large, but well filled. Tree an abundant bearer.

HIGHFLYER.—Middle size, remarkably thin-shelled, and well filled. Ripens early. One of the best.

LARGE DOUBLE (Noyer à bijoux).—Fruit very large, double, kernel good, but soon shrivels. The shells are frequently used by ladies for holding trinkets, hence its French name.

LARGE LONG-FRUITED.—Fruit thin-shelled, very full, of excellent flavour, and produced in great abundance.

LATE (Noix Saint-Jean) (fig. 228, c).—The principal merit of this is in its not flowering till the end of June, so that the crop is not exposed to injury from late spring frosts.

PARISIENNE (French Walnut) (fig. 228, a).— Fruit very large, but must be eaten soon after gathering, otherwise it becomes hard and shrivelled. Tree not a great bearer.

PROLIFIC.—Said to come into bearing when the seedlings are three years old, and to reproduce itself true from seed. It may be trained as a pyramid, but the pruning for this purpose should be performed in summer, whilst the shoots are soft.

PYRIFORMIS (fig. 228, b).—Remarkable for its Pear-shaped fruit, containing an oval nut of good quality.

THIN-SHELLED.—Fruit double, longer, earlier, and of better quality than the others. It has a very thin shell, which is frequently pierced by birds in order to get at the kernel.

YORKSHIRE.—Large but not double, well filled, shell moderately thin. It ripens well.

QUINCE.

QUINCE.—Several species of Cydonia are cultivated under the name of Quince, viz. *C. vulgaris* (the common Quince), *C. sinensis* and *C. cathayensis* (Chinese Quinces) and *C. japonica* (Japanese Quince). The last named is grown as a decorative plant, but it crops very freely, and its fruits are useful for jellies, flavouring, &c. The best known is *C. vulgaris* (fig. 229, a), which is supposed to be a native of South Europe,

but this is uncertain. It forms a low, deciduous tree, of crooked, branching irregular habit. The fruit, which is powerfully odoriferous, and in its raw state acid, astringent, and unfit for eating, is principally used for flavouring, and for making Quince marmalade and other preserves.

The tree itself is largely used as a stock for certain varieties of Pear.

C. cathayensis and *C. sinensis* (fig 229, c, b) are not unlike each other in general characters; they have ovate fruit 5 to 7 inches in length, and have all the properties of the common Quince. They require the protection of a south wall, and even then they only ripen fruit in England in exceptionally warm summers.

The common Quince (fig. 229, a) succeeds in any soil, but prefers one of a rich, somewhat light, and moist nature. To ripen the fruit properly, a sunny situation is necessary.

Pruning and Training.—The Quince is apt to grow up with long flexible shoots, inclined to branch and twist. A tree planted where it is intended to remain should be allowed to grow at will for a season. It ought then to be cut back, in autumn, to within 18 inches of the ground, and then several shoots will push, the strongest of which should be trained upright to a rod, and shortened a little at every autumn-pruning. If the one highest up be the strongest, so much the better, if not, the shoot or shoots above it must be rubbed off, and those below it should be pinched when 1 foot in length. Laterals on the young upright ought to be allowed to grow during the summer, but they should be shortened to a few inches at the autumn-pruning; at the same time the shortened shoots between the base of the one trained upright and the ground ought to be cut clean off. By continuing to train the young shoot quite upright, an erect stem will be ensured; and by allowing plenty of laterals to grow, and gradually reducing them, the stem will be rendered strong enough in course of a few years to be self-supporting. When the stem has attained the required height the head should be formed as directed for the Apple. After the principal branches have been originated, very little pruning will be necessary. Over-luxuriant shoots should be checked at an early period of their growth, and weak spray and cross shoots cut off.

The fruit ripens in October or November, and may hang on the tree as long as there is no danger of frost. After gathering, it should be wiped with a clean cloth and laid on a shelf in some cool place, apart from other fruits, to which it is apt to communicate its peculiar odour and flavour. It does not keep longer than a month or six weeks.

Propagation is effected usually by cuttings early in autumn. If intended for plants may thus be obtained every two years.

Plants intended for stocks should be shortened back to 18 inches, but if for standards, they ought to be trained upright and at full length to a rod. Those for stocks should, in the summer after planting, have the lateral shoots cut entirely off to the height of 6 inches above

Fig. 229.—Quinces

a, Common (*C. vulgaris*). (Nat. size.)   *b*, Chinese (*C. sinensis*). (¼).   *c*, Chinese (*C. cathayensis*). (¼)

stocks, they are fit for use in their second or third year.

If propagated by layers, the stem of a Quince tree is cut down in autumn to form a stool, and the young shoots which are put forth in consequence are layered in the following autumn. The shoots soon strike root, and may, for the most part, be severed from the " stool " and planted in the autumn of the succeeding year. The stool will continue to produce shoots, which may be treated in the same way, and young

the ground, in order to form a clean stem near where they are to be worked.

The principal varieties cultivated for fruit are:—

APPLE-SHAPED QUINCE.—Leaves ovate, downy beneath. Fruit roundish, 2½ inches in diameter, of a rich golden colour. Very productive; ripens more readily than the other sorts.

CHAMPION. — Fruit very large, round; skin bright-yellow; flesh very tender when cooked; flavour delicate. Tree very productive, commencing to bear when young.

PEAR-SHAPED QUINCE. — Leaves oblong-ovate,

downy beneath. Fruit large, pyriform, or sometimes roundish, with a short neck, more or less
ribbed towards the eye, of a somewhat paler colour
than the Apple-shaped, and ripening later.

PORTUGAL QUINCE.—Leaves very large, broad
oval or ovate, downy on the upper side, very
downy beneath. Fruit 4 inches in length, and
3½ inches in diameter at the widest part, from
which it is most elongated towards the stalk,
tapering more abruptly towards the eye, where it

it acquires an agreeably acid somewhat
astringent flavour. It is generally eaten
raw, but is also occasionally made into
preserves with sugar.

The Medlar is raised from seeds, which
should be sown as soon as ripe. They
take two years to germinate. The seedlings should be trained to a stake in order

Fig. 230.—Medlar (*Mespilus germanica*)

again projects, forming irregular ribs; skin
thickly covered with grey wool, beneath which it
is deep yellow; flesh tender, juicy, much better
than the other sorts. The tree is tall and vigorous,
is not quite hardy, and is a shy fruiter. It is frequently planted for the ornamental appearance of
its flowers and fruit; also, from its vigorous
growth and forming thicker annual layers of wood,
it is well adapted for stocks for the Pear.

MEDLAR (*Mespilus* or *Pyrus germanica*)
(fig. 230) is a low, deciduous tree, a native
of Asia and Europe, including the British
Islands, where it grows wild in hedges,
woods, and copses. Its fruit is hard, acid,
and unfit for eating till it loses its green
colour and *blets*, or begins to decay, when

to get an upright stem. The varieties are
propagated by budding or grafting upon
Pear, Quince, or Thorn, the last-named
being preferred on the Continent. Pear,
as a stock, if grafted standard-high, gives
a straight stem and is probably the best.

The Medlar is not particular as to soil,
growing in any that is not over dry or
swampy, but it produces the largest and
best fruit in rich, loamy, somewhat moist
ground.

The tree may be trained either as a standard or as a pyramid, in the same way as
the Pear. The Nottingham Medlar, which
takes an upright growth, requires very little

pruning; but the Dutch and others of similar crooked growth require some regulation to prevent the branches from crossing and rubbing against each other. More than this need not be attempted, for the branches are naturally so inclined to assume an elbowed form, turning frequently at right angles in any direction, that to keep them straight is almost an impossibility.

The varieties worthy of cultivation are:—

DUTCH MEDLAR.—Fruit bright reddish-brown when ripe, and of good flavour.

NOTTINGHAM MEDLAR. — Fruit obovate, yellowish-brown spotted with russet; flavour rich, sub-acid. Tree of upright growth; leaves small.

STONELESS.—Fruit small, obovate, russet-brown when ripe, stoneless. Inferior in flavour, but keeps well.

Fig. 231.—Date Plum (*Diospyros Kaki*)

The fruit should remain on the tree until the end of October or beginning of November; and when the stalk parts readily from the shoot it should be gathered on a dry day and placed in the fruit-room. It is a good plan to dip the end of the stalk in a solution of common salt to prevent the attacks of fungus. The fruit should be looked over from time to time, and any affected with fungus removed. It becomes fit for use in two or three weeks after gathering, and may keep good till January.

DATE PLUM (*Diospyros Kaki*), also called Japanese Persimmon and Kaki, is scarcely known in English gardens, although cultivated in the south of Europe for its fruits, which find a ready market in Continental towns. Professor Sargent is of opinion that some of the varieties cultivated in Japan would thrive in England. In a few gardens in the south fruits have grown and ripened in the open air, and in a sunny greenhouse at Kew a healthy tree fruits every year.

The requirements of the Date Plum are essentially those of the Apple or Peach; it is certainly easily grown, and it flowers freely.

The varieties are propagated by grafting only. Females are cultivated, but they mature their fruits without the aid of fertilization, as in the case of the Banana, &c. Fruits matured at Kew are as large as a Blenheim Orange Apple, and when ripe are bright scarlet and as soft as a ripe

of Persimmon sap. The tree is distinguished for the excessive hardness of its wood and its black ebony-like colour.

In Japan the Kaki has long been subject to improvement by culture and selection of the best varieties, of which there are now many, differing greatly in size, shape, and quality; some being oblong, others resembling, both in shape and colour, a large, red, smooth Tomato.

Fig. 232.—Mulberry. (¼)

Tomato, quite as juicy, and very sweet.

The Date Plum has been abundantly grown from the earliest period in all the Japanese provinces, except in those where the climate is excessively hot or cold.

The fruits are very harsh and astringent before maturity, but become luscious and highly nutritious when ripe, more especially after exposure to frost. They are eatable in the raw state when ripe, or made into very delicious sweetmeats and dried fruit. From the unripe fruit a juice is expressed, which is used instead of varnish for many purposes under the name

The soil most suitable for the Kaki is a gravelly clay-loam, in an open situation. The trees are manured once in winter, preferably with night-soil applied in a circular furrow around each. They are pruned, in early spring or in late autumn, by breaking the branches with the hand without using any knife, because this tree, the Japs say, should not be touched with iron.

Professor Charles Sargent, in *The Forest Flora of Japan*, says:

"The Kaki is planted everywhere in the neighbourhood of houses, which in the interior of the main island are often embowered in small groves of this handsome tree. In shape it resembles a well-grown Apple tree, with a straight trunk, spreading branches which droop toward the extremities and form a compact round head. Trees 30 to 40 feet high are often seen, and in the autumn, when they are covered with fruit, and the leaves have turned to the colour of old Spanish red leather, they are exceedingly handsome.

exposed for sale was the orange-coloured variety, which, fresh and dried, is consumed in immense quantities by the Japanese, who eat it, as they do all their fruits, before it is ripe."

MULBERRY (*Morus nigra*) (fig. 232).— A deciduous tree, native of Persia, whence it is supposed to have been introduced into Europe by the Greeks. The fruit, which is composed of a number of grains, is oval,

Fig. 233.—Mulberry Tree, Chesterfield House, Edge Lane, Liverpool.

"Perhaps there is no tree except the Orange which as a fruit-tree is as beautiful as the Kaki. In central and northern Japan the variety which produces large orange-coloured, ovate, thick-skinned fruit is the only one planted, and the cultivation of the red-fruited varieties with which we have become acquainted in this country is confined to the south. A hundred varieties of Kaki, at least, are now recognized and named by Japanese gardeners, but few of them are important commercially in any part of the country. The only form I saw

1 inch or more in length, and about ¾ inch in diameter at the widest part, of a dark-purple colour approaching to black, very juicy, and having a sub-acid flavour. It is occasionally eaten raw, and sometimes preserved, or made into wine. A syrup known as *syrupus mori* is prepared from the berries gathered before they are ripe; it is principally used by chemists and others for colouring medicines.

The Mulberry succeeds best in a rich deep, rather light, and somewhat moist loam. In very dry shallow soils, as well as in those which are heavy, cold, or wet, the fruit rarely acquires any degree of perfection, and generally drops before it is fully ripe. The tree requires shelter from northerly winds. In the neighbourhood of London, and in all the warm parts of the kingdom, it grows well, and ripens its fruit; but in the cold parts of Scotland, and in the north of England, it requires a warm wall.

Propagation is effected by seeds, cuttings, and layers. The seeds are separated from

light rich mould, in a shady border; or in pots, and plunged in a moderate hotbed till they strike root, when they may be hardened off.

Autumn cuttings are taken off when the shoots are well matured.

Bearing branches, and even large limbs, will strike root, and are sometimes employed when the object is to obtain a tree which will bear in two or three years. They should be inserted in autumn in good soil, to the depth of a foot or so, according

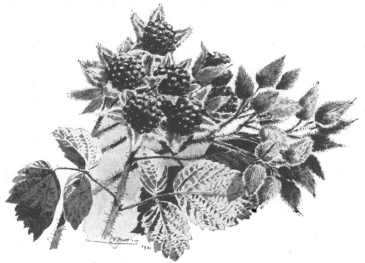

Fig. 234.—Japanese Wineberry (*Rubus phœnicolasius*)

the fruit by bruising the latter between the hands, and washing them free from the pulp in a basin of water. The seeds should then be thoroughly dried, put in paper or canvas bags, and kept in a cool, dry place till spring. They may be sown in March, in pans filled with light rich mould, placed in gentle heat, the seedlings being potted off or planted out in the course of the summer. Propagation by seeds, however, is seldom practised, as plants so raised, unless grafted, are long in coming into bearing, and may produce only male blossoms.

Cuttings made in spring or autumn should be taken from the upper branches of the tree. Spring cuttings should be well-ripened shoots of the preceding year. They may be planted 6 inches apart, in

to the size of the branch and the depth of the soil, and supported by a stake. Afterwards a good supply of water should be given, and when the branch has taken root a portion of the lower branches should be removed every year in order to form a clean stem.

The Mulberry is generally planted in the orchard, or on lawns, in order that the fruit may not be damaged by its fall from the tree, but it is always better to keep the ground beneath dug. The tree will also succeed, spur-pruned, as an espalier, and in cold localities it may be trained against a wall with a south aspect.

As a standard the tree requires little pruning and but little culture, it being merely necessary to dig over the ground about the roots in autumn and spring. The fruit ripens in succession in August and September, and should be gathered when about to drop. If the tree is not growing on a lawn, grass mowings should be spread out in a layer, not so thick as to ferment, in order to prevent injury to such fruit as may fall before it can be gathered. It does not keep good more than a day or two, and the sooner it can be used after gathering the better.

WINEBERRY.—The Japanese Wineberry (*Rubus phœnicolasius*) (fig. 234) is another Blackberry-like plant. In addition to producing an abundance of ripe fruit early in August, it is distinctly ornamental —sufficiently so to merit a place in the " wild garden " if only the birds would

of Cranberries in wet soil, especially where there is peat. In some of the North American States large areas of land, which for other purposes is valueless, is made to yield a considerable profit annually by the cultivation of Cranberries. The species grown there is:—

O. macrocarpus (fig. 235), a native of North America. It was first cultivated about 1810, but its culture had not become general until forty or fifty years later. The berries vary in size, shape, and colour, and three general types, named in reference to their forms, are known as the Bell, the Bugle, and the Cherry. There are many other named sorts in cultivation, such as

Fig. 235.—American Cranberry (*Oxycoccus macrocarpus*)

not interfere with the fruit. It is of the same habit of growth as the Bramble, the stems, which are covered with reddish hairs, growing to a length of from 6 to 10 feet. The fruit, borne closely together in clusters, is wine-red in colour, juicy, and agreeably acidulous. It ripens very evenly, thus admitting of whole sprays being cut for dessert purposes. The fruit also makes excellent jam.

CRANBERRY.—Two species of *Oxycoccus* (a near relation of *Vaccinium*) yield Cranberries, namely, *O. palustris*, a widely-distributed little plant which is abundant in peat-bogs in some parts of the British Islands. It is of creeping habit, with thin wiry stems, tiny ovate leaves, deep-green above, glaucous beneath, and small red flowers succeeded by dark-red globose berries, which ripen in August, and are gathered by poor people and sold to fruiterers, &c.

It would be easy to establish a plantation

Early Black, Dennis, M'Farlin, Gould, Franklin, &c.

Although the Cranberry thrives in swamps and endures flooding at certain seasons, it nevertheless demands comparative dryness during the growing and fruiting season.

Fifty barrels per acre is said to be a good crop of Cranberries, yet 200 barrels have been produced. Bogs that have been cultivated thirty years have yielded a crop annually and are still good.

The plantations are made by putting in cuttings 6 inches long—two-thirds of which is thrust obliquely into the soil—and a foot apart each way. This is done in early spring, and the plants root in about three weeks; in three or four years a full crop of berries is obtained. The plantations are flooded in December, and the water is drawn off again in April.

The Common Cranberry (*O. palustris*) may be grown in beds formed by digging out the ground at the side of a clear pond or running water, so that the bottom of the excavation may be about 6 inches below the surface of the water, and then filling in a layer of loose stones and peat earth to the depth of about 9 inches. The bed may then be planted and the water let in.

BILBERRY or **BLAEBERRY** (*Vaccinium Myrtillus*) (fig. 236) is a deciduous

Fig. 236.—Bilberry (½)

shrub, growing to the height of 1 or 2 feet, and commonly found on stony heaths in various parts of Britain. The fruit, a small dark-purple berry, has an agreeable acid flavour. It makes excellent tarts and preserves. The plant is propagated by layers, and may be grown in peat soil mixed with garden mould.

BERBERRY (*Berberis vulgaris*) is a deciduous shrub, growing to the height of 7 or 8 feet, a native of Britain and most parts of Europe and North America. It is found wild in woods and coppices in dry soil, and was formerly common enough in hedgerows, but is now everywhere banished from these in consequence of the plant being very generally supposed to be a host for the fungus which causes rust on corn growing in its vicinity. The fruit when ripe is acid and astringent, but it makes excellent preserves; those made at Rouen from the stoneless fruit are held in high estimation. In a green state the berries are pickled in vinegar.

The Stoneless Berberry, supposed to be a distinct variety, is propagated by layers.

ELDER (*Sambucus nigra*).—A low deciduous tree, a native of Britain and other parts of Europe, as well as of North Africa. The berries are employed in making wine, of which large quantities are consumed at Christmas, and for the production of a jelly which is said to be useful in cases of severe cold and sore throat. Elder-flower water, which is used for flavouring confectionery, and as a lotion for the skin, is obtained from the flowers; and the whole tree is held in great estimation by country people for its medicinal properties.

Besides the common sort with black berries, there is a variety with green, and another with yellow fruit, but these are chiefly planted for ornament.

The Elder is propagated with great facility, either by seeds sown in autumn or spring, or by cuttings. The latter method, being the most expeditious, is that usually adopted. If the trees are to be grown as standards, they may be planted 20 feet apart; sometimes, however, cuttings are put in 1 foot apart, so as to form a hedge. The Elder will grow luxuriantly in any good garden soil, and is not particular as to situation; but a sunny spot is preferable, if good fruit is required. Beyond the removal of suckers when the tree is young, and helping it to form a regular head, no other treatment is required.

Ingram Content Group UK Ltd.
Milton Keynes UK
UKHW021111030523
421135UK00002B/15

9 781446 512999